The Philosophy of Jos Soloveitchik

MW00576229

Providing a concise but comprehensive overview of Joseph B. Soloveitchik's larger philosophical program, this book studies one of the most important modern Orthodox Jewish thinkers. It incorporates much relevant biographical, philosophical, religious, legal, and historical background so that the content and difficult philosophical concepts are easily accessible.

The volume describes his view of Jewish law (Halakhah) and how he answers the fundamental question of Jewish philosophy, namely, the "reasons" for the commandments. It shows how many of his disparate books, essays, and lectures on law, specific commandments, and Jewish religious phenomenology can be woven together to form an elegant philosophical program. It also provides an analysis and summary of Soloveitchik's views on Zionism and on interreligious dialogue and the contexts for Soloveitchik's respective stances on issues that were pressing in his role as a leader of a major branch of post-war Orthodox Judaism.

The book provides a synoptic overview of the philosophical works of Joseph B. Soloveitchik. It will be of interest to historians and scholars studying neo-Kantian philosophy, Jewish thought, and philosophy of religion.

Heshey Zelcer is a founder of *Hakirah: The Flatbush Journal of Jewish Law and Thought* and a member of its editorial board. He has published books and articles on Jewish law, philosophy, history, and liturgy.

Mark Zelcer is Assistant Professor of Philosophy at Queensborough Community College, City University of New York. He has published in various areas of philosophy including the philosophy of mathematics and ancient philosophy. He co-authored *Politics and Philosophy in Plato's Menexenus* (Routledge, 2015).

Routledge Jewish Studies Series

Series Editor: Oliver Leaman, *University of Kentucky*

Jewish Studies, are interpreted to cover the disciplines of history, sociology, anthropology, culture, politics, philosophy, theology, religion, as they relate to Jewish affairs. The remit includes texts which have as their primary focus issues, ideas, personalities, and events of relevance to Jews, Jewish life, and the concepts which have characterized Jewish culture both in the past and today. The series is interested in receiving appropriate scripts or proposals.

For more information about this series, please visit: https://www.routledge.com/middleeaststudies/series/JEWISH

The Philosophy of Joseph B. Soloveitchik

Heshey Zelcer and Mark Zelcer

LONDON AND NEW YORK

First published 2021
by Routledge
2 Park Square, Milton Park, Abingdon, Oxon OX14 4RN

and by Routledge
52 Vanderbilt Avenue, New York, NY 10017

Routledge is an imprint of the Taylor & Francis Group, an informa business

British Library Cataloguing-in-Publication Data
A catalogue record for this book is available from the British Library

Library of Congress Cataloging-in-Publication Data
Names: Zelcer, Heshey, author. | Zelcer, Mark, author.
Title: The philosophy of Joseph B. Soloveitchik /
Heshey Zelcer, Mark Zelcer.
Description: First edition. | New York, NY : Routledge, 2021. |
Series: Routledge Jewish studies series | Includes bibliographical
references and index.
Identifiers: LCCN 2020047715 | ISBN 9780367698942 (hardback) |
ISBN 9781003143765 (ebook) | ISBN 9781000368734 (adobe pdf) |
ISBN 9781000368772 (epub)
Subjects: LCSH: Soloveitchik, Joseph Dov--Philosophy. |
Jewish philosophy.
Classification: LCC BM755.S6144 Z45 2021 | DDC 181/.06--dc23
LC record available at https://lccn.loc.gov/2020047715

ISBN: 978-0-367-69894-2 (hbk)
ISBN: 978-0-367-69895-9 (pbk)
ISBN: 978-1-003-14376-5 (ebk)

Typeset in Times New Roman
by MPS Limited, Dehradun

Contents

Acknowledgments

We owe thanks to many people, individually and together. Mark (Meir) first: Brad Wray, David Vampola, Lori Reitmeier, Jared Peterson, Lori Nash, David Lambie, Craig Delancey, Richard Cocks, Jean Chambers, Robert Card, and many great students at SUNY Oswego provided a wonderful and open-minded environment to do philosophy. The Social Sciences faculty at Queensborough Community College, CUNY, where I currently teach, has been particularly helpful during these trying pandemic times as we completed work on this book, especially the philosophers Phil Pecorino and Shannon Kincaid, and the chairs Joe Culkin and Jeff Jankowski. Rabbi Aaron Raskin and Congregation B'nai Avraham of Brooklyn Heights invited me to speak about Soloveitchik. Thanks for their encouragement throughout and also for Yankel's help. USACAPOC 351st Tactical PSYOP Co. was an important focus of my life while writing this book. I had the privilege to serve with some great people including MAJs Jim G., Elena H., Erik K., CPT Alice K., SSG Ben A., SGT Devin K., and many others. Tango Mike. I am grateful to two philosophers who have been role models: Nick Pappas and Doug Lackey. Both served as my Department Chair when I taught as a graduate student, and both taught me much about doing philosophy. Doug invited me to speak at the Michael Wyschogrod memorial which forced me to think about Soloveitchik's reception. Leib Litman has been a valuable sounding board and a great friend since we met in yeshiva a lifetime ago. His thoughtful remarks on everything we talk about has been a constant source of stimulation since our adolescence. Thanks also to Noson Yanofsky for help in so many things throughout the years, including very thoughtful remarks on an early draft of this book.

Heshey: Shmuel Lichtenstein, OBM, was the rabbi of the shul in Flatbush which my wife, Temy, and our children attended during the formative years in which our family was being forged. He appeared in shul one morning carrying a fistful of cassettes. He walked over to me and declared, "Heshey, listen to these. I believe you will enjoy them." A few days later, during a long drive to Syracuse, I listened to them, and again and yet again. The cassettes were recordings of Yiddish lectures by Rabbi J. B. Soloveitchik. On that day my infatuation with Soloveitchik's thought began and has remained ever since.

During those same years, I was part of a study group including Asher Benzion Buchman, Sheldon Epstein, David Guttmann, Chaim Lam, and Yonah Wilamowsky, which met on Saturdays to discuss issues in Jewish law and thought. This group introduced me to a wider world of Judaism and Jewish thought. This same group also founded *Ḥakirah: The Flatbush Journal of Jewish Law and Thought*, a journal, which during the past sixteen years, has published twenty-eight volumes of interesting scholarly research.

Since 2010, Professor David Shatz, a philosopher and an expert on Soloveitchik's thought, has been a dear and kind friend. He graciously read and reviewed an early draft of our book and provided us with feedback which greatly improved its quality. He also helped us understand the dynamics and the culture within Yeshiva University as it related to Soloveitchik, and his lengthy tenure there as a lecturer, a leader, and a molder of Jewish minds and souls.

Sylvia Lam, Mindy Schaper, Judith Tiger, and Max Wagner all read earlier drafts of this work. I thank you all. Your feedback and comments prevented mistakes and improved our book.

This book, along with other areas of research and writing, has occupied my free time and has helped nourish my soul. The body, alas, requires more mundane efforts to survive and thrive. My brother-in-law and business partner for forty-five years, Jerry Solomon, has been my constant friend and confidant, working together, helping our business thrive. He is smart, generous, and resourceful, and he complements me in areas in which I am deficient. Thank you Jerry for always being there for me, in business and in life, in good times, and during challenging days.

We thank David Shurin for sharing his father's *Rabbi Aaron Ben-Zion Shurin Archive on Rabbi Dr. Joseph B. Soloveitchik* and for allowing us to make it publicly available. This archive introduced us to additional—and often surprising—information on Soloveitchik's life and times.

Together the authors acknowledge Oliver Leaman, the editor of the Jewish Studies series at Routledge, and Joe Whiting and Ella Panczel in the editorial offices who made the publication process seamless. Thank you. We also appreciate the anonymous reviewers for Routledge (who we wish we can thank by name) for urging us to improve upon the manuscript in various ways.

The authors are related, and it is our privilege to express appreciation to our family. Heshey notes with gratitude the help and encouragement offered to his dear wife Temy and himself by their kind and caring children—good people all of them—Meir and Dahlia Zelcer, Esty and Yehuda Herskowitz, Shloimy and Aliza Zelcer, and Malky Zelcer. You and your children—our grandchildren—cause our hearts to overflow with love, joy, and hope. Meir's debts are to the same people but in different ways. Temy (mom) and Dahlia made this book, like so much else, possible. Thanks to my siblings and their families for a lifetime of understanding. You have always been there for me. Alex and Rachel Kozlowsky are wonderful, kind, and caring. Max Rocky and Julian K, you make it all worthwhile.

We dedicate this book to two outstanding women who significantly shaped our lives: Rivka Solomon and Roza Zelcer, mother-in-law and mother, respectively, to Heshey, and Meir's grandmothers. They survived the greatest existential crisis Judaism has ever faced and emerged stronger for it. Their influence on our lives has been incalculable. *Te'hei nafshan tzrurah be-tzror ha-ḥayyim.*

Notes to the reader

Note 1: When capitalized, "Halakhic Man," "Cognitive Man," "Economic Man," "Religious Man," etc. refer to personality types, not individuals. "Adam the First" and "Adam the Second" refer to the two descriptions of Adam described in the Bible. For clarity, we use "Religious Man" to refer to a personality type in place of Soloveitchik's "*homo religiosus.*"

Note 2: We take minor liberties with spelling and transliteration for clarity. Titles of books and foreign words are italicized. Thus, *Halakhic Man* refers to the book, not the personality type. When it does not seriously do violence to the text, we replace Hebrew, Yiddish, Latin, and German words with the English translations in [brackets]. We use the words *Halakhah*, halakhic, etc. throughout.

Note 3: There is no obvious reason to believe that Soloveitchik does not usually use the term "Man" in a gender-inclusive way when discussing personality types. "Man" is generally a substitution for the Latin "*homo*," a term generally denoting "human." However, to avoid anachronism, we follow his usage, using "Man" when discussing personality types.

Note 4: Following convention, we typically omit titles such as Dr., Rabbi, Ms., etc.

Note 5: Works by Joseph B. Soloveitchik are referred to by a two-word (or acronymic) abbreviation listed alphabetically in the bibliography.

Foreword

Abstract Soloveitchik's philosophical work is worth reading because (1) of his impact on Jewish history, (2) of his advocacy of religious Zionism, (3) it helps us understand a figure who is at the intersection of the analytic Talmud method of Brisk and the philosophy of Weimar Berlin, and (4) it is innately interesting philosophy.

For those familiar with his legacy, there is little need to justify the value of understanding Joseph B. Soloveitchik's works. For those less familiar, it is worth rehearsing the relevance that his, at times, arcane intellectual legacy can have for us. A strong case can be made that Soloveitchik's thought ought to be more widely understood both by those familiar with the position he held in the Jewish world and also by those for whom Soloveitchik's cultural and intellectual milieu is unfamiliar.

If nothing else, Soloveitchik's impact on Jewish history justifies further study of his work. He left multiple intellectual legacies of which at least two left indelible marks on the daily lives of entire significant Jewish communities. His first legacy is that—though he may not have seen himself in this role—he carried the banner of Modern Orthodox Judaism (Waxman 2010, 374) and provided it with an unparalleled pious and intellectual leader. Modern Orthodox Judaism sees a synthesis of traditional Jewish practice with modern culture as an ideal. Ashkenazi Orthodox Jews in the Jewish diaspora who do not consider themselves ultra-Orthodox owe much of their religious intellectual respectability to Soloveitchik. Chances are their congregational rabbi was educated and ordained by Soloveitchik, or more recently by one of his students.

Soloveitchik was a leader of American Orthodoxy in a period when it was seeking a *modus vivendi* with the modern world. After World War II, Jewish life, especially Orthodox Jewish life, in Eastern Europe practically ceased, and many of its refugees to the United States sought to chart a course between traditional observance and American modernity. Soloveitchik, implicit in his daily life and his affiliation with Yeshiva University (YU) and perhaps explicitly too, defended the *Torah u-Madda* (Torah and knowledge) ideology for generations of American Jews (see Shatz 2008b).

Second, from the end of World War II through the early days of the State of Israel when ultra-Orthodox Jewish leaders in the diaspora transplanted anti-Zionism from pre-war European *shtetls*, Soloveitchik advocated for a religious Zionism intellectually independent of political Zionism. He sanctioned a pro-Israel ideology for those who could not conceive of a Judaism that rejected the new Jewish state or its religious significance. His defense of religious Zionism gave Modern Orthodox Jewry the confidence to remain inside the observant fold and concurrently support the then fledgling State of Israel.

Few individuals in the United States could have accomplished this dual mission. Soloveitchik's credentials as the scion of a family of formidable and innovative Talmud scholars and as one of the foremost Talmudists of his generation enabled him to speak with an authority that was accepted among a wide swath of Orthodox Jews. His detractors may not have liked what he had to say, but they could not easily dismiss him.

Third, going beyond post-war Judaism, his life and work significantly illuminate its various contexts. He studied Talmud with his grandfather, Hayyim Soloveitchik, the locus of the analytic Talmud circle centered on the Yeshiva of Volozhin that revolutionized religious study of Talmud and Jewish law. He also studied philosophy and Judaics in Berlin in the heyday of the cultural upheaval that was the Weimar Republic. That these worlds converged in his person is reason enough to take a closer look at his intellectual output.

Finally, Soloveitchik's works, although often difficult, are innately interesting. He did not leave a clear, simple picture of his philosophical program, but piecing together his philosophical essays and speeches to form a coherent program is quite rewarding.

Soloveitchik studied at the University of Berlin during an important period in the history of philosophy. It was in this period that the Vienna Circle was meeting in Austria and Martin Heidegger rose to intellectual prominence first in Marburg and then in Freiburg. At the time, German-speaking philosophers were forging new approaches that would divide them into two camps, now called "analytic" and "Continental." The two are typically thought to differ on the proper objects of philosophical study as well as the proper methods for philosophers to employ in their investigations of them. They are often said to disagree over whether or not science is adequate to explain the world and if science is even the right lens with which to view it. Aware of these discussions, Soloveitchik produced work that shows sympathy with each camp, all in the service of answering perennial questions in Jewish thought.

We are now among the second generation of students, scholars, and devotees trying to make sense of Soloveitchik's philosophical legacy. It can presently be read with a level of detachment that may have been difficult for the previous generation of scholars. We also have a rich layer of secondary literature now, which adds to his legacy and makes it easier to interpret his work.

Scholars of the philosophy of religion, modern Jewish philosophy, Judaism in general, and the legacy of neo-Kantianism, could all benefit from studying Soloveitchik's work. We hope our emphasis on Soloveitchik as a philosopher helps more people see the interplay of the history of philosophy and modern Jewish thought.

Few intellectuals and philosophers in the course of human history can be said to have had an important impact on the practical lives of hundreds of thousands of people. Soloveitchik, through his communal work, activism, teaching, scholarship, and rabbinic leadership, did. He influenced the religious, theological, intellectual, and political lives of many Jews at a particularly sensitive time in Jewish history. As Judaism was rebuilding from the Holocaust, Soloveitchik was one of the architects of its new edifice. He ordained a great many rabbis and was by far the most significant teacher for an entire generation of Modern Orthodox Jewish leaders. In the diaspora, he can reasonably be called the godfather of both Modern Orthodoxy and contemporary religious Zionism.

1 Overview

Joseph B. Soloveitchik has a clear and coherent philosophical project that extends throughout many of his numerous lectures and essays, and much of his work has an intellectual pedigree that winds its way through the history of philosophy, a subject he studied at the University of Berlin. This book spells out Soloveitchik's most significant philosophical preoccupations.

In the 1940s Soloveitchik wrote three important and related essays, whose subsequent publication history has done much to impede understanding of his project. The most famous essay, *Halakhic Man*, was published in Hebrew in 1948 as "Ish ha-Halakhah." *And From There You Shall Seek* was also published first in Hebrew, in 1978, as "U-Vikkashtem mi-Sham." Finally, in 1986 at the twilight of his career, after the manuscript had been set aside for about four decades, *The Halakhic Mind* was published.

When read together, and only when read together, these three works comprise a three-part structure which jointly articulate Soloveitchik's philosophy of Judaism. Ironically, it is the book that was published last, *The Halakhic Mind*—a notoriously difficult, jargon-laden work with little apparent Jewish content in its first three Parts—that spells out the foundation for Soloveitchik's philosophical approach. People studying Soloveitchik's work in the 1960s or 1970s had no access to this manuscript or to most of Soloveitchik's philosophical output. Soloveitchik's fame as a philosophical thinker and expositor at that time rested largely on an oral tradition emerging from students' discussion of his lectures. They had few means of determining the scope, nature, or goals of Soloveitchik's philosophical project. The interpretations that have emerged from that period—prior to the publication of *The Halakhic Mind* or even subsequent to its publication but which did not take it seriously enough—often miss key components necessary to understand the elegant coherence of Soloveitchik's many essays and lectures.

In trying to make sense of *Halakhic Man* in the 1960s and 1970s, many commentators spoke of it as a phenomenological study of the subjective religious experience of a Halakhic Man or a personality profile of the kind popular in those early days of German psychoanalytic theory when Soloveitchik was in University. Soloveitchik's contribution was to provide a profile of a Halakhic Man as a unique personality alongside other better discussed personality types. In Chapter 4, Section "Personality," we explain *Halakhic Man* in detail and show how the above description of Soloveitchik's project is correct but incomplete. We show how *Halakhic Man* fits into Soloveitchik's overall philosophical project. We also discuss his other works which can be classified as "Personality studies" which round out this aspect of his project.

With the publication in 1986 of *The Halakhic Mind*, what we think of as Soloveitchik's "Foundational" essay, scholars had what they needed to understand the big picture of his philosophical approach to halakhah and Judaism. We see him addressing one of the most quintessentially Jewish questions in philosophy—the *ta'amei ha-mitzvot* problem—not by answering it in a traditional way but by rephrasing the question and pursuing a novel kind of answer. One of this book's contributions to the scholarship of Soloveitchik is to take the bulk of his philosophical corpus seriously as a unified project and spell out his larger philosophical structure rather than explicating his work piecemeal.

Soloveitchik argues, like others before him, that Maimonides' approach to the *ta'amei ha-mitzvot* problem—which tries to determine the moral, ethical, or scientific purpose of each commandment—is misguided. The approach does nothing to describe the Jewish religious experience. Judaism ought not try to determine moral or scientific reasons for the commandments, Soloveitchik argues, for doing so reduces the commandments to mere "handmaidens" of those considerations. Furthermore, "reformers" within Judaism mistakenly went down this path and wound up replacing the eternal commandments with in-vogue societal values. If morality, ethics, and social considerations are the supreme values, then it is the values and not Judaism that is sacred or absolute. Everything in Judaism then becomes subject to change, and all that is unique in it ultimately disappears.

Soloveitchik therefore reformulated the *ta'amei ha-mitzvot* question. Instead of asking for the reason something is commanded, or for what purpose, he tells us to ask instead what effect the commandment has upon the person performing it. The Hebrew word "*ta'am*" here means "taste" rather than "reason." In Soloveitchik's philosophical program, the *ta'amei ha-mitzvot* problem asks how a specific commandment "tastes" to the one who performs it. More precisely, if slightly less literally, what is the experience of fulfilling a commandment? To understand the totality of what it is to be a Halakhic Man, one thus needs to study and define that which shapes his world, the facts of his religion, its objective data—the Halakhah, in its broadest sense.

The sum total of all Halakhot—all the objective data of Judaism—create the world of a Halakhic Man. We do not mean that Halakhah creates objects *yesh-me-ayin* (*ex nihilo*) but rather that the Halakhah embeds constructs that exist only for a Halakhic Man. For example, a Non-Halakhic Person, looking around outside, may see a large field, with fallen branches, and a pond. Perhaps there is an aesthetic experience accompanying the scene.

A Halakhic Man, experiencing the exact same scene, perceives objects of Halakhic significance: a *reshut ha-rabbim*, *sekhakh*, and a *mikveh* (a public domain, roofing for a sukkah, and a ritual bath). Perhaps the time of day, the season, or the flora is significant too in addition to the acknowledgement of the majesty of creation. The Halakhah which he has internalized imposes these constructs on his subjective experience. We explain and justify this in our discussion of *The Halakhic Mind*, in Chapter 4, Section "Foundation."

A lifetime spent seeing the world through a Halakhic lens creates a very specific type of personality, a Halakhic Man, who is at once grounded, creative, dialectical, lonely, conflicted, thoughtful, cooperative, analytical, redeemed, and deeply spiritual. How exactly does Halakhah give rise to such an individual? In Chapter 4, Section "Development," using material from *And From There You Shall Seek* as well as Soloveitchik's writings on specific areas of Jewish law including mourning, prayer, and repentance, we describe Soloveitchik's vision of how such a person emerges organically from a Halakhic life. We begin to understand how creativity, dialectical reasoning, and the tension of incompatible personality types help develop the ideal (idealized) Jew, the Halakhic Man.

The Halakhic Mind thus lays the foundation of Soloveitchik's philosophy of Judaism. *Halakhic Man* describes the individual who struggles with and has internalized the Halakhah. *And From There You Shall Seek* explains how one develops into that individual. Throughout Chapter 4 we review and explain the three works mentioned previously. We show how so many of Soloveitchik's other works also fall neatly into a coherent philosophical program, helping him depict new faces of Halakhic Men, or articulate how a specific law contributes to the ideal personality.

To understand how Soloveitchik's philosophy fits into the continuum of intellectual history, how it draws and builds upon earlier philosophic thought, we review the most relevant philosophical concepts, arguments, and background from the ancient Greek philosopher Plato, through German philosophy in the inter-war years, and contemporary philosophy of science. We also provide enough of Soloveitchik's biography to put his thought into the context of his own life and the historical events through which he lived.[1]

***

The philosophical program just described is the one that Soloveitchik most thoroughly worked out and in fact pervades much of his writing and lecturing (especially the philosophy published in his lifetime). However, it is hardly his only philosophical thought. Some of the philosophical ideas for which he is best known regards his stance on Zionism and on interfaith dialogue. These works are not part of Soloveitchik's philosophy of Judaism but rather pertain to important issues emerging from the historically contingent circumstances in which Soloveitchik and his generation found themselves. We may think of these arising as *horoat sha'ah*, discussions of and solutions to challenges facing the Jewish people at that particular moment in history. The Holocaust and the subsequent establishment of the State of Israel loomed large in the Jewish consciousness of Soloveitchik's time. Soloveitchik gave expression and sanction to the sentiment of a large segment of the Jewish world in his outspoken support for Zionism. Chapter 5 covers this. Chapter 6 is concerned with a question that arose in response to an evolution in the attitude of the Catholic Church upon which Soloveitchik was compelled to weigh in: May Jews engage in theological discourse with other religions?

Finally, Chapter 7 speculates on the direction that Soloveitchik's philosophy can take. What can be done to further Soloveitchik's philosophical program and build upon his work? We tentatively suggest ideas, questions, and approaches for building upon and advancing his approach to the philosophy of Judaism.

This book provides a synoptic picture of many of Soloveitchik's central and well-known philosophical writings and theses, generally in the form of summarizing and contextualizing many of Soloveitchik's essays and speeches. We are less focused on detailed exegesis of his individual works. Much of that is widely available—some of it of excellent quality. We also focus less on some of the more recently published posthumous material which scholars have yet to carefully scrutinize. We do not expect the reader, lay or scholarly, to agree with all of our analyses just as we have disagreed, sometimes quite significantly, with many commentators who preceded us. In the notes we point to earlier scholarship, some of which we agree with, much of which we do not. We rarely, however, take issue with other thinkers on these pages. Stating each point of disagreement with other scholars, explaining why we disagree, and arguing our case over theirs would make for a very different kind of book, one we did not wish to write. We are also less focused on defending Soloveitchik against criticism or potential criticism. We wish to present his system as we believe he understood it, to the reader in its philosophical and historical context. We hope that the ideas are challenging and stimulating and that they motivate the reader to delve deeper into the words of Rabbi Dr. Joseph B. Soloveitchik, *zt"l*, one of Judaism's greatest Talmudists, philosophers, teachers, and advocates.

Note

1 See Sherlo (1999/2000). Ziegler (2012, 23–24) and Shatz (2017, 175ff) argue for the intellectual relevance of Soloveitchik's biography.

2 Biography

Childhood[1]

Joseph B. Soloveitchik,[2] eldest of Moshe and Pesha's five children, was born on February 27, 1903, in Pruzhany,[3] Poland (now in Belarus), where his maternal grandfather, Elijah Feinstein[4] (1842–1928), served as rabbi to a Jewish population of about 5,000.

Generations of Soloveitchik's ancestors were among the foremost proponents of the Lithuanian *mitnaged* (Orthodox anti-Ḥasidic) tradition. His paternal grandfather, R. Ḥayyim Soloveitchik,[5] developed what is known as the *Brisker* method of Talmud study, now standardly employed by Orthodox Jews.[6] The family traces its lineage back to the Luria family and to Ḥayyim of Volozhin (1749–1821), a disciple of Elijah ben Shlomo Zalman Kremer, the "Gaon of Vilna" (1720–1797), the foremost opponent of the then nascent Ḥasidic movement and a towering figure of the Talmudic tradition.

When Soloveitchik was a young child, his parents relocated to Raseiniai, Lithuania, where his father Moshe served as a rabbi for three years (Meiselman 1995, 114) in a sizable Jewish community. Although his family was poor (*Vision and Leadership*, 26), he had warm memories of this period of his life. He recalls, "I used to sit in bed and listen to my father talk … Father would always find that the Rambam [Maimonides] had offered a different interpretation and had deviated from the simple path … Father strode boldly and bravely … The difficulties were resolved, the passage was explained … But occasionally the Rambam's [Maimonides'] luck did not hold … Father was unable to follow the logic of his position … Slowly I would go to Mother and tell her with a broken heart, 'Mother, Father can't resolve the Rambam—— what should we do?' 'Don't be sad,' Mother would answer, 'Father will find a solution for the Rambam. And if he doesn't find one, then maybe when you grow up you'll resolve his words …'" (*AFTYSS*, 143–46).[7]

From 1913 to 1921, the family lived in Khislavichi, Belarus (now in Russia), a town comprised mostly of Lubavitch Hasidim, but interestingly, and again seminally, traditionally led by a *mitnaged* rabbi.[8] Soloveitchik's teacher in ḥeder (school), Barukh Ya'akov Reisberg, a Ḥasid of Lubavitch, taught his class *Tanya*, the central book of the Lubavitch movement.[9] When

R. Ḥayyim tested his grandson, he realized he knew very little Talmud. When pressed as to what he did know, the young Soloveitchik recited passages of *Tanya* from memory. R. Ḥayyim then advised his son Moshe to personally teach his child Talmud.[10] Indeed, during the next twenty-nine years, Soloveitchik would study Talmud with his father, and for much of that time, his father was his primary teacher [*rabbi muvhak*] (*On Prayer* 64n75). Both his early exposure to Hasidic teaching and his intense study of Talmud would leave a deep impact on Soloveitchik's thought.

Moshe was strict and demanding while teaching his son. His sister recalled, "Quite frequently, Father would become indignant at him when the right answer did not come fast enough. Father was a hard taskmaster ... With tears in his eyes, he [Soloveitchik] would continue to ponder the difficult Talmudic problems until he could solve their intricate mysteries" (Meiselman 1995, 153).

He was encouraged to write his thoughts on the Talmud in a notebook, and it became a habit that remained with him the rest of his life. As a twelve-year-old, the young Soloveitchik wrote novella on Talmud which was shared with his illustrious grandfather. "Reb Chaim began to read his grandson's Talmudic expositions. Finishing the last page, he rose from his seat, put on his heavy overcoat, and left the house with his grandson's notebook ... When he returned home, his daughter asked him where he had been for so long. 'At my friend Reb Simcha Selig's house,' was his reply. 'How often does a grandfather receive such *nachas* [pride in accomplishment, especially of a descendant]——to be a witness to the birth of a great Talmud scholar'" (Meiselman 1995, 154).

After accepting an offer to head Talmud studies at the Tahkemoni School, Moshe Soloveitchik moved his family to Warsaw. Tahkemoni was a liberal, religious, Zionist school which offered both Talmud and secular courses. The job was not to last. After various disagreements with the school,[11] some of which were resolved to Moshe's satisfaction, he lost his job. The school had insisted that ordination be granted upon completion of a course of study. He, however, refused to ordain students who did not pass a written or oral exam. This experience appears to have left Soloveitchik with a distaste for the Mizrachi movement which ran the school and for the Zionism which the movement defended (Rakeffet-Rothkoff 2013, 1). Now unemployed, in September 1929, Moshe Soloveitchik accepted a position as lecturer of Talmud at Yeshiva University in New York City, a position Soloveitchik himself would one day assume.

University

Until his early twenties, Soloveitchik devoted himself mostly to the study of Talmud and Jewish law. He also received the equivalent of a *gymnasium*, high school education. This was rare for someone of Soloveitchik's insular Eastern European religious milieu. With his mother's encouragement, he read and acquired a taste for secular literature including the fiction of Pushkin, Lermontov, Ibsen, and Bialik (Rakeffet-Rothkoff 1998, 256).

Soloveitchik's parents decided he should enroll in university and obtain an advanced secular education. As could have been expected, this decision was unpopular with some leaders of their ultra-Orthodox Jewish community. His sister recounts, "Early one morning the bell rang. Opening the door, I was confronted by a very distinguished-looking rabbi ... Father [Moshe Soloveitchik] immediately went to receive his guests. Suddenly, we heard excited noises coming from the direction of Father's study ... Then we heard an uproar like the sound of thunder. Rushing into the study, we found Father shouting at his guest, 'How dare you come to me with such a message! Who sent you? What right do you have to meddle in my affairs? If I want to send my son to the University of Berlin, it's my business and no one else's. My son will never come under foreign influences ... Take a message back to your friends: Joseph Dov Soloveitchik will one day be the world spokesman for Talmudic Judaism'" (Meiselman 1995, 226). Years later, when asked why he went to university, Soloveitchik answered simply, "My mother sent me. She felt that to make a mark, even as a Rav [Rabbi], in the new world and a new time, you needed to go to university" (Charlop 2003, 154). This was a bold move and a social risk for someone in Soloveitchik's cultural position.

In 1922, Soloveitchik graduated from the liberal arts gymnasium in Dubno,[12] and in 1924, he began studying at the Free Polish University in Warsaw, where he spent three terms taking classes in political science.[13] In 1926, he moved to Berlin[14] and entered the Friedrich Wilhelm University of Berlin (now Humboldt University). He passed the examination for supplementary subjects at the German Institute for Studies by Foreigners and matriculated at the university. He then studied philosophy,[15] economics, and the Hebrew language.

To the religious Jewish community in Berlin, Soloveitchik epitomized the best of Eastern European Talmud scholarship and Western European scientific culture. "You have no idea what the young Rabbi Soloveitchik signified in Berlin then. He was the pride, the ornament, of the Berlin Jewish community ... They knew he was the grandson of Reb Ḥayyim ... and that, at the same time he was the '*liebling*' [darling] of the academic community at the University of Berlin; yet, all the while, remaining in learning and absolutely singular in his astonishing *hasmadah* [passionate commitment to Torah study] ..." (Charlop 2003, 153).

The Weimar Republic, the government in Germany from 1919 to 1933, had an incredibly vibrant artistic and cultural scene. Wassily Kandinsky, Paul Klee, and Bauhaus design were at the apex of their popularity. Thomas Mann had just published *The Magic Mountain*, Bertolt Brecht was in his prime, and *The Threepenny Opera* came out, and Marlene Dietrich catapulted to international film stardom. But Soloveitchik was absorbed in a small part of the equally vibrant Jewish life in Berlin. Soloveitchik met

Jehiel Jacob Weinberg who headed the Berlin Rabbinical Seminary, and he befriended people like Alexander Altmann (1906–1987) who would go on to become an important scholar in Jewish studies. He also interacted with a number of individuals who would leave a lasting impression on twentieth-century Judaism and join the ranks of Weimar exiles: Yitzhak Hutner would later lead Yeshiva Rabbi Chaim Berlin in Brooklyn; Menachem Mendel Schneerson would become the seventh (and final) Lubavitcher Rebbe; and Abraham Joshua Heschel[16] would go on to become a prominent Jewish theologian active in the U.S. civil rights movement.

Soloveitchik registered at the famed Berlin Rabbinical Seminary founded by Azriel Hildesheimer, which offered courses in Jewish and scientific studies. He also took an interest in the Academy of Higher Jewish Learning (*Beit ha-Midrash Elyon*), an institute for advanced Talmudic scholarship under the direction of Hayyim Heller (1880–1960). The academy combined Lithuanian Talmudic learning with modern critical historical scholarship. A deep friendship developed between Heller and Soloveitchik who revered his older friend as a father figure. In 1929, Heller left Berlin and joined the faculty of Yeshiva University.

Soloveitchik passed his oral exam on July 24, 1930, and (after requesting extensions) graduated with a doctorate[17] awarded on December 10, 1932. The dissertation was about Hermann Cohen's epistemology.[18] Later in life Soloveitchik would at times identify with the Biblical Joseph, which may explain his reference to his time in Berlin as "the seven good years."[19] In Berlin he was free to pursue his religious and secular studies. It was there where he would also meet his future wife, Tonya.

Tonya

Soloveitchik was introduced to Tonya Lewit by her brother, a fellow student at the University of Berlin. She had grown up in Vilnius (Vilna), Lithuania, and was a year younger than Soloveitchik. Tonya studied philosophy, pedagogy, psychology, and history at the University of Jena where she received her doctorate for a dissertation on the development of Jewish popular education in Poland (Lewit 1931). Though she hailed neither from prominence nor from wealth, and though Soloveitchik was expected to marry through formal matchmaking, they fell in love and married.

For a few months in 1931, Soloveitchik lived in Vilnius, his fiancée's hometown. In a letter to Altmann, Soloveitchik describes Vilna as "the cradle of the strict, I could even say 'puritanical,' Lithuanian scholarly persona, the *Lamdan*, the home of the Vilna Gaon, and [yet] also the nest of the Haskalah, the Jewish Enlightenment, which revolts against Halakhah. The rigid conservatism and the thrust toward the new are intertwined. Today Vilna is the fortress of an extremist orthodoxy which seeks to close off the Jewish soul from any new fresh breath, as well as the center of radical Jewish Marxism ... The two elements penetrate and reach into each other. In most cases, one and the same family is gripped by these two opposing forces" (Helfgot 2009, 1:316–18).

Soloveitchik and Tonya were married in Vilnius on June 16, 1931. Shortly after their wedding, they moved back to Berlin. Although the new couple had intended to remain in Berlin, the increased anti-Semitism convinced them it was time to leave. Just three months after their first child, Atarah, was born,[20] the young Soloveitchik family left Berlin for the United States[21] via boat from Liverpool, England, and joined the ranks of prominent Weimar exiles. They would arrive in New York nine days later on August 29, 1932. On the way Soloveitchik realized that he had forgotten to bring the most important document he would need in his new home.

Arrival in the United States

Although he had been awarded *semikha* (rabbinic ordination) verbally a number of times, he did not possess a formal written certificate. Avraham D. Kahana Shapiro, a distant relative, the last Chief Rabbi of Lithuania and the rabbi of Kovno (Kaunas), was more than pleased to provide the formal document, adding,[22] "The spirit of his illustrious grandfather, the leading rabbi of his time, Rabbi Hayyim Soloveitchik, rests upon Rabbi Joseph Dov Soloveitchik ... Happy is the country that will be the home of this great sage. The sages have ordained him to be the true interpreter of all religious problems, and the Halakhah shall always be decided in accordance with his rulings" (Rakeffet-Rothkoff 1998, 256).

In August 1932, Soloveitchik arrived at Ellis Island,[23] joining his parents who had arrived three years before in the United States, but the promise of employment teaching Talmud at the Hebrew Theological Seminary in Chicago did not materialize. In December 1932, however, Soloveitchik was accepted as chief rabbi of the Orthodox community of Greater Boston.[24] There, he would use his expertise in Jewish law, his intellect, and his family's reputation to influence and guide the Jewish community that included eleven congregations. But Soloveitchik would not be a copy of his father. Gone was the traditional long black coat of the European rabbinic elite.

Soloveitchik was determined to reform Jewish education. Eventually, he would also try to improve kosher standards in the local meat and poultry industry. The Jewish community, however, had its own ways of operating, and Soloveitchik would learn that imposing his will on the community would be a daunting task.

In January 1933, Soloveitchik organized a series of meetings with school and lay leaders. Instead of trying to improve the traditional Orthodox schools, he turned his attention to the community Board of Jewish Education (BJE) schools. He tried to reorganize their curriculum to teach not only Hebrew reading, writing, and spelling but also the meaning of prayers, Bible with Rashi's commentary, and Mishnah and Talmud. For practical reasons, however, this became impossible to implement.

Soloveitchik's initial failure did not deter him. He turned to Yeshiva Torat Israel, a co-ed supplementary (afternoon) school for elementary and high school students. Although originally founded in 1919, in 1934, its existence was largely unknown to the vast majority of Boston Jewry. Chevra Shas, the most prominent Orthodox organization in the Greater Boston area, voted to give control of the yeshiva to Soloveitchik who sought to turn Torat Israel into a school similar to Yeshiva University in New York. Teachers were recruited from both BJE schools and more Orthodox schools. A traditionally educated teacher directed the Talmud program, while a teacher trained in Hebrew oversaw the language program.

Vying for Chief Rabbi of Tel Aviv

On April 4, 1935, just after the death of Solomon Aaronsohn, the Chief Rabbi of Tel Aviv, Soloveitchik was nominated by his father via a letter (Soloveitchik 2010) to R. Dov Katz for Aaronsohn's position. Vying for the job were Rabbis Moses Avigdor Amiel and Isaac Herzog (who would become chief rabbi of Palestine in 1936[25] and then of Israel), both substantially older than Soloveitchik. In June 1935, Soloveitchik left Boston for Palestine (apparently) to lobby for the position. On June 12, he gave a lecture at Yeshiva Merkaz HaRav in Jerusalem (Rakeffet, 1996, 24; Dalfin 2016, 130). He also met with Abraham Isaac Kook, who remarked that the young Soloveitchik reminded him of his earlier years when he was a student attending the lectures of Hayyim Brisker at the Volozhin yeshiva. He also said that the genius of the grandfather now resided with the grandson.[26] Ultimately, for reasons still obscure,[27] Amiel secured the position.

Boston

Back in Boston, Soloveitchik once again immersed himself in improving and expanding the Torat Israel School. Some of the faculty members were now young Americans rather than former *heder* teachers, and classes were conducted with both Hebrew-Yiddish and Biblical Hebrew-Modern Hebrew translation. By 1936, the yeshiva employed teachers who were living examples of the ideology that the school attempted to infuse.

In 1937, despite much community opposition, Soloveitchik created the Maimonides Educational Institute, the first all-day Jewish school in New England. At its inception, the Maimonides day school, housed at Soloveitchik's home,[28] had six students and a single faculty member. By the mid-1990s, enrollment would peak at about 700 students. Classes at the Maimonides school were co-educational at all grade levels, and as such, the girls too studied Talmud, a radical curriculum move at the time. In a 1953 letter to Rabbi Leonard Rosenfeld, Soloveitchik would state explicitly that girls should be taught Talmud: "Not only is the teaching of *Torah she-be-al peh* [Talmud] to girls permissible but it is nowadays an absolute imperative.

The policy of discrimination between the sexes as to subject matter and method of instruction which is still advocated by certain groups within our Orthodox community has contributed greatly to the deterioration and downfall of traditional Judaism. Boys and girls alike should be introduced into the inner halls of *Torah she-be-al peh*" (*CCC*, 83). In 1977, Soloveitchik implicitly reiterated his position by delivering the inaugural Talmud lesson for girls at YU's Stern College for Women (Gorelik 2008, 181). While teaching at Yeshiva University, Soloveitchik continued to have a soft spot in his heart for graduates of Maimonides and granted them greater access to himself (Gopin 2006, 27).

To further intensify the level of Torah scholarship in Boston, Soloveitchik, together with his father, opened a full-time yeshiva and rabbinical training program for advanced male Talmud scholars. It was modeled after the classical European Yeshivot and called Heikhal Rabbenu Hayyim ha-Levi. Its students were mostly recent immigrants from Europe.

During the month of *Elul* (August/September) 1937, Yaakov Kamenetsky visited Soloveitchik in Boston and proposed that they jointly open a traditional yeshiva (school) in which Soloveitchik would serve as the Rosh Yeshiva (dean) and Kamenetsky would serve as the spiritual guide, *menahel ha-ruhani* (Schachter 2001, 12–13 citing Kamenetsky 2002). Perhaps Kamenetsky was not aware that Soloveitchik was already working with his father on such a yeshiva.

In early 1940, Soloveitchik attempted to merge Heikhal Rabbenu Hayyim ha-Levi with Yeshiva University College. However, with the death of Soloveitchik's father, Soloveitchik succeeded him at YU's Rabbi Isaac Elchanan Theological Seminary (RIETS), and the planned merger did not materialize. In 1941, Soloveitchik merged the yeshiva with Yeshivat Torat Israel, and the Maimonides Educational Institute, forming the Boston Yeshiva Academy. It was to the Maimonides day school that the Soloveitchiks, especially Tonya, continued to dedicate their efforts in Boston (Farber 2004, 31–57). Had Soloveitchik been content to focus only on education he might have avoided one of the most challenging periods of his life. Instead, he decided to take on the kosher meat and poultry industry.

Boston's Kosher problem

When Soloveitchik arrived in Boston, he believed that much of the meat and poultry that was presented as kosher in fact was not. This was scandalous and unacceptable. In 1937, Soloveitchik advocated the use of markers (*plumbas*) on poultry to certify their *kashrut* (kosher status). He instituted a one-cent surcharge for each *plumba* and directed the profit to the slaughterers who were underpaid and worked under difficult conditions. Soloveitchik also participated in demonstrations for the slaughterers (one of which turned violent) demanding improved working conditions (Farber 2004, 60).

In apparent retaliation for Soloveitchik's participation, accusations were spread that he was running a racket and financially benefiting from his supervision. In 1941, fraud and corruption charges against Soloveitchik were brought before Judge Robert Bushnell, and at his behest, Judge Abraham Cohen was appointed to conduct an independent investigation.

This was a difficult period for Soloveitchik whose father would not live to see him exonerated. He passed away before Cohen's report in November 1943 praised Soloveitchik and cleared him of all charges. Seth Farber notes, "[M]any of Rabbi Soloveitchik's early activities ended in failure, and during the late 1930s and early 1940s he was alienated from the majority of Boston Jewry" (Farber 2004, 151). This largely stemmed from his confrontation with the kosher meat and poultry industry.

While Soloveitchik's affiliation with the Boston community continued throughout his life, his focus shifted. His efforts would no longer be directed toward community and religious reforms but to teaching.

Appointment at Yeshiva University

At his father's invitation, he had acted as a guest lecturer in Talmud at Yeshiva University throughout the 1930s and was an instructor in Jewish philosophy from the spring of 1936 to the fall of 1937 (*CCC*, xx). On his father's passing in 1941, Soloveitchik succeeded him as lecturer of Talmud at YU's RIETS despite some vehement opposition from its board members. Soloveitchik would now be able to dedicate himself to teaching, in a position he would hold for forty-four years.

Hershel Schachter describes Soloveitchik's schedule: Each week he would fly to New York to teach Talmud at RIETS. On Tuesdays, he gave two two-hour lectures in the morning, one to younger students and the other to older students who were studying for ordination. At night he gave a lecture for laypeople at Congregation Moriah,[29] a second-story synagogue on the Upper West Side of Manhattan. On Wednesdays, he would again give two morning lectures, after which he would return to Boston (Schachter 1994, 27, 28). In addition, he resumed teaching courses in Jewish philosophy in the late 1940s and the 1950s[30] in the university's Bernard Revel graduate school (Shatz 2018, 152).[31]

As Rosh Yeshiva (dean), he ordained some 2,000 students (Lamm 1993, 13) whose ordination certificate he cosigned with Rabbi Samuel Belkin (*CCC*, xvii).

Zionism

In the late 1930s, Soloveitchik had not as yet fully developed the attitude toward Zionism for which he would later become known. Would he continue along the path of his grandfather, Ḥayyim, who in line with Eastern European Orthodoxy was an anti-Zionist, or would he follow his father, who had already taken steps in the direction of religious Zionism?

Soloveitchik appears to have initially been leaning toward the non-Zionist (anti-Zionist) policies of the Agudath Israel movement.

In 1937, Rabbi Eliezer Silver, a close friend of Soloveitchik, led the American delegation to the last European Agudah conference and received a mandate to establish Agudah in the United States. Soloveitchik joined Agudath Israel and was enthusiastically welcomed by its members. Firmly committed, he played a leading role in the organization.[32] He was appointed to head its national executive committee, and he served as an active member of the newly formed American Council of Torah Sages (Rakeffet-Rothkoff 1999, 1:52). In the late 1930s, following Agudah's policy, he refused to support a boycott against Germany (Rakeffet-Rothkoff 2013), and in the early 1940s, he worked with Agudath Israel to raise money for the Jews of Europe.[33]

Soloveitchik also took part in a public protest on behalf of the Jews in Europe. In 1943, the Union of Orthodox Rabbis of the United States and Canada organized a March on Washington to persuade the administration to help the European Jews being killed by the Nazis. Soloveitchik, one of the 400 rabbis who participated, recalled bitterly how President Franklin Roosevelt refused to meet with them and instead sent his vice president, Henry Wallace. Soloveitchik was dejected over the seeming failure of the march to achieve its stated goals, and years later, he expressed guilt for not having done enough to help the Jews during the Holocaust. "I am not blaming anybody. I am blaming myself. Why didn't I act like [the biblical] Mordechai when he heard the news about the evil decree issued by Haman and Ahasuerus? Why didn't I go into the center of the city and shout bitterly and loudly? Why didn't I shout, yell and cry? Why didn't I tear my clothes like Mordechai?" (Rakeffet-Rothkoff 1999, 2:156). He was determined not to repeat this mistake. He would not let down the Jews of Palestine.

Prior to the establishment of the State of Israel, Soloveitchik advocated for Jewish settlement in Palestine. In January 1948, he keynoted the YU Student Drive on behalf of new Palestine settlements, declaring, "The number of religious colonists will decide the future of Palestine rather than any political triumphs."[34]

In contrast with many ultra-Orthodox Jews of his time, he proclaimed as false the argument that a Jewish state run by non-observant Jews should be shunned. "The first Temple was under the control of idolaters most of the time. The Sadducees were in power at the time of the Second Temple, even though the prophets and the sages fought bitterly against these foes of Judaism, still they did not desert the state." Soloveitchik predicted that although "Orthodoxy may not have a big share in the new state yet Torah will be fruitful in Palestine. Religious Jews will be able to live better in a Palestine ruled by Hashomer Hatzair (a secular Marxist-Zionist youth movement) than in an American Jewish ghetto like Williamsburg."[35]

From 1946, Soloveitchik served as honorary president of the Religious Zionists of America and then became the honorary president of Mizrachi-Hapoel Mizrachi World Organization (Goldberg 2010, 107).

Years later, on Israel Independence Day in 1956, at a public convocation at Yeshiva University, Soloveitchik would deliver in a poetic Yiddish his case for Zionism. It was later published in Hebrew as *Kol Dodi Dofek* (*Listen, My Beloved Knocks*) and was to become one of his most endearing works.

Two years later, on Israel's tenth anniversary year, Soloveitchik would again give an impassioned speech about his love for Israel. Soloveitchik explained that bread, after which we recite three blessings, is more special than the seven species of grain for which Israel is known, which after eating one recites only one blessing. This, he explained, is because when we create bread, we partner with God in its production. In a similar vein, the sanctity of Mt. Moriah remained, while that of Mt. Sinai did not. This is because on Mt. Moriah, mankind, that is, Abraham and Isaac, partnered with God to make it holy. So too we are partnering with God in redeeming the Land of Israel, and, therefore, the Land is so beloved to us.[36]

Earliest Jewish philosophy

Some of Soloveitchik's most important philosophical works were written in the early 1940s. *Ish ha-Halakhah* (*Halakhic Man*) was published in 1944, the same year Soloveitchik wrote *The Halakhic Mind*, although that would not be published for another forty-two years. *U-Vekashtem me-Sham* (*And from There You Shall Seek*) was likely written at this time as well.

Declining the Chief Rabbinate

Shortly after the death of Chief Rabbi Isaac Herzog (1888–1959), the Mizrachi leader Moshe Ḥayyim Shapiro came to America and, with the consent of Prime Minister David Ben-Gurion, offered the Chief Rabbinate of Israel to Soloveitchik,[37] who ultimately turned it down. When Shapiro asked him why he had previously campaigned for the Chief Rabbinate of Tel Aviv, Soloveitchik responded, "… Tel Aviv is a city with [Jewish courts], butcher shops, [synagogues], [study halls], people in need of pastoral tending. The Chief Rabbinate is a bureaucracy" (Genack 1998, 217). Soloveitchik also explained that he was reluctant to become an officer of the state; a rabbinate linked with the state cannot be completely independent. In a letter to Dr. Milton Konvitz, Soloveitchik describes his refusal to serve in more detail: "… the idea of [the Rabbinate] may be placed in either of these two perspectives. If interpreted in terms of personal participating and sharing in the existential experience through the act of Judaic living and teaching, then the rabbi-teacher comes to the fore. If, however, the [Rabbinate] is institutionalized, depersonalized, and the rabbi's educational task reduced to nil, the rabbi-administrator appears in the public arena. Unfortunately the makeup of the Chief Rabbinate in Israel fits more easily into the latter category."[38]

Soloveitchik's refusal to serve as chief rabbi did not diminish his stature. On the contrary, many viewed it as a principled stance (Elberg 1960).

Second Kosher meat crisis

Soloveitchik's stature was now firmly established in the broader Jewish community. In 1958, when Congress enacted and President Eisenhower signed into law humane slaughtering legislation, the Jewish establishment turned to Soloveitchik, among others, for guidance.

Although the legislation defined *shehitah*, Jewish ritual slaughter, as humane, only a special amendment exempted how livestock were handled prior to *shehitah*, a method which included shackling and hoisting, and which was widely viewed as inhumane.[39]

Fearing that state legislatures might impose their own restrictions on the *shehitah* process, and fearing that a future federal administration might revoke the *shehitah* exemption, Soloveitchik in 1959 galvanized not only the Rabbinical Council of America (RCA) but also the Synagogue Council of America (SCA) and the National Community Relations Advisory Council (NCRAC), which at that time represented almost the entire range of religious and secular Jewish organizations in the United States. Their mission was to protect *shehitah* by instituting practices that avoided any unnecessary pain or discomfort to the animal.

The legislation enacted in 1958 also authorized the Secretary of Agriculture to conduct research to identify humane methods for handling livestock prior to slaughter. Soloveitchik was nominated by the RCA in late 1958 and was endorsed by all major rabbinic and secular Jewish organizations. In 1959, he was appointed by U.S. Agriculture Secretary Ezra Taft Benson to serve as the Jewish religious authority on the advisory committee to help implement the Humane Slaughter Law.[40] In this capacity, he would testify in 1961 and again in 1964 regarding the humane process of Jewish ritual slaughter.

Soloveitchik worked with the committee to identify restraining pens which do not utilize shackling and hoisting, and which are efficient and humane. The American Society for the Prevention of Cruelty to Animals (ASPCA) allocated $250,000 to this process and bought all patent rights to the technology of handling animals prior to slaughter. The patent rights owned by the SCA and the NCRAC[41] were turned over gratis to the ASPCA, and the ASPCA in turn made them available free of charge to any slaughterhouse. Kosher slaughterhouses across the country, and in Canada,[42] began implementing these methods.

While dealing with the *shehitah* issue, Soloveitchik also needed to focus on a more personal crisis. In 1959, he was diagnosed with cancer, and in 1960, he underwent surgery. Although his surgery was successful, Soloveitchik tempered his teaching ambitions. He no longer gave courses in philosophy and concentrated on teaching Talmud.

The teacher

Of all his roles, the one to which Soloveitchik devoted the majority of his efforts was that of a *melamed*, a teacher of Torah.[43] Soloveitchik would point out that God too is referred to as a teacher: "One who teaches Torah to his nation Israel" (*Berakhot* 11b). Soloveitchik poetically described his own role as a teacher of Talmud:

> Whenever I start a [lecture], the door opens. Another old man walks in and sits down. He is older than I am. All the [students] call me the Rav. He is older than the Rav. He is the grandfather of the Rav. His name is Reb Ḥayyim Brisker. Without him, no [lecture] can be delivered nowadays. Then the door opens quietly again and another old man comes in. He is older than Reb Ḥayyim. He lived in the seventeenth century. What is his name? Shabsi Kohen. He is the famous Shach who must be present when [laws involving money] are being discussed, and when we study [the Talmudic tractates] *Baba Kamma, Baba Metzia.* And then more visitors show up. Some of the visitors lived in the eleventh century, some in the twelfth century some in the thirteenth century. Some lived in Antiquity. Rabbi Akiba, Rashi, Rabbeinu [Tam], the [Ra'avad], the Rashba. More and more come in, come in, come in.
>
> Of course, what do I do? I introduce them to my pupils, and the dialogue commences. [Maimonides] says something, The Ra'avad disagrees sharply ... A boy jumps up to defend [Maimonides] against the Ra'avad ....
>
> We are all committed to a common vision, and we all operate with the same categories ... This community of generations, this dialogue between antiquity and present will finally bring the redemption of the Jews.
> (Kashkin 2012, 56–57)[44]

His own romanticized perception of his lectures notwithstanding, Soloveitchik was a strict and demanding teacher. Norman Lamm recalls a frequently heard refrain: "He was a terror, a holy terror. I mean, he terrorized his students" (Eisenberg 2006, 00:38:48).[45] But they also greatly admired him. Fred Sommers, for example, who was in Soloveitchik's lecture for five years in the 1940s and went on to become a rather formidable philosopher, complained that no one he encountered in his graduate school days at Columbia University had Soloveitchik's intellectual stature or independence of mind (Sommers 2006). In his lectures to laypeople, Soloveitchik's teaching demeanor was very different. He could be charming and even entertaining. Referring to his lectures at Maimonides school, he once quipped, "Remember, this is Saturday night. I'm in competition with all the movie houses, so I've got to be able to entertain the same time that I teach" (Eisenberg 2006, 00:59:55).

Although Soloveitchik might have remained content devoting his efforts to teaching, there were other issues affecting the Jewish community demanding his attention.

Soloveitchik was called upon to help battle Christian influence on Jews in Israel. In the early 1960s, the issue of Christian missionizing in Israel came to the forefront. In the following year, Soloveitchik wrote a private letter stating that if he were a member of Knesset, he would introduce legislation prohibiting missionary activity in Israel. In 1963, Soloveitchik cosigned a letter with other leading rabbis encouraging Prime Minister Levi Eshkol to enact legislation prohibiting Christian missionizing in Israel (*CCC*, 208).

Soloveitchik would soon be called upon to deal with Christianity (specifically, Catholicism) on a much broader and global level.

"Confrontation"

To modernize Catholic dogma and revise its historic contempt for the Jewish people, the Catholic Church in 1960 convened Vatican Council II. In 1965, it would issue its document *Nostra Aetate* absolving Jews from the charge of deicide. During that period Soloveitchik, as head of the Halakhah committee of the RCA, was asked by Nahum Goldmann, president of the World Jewish Congress, to formulate the Orthodox reaction to the Vatican Council. Soloveitchik insisted that the Vatican Council was a Catholic affair and that Jews should not attend or tell the Church what to do. In 1964, Soloveitchik published "Confrontation" formalizing what he believed should be the Orthodox attitude: cooperate with other faith communities in social causes but not engage in dialogue concerning issues of faith or religion.[46]

Closely overlapping his involvement with *Nostra Aetate*, in the years 1961–1966, Soloveitchik summoned his most impassioned rhetoric on behalf of religious Zionism. During this period, Soloveitchik delivered his *Five Addresses* at the annual Mizrachi (Religious Zionists of America) conventions held in November in Atlantic City, New Jersey, justifying and advocating for Mizrachi and religious Zionism.

Soloveitchik's relationship with right-wing Orthodoxy became strained due to his advocacy of secular education and Zionism. These same issues may have also played a role in his relationship with the Lubavitch Ḥasidic sect.

Lubavitch

Soloveitchik's warm feelings toward Lubavitch began in his childhood and were fostered by a long-term relationship with Menachem Mendel Schneerson (the "Rebbe") that began while they were university students in

Berlin.[47] In 1964, Soloveitchik visited Schneerson to comfort him when he was mourning for his mother, and in 1980, he visited him at a *farbrengen,* a public gathering, in honor of his thirtieth anniversary as the Rebbe of Lubavitch.[48] Soloveitchik's visits may have been in part an acknowledgment of an old but important favor: the previous Lubavitcher Rebbe had played a crucial role in helping Soloveitchik succeed his father as Rosh Yeshiva (senior lecturer of Talmud) at RIETS.[49]

Soloveitchik viewed Schneerson's philosophy not as one based on Halakhah but as a mystical conceptual system with its own trajectory. Nevertheless, he was impressed with Schneerson's organized army of volunteers reaching out to the less affiliated, and he favorably viewed Schneerson's willingness to fight for his ideals. He also agreed with Schneerson that a Jew should live where he can be productive and do the most good, even if that means living outside the Land of Israel (Holzer 2009a, 172, 156, 160, 241).

There was, however, a less amicable side to their relationship. Soloveitchik's son Haym relates, "In 1951–52, my father offered to come see the Rebbe. His invitation [sic] was refused by the Rebbe. From that point forward, the relationship was almost non-existent ... In 1954, my father was invited to give a lecture at YIVO [Yiddish Scientific Institute]. It was at that time that he received a letter from the Rebbe. The Rebbe wrote my father asking him to mention in his speech the *Chilul Shabbos* (desecration of *Shabbos*) that was taking place at YIVO, since they were open on *Shabbos*. My father didn't even bother to answer" (Deutsch 1997, vol. II, 118). Haym Soloveitchik also relates that his father feared "The Rebbe will turn Lubavitch into a messianic movement ..." (Deutsch 1997, vol. II, 122).

1967

In 1967, as Israel faced an existential threat from Egypt, Soloveitchik was facing his own personal crisis. Early in the year, Egyptian forces mobilized along their border with Israel as Gamal Abdel Nasser threatened to annihilate the State of Israel. Fear and dread would soon turn into jubilation and a newfound self-confidence. Following Israel's pre-emptive attack which debilitated the Egyptian, Jordanian, and Syrian armies, Israel found itself in possession of a vastly enlarged country that now also included East Jerusalem, Judea and Samaria (the West Bank), the Golan Heights, and the Sinai Peninsula. The war electrified the Jewish people and their young State. Jews worldwide claimed a new sense of pride, and those in Israel were granted a new holiday celebrating the reunification of Jerusalem.[50]

But for Soloveitchik, 1967 was the saddest year of his life. His wife passed away on March 23, and he was inconsolable. "... He said *Kaddish* for at least five years. Every day, every *Kaddish*."[51] He would visit her grave site every week. When it was pointed out to him that his family's custom was to avoid visiting the cemetery, he shrugged his shoulders and replied, "What can I do?"[52]

He had also lost his mother on January 2[53] and his brother, Shmuel, a chemistry professor, on February 25.[54] Despite this triple tragedy, on July 25, Soloveitchik took the time to answer a letter from a Zionist teacher in Israel asking him why he did not make *aliyah*. In his reply Soloveitchik laments his cruel fate, "Last year, we——my wife *z"l* and I——decided to come to Israel and remain for about six months, to see the land and the people who dwell therein. However … what happened, happened …" His main answer though seems to be at the end of the letter, "One may do much or one may do little; it is all one, provided he directs his heart to Heaven [*Berakhot* 5b]. All our work is dedicated to the flourishing of the values of Judaism, the tradition of our forefathers and our sages, the bearers of the tradition and its scholars" (*CCC*, 228–29).

These tragedies took their toll.[55] From that point on, he was easier on his students and became more tolerant of their weaknesses. He also allowed more of his work to be published. In the 1970s, a number of Soloveitchik's public lectures appeared in print. Five were published in *Tradition:* "The Community," "Majesty and Humility," "Catharsis," "Redemption, Prayer and Talmud Torah," and "A Tribute to the Rebbitzin of Talne."

Begin and Sharon

As a leader of Modern Orthodox Jewry in America, Soloveitchik's residence became a stop for Israeli politicians. In July 1977, Prime Minister Menachem Begin visited the United States and met with Soloveitchik in New York. The two had strong family ties. Begin's father Ze'ev Dov had been the *gabbai* (sexton) in the synagogue where Soloveitchik's grandfather Rabbi Ḥayyim was the rabbi. When Begin and Soloveitchik met, they embraced warmly and recounted how Begin's father Ze'ev Dov, over the objection of R. Ḥayyim, arranged for a eulogy of Theodor Herzl to take place at the synagogue.[56]

Their warm encounter, however, was not an endorsement of Begin's politics. During that same visit to New York, Begin gave a speech at Yeshiva University. Soloveitchik was about a hundred feet away and chose not to attend. Marc (Mendi) Gopin, who was then with Soloveitchik, asked him why he was not attending. Soloveitchik is purported to have answered, "Why should I listen to a person who blew up people in a hotel," referring to Begin's role in blowing up the King David Hotel in 1946 as part of the campaign to expel the British from Palestine (Feldinger 2010).

On June 6, 1982, following negotiations with the Christian ruling party and the assassination attempt of an Israeli diplomat in London, the Israel Defense Forces entered Lebanon in the midst of their civil war. The Israeli role was brought to an end on August 21, 1982, with a U.S.-brokered agreement. On September 16, 1982, following the assassination of the

Lebanese prime minister but prior to Israel's withdrawal, a militia made up of Christian Lebanese right-wing loyalists entered the Sabra and Shatila refugee camps in Beirut and killed many civilians, mostly Palestinians.

Following widespread condemnation of these killings, with much of the anger directed at then Israeli defense minister Ariel Sharon, Soloveitchik in his last public act as a Jewish community leader instructed Louis Bernstein to contact the leaders of the National Religious Party in Israel to demand they support an investigation into the incident. If they failed to do so, Soloveitchik warned that he would resign as head of Mizrachi. Soloveitchik's will prevailed, and in September 28, 1982, the MafDa"L religious Zionist party participated in the Kahan Commission inquiry into the massacre at Sabra and Shatila.

Death

In 1986, after forty-four years at Yeshiva University, Soloveitchik retired from teaching. He had become incapacitated by Parkinson's disease and later from Alzheimer's. He remained secluded and was cared for by his daughter Atarah, and his son-in-law, Yitzchak (Isadore) Twersky.

On the fourth day of Passover, the night of April 8, 1993 (18 Nisan 5753), at the age of 90, Soloveitchik died of heart failure and was buried next to his wife Tonya in West Roxbury, Massachusetts.

Legacy

Soloveitchik left behind many recorded lectures in Yiddish and English and approximately 200 manuscripts containing his Hebrew writings on Halakhah and English writings on philosophy.[57] Many of these appear to be the manuscripts currently being edited by the Toras HoRav Foundation, an organization dedicated to publishing Soloveitchik's manuscripts, which as of 2020 has published about a dozen books.

Soloveitchik's legacy continues through his descendants, which number among them scholars, rabbis, and leaders, and in the thousands of rabbis he ordained and the students he taught.

"The righteous, even in death, are said to be alive" (*Berakhot,* 18a). To his students and his followers, Soloveitchik continues to be referred to admiringly as "the Rav," the Rabbi *par excellence.*

Notes

1 A scholarly biography of Soloveitchik is still a desideratum (Ziegler 2012, 38, reiterated in Shatz 2017). We draw primarily, but not exclusively, on Schachter (1994, 2001, 2010), Meiselman (1995), Rakeffet-Rothkoff (1998, 1999), Farber (2004), *CCC* (2005), Helfgot (2009), and Soloveitchik's own works.
2 As is not uncommon with Jews, Soloveitchik used different names in different circumstances: Yosef Dov ben Moshe ha-Levi on religious occasions and

documents; at home and among friends, his name was Yiddishized to Berel or Yoshe Ber; his Anglicized legal name was Joseph B. Soloveitchik and Josef Solowiejczyk in Polish.Soloveitchik was also diminutively referred to as "J. B." (his initials) by some of his ultra-Orthodox detractors (Rakeffet-Rothkoff 1996, 32, 41n41), a moniker that dates back to at least 1958 when Archibald MacLeish's play, *J. B.*, a retelling of the Biblical story of Job, appeared on Broadway. A press release from Yeshiva University dated December 12, 1958 reads, "There'll be standing room only for JB at Yeshiva University, Sunday, January 11. But it won't be for the Broadway play of the same name. The 'JB' we have reference to is less euphemistically known as Dr. Joseph B. Soloveitchik, Yeshiva University renowned Talmudic scholar" (www.Hakirah.org/ShurinArchive/Doc0105.pdf).

3 Though small, Pruzhany had been the home of distinguished rabbinic scholars including Joel Sirkes (1561–1640), author of *Bayit Ḥadash (Ba"ḥ)*, and his son-in-law David b. Samuel ha-Levi Segal (1586–1667), author of *Turei Zahav (Ta"z)*. See *Encyclopaedia Judaica*, s.v. "Pruzhany" (vol. 13, Jerusalem: Keter, 1972, col. 1294).

4 Soloveitchik was distantly related to Moses Feinstein, a leading American post-war halakhic authority. See Chapter 6.

5 Ḥayyim Soloveitchik, also known as R. Ḥayyim Brisker (1853–1918), so called after Brisk (Brest-Litovsk, Lithuania) the city in which he served as rabbi, was the grandson-in-law of Rabbi Naftali Zvi Yehuda Berlin, the Netziv (1816–1893).

6 See Chaper 3, Section "The Brisker method."

7 Kolbrener (2016, 67–75) takes this story as key to understanding Soloveitchik's thought.

8 Schachter (2010, 110) paraphrases a story Soloveitchik told on 19 Kislev (the Hebrew day on which Rabbi Shneur Zalman of Liadi was released from prison in 1798), in 1968 to a group of Lubavitch hasidim in Boston to explain why a town comprised mostly of Lubavitch hasidim had a *mitnaged* rabbi. The rabbi, by tradition, was selected from the descendants or disciples of Hayyim Volozhin. During the French invasion of Russia, Shneur Zalman of Liadi spoke out in support of the Tsar. When Napoleon found out that Shneur Zalman was in Khislavichi, he ordered him arrested. Knowing that no one would believe he was hiding in the house of a *mitnaged*, Shneur Zalman appealed to the rabbi of the city—a student of the Gaon of Vilna—to hide him. In gratitude, the Lubavitch town established that its rabbi would always be a *mitnaged*. A (truncated])audio recording of Soloveitchik telling this story can be found at https://www.torahrecordings.com/classes/by_month/003_kislev/kislev19/023.

9 In the recording cited in the previous note, Soloveitchik is recounting the "mitnaged version" of the story of Shneur Zalman of Liadi and Levi Yitzhak of Berditichev's attempt to visit the Goan of Vilna. In that speech he claims that Reisberg directed his *Tanya* lessons particularly at him, as the representative of the Brisk tradition. He also notes that he is a great-great-grandson of Ḥayyim of Volozhin, the chief opponent of hasidim in general and Habad in particular. Nonetheless, he knows much about Habad and in fact claims (somewhat light-heartedly) to be a "clandestine Habadnik." Wolfson (2015, 200n11) takes that as "[o]ne of the most unequivocal affirmations of the influence of Habad on Soloveitchik ..." See there for a reference to a paraphrase of the talk. See also Schachter (2010, 108–11). Solomon (1993, 49) notes Ḥayyim Soloveitchik's appreciation for some aspects of the Hassidic movement.

10 There are a number of versions of this story. See Rakeffet-Rothkoff (1998, 255, 1999, 1:149) and Lamm (1993, 4). Shlomo Riskin provides yet another—more colorful—account: "One afternoon, when young Yosef Dov was no older than

seven or eight, he came home with smack marks (apparently from his rebbe) on his cheek. When his father demanded an explanation, and when the hapless student repeated his unfortunate questions that caused the slaps, his father, Rav Moshe, admitted that his wife had been right in the first place. From then on, he himself taught his brilliant son. Rav Soloveitchik looked at us and smiled. 'Apparently there were two of us who didn't know *Bava Metzia*: the *melamed dardeke* [teacher of children] and I. But my father agreed that the *melamed dardeke* should continue to teach me *Tanya*. I loved those classes with him and they left an indelible impression on my life-long interest in *Torat HaNistar*'" (Riskin 2010, 233).

11 A. I. Kook, for unrelated reasons, also became disillusioned with a Tahkemoni School in Jaffa (Mirsky 2014, 62–63).
12 It is unclear whether Soloveitchik ever attended classes or was just awarded a certificate from the gymnasium. See Rakeffet-Rothkoff (1999, vol. 1, 68n9).
13 At the time, the diploma was equivalent to a high school certification. About one-third of the students there were Jewish as were many of the faculty, who were also politically quite radical.
14 See Rakeffet-Rothkoff (1999, vol. 1, 68n11) and Rutishauser (2013, 7) regarding the claim Soloveitchik left Poland to avoid the Polish military draft. See, however, Schacter (1998, 218–19) for an analysis of the accuracy of this claim.
15 The reason Soloveitchik was drawn to philosophy is a matter of some speculation (see Shatz 2017, 176ff).
16 Max Dessoir, a co-sponsor of Soloveitchik's dissertation, was also one of Heschel's sponsors. See Kimelman (2004) for a discussion of the relationship and similarities between Heschel and Soloveitchik, but see Kaplan (1987, 194) regarding important differences.
17 A pre-war German doctorate was not quite the equivalent of an American doctorate of the period. It granted a title but did not qualify one to teach as an ordinary professor in a German university. The highest degree, the one needed to teach in a German university, is earned once a *habilitationsschrift*, a more significant dissertation, is accepted by a university. (Thanks to David Vampola for clarification.)
18 Soloveitchik had originally intended to write a dissertation arguing, against the prevailing opinion (but in line with Hermann Cohen's), that Maimonides was a Platonist (see Cohen 2004). There was no one in the university, however, qualified to supervise such a thesis (Lichtenstein 1963, 285; Rakeffet-Rothkoff 1996, 21). See Ravitzky (1986) and the Editor's Introduction to *Maimonides Course* as well as p. 118f for a discussion of Soloveitchik's relationship to Cohen's Platonism.
19 Rakeffet-Rothkoff in Eisenberg (2006, 00:22:23).
20 They would have three children, Atarah (who married Isadore Twersky), Tovah (who married Aharon Lichtenstein), and Haym.
21 Moshe Soloveitchik enlisted the help of Yaakov Yisroel Korff, the Zvhiller Rebbe, to help Soloveitchik come to the United States (Dalfin 2016, 18–19).
22 Shapiro's letter was first published in the rabbinic journal *HaPardes* 6 (7): 6 (October 1932) on the occasion of Soloveitchik's arrival in America and was reprinted in *Mesorah* 9: 7 (1994) (see Bierman 2003, 28n23). See also Rakeffet-Rothkoff (1996, 20).
23 See "Rabbi is Detained," *The New York Times*, 8/30/32.
24 See "To Install Rabbi Soloveitchik as Chief Rabbi of Boston," *The Wisconsin Jewish Chronicle*, 12/30/32, p. 8, available at www.hakirah.org/ShurinArchive/DOC2000.PDF.
25 After Isaac Herzog became Chief Rabbi of Palestine, the post he vacated, Chief

Rabbi of Ireland, was offered to Soloveitchik (*Herald Tribune* 5/11/1937. Available at www.hakirah.org/ShurinArchive/DOC0024.PDF).

26 See Saks (2006a, 2006b, 90, 95n2).

27 Some claim that Meyer Berlin, president of the World Mizrachi movement, believed Soloveitchik, although possibly the greatest scholar among the contenders, was not the most suitable for Tel Aviv's Jewish community (Rakeffet-Rothkoff 1998, 268–69, 273n29). Perhaps he was too young (Rakeffet-Rothkoff 1996, 25), or perhaps he was too far to the religious right, being affiliated at that time with Agudath Israel (see Rosensweig 1998, 250).

28 Aharon Ben-Zion Shurin writes that realizing that the students in her home were interfering with her husband's study, Tonya remarked to him, "I was born in Vilna and I would like to tell you what the Vilna Gaon repeated about his wife in his eulogy for her. This is how it was told-over in Vilna. The Vilna Gaon's rebbetzin was once speaking with her husband. 'Listen to me, my husband, we both suffered from starvation, but I also suffered from the cold and therefore my reward in the other world is greater.' Rebbitizen Tonya elaborated to her husband, Rabbi Yosef Ber, as follows: 'You, my husband, are warmed by the Torah which you study day and night. You create *hiddushim*, you offer opinions and sharp thoughts from which you have spiritual joy. You give lectures to students and addresses to laymen. This warms you but I remain cold. I cannot do what you do. Therefore, I need to warm myself a bit with my small accomplishments. Behold these young children who learn Torah—this will warm me a bit. This will be my reward'." ("An Interesting Woman Departed from the World." *Forward* 4/18/67 available at www.Hakirah.org/ShurinArchive/Doc0109.pdf.)

29 Soloveitchik was the rabbi of Congregation Moriah from 1950 to 1960 (Rakeffet-Rothkoff 1996, 33).

30 The first term of his 1950–1951 philosophy lectures on Maimonides' *Guide of the Perplexed* was published as *Maimonides Course.*

31 Following the style of German university professors, Soloveitchik, at YU's Revel graduate school, would often read from a prepared text, look up, and elaborate. His transition from the written to the oral was frequently introduced by the expression, "I mean" (Blau 2008, 67). Sid Leiman told us (personal communication) that when reading from his text, he would often look up from the page and say, "Now I will tell you what is *not* on the paper."

32 At the 1940 Agudah Convention, Soloveitchik delivered a eulogy for Ḥayyim Ozer Grodzinski of Vilna, the leading sage of Eastern Europe, who had recently passed away. See Rakeffet-Rothkoff (1999, 1:52). Grodzinski was a participant in the founding conference of Agudath Israel (in Kattowitz, Silesia, in 1912) and served on its Council of Sages.

33 The rabbinical journal *Ha-Pardes* (14 (11): February 1941, 7) published Agudath Israel of America's emotional appeal to raise money prior to Passover for the Jews in Europe, "All their possessions and assets were looted and they find themselves bereft of all. Millions of our Jewish brothers and their families are dying of hunger …" Rabbi Eliezer Silver is signed as president, and Yosef Dov ha-Levi Soloveitchik of Boston is signed as head of the national executive committee.

34 *The Commentator,* vol. XXVI (6), 1. 1/15/48.

35 Ibid.

36 See YUTorah.org, "Yom Haazmaut–Ezra, Yeshaya, Koach and Gvura (Yiddish)," 1958, www.yutorah.org/lectures/lecture.cfm/751426/Rabbi_Joseph_B_Soloveitchik/Yom_Haazmaut_-_Ezra,_Yeshaya,_Koach_and_Gvura_(Yiddish)_.

37 Soloveitchik was also considered for the position of Chief Rabbi of Great Britain

a number of times. The first time his name came up, it was to replace Joseph Herman Hertz on his death in 1946. It was immediately rejected as word got out that Soloveitchik could not use a knife and fork properly, that is, he ate like an American. The second time he was suggested was in 1965 to succeed Israel Brodie, but he refused to allow his name to go forward (https://www. torahmusings.com/2011/07/british-chief-rabbis-who-never-were/).

38 Letter dated 1/30/61 (Helfgot 2009, 1:321).

39 See the introduction to *CCC* (xviii–xix) and the three reports by Soloveitchik on pp. 61–74.

40 From a biographical sketch of Soloveitchik, *Yeshiva University* (8/1/59) available at www.hakirah.org/ShurinArchive/DOC0025.PDF.

41 The patent can be accessed at https://patentimages.storage.googleapis.com/96/8a/ 7c/fb9659c1479303/US3113340.pdf.

42 See "Canadians Find New Animal Handling Method," *Wisconsin Jewish Chronicle*, 9/16/60, p. 6, available at www.hakirah.org/ShurinArchive/DOC2009. PDF; "Shechitah System in Can. Begun in Major Cities," *Wisconsin Jewish Chronicle*, 12/9/60, p. 5, available at www.hakirah.org/ShurinArchive/ DOC2011.PDF.

43 Cf. Lichtenstein (1996, 52): "[Soloveitchik] often—albeit, at times, with a note of conveniently feigned self-deprecation—described himself as a *melamed* [teacher]; and that he was, without peer ...."

44 Kashkin notes (57n26) that this was said at a *pidyon ha-ben* (ceremonial redemption of a first-born son) in 1974. See there for a reference to an audio recording. See the summary in Besdin (1989, 15–24). Cf. *AFTYSS* 143–45.

45 See Blau (2008, 67) for another account of Soloveitchik's lectures and Boylan (1996) for a somewhat hagiographic description of Soloveitchik's Talmud lectures.

46 Soloveitchik's attitude toward interfaith dialogue parallels his attitude toward membership in the Synagogue Council of America in which Orthodox, Conservative, and Reform rabbis cooperated on social issues. See Chapter 6.

47 Adin Steinsaltz recounts that Soloveitchik recalled having once rescued Schneerson from jail: Once on Purim the Rebbe was on the Humboldt University campus somewhat tipsy where he climbed onto a chair and began to speak loudly about religious observance and the meaning of the holiday. He was promptly arrested for creating a public disturbance. A man on the scene telephoned Soloveitchik and reported this to him. After securing his release, Soloveitchik joked with Schneerson, telling him he could now be the Rebbe, as all previous Rebbes had been in jail (Steinsaltz 2014, 40).

48 Soloveitchik's son, Haym, claims that "he later expressed regret for attending even the one gathering in 1980 in honor of the Rebbe's thirtieth anniversary as the Rebbe of Lubavitch" (Deutsch 1997, 2:119).

49 Haym Soloveitchik mentioned in an interview, "The committee was split in their opinion about my father ... The previous Rebbe called Mr. Mazer and asked him to support my father. His vote was the key factor in the committee's decision to offer my father his job" (Deutsch 1997, 2:116).

50 See Sagi and Schwartz (2019) for a broad discussion of the religious Zionist response to the Six Day War, including Soloveitchik's. See also the discussion of *KDD* in Chapter 5, Section "Kol Dodi Dofek (1956)."

51 It is customary for a son to recite *Kaddish* for his parent, and even then, for only eleven months.

52 Joseph Abelow in Eisenberg (2006, 01:16:05). Gopin (2006, 30) adds, "I once saw

the Rav with two different-colored socks. He grew his beard longer, said *Kaddish* the entire year ..."
53 See www.hakirah.org/ShurinArchive/DOC0209.PDF.
54 See Yeshiva University, Press Release "Dr. Samuel Soloveitchik of Yeshiva University, Authority on History of Chemistry, Dies at 58," 2/27/67, p. 1, available at www.hakirah.org/ShurinArchive/DOC0208.PDF.
55 Koenigsberg (2007, 1) relates that in early 1967, Soloveitchik was teaching his Talmud class Tractate *Bava Batra*. Shortly into the year, he stopped. When he returned to Yeshiva after Passover, he did not continue with that tractate but instead lectured on topics related to the laws of mourning.
56 Riskin (2010, 77–78) recounts how at their meeting Soloveitchik added that "Reb Ḥayyim, who was generally a lion in defense of what he considered proper Torah values, told his son that he decided not to react, that he inquired how many people had attended the eulogy, and found out that the shul [synagogue] was filled to the rafters with a large overflow outside, many more congregants than for [the] Ne'ila [prayer] on Yom Kippur. Reb Ḥayyim explained that "*a rav muz vissen ven tzu reden, un a rav muz vissen ven tzu shveigen*, a rabbi must know when to speak out, and a rabbi must know when to remain silent."
57 "Why has he not published? 'I am a funny animal,' he replied. 'I am a perfectionist. I am never sure something is the best I can do ...' 'I don't know how many manuscripts there are,' he remarked. 'I've never counted them. But there must be 200 and at least that many tapes'... Rabbi Soloveitchik said he wrote on philosophy in English and on law in Hebrew, always in long hand" (Fiske 1972). Later in life he became more interested in publishing, though he placed a higher priority on his popular works, which would serve the general Torah public, "rather than to those which were geared to his indigenous '*lomdische*' constituency" (Lichtenstein 1996, 53). See also Shalom Carmy in Eisenberg (2006, 01:29:10): "His public claim was that he was a perfectionist ... On a few occasions, he also told me, he just felt that there had been no interest ... He didn't think people understood what he was trying to do ... He just felt that there was nobody 'out there'."There are a number of challenges related to many of his writings that were published posthumously. See Freedman (1999), Schwartz (2017), and e.g., Kaplan (2007b, 102–14).

3 Background

While Soloveitchik's approach to Jewish philosophy is novel, he draws upon and reacts to numerous sources from the broader history of philosophy and theology and early-twentieth-century science and psychoanalytic theory. Before delving into his work, however, it is worth reviewing some philosophy that Soloveitchik knew well to understand his place in its history and his use of its ideas.

Situating a figure within the history of philosophy by presenting the historical antecedents allows us to describe the intellectual framework within which they worked. If Soloveitchik used the tradition, it is worth our while to understand it. The figures we address laid groundwork for Soloveitchik's system of philosophy. Most saliently, it is difficult to understand some of the main features of Soloveitchik's program without reference to his intellectual predecessors and contemporaries. Much of our background uncovers just how much Soloveitchik's philosophical output is a product of early-twentieth-century German thought.

The history of philosophy is also important for a reason somewhat inspired by Soloveitchik himself. Soloveitchik believed that with respect to some features of Jewish law, there is an important way in which present actions reorient the trajectory of the past and its effects on the future (see Chapter 4, Section "Max Scheler on repentance"). Similarly, if we understand the intellectual space Soloveitchik occupied, we know how he thought about the past and how to build on his work in the future. If we do not properly contextualize Soloveitchik's philosophy, it is difficult to comprehend how to augment, amplify, continue, or challenge it.

Additionally, we obtain a fuller picture of Jewish philosophy as Soloveitchik conceived it if we understand what he was thinking when he put it together. What sorts of examples was he specifically excluding? How should we *not* think about Jewish philosophy? It is sometimes difficult to understand Soloveitchik, but knowing how his predecessors thought and how he differed from them can take us quite far in making sense of his ideas.

It is difficult to appreciate the wide range of sources upon which Soloveitchik drew without good backgrounds in both Jewish thought and in the history of philosophy. First, he drew from the gamut of religious Jewish texts. Second, he marshalled the Western philosophical, psychological, political, scientific, and theological canons from the works of the pre-Socratics (ca. 500 BCE) through his own time.

We first briefly review some terminology that may be unfamiliar to those with little exposure to Western philosophy or Jewish law. This is necessary for the uninitiated to obtain a basic sense of Soloveitchik's goals, methods, and vocabulary. We then provide a quick guide to the sources and history of Halakhah, the Brisker method of Torah study, and the *ta'amei ha-mitzvot* problem. Interspersed throughout this book we take very brief tours through some relevant episodes in the history of Western thought from the ancients to the neo-Kantians and beyond. Our summaries contain only those ideas that help illuminate Soloveitchik's work.[1] They are not comprehensive. They do not follow one theme; they highlight some—and only some—of the main ideas Soloveitchik draws upon in his philosophical works and present them in the manner that he is likely to have understood them.

While Soloveitchik was attending university in Berlin, Freud and Jung were developing modern psychology; chemistry was becoming the mathematical discipline we know today; Einstein, Eddington, Planck, Bohr, and Heisenberg were remaking physics by working out relativity theory and quantum mechanics; and phenomenology and logical positivism were taking philosophy in new directions. Soloveitchik's early work gives pride of place to the ongoing scientific controversies and new philosophical methods being discussed at the time, mostly in vibrant Weimar Germany, then the center of the intellectual, artistic, and cultural universe.

We beg the indulgence of those whose knowledge of Western philosophy and/or Jewish law and their jargon makes the following sections unnecessary. We wish this book to be self-contained to benefit those readers whose knowledge of both may be minimal.

Philosophy

Philosophy encompasses a wide range of questions and methodological strategies for addressing them. Historically, the central questions involve metaphysics, epistemology, and ethics.

Metaphysics is largely concerned with understanding existence or being. One might think it would be easy to articulate what exists, what is real, and what reality is like. People are real, coffee mugs are real, the Atlantic Ocean is real, Pluto is real, and they are all made of atoms and molecules configured in ways studied by scientists. Unicorns are not real. Neither are dragons, the tooth fairy, or the planet Vulcan.

Those, however, are the easy cases. Many questions about reality are far more difficult. Philosophers linger on questions about things in between the obviously "real" and the obviously "not real." Philosophy of science, for example, is concerned with objects whose ontological status (existence) is more difficult to make sense of. These may be different kinds of things, such as force fields, causes, empty space, quarks, mathematical sets, time, minds, and infinitely small numbers. Justifying an answer to a question about the existence or nature of any of these things is a major philosophical challenge. These cases are not studied using standard tools of physics but rather metaphysics. Metaphysics studies reality but generally confines itself to objects whose reality itself is in question and whose natures are hard to make sense of scientifically.

One can imagine how reasonable people throughout history could disagree about basic metaphysical questions, most significantly "Does God exist and if He does, what is He like?" Historically, God represents the ultimate metaphysical concern. Not for Soloveitchik though (see *TLMOF* 52n). The metaphysical questions that most interested him are analogous to those that concern scientists: what is the nature of reality? By and large he thought the world is not significantly different than science describes it, though he was quick to point out that he lived in a time with little scientific consensus about some very fundamental questions.

However, he also took the world, or at least his world, to be the one described by Judaism. What this means is complicated and will later be thoroughly discussed, but for now we can consider the following: A religious Jew may take some objects to exist or have certain properties that may make little sense to someone not conditioned to experience them. Take, for example, a kosher meal, which may be physically identical, molecule for molecule, to a nonkosher meal. Or consider an object that is ritually impure. The latter object is physically identical before and after becoming impure but has an additional metaphysical characteristic (namely being impure) that only makes sense or exists to one who understands and accepts the legal category of "ritual purity."

Similarly, the Jewish concepts of legal private property (*reshut ha-yaḥid*), a valid ritual bath (*mikvah*), or a kosher Torah scroll all depend for their very existence on a particular Jewish worldview. Without such a worldview, these objects literally do not exist. There could be Torah scrolls without Jews, but not kosher ones. Soloveitchik was largely concerned with the way these "Jewish objects" interact with those who experience and construct them, just as philosophers of physics are interested in the way the physical objects of the world relate to the people who experience them. Remember, we do not experience the world as it is; rather, we experience the world as mediated through our physical senses. For reasons stemming from these considerations, we will see that examining the existence and nature of the world will prove more complicated than we might have initially anticipated. Soloveitchik develops a philosophical worldview around these complications.

Each time we assert that something exists, we take on an epistemological debt. When we claim something in the world is real or that we have established its nature, we owe an answer to the corresponding question: how do we know? This question is independent of the metaphysical one. How one comes to know something is different than whether or not that thing is real. Epistemology studies knowledge. What is knowledge? How do humans come to know things? What are the limits to human knowledge? Do humans innately know anything? What differentiates knowledge from other epistemological stances one may take, such as belief, understanding, wishing, etc.? Are there structures to human knowledge? What is a structure of human knowledge? Can we really know what the world is like? What stands in the way of human knowledge? Are there different ways of knowing about the world? Do different kinds of things in the world require different types of epistemological stances? Are some ways of knowing better than others? Philosophers want a universal way of talking about what one knows and what it means to have knowledge. Providing such descriptions only seems simple until one attempts it.

In a way, Soloveitchik's philosophical work can be said to be concerned primarily with epistemology. He attempts to understand what we might call epistemic constraints and conditions for Jewish ways of knowing. He wants to understand the relationship between the Jewish world and a Jewish mind. What is a halakhic person doing when they apprehend the world?

Soloveitchik is interested in understanding the relationship between the way the world is *objectively* and the way we *subjectively* perceive it, especially given the unique Jewish mind conditioned by a lifetime of exposure to a Jewish worldview and ontology (the objects Jewish law takes to exist). To what extent does the subjective experience shape the objective world, and how does the world shape subjective experience?

The third set of questions that philosophers address pertains to normativity, ethics, and values. These should be more familiar, so we only remind the reader of the basic questions: What is the right thing to do? How should I act? How should I live my life? How should I behave? What worth should I place on different objects and actions? How should I judge the actions of others? How should I evaluate objects? Are there better and worse things in the world? Are there formulas that tell me how to go about doing each task? What duties do I have? What duties does my society have? How is the ideal society best organized and governed? What is the moral relationship between an individual and the society?

Much in these questions pervade Soloveitchik's thought, and we will encounter them in due course. Most significantly, Soloveitchik is concerned with the way the normative structure of Judaism influences the metaphysical categories of Jewish experience.

Halakhah, Torah study, and the Brisker method

Halakhah

Soloveitchik's life and thought were dominated by Halakhah, its structures, and distinctions. It is infused in all his writings, is the overarching narrative in his thinking, and is the foundation upon which his thinking is based. It is impossible to exaggerate the centrality of Halakhah within Soloveitchik's thought. Not only is his philosophical thought derived from Halakhah but he was also concerned with the Halakhah itself. He was a philosopher who saw Halakhah as central to his project, and he was also a creator and decisor of Halakhah.[2]

Before we describe what Halakhah is, it is worth pausing to understand the role Halakhah plays in Jewish history. Halakhah was once the definitive focus in the life of a Jew. Its centrality has eroded considerably over the past 200 or so years, but prior to that, in almost every Jewish community, Halakhah defined the Jew's space within that community and their relationship toward the non-Jew and the nation-state in which they lived. There was once no such thing as a secular or cultural Jew or a Jew of a different denomination. A Jew either followed Halakhah, to a lesser or greater degree, or became a member of another religion (Katz 1975, 215).

Soloveitchik is one of very few Jewish philosophers to speak within this tradition and from this perspective. Yeshayahu Leibowitz (1903–1994), a philosopher Soloveitchik once called the only interesting thinker in the State of Israel (Harvey 1996, 106n16), writes that "[a]part from Halakhah, all flowering of creativity within Judaism was but episodic and fleeting" (Leibowitz 1992, 8). Eliezer Berkovits (1908–1992) and Eliezer Goldman (1918–2002) are other prominent philosophers and contemporaries of Soloveitchik who put Halakhah at the center of their philosophical thought (Sagi 2012). All three, however, interacted surprisingly little with his work, perhaps because of the infrequency with which Soloveitchik published his essays. (Goldman was a student both of Joseph Soloveitchik and his father, Moshe.) Given Soloveitchik's halakhic authority, he is one of the few philosophers, certainly in modern times, to speak from within the historical mainstream of Jewish practice with such a prominent voice. Moreover, putting Halakhah at the center of one's philosophical project is an unusual move even for Jewish thinkers.[3] Traditionally, the project of Jewish philosophers was similar to that of their Christian and Muslim counterparts, often taking cutting-edge philosophical thought and applying it to argue for religion in general, and where possible, for the truth of their own particular religious beliefs. Soloveitchik, instead, considered Halakhah as the only basis for a proper Jewish philosophical system and drew upon the history of Western thought to bolster and flesh out this approach.

Definition

Halakhah, from the root *halakh*, "to go" (though the word may have its actual origins in the Akkadian word for a kind of property tax), is the legal aspect and framework within Judaism that dictates how Jews should live their lives. It governs personal, social, civil, and commercial relationships, as well as all religious ritual practices and observances.

The word "halakhah" refers either to a specific legal ruling (as in, "The halakhah in this case dictates that ...") or to the legal system as a whole. The halakhah includes both ritualistic and civil law, *issurim* and *mamonam*. Halakhah, the legal aspect of Jewish thought, is often (though not as clearly for Soloveitchik) contrasted with aggadah, its nonlegal counterpart which is about topics such as ethics, philosophy, history, etc.[4] Regardless, it incorporates law, literature, and interpretive strategies.

Sources of Halakhah

WRITTEN LAW AND THE ORAL LAW

An important tenet of halakhic Judaism and a guiding principle of the halakhists is that together with the Written Law (*torah she-be-ketav*) and the 613 commandments it is traditionally said to contain, Moses also received and passed down an Oral Law (*torah she-be-al-peh*) which clarifies, explains, and amplifies the Written Law (Elon 1975, 53). The Written Law refers to the Five Books of Moses (Pentateuch) containing the laws said to have been received by Moses from God at Sinai approximately 3,300 years ago. In its narrow sense, Oral Law refers to the explanations and details of the Written Law that were passed down orally at Sinai simultaneously with the Written Law. In a wider sense, the Oral Law refers to all law not directly derived from the Pentateuch, whether given to Moses at Sinai or enacted later by Sages throughout the generations.

BIBLICAL LAW AND RABBINIC LAW

Distinguishing between Biblical Law (*de-oraita*) and Rabbinic Law (*de-rabbanan*) can be difficult. Certainly, laws expressly stated in the Pentateuch are Biblical, while those originating from the enactments or decrees of Sages are rabbinic. More difficult is the classification of laws derived by hermeneutical rules of Biblical exegesis (Elon 1975, 9).

Elon (1975, 14) identifies six legal sources of Jewish law: (1) *Kabbalah*, a tradition transmitted from person to person going back to Moses at Sinai; (2) *Midrash*, exegesis and interpretation of the Written Law; (3) *Takkanah and Gezeirah*, the legislative activities of halakhic authorities in every generation; (4) *Minhag*, custom; (5) *Ma'aseh*, derived from judicial decision; and (6) *Sevarah*, originating from legal-human logic of halakhic scholars.

Who decides Halakhah?

Who decides the law when there is a dispute among scholars? *Deuteronomy* (17:8–11) states, "If a case is too baffling for you to decide, be it a controversy over homicide, civil law, or assault—matters of dispute in your courts—you shall promptly repair to the place that the Lord your God will have chosen, and appear before the Levitical priests, or the magistrate in charge at the time, and present your problem ..." How was this accomplished in practice?

Tractate *Sanhedrin* in the Mishnah deals with the laws associated with the Jewish court system, including the Sanhedrin, comprised of seventy-one ordained scholars. Subordinate courts consisting of twenty-three judges were situated in various towns. There was also a plethora of minor courts, each a three-member *bet din* (pl. *batei din*). The Sanhedrin was the supreme religious and judicial body both before and after the destruction of the Temple in 70 CE, until the abolishment of the patriarchate (ca. 425 CE). Josephus and the Gospels portray the Sanhedrin as a political and judicial council headed by a ruler. Tannaitic sources (see later for discussion) depict it chiefly as a legislative body dealing with religious matters and, in rare cases, acting as a court.

After the destruction of the Temple, a politically weakened Sanhedrin was reconvened in the Land of Israel in Jabneh presided over by its president (*nasi*). When Judea was destroyed following the failure of the Bar Kokhba revolt (ca. 132–136 CE), the Sanhedrin moved to the Galilee. The Romans apparently withdrew their recognition of the Sanhedrin when they dissolved the patriarchate around the year 425.

Toward the end of the patriarchate and afterward, halakhic authority was generally centered on an academy. Initially the main academies were in the Land of Israel, but the academies in Babylonia eclipsed them. As history progressed, Babylonian academies were in turn superseded by those in North Africa, Spain, Germany, France, and Eastern Europe. Today, supremacy in halakhic authority appears to have reverted back to Sages residing in the State of Israel.

Today, there are no formal rules as to which academy or individual is authoritative in Jewish law. A decider of Jewish law (*posek*) will often publish a code of Jewish law, a commentary on Jewish law, and/or his own responsa. Rabbis and the Jewish laity, after reviewing and relying on these works over a period of time, will ultimately decide which is authoritative and whose halakhic decisions should be followed and canonized. Different communities—geographic and otherwise—often have preferences for different *poskim*.[5]

Poskim (decisors) use various rules to establish the proper halakhic ruling for new situations. Some rules like following the majority opinion, or an argument a fortiori are clear-cut and universally accepted. Other rules, less so. In 1767, Malakhi ben Jacob Ha-Cohen (1695/1700?–1772) published *Yad Malakhi: Kelalei ha-Shas*, a book which lists 667 rules for determining the proper Halakhah. Often though, rules have exceptions, and there is much more that *poskim* need to take into account—human nature, social conditions, knowledge of the relevant science and technology, not to mention their own intuitions and philosophical predilections—to make a halakhic ruling.

Development of Halakhah

FROM SINAI TO THE DESTRUCTION OF THE SECOND TEMPLE

The Pentateuch is the foundational text from which Halakhah is derived, though it is actually the Oral Law, in its broad sense, which specifies how Jews ought to act and clarifies the details of daily religious life. Second only in importance to the Pentateuch as early sources for Halakhah are the Books of the Prophets (*Nevi'im*) and the Hagiographa (*Ketuvim*).

With the destruction of the second Temple and the inability to worship through Temple rites, rabbinic Judaism introduced new means of religious service. An early rabbinic innovation was the introduction of the morning and afternoon (and evening) *Shemoneh Esreh* (lit., Eighteen) prayers whose recitation was timed to correspond to the morning and afternoon sacrificial offerings (the *Korban Tamid*) of the Temple.

THE MISHNAH: THE TANNAITIC ERA (CA. 70-220 CE)

The main halakhic document of the Tannaitic era is the Mishnah, compiled and edited by Judah ha-Nasi, and covers, in a very concise manner, all areas of Jewish law. It is organized into six orders, or *sedarim* each of which deals with a broad area of law: *Zera'im* ("Seeds," i.e., Agriculture); *Mo'ed* ("Appointed Times," i.e., Sabbath and Festivals); *Nashim* ("Women," i.e., Marital Laws); *Nezikin* ("Damages," i.e., torts); *Kodashim* ("Consecrated Articles"); and *Tohorot* ("Purities"). These six orders are further subdivided into some sixty tractates (*Mesekhtot*).

The Mishnah is not what we would today consider a code of law, as it often records within it conflicting opinions of the *zugot* ("pairs") and tannaim ("repeaters") without offering definitive rulings. Another halakhic text from this era is the *Tosefa* ("*Addendum*") compiled by two disciples of Yehudah ha-Nasi: Ḥiyya and Oshiya. Other halakhic midrashic texts include *Mekhilta* (on Exodus), *Sifra or Torat Kohanim* (on Leviticus), and *Sifre* (on Numbers and Deuteronomy). Numerous commentaries and glosses have been written on the Mishnah. Among the most popular are those of Ovadiah of Bertinoro (ca. 1445–1510), Yom Tov Lipmann Heller (1579–1654) (*Tosafot Yom Tov*), and recently, Pinḥas Kehati (1910–1976).

THE TALMUDS: THE AMORAIC ERA (CA. 220-500 CE)

The concise nature of the Mishnah and the fact that it contains numerous contradictory opinions necessitated a more elaborate work to amplify its laws and to resolve conflicting rulings. The results of this effort were the Palestinian Talmud developed in the Land of Israel and the Babylonian Talmud developed in Babylonia (the approximate geographic area of modern-day Iraq.) The two Talmuds contain detailed discussions of most of the Mishnah. Of the two Talmuds, the Babylonian Talmud became more authoritative. It discusses the rulings of numerous scholars (both Palestinian and Babylonian, and *tannaim* and *amoraim*).

In the Talmud the opinions of one Talmudic sage, or *amora* ("sayer"), are often contrasted with those of another. Examples of notable pairs of *amoraim* include Yoḥanan and Resh Lakish, and Ravina and Rav Ashi. Sometimes an opinion of one study hall (academy) is contrasted with those of another study hall, such as the academy of Shammai and the academy of Hillel.

Following the destruction of the Temple and the subsequent failed Bar Kokhba revolt, the Romans no longer permitted Jews to live in Jerusalem. Thus, in the third century CE, the prominent centers of learning within the Land of Israel were in Sepphoris and Tiberias (in the Galilee), in Caesarea, and in southern coastal areas referred to as *darom*, the south. Meanwhile, academies continued to flourish in Babylonia, which eventually eclipsed those of the Land of Israel.

The Babylonian Talmud contains commentary on thirty-seven tractates of the Mishnah and spans 2,711 double sided pages in the standard Vilna edition. A typical page of a modern printed Babylonian Talmud has the text of the Talmud in the center of the page, the explanation of Shlomo Yitzḥaki, "Rashi" (1040–1105) on the inner margins, and the commentary of the Tosafot (12th and 13th Ce.) on the outer margins. The extreme inner and outer margins contain additional commentaries and references. In many printed editions of the Talmud, additional commentaries appear after the main text.

A passage (*sugya*) of Talmud often starts with a quote from the Mishnah followed by a discussion of its meaning. The discussion often quotes what appears to be a contradictory statement from a different Mishnah or from a *baraita*. It then attempts to reconcile the two statements. Sometimes the Talmud declares that the conflicting statements represent two different cases, that the views are of two different scholars, or that the two sources reflect different recollections of the same discussion. A passage may also start by quoting a source external to the Mishnah. It may then work toward determining its source or reconciling it with other quoted statements. A passage may or may not contain material of any legal significance.

A typical passage often contains three distinct layers from three different time periods: statements by Tannaim, the earliest time period (usually in Mishnaic Hebrew); statements of Amoraim (usually in Aramaic); and anonymous text attributed to the Stammaim, the latest time period. (The *Savoraim* ("reasoners") are often said to close the Talmudic era.) On the prevailing view (due to Halivni, e.g., 1986, 76–92), the Talmudic passage was structured by Stammaim, editors, who provided their own additions to the Talmud anonymously in order to distinguish their additions, which they considered of lesser worth, from the "give and take" of the Tannaim and Amoraim whom they quoted with attribution.

The *Jerusalem* (*Palestinian*) *Talmud*, popularly known as the *Yerushalmi*,[6] is considered of lesser halakhic authority than the Babylonian Talmud. The Jerusalem Talmud was compiled by *amoraim* in the northern part of Israel ca. 220–375 CE. Yoḥanan, who is quoted in both Talmuds, played a major role in the Jerusalem Talmud's halakhic infrastructure, and his students continued to be involved in its development. The tumultuous political climate in the Land of Israel during the development of the Jerusalem Talmud and its incomplete editing account for the preeminence of the Babylonian Talmud over its Palestinian counterpart (Zelcer 2002, 49).

The Talmuds' ostensive overarching aim is not to set the law but rather to record and preserve the discussions, debates, and arguments about the laws for future study and reference. Indeed, they contain much nonhalakhic material, known as *aggadah*, which is comprised of stories of a didactic nature, Biblical interpretation, philosophical speculation, psychological analysis, historical information, advice of the rabbis on all sorts of topics, and much more.

DIFFERENT TYPES OF HALAKHIC WORKS

Post-Amoraic halakhic works continue to be produced in every generation. They can be divided broadly into commentaries and novellae, responsa, and codes of law. Commentary literature represents the efforts of scholars to elucidate earlier halakhic sources. A classic commentary on the Babylonian Talmud is that of Rashi. Novellae involve the study and analysis of different sources of halakhah with an effort to reconcile conflicting or difficult statements. Classic novellae on the Babylonian Talmud are those of the tosafists. Responsa literature (*she'elot u-teshuvot,* questions and answers) contain questions directed to a halakhic authority (*posek*) and his answers. The questions arise, for example, from changes in technology, community situations, one's occupation, interactions with non-Jews, or social sensibilities. The answer is determined by the halakhic authority based on their knowledge of Halakhah, their ability to establish analogies with similar cases, and by determining the relative authority of one decider of Jewish law over another. Responsa literature are expansive in nature as these create Halakhah to address new realities. Finally, many and varied codes of Jewish law, some more authoritative than others, have been produced over the generations.

GEONIC PERIOD (CA. 500–1040 CE)

Traditionally, halakhic works in the post-Talmudic era are divided into three chronological eras: that of the Geonim, Rishonim, and Aḥaronim. *Gaon* (pl. *Geonim*) is the title of the head of academies in Sura and Pumbedita in Babylonia from approximately the end of the sixth century to the middle of the eleventh. ("Gaon" eventually became an honorific title for someone with a great knowledge of Torah.) Geonim were appointed by the exilarchs and were considered the intellectual leaders of the Diaspora. Their decisions and re-sponsa had absolute legal authority in most Jewish communities.

Outstanding Geonim include Yehudai, Amram, Saadiah, Sherira, Samuel b. Hophni, and Hai. The main works of the Geonic period include *Sefer ha-She'iltot* of Ahai Gaon, a collection of halakhic discussions which follow the order of the Pentateuch. Each discussion usually starts with a question; hence, *She'iltot*. Another important work, *Halakhot Pesukot* of Yehudai b. Nahman Gaon, is organized by both subject matter and Talmudic tractates and includes only those halakhot with practical relevance. *Halakhot Gedolot*, the greatest halakhic work of the geonic period, is believed to have been written by Simeon Kayyara of Basra (Bassora), Babylonia. The decline of the Baghdad Caliphate, the impoverishment of Babylonian Jewry, and the concurrent intellectual development in the Diaspora put an end to the in-stitution of the geonate around the year 1040.[7]

The Spanish-Jewish philosopher Abraham ibn Daud (ca. 1110–1180) re-counts a now famous, though perhaps apocryphal, tale about the dispersal of the final geonim from Babylonia. In ca. 960 CE, four Gaonim embarked on a ship from Bari to Siponto in southern Italy to attend the wedding of a colleague's daughter. On the journey they were kidnapped and sold as slaves, each in a different city, where they were redeemed by the local Jewish communities. Each community subsequently took note of the erudition of their redeemed captive and appointed him to head their academy. Shemariah, redeemed in Alexandria, made his way to Fustat, the old Jewish neighborhood of Cairo. Hushiel, father of Rabeinu Hananel, was redeemed by the community of Kairouan, Tunis. Moshe, his wife, and young son Hanokh were redeemed by the community of Cordoba in Moorish Spain. Ibn Daud writes that the name of the fourth captive is unknown (Cohen 1967). Regardless of whether this event occurred, this tale signifies the transition of the halakhic authority from the Geonim to the Rishonim.

RISHONIM (CA. 1000–1500 CE), EARLY DECIDERS OF JEWISH LAW

The works of the Rishonim, their codes of law in particular, are of special importance for Soloveitchik. Some of the names should sound familiar from the story in Chapter 2, Section "The teacher." Sages of Germany (*Hakhmei Ashkenaz*) include Gershom b. Yehuda (ca. 955–1028) known as Rabbenu Gershom; Rashi, renowned for his comprehensive and lucid explanatory glosses on the Hebrew Bible and the Babylonian Talmud; the group known as the *Ba'alei Tosafot* most notable of whom is Ya'akov b. Meir (ca. 1100–1171) known as Rabbenu Tam; and his nephew Yitzhak b. Shmuel of Dampierre (c. 1115–c. 1184). Other *poskim* at that time include Moshe of Coucy known for his *Sefer Mitzvot Gadol* and Meir b. Barukh (ca. 1215–1293) known as the Maharam mi-Rothenberg (Lewittes 121–28).

Southeastern France (Provence) includes the communities of Narbonne, Lunel, Montpelier, and Marseilles. Important halakhic works from that region and nearby include *Sefer ha-Ittim* of Yehudah b. Barzilai of Barcelona (d. 1158) on the laws of Sabbath and Festivals, *Sefer ha-Eshkol* of Avraham b. Yitzḥak of Narbonne (1110–1179), based on *Sefer ha-Ittim*, and followed by the *Sefer ha-Ittur* of Yitzḥak b. Abba Mari of Marseilles (1122–1193). Abraham b. David of Posquières (ca. 1120–1198) known as Rabad, in addition to his glosses on the *Mishneh Torah* (see later) and other texts, wrote important legal works (Twersky 1962), as did his interlocutor Zerahiah ha-Levi of Gerona (d. 1186).

One of the primary works of the rishonim is *Sefer ha-Halakhot* of Isaac b. Jacob ha-Kohen Alfasi, "Rif" (1013–1103) from Algeria. It is arranged in the order of the Talmudic tractates and includes only the laws practiced in its time. A large body of literature (known as its *nosei kelim*, "arms-bearers") developed around this work, partly in disagreement with it, partly in its defense, and partly as an interpretation. *Halakhot Ketannot,* also by Rif, contains relevant laws that are dispersed in the orders *Kodashim* and *Toharot,* which primarily deal with laws which were not applicable at that time. They do, however, also contain relevant laws such as those of *Sefer Torah, mezuzah, tefillin, tzitzit,* etc. Rif also wrote many responsa, the majority in Arabic, hundreds of which have survived.

Sages of Spain (*Ḥakhmei Sepharad*) include Joseph ibn Migash (also known as Ri Migash), a twelfth-century Talmudist and teacher of Maimon, father of Maimonides; Maimonides; Asher ben Jehiel (known as the Rosh), a thirteenth-century German-Spanish Talmudist; and Jacob ben Asher (*Ba'al ha-Turim*) (1269–ca. 1343), a German-Spanish halakhist (see later).

Moses ben Maimon, Maimonides (1135/38–1204), was born in Córdoba and served as rabbi and physician in Morocco and then Egypt after he was forced to flee Spain. He is sometimes known as "*ha-Nesher ha-Gadol*" (the great eagle) in recognition of his outstanding mastery of the Oral Torah. One of his earliest works was a commentary on the Mishnah. He also authored *The Guide of the Perplexed*, perhaps the most significant work of midieval Jewish philosophy. Maimonides also figures prominently in the history of Islamic and Arab medicine and sciences, as the author of a number of books on medicine, illness, and health.

Maimonides' *magnum opus*, the fourteen-volume *Mishneh Torah*, is generally hailed as the greatest code of Jewish law ever produced. Subsequent codes of Jewish law reckon with its rulings and often cite its conclusions. In creating his *Mishneh Torah*, Maimonides followed four guiding principles: he included all of Jewish law, from the Written Law and the Oral Law until his time, in a scientific and systematic manner, regardless of its practical relevance in his time; he subdivided and classified the material according to subject matter; he decided on the definitive halakhic ruling without reference to conflicting opinions and without citing his sources; and he wrote in Mishnaic Hebrew (Elon 1975, 130). During Maimonides' lifetime and continuing to this day, hundreds of commentaries on *Mishneh Torah* have been produced. For many nineteenth- and twentieth-century Torah scholars, including Soloveitchik, Maimonides also stands as the most significant codifier of Jewish law upon which they expend much energy understanding and explicating.

Asher b. Jehiel, known as Rabbenu Asher or simply as "the Rosh" (1259–1327), was probably born in Cologne and died in Toledo. His halakhic work quickly superseded that of Alfasi, and, within a short time, it began to be printed with almost every edition of the Talmud. It would be his son Jacob, however, who would rearrange his father's rulings into an original and more logical structure that established four main areas of Jewish law, known as *Arba'ah Turim* (the "four rows") or simply, the Tur. The four main areas are *Oraḥ Ḥayyim*, "Way of Life" containing the laws of prayer, Sabbath, and Festivals; *Yoreh De'ah*, "Instructor of Knowledge," the dietary laws, laws of the menstruant, the laws of charity, circumcision, mourning, and more; *Even ha-Ezer,* "Stone of Help" the laws of marriage, divorce, and *ḥalitzah*; and *Ḥoshen Mishpat*, "Breastplate of Judgment," the laws of judgement (courts, judges, and witnesses) and property (contracts, loans, damages, etc.). This structure would be adopted later by Joseph Karo for his *Shulḥan Arukh* as well as by many later halakhic works.

AḤARONIM (CA. 1500-CURRENT), LATER PERIOD OF JEWISH LAW

The early modern period saw vast movement in Jewish law, which can be attributed to significant changes in the structure of Jewish communities, rabbinic jurisdiction, the establishment of rabbinical courts, Jewish mobility, book printing, and other social and economic factors. The enlightenment eventually seeped into rabbinic and lay culture forcing shifts in halakhic thinking as well (Berkovitz 2017). Some halakhic writing and rabbinic authority and practice accommodated these developments; some pushed back against them.

Joseph b. Ephraim Karo (1488–1575), born in Spain, spent twenty years writing a comprehensive commentary on the *Tur* entitled *Bet Yosef*. Before publishing this work, he had settled in Safed, a city containing many halakhic scholars and mystical kabbalists. In his *Bet Yosef*, he first cites Talmudic sources and then elaborates upon the opinions of the Rishonim, especially those of Sephardic descent. Finally, he offers his own definitive ruling. He also authored the *Kesef Mishnah*, a commentary on Maimonides' *Mishneh Torah*, giving the sources of Maimonides' rulings and defending him against the strictures of Rabad. Karo was also the author of numerous responsa.

Foremost among the halakhists of this period was Yaakov Berab (1474–1546), born in Castile, who fled the inquisition and also ended up in Safed, via Fez. Karo, the youngest of Berab's four students to receive ordination, produced a work, the *Shulḥan Arukh,* based on his own *Bet Yosef*, that anyone could use to consult the proper ruling. The *Shulḥan Arukh,* in a relatively short time, with some reservations, became the basis for subsequent halakhic decisions in the "Orthodox tradition." In preparing the *Shulḥan Arukh*, Karo intended to provide a handy yet comprehensive digest of Jewish law that would unite Jewish practice. He often used the majority opinion of Isaac Alfasi, Maimonides, and Rosh as his guide to a final ruling, naturally, often favoring the customs of Spanish Jews.

Meanwhile, Moshe b. Yisrael Isserles (1530–1572) of Lublin, Poland, known as the Rema, wrote a commentary on the Tur clarifying its sources and bringing it up to date. When the *Shulḥan Arukh* reached Poland, Isserles was dismayed; the work he had envisioned had already been done. Nevertheless, he published his commentary called *Darkhei Moshe*.

The *Shulḥan Arukh,* as the work of a Sephardic *posek,* could not very well serve Ashkenaz Jewry who were obligated to follow decisions and customs of their own authorities. (The *Shulḥan Arukh* also served to help solidify the Ashkenazi/Sefardi halakhic divide.) Isserles thus added his own notes (*hagahot*) specifying Ashkenaz practices which conflict with the rulings of Karo. He called these notes a *mapah,* a "tablecloth," covering the *Shulḥan Arukh*, the "set table" of Karo. The *Shulḥan Arukh* printed together with the comments of Rema thus became the authoritative code of Jewish law: Sephardic Jews, following the decisions of Karo, relied on the ruling of the composer, the *meḥaber,* and Ashkenazi Jews followed the rulings of Isserles.

While the *Shulḥan Arukh* achieved widespread acceptance, it did have its detractors. Chief among them was Judah Loew, the Maharal of Prague (ca 1512/26–1609) and his brother Ḥayyim. In his *Netivot Olam*, the Maharal argued that it is preferable for rabbis to determine the law based on the Talmud, using their own reasoning rather than resort to a code like the *Shulḥan Arukh* as an intermediary. Ḥayyim's most significant complaint was that the *Shulḥan Arukh* is a code for Polish Jews and thus not acceptable for German Jews (Davis 2002, 262f).

The *Zohar*, a foundational text of Kabbalah, Jewish mystical thought, attributes many of its statements to the Tannaitic era and often to Shimon b. Yoḥai specifically. The text of the *Zohar*, however, has its origin in Spain where it was published in the thirteenth century by the Jewish writer, Moses de León. Decisors of Jewish law have generally been reluctant to grant halakhic authority to the *Zohar*, nonetheless Yosef Karo, in his *Shulḥan Arukh,* did include halakhic rulings that can only be attributed to the *Zohar*.

The period of Aharonim continues to this day providing notable works of halakhah. From the early 1900s, we have the code of law of Yeḥiel Mekhel Epstein (1829–1908), the *Arukh ha-Shulḥan,* which is often contrasted with the code of law of Yisrael Meir Kagan (1839–1933), the *Mishnah Berurah*. Of the two, it is the *Mishnah Berurah* which has become more authoritative, perhaps as a result of the great reputation of Yisrael Meir Kagan, the *Chofetz Ḥayyim*. Interestingly, disputes over which of the two to prioritize sometimes hinge on the respective positions of the authors; Kagan was the head of a school and Epstein was a community rabbi . Whether one favors theory or practice may determine one's preference for which halakhic work to utilize (Henkin 2018, 311–17).

The responsum of Moshe Feinstein (1895–1986), *Iggerot Moshe,* has become, in the United States, a popular and authoritative halakhic work.

Among the ultra-Orthodox in Israel, Shlomo Zalman Auerbach's (1910–1995) responsum, *Minḥat Shlomo*, has achieved similar status. For the Sepharadic community in Israel, the responsa of Ovadia Yosef (1920–2013), *Yabia Omer* and *Yeḥaveh Da'at,* are similarly authoritative.

Halakhic works continue to be produced. Two recent examples are the code of law, *Badei ha-Shulḥan* by Shraga Feivel Cohen in the United States and the responsum *Tzitz Eliezer* of Eliezer Yehuda Waldenberg (1915–2006) in the State of Israel. Only history will determine whether they become authoritative and canonical and for whom. We do know, however, that within the past few generations, the transmission of Halakhah has undergone a considerable sociological shift, with halakhic texts rising in importance, even over family and community oral tradition, which had priority in the past (Soloveitchik 1994).

This brief whirlwind tour through the highlights of the history of Jewish law[8] should give us a sense of a number of things that are vital to understanding Soloveitchik's thought. Most important for us is that it shows two seemingly contradictory features of Jewish legal history: on the one hand, it illustrates the continuity of the mesorah, the continuous tradition of halakhic law, thought, and texts over 2,000 years to the present time. On the other hand, it allows us to appreciate the dialectic, disagreement, and diversity in Halakhah over the same period. Both the continuity of tradition and the diversity of dialectic strongly influenced Soloveitchik's philosophical outlook about the law itself and its philosophical repercussions.

Halakhah in the different streams of Judaism

As is frequently noted, Judaism is not and never has been monolithic, and neither has Rabbinic, or Orthodox Judaism. The history of Halakhah encapsulated above reveals but a fraction of its diversity. Soloveitchik professed a kind of Orthodoxy that can be located on the Orthodox spectrum. Other spectra exist as well, and each stream of Judaism has a different relationship with and philosophical approach to Halakhah. In this book we are primarily concerned with how Soloveitchik saw Halakhah. But it is useful to contrast his understanding of Halakhah with those of other groups of Jews.

Soloveitchik's approach is not idiosyncratic, but neither is it standard given the range of Jewish thinkers who write about Halakhah. His approach is typical of a certain swath of Orthodox Jewry, and his occasional polemical vociferousness reflects the internecine debates going on in his lifetime over the place and nature of Halakhah in Jewish life and thought. The history of the divergence of the various groups of Jews is not relevant right here, but we should note that Soloveitchik was typically intellectually hostile to the approach of what he sometimes referred to as "liberal Judaism," Judaism that is of a non-Orthodox strain.[9]

For Orthodox Jews Halakhah dictates how to live: what ought to be done and what may not. While some Orthodox Jews are more punctilious in their halakhic observance than others, they share a consensus that faithfulness to Halakhah, as the Orthodox Jews construe it, is an ideal. There is also a consensus among Orthodox Jews that the study of Halakhah or Torah is itself an ideal. There is general agreement about canonical halakhic texts and the structure of religious authority even with radical disagreement over the status of specific texts and specific authorities.

Halakhah unites Orthodox Jews across different communities and geographic areas. Although there are differences in Halakhah from one community to another, and even more so, in *minhagim* and *takanot*, customs and edicts, nevertheless, most Orthodox Jews would feel comfortable participating in Jewish ritual—daily prayers, holiday celebration, and most events involving food—with most other Orthodox Jews.

While levels of adherence to Halakhah vary significantly among the Orthodox, there is widespread agreement that at least a minimum halakhic observance—including a basic observance of Sabbath and Festivals, and kosher dietary laws—is an ideal.

Conservative Judaism. American Conservative Halakhah is more centralized than Orthodox Halakhah and is generally not accepted as Halakhah by the Orthodox. Halakhic rulings in Conservative Judaism are decided by their Rabbinical Assembly's Committee on Jewish Law and Standards, the Law Committee. It consists of twenty-five voting members, all rabbis, and six nonvoting members, one of whom is a cantor and five laypeople. Any decision which receives at least six votes is considered a valid position which a rabbi may implement for their congregation. Conservative Judaism has published its own codes of Jewish law, for example, Klein (1979; an earlier code) and Cohen (2012), which dictate the proper halakhic practices, or, the range of acceptable halakhic practices for members of the movement.

Conservative Halakhah may change rapidly to adapt to modern values and sensibilities. An early Conservative innovation which is contrary to Orthodox halakhic self-understanding (and bothered Soloveitchik [*Seating Sanctification*]) is their acceptance of mixed male/female seating during prayer services. A more substantial break with Orthodox Halakhah came about in its ruling regarding driving a car on the Sabbath. Cohen's code (2012, 132–33) states, "A majority opinion allowed for driving to the synagogue on Sabbath when walking would be unreasonably difficult. This ruling was a concession not only to the realities of life in the suburbs, where Jews lived at great distances from the synagogue, but also to the fact that many synagogues remained in downtown areas that were suddenly very far from their constituencies ..."

Another prominent area in which Conservative Halakhah differentiates itself from Orthodoxy is in its equality for women in ritual practice: counting women for a *minyan*, a ritual quorum, and accepting them as valid witnesses in a *bet din*, a Jewish legal court, and ordaining them into the rabbinate.

Reform Judaism. Washofsky (2010) writes that "[r]eform Judaism does not accept the notion that a particular observance or action is either obligatory or forbidden solely because some book or set of books—the Bible, the Talmud, or a code of halachah—says so." Rather, that "... innovations have historically taken place within a context of practice that is inextricably rooted in the traditional rabbinical literature."

In the American Reform Movement, halakhic decisions are generally arrived at by its Responsa Committee of the Central Conference of American Rabbis, which to date has issued approximately 1,300 *teshuvot* (lit. answers) or opinions.[10] In contrast with the authoritative role of Halakhah and responsa for the Orthodox and Conservative movements, American Reform Halakhah and responsa are advisory but not authoritative. It is essentially an argument, a reasoned attempt to justify one or more courses of action. It seeks to win its point through persuasion rather than as an act of religious authority.[11]

There are two distinctive features of the Reform halakhic enterprise. First, that Reform responsa will often read the Halakhah in ways that differ from decisions reached by Orthodox rabbis. Second, Reform Judaism does not recognize the absolute binding authority of a rabbinic ruling, practice, belief, or doctrine (Washofsky 2010).

Reconstructionist Judaism. In 1920, in one of the five planks of the Society for the Jewish Renascence, which Mordecai Kaplan (1881–1983) helped found, it states that "[w]e accept the halakha, which is rooted in the Talmud, as the norm of Jewish life, availing ourselves, at the same time, of the method implicit therin to interpret and develop the body of Jewish Law in accordance with the actual conditions and spiritual needs of modern life." In 1948, in his *The Future of the American Jew*, Kaplan emphasized that Jewish life is meaningless without Jewish Law.

Daniel Cedarbaum[12] writes that Reconstructionist Judaism believes that "... the traditional halakhic system is incapable of producing a code of conduct that is meaningful for, and acceptable to, the vast majority of contemporary Jews." Instead, Cedarbaum suggests, "Drawing on the wisdom that we have received from centuries of Jewish legal thinking, we, as a community, must construct for ourselves a set of rules that are at once rooted in our tradition and consonant with the actual conditions and spiritual needs of modern life. We must then commit ourselves to obeying those rules."

The Reconstructionist Rabbinical Association (RRA) serves as the collective voice of Reconstructionist rabbis and issues guidelines which serve as statements of beliefs about, and guidance for, rabbinic Jewish practice and behavior. While these guidelines are not understood as binding Halakhah, they are seen as akin to responsa. Guidelines are the product of study, discussion, and deliberation by its membership. The process for reaching consensus on a set of guidelines may take up to two years. Guidelines are adopted through a vote at plenary meetings of the RRA at either its biennial North American Convention or Virtual Business Meeting.[13]

In the state of Israel

For two millennia, Halakhah was studied, developed, and documented to serve the needs of Jewish communities in exile. Much of the philosophical discussion among eighteenth-, nineteenth-, and twentieth-century halakhic thinkers can be seen as grappling with the interplay of Jewish and state law. Restored Jewish sovereignty in Israel saw a lack of halakhic precedent and case law to address the new reality. Halakhah now had to grapple with a legal system that had evolved and adapted to a Jewish diaspora. Can Halakhah "scale-up," so to speak, to play the role of law for a modern nation state? Can it accommodate contemporary thinking on the status of women? Can it be reconciled with having non-Jews as citizens? Does it have a concept of citizenship? Can it speak the language of human rights or international law? How does Halakhah see a state's responsibility toward a population made up of mostly Jews who do not acknowledge Halakhah's authority and toward people of other faiths? How is Halakhah observed at an army base, and how does it adapt to wartime or military operations? (Israel's Chief Rabbi, Shlomo Goren, famously opposed the 1982 siege of Beirut on halakhic grounds and started a heated public halakhic debate.) What does Halakhah have to say about the operation of national utilities by Jews on the Sabbath and on Jewish festivals? Is Israel's Independence Day a Jewish holiday with all the concomitant halakhic repercussions? How must Israeli Jews make sense of the halakhic principle that one must generally respect the law of the land, when the assumption behind this principle is that the law of the land is non-Jewish? These and related problems occupied the minds of both secular and observant Jews in Israel. Yeshayahu Leibowitz (e.g., 1992, ch. 16) was a religious outlier in (sometimes) completely opposing any relationship between Halakhah and national law. Most prominent of the religious voices, however, to advocate for halakhic inclusion of non-Jews and nonobservant Jews include some of mandatory Palestine and Israel's chief rabbis: A. I. Kook, Shlomo Goren, and Isaac Halevi Herzog (Batnitzky and Brafman 2018, 161ff).

Upon the establishment of the State of Israel, Halakhah, as the greater Orthodox communities understand it, was incorporated into official law but only in regard to personal status issues such as marriage, divorce, and Levirate marriage (*yibbum* and *ḥalitzah*). Legislation was also enacted regarding certain ritual law. In 1948, the Provisional Council of State mandated that kosher food be provided to all Jewish soldiers of the Israel Defense Forces. The Law and Administration Ordinance of 1948 specified that the Sabbath and Jewish festivals be designated as days of rest, and it allowed for non-Jews to observe their own Sabbath and festivals as days of rest. In 1952, a law was enacted prohibiting raising, keeping, or slaughtering pigs in Israel, except in specific areas populated mainly by non-Jews.

The State of Israel has two court systems: the rabbinical courts and the general courts. Rabbinical courts have exclusive jurisdiction in matters regarding personal status, including marriage and divorce. As regards to a wife's claim for maintenance, however, jurisdiction is given to the court to which the wife applied, the rabbinic or the district (general) court.

Generally, rabbinic courts decide based upon Halakhah. Sometimes, however, even the rabbinical courts must decide based on general law. For example, the Succession Ordinance of 1923 provides for the equal treatment of son and daughter, husband and wife, in the division of certain property in inheritance. In the Women's Equal Right Law of 1951, the equal division was extended to all property.

General courts have jurisdiction in all matters not entrusted to rabbinical courts. General courts may also rule on matters of personal status when they arise incidentally to the matters before court. For example, general courts must first resort to private international law before applying Halakhah and therefore must recognize a marriage entered into while abroad as valid even when Halakhah would not (Elon 1975, 39–46).

Torah study

Following the destruction of the Second Temple in Jerusalem, Torah study became a significant mode of Jewish worship. The rabbis of the Talmud even considered whether Torah study or religious practice is the highest ideal. The Talmud recounts that "Rabbi Tarfon and the Elders were reclining in the loft of the house of Nitza in Lod when the following question came before them: Is study greater or is practice greater? Rabbi Tarfon answered and said 'practice is greater.' Rabbi Akiva answered and said, 'study is greater.' Everyone then answered 'Study is greater as it leads to action'" (*Kiddushin* 40b). Yet, as we will see later, the debate was never quite settled.

The word "Torah" refers broadly not only to the vast corpus of literature which discusses Bible and Jewish law, that is, Halakhah, but also to Talmudic aggadah, Midrash, and more. For decisors of Jewish law, the focus of Torah study is to determine halakhic answers for real-life situations. For those who study Torah for its own sake, however, the goal is not necessarily the determination of what may or may not be performed, but Torah study itself.

Though our discussion of Halakhah focused on legal works, Soloveitchik's view of Halakhah is much broader than the confines of Jewish law and includes much of what might be included in "Torah" (see *Halakhic Mind*, 90–91). He thinks of a wide swath of classical religious literature as comprising the halakhic corpus. While he often draws directly upon literal Halakhah itself, for example, the laws of mourning or repentance, for philosophical insight, he also draws upon the Bible, Midrash (ancient texts of Biblical hermeneutics), Jewish philosophical and mystical texts, Talmud, or Hasidic thought. He also thinks of Halakhah as a learning style (Schwartz 2012, 308n81). In a different context, Shatz (2009, 164) writes, "Now no doubt the supposition that the philosophical content of R. Soloveitchik's writing arises organically and naturally from 'the Halakhah' is too simple ... [The] magnificent philosophical castles that he built are ... first-order religious activities: *divrei Torah*, efforts at halakhic interpretation—which I think really means the interpretation of the entire Jewish tradition, including the Bible, law, philosophy, mysticism, and so forth."

But Torah study as the ideal may not reflect the whole story. On one way of looking at the history of Torah study, there was a shift that coincides, not accidentally, with the Enlightenment. Since Talmudic times, Torah study was a central Jewish ideal. However, so was its practice. The European Jewish Enlightenment (ca. eighteenth century) saw the weakening of Jewish communal power structures. Jews were now becoming more integrated into the legal infrastructures of their larger societies, and the rabbis had less power over the day-to-day lives of average Jews. Accordingly, rabbinical legal philosophy shifted too. In some areas of Europe, the Hasidic movement emerged and thrived, reinforcing the power of the rabbis as holy men and not necessarily Torah experts. In other regions, however, Torah study itself, the aspect of Jewish life in which the rabbis excelled, became the highest religious ideal. The rabbis were free to focus on ritual laws that may or may not have had relevance to Jewish life and stress theory in general over practice. Eliyahu of Vilna (the "Vilna Gaon" 1720–1797) and his student Ḥayyim of Volozhin (1749–1821) and his school were at the center of anti-Hasidic resistance and also the locus of a revolution in Torah study, emphasizing the study of law over its practice, the primacy of rabbinic interpreters, and the downplaying of the codes of law (Batnitzky and Brafman 2018, 45ff). While the Vilna Gaon saw Torah study as the ideal, the Hasidic text *Tanya* saw *practice* as being primary (48b–49a).

For the rabbis who prioritize Torah study, learning involves not merely knowing the Torah but also becoming a participant in its continued creation. Soloveitchik's work is preoccupied with the inherent creativity involved in creating Jewish law. Making law is a complex process of synthesizing a vast amount of Jewish texts, applying the right rules to a situation, taking into account relevant distinctions, conflicting values, arguments among sources, precedent, custom, context, intuition, and mitigating factors to come up with an answer to a concrete or hypothetical halakhic question (see Soloveitchik's letter on military chaplains in *CCC* 23–60 for an example). Like the practice of secular law, this requires creativity[14] and a broad and deep understanding of Jewish law, literature, and life. Importantly for Soloveitchik, creativity literally means to create new concepts where there were none before. New concepts translate to new objects that shape the world of Halakhic Man in a way that will become clear as we progress. How does Halakhic Man create new insights when he studies Torah? To start answering this question, we turn to the Brisker method of Torah study, what became for a certain school of Talmud study, the ultimate tool for halakhic analysis and creativity.

The Brisker method

While the Talmud is the main source for Halakhah, it is not a law book in the classic sense. It does not contain lists of laws, commandments, or halakhot. Even those sections that discuss Halakhah do not contain definitive rulings but rather lengthy records of conflicting opinions and their opposing rationales. It is, therefore, difficult to derive definitive law from the Talmud; hence, the need for the codes discussed previously. R. Ḥayyim of Brisk, Soloveitchik's grandfather and a great Talmudic scholar, perfected a method (which had various historical antecedents) of analyzing a portion of a Talmudic text (a *sugya*) that discusses a particular halakhic issue. This method is now referred to as the Brisker method (sometimes "the method of the Analytic Movement," "conceptualism," or in Hebrew "*havanah ḥaqirah*" or "*higayon*"). It was a method of analysis Soloveitchik took quite seriously. In a preamble to a lecture on religious conversion, he remarked:

> You know very well that I place a great deal of emphasis upon the intellectual understanding and the analysis of the *halachos*; you know that this is actually what my grandfather *zt"l* introduced, and you know, I have told it so many times and I will tell it again, our methodology, our analysis, and our manner of conceptualizing, and inferring, classifying, and defining things, halachic matters, does not lag behind the most modern philosophical analyses, [which] I happen to know something about. We are far ahead of it. The tools, the logical tools, the epistemological instruments which we employ in order to analyze a *sugya* in say [the Talmudic discussions of] *Ḥeskas ha-Batim*, or in *Shabbos* or *Bava Kamma* are the most modern, they are very impressive, the creations of my grandfather. Anyway, we avail ourselves of the most modern methods of understanding, of constructing, of inferring, of classifying, of defining, and so forth and so on.[15]

These "most modern methods of understanding" are those of the Brisker method, a style of learning so sophisticated, Soloveitchik believed, that it was able to compete with the most demanding secular studies. Soloveitchik believed that it was this method of Torah study that held the attention of the most advanced of the Eastern European Yeshiva students, keeping them from seeking intellectual stimulation elsewhere (*Eulogy Velvele* 213; Kaplan 1992, 153). Moreover, the method allows for so much halakhic individual creativity that at least one prominent Lithuanian ultra-Orthodox thinker, the Ḥazon Ish, opposed it on principle (Kaplan 1992).

We are interested in the method here first because Soloveitchik's grandfather, R. Ḥayyim, perfected it, and it is a part of the legacy the Soloveitchik family bequeathed to contemporary Talmud study but also because Soloveitchik himself used it to analyze the Talmud and the halakhic rulings of its commentators (most notably Maimonides). Most important for us, however, is that the method is integral to Soloveitchik's whole thought process (recall the story in Chapter 2, Section "The teacher"), both in religious and secular matters. One of many standard canonical examples, the subject-object dichotomy which we address in this section, echoes throughout Soloveitchik's philosophical works.

What is the Brisker method?[16] The method is a style of critically inter-rogating halakhic texts in a way first practiced by a group of scholars including Ḥayyim Soloveitchik, Jacob Isaac Rabbinowitz, Joseph Leib Bloch, Shimon Shkop, Ḥayyim Telzer (Rabbinowitz), Moshe Mordecai Epstein, Issur Zalman Meltzer, Naftali Trop, Elhanan Wasserman, Moshe Avigdor Amiel, and Abraham Isaac Bloch. Most of them studied at the Yeshiva in Volozhin or Kelm, and all ended up teaching and subsequently spreading the method to yeshivot in Ponevezh, Slobodka, Mir, and Telz, and eventually to the United States and Israel. They were all hostile to the Haskalah (Jewish Enlightenment), and many were hostile to secular education and learning in general (Solomon 1993, 81).

Foremost among the circle was R. Ḥayyim (Soloveitchik's grandfather) who focused on the *Rishonim* and emulated their analysis of the Talmud. To be sure, his expressions and delivery were quite different than theirs, but he followed the same path and employed the same methodology of critically scrutinizing religious texts. R. Ḥayyim's analytical task was different from that of the commentators he was studying. "Whereas the Rishonim explained the Talmud, it is our duty to explain the Rishonim. R. Ḥayyim takes this very seriously—it is not for us to challenge or debate with the Rishonim, or to choose between them; our task is to understand them. Thus if Ra'avad disagrees with Maimonides, we are not to decide between them, but to understand the rationality of both their points of view" (Solomon 1993, 98, summarizing Zevin).

When R. Ḥayyim would dissect a halakhic subject, he would typically begin by clarifying the relevant concepts and then point out a distinction. Generally, he would clarify that two principles are involved: for example, the subject and the object, the item (*heftza*) and the person (*gavra*), the act and what is being acted upon, or a general rule and a specific rule. He would then establish the role that each principle occupies in the respective ruling to determine whether there are two different laws in play or whether the ruling is only over a single law. If related topics point to different halakhot, he established which one applies to the case at hand.

When executed well, this type of analysis yields clarity. Contradictions fall away, and the main points and real disagreements emerge. R. Ḥayyim institutionalized the Brisker method. His posthumously published book *Ḥiddushei Rabbenu Ḥayyim Ha-Levi Al Ha-Rambam* (*Novellae of Our Rabbi Ḥayyim the Levite on Maimonides*) is a classic of the school, and subsequent generations of scholars continue to follow his methodology to gain a better understanding of Talmud and Halakhah.

Prior to the development of the Brisker method, one of the primary aims of Talmud study was to reconcile contradictions in the text and resolve discrepancies. Often this was done in a pilpulistic manner. *Pilpul* is the style of attempting to reconcile or explain contradictory texts (see Solomon 1993, 4–5, 94, 105f, 113). After the promulgation of the Brisker method, the pilput style lost favor among *mitnaged* Talmud students, though its most well-known detractor might be the novelist Chaim Potok. In his novel *The Chosen*, set in the 1940s, Rav Gershenson appears sympathetically as a thinly veiled stand-in for Soloveitchik. At one point in a particularly memorable scene, the narrator, Reuven Malter, is discoursing for hours in Gershenson's class about a particularly knotty portion of the Talmud. He resolves the crucial questions posed by the passage. When Gershenson asks him if he is really satisfied with the answer, he replies that he is not, because it had been resolved pilpulistically. Reuven's best friend, representing the Ḥasidic view, disapproves of the derogatory reference to pilpul. Subsequently, Potok makes clear that he is contrasting pilpul with a source critical approach to the text, which Gershenson cautions him against using in class (Reuven is a veiled reference to David Weiss Halivni, a pioneer of the modern source critical approach to Talmud study). But the Brisker method is different from both of those. It is an approach that involves the conceptual underpinnings of the respective texts. Definition, structure, and the application of principles are prioritized (Boylan 1996, 136). It is a way to analyze the text that makes sense of the debates in the Talmud and subsequent Medieval halakhic thinkers. Pilpul resolves many questions by showing that two apparently dissimilar things are really the same. The method involving *ḥilluk* and *ḥakirah*, the Brisker method, shows that some questions themselves are dissolved when we realize that things that sound synonymous or similar are actually different concepts, categories, phenomena, or legal statuses.

Consider a straightforward example. As a matter of Jewish law, on Passover one may not eat or obtain any benefit from bread. There is also a halakhic prohibition against merely owning bread on Passover. So, what does one do with leftover bread as Passover approaches? In the Talmud (*Pesaḥim*, 21a) R. Yehuda rules that the bread must be burned, while the Sages rule that the owner may dispose of it in any manner he chooses. This seems like a straightforward difference of opinion, and it was generally treated as such. R. Ḥayyim, however, assumes there is a more fundamental disagreement behind the respective rulings.

R. Ḥayyim explains that the respective opinions of R. Yehuda and the Sages hinge upon their understanding of whether the law applies to the object (*heftza*), the bread: i.e., that *it* must be destroyed before Passover, or whether it applies to the person (*gavra*), that is, that the *individual may not own* bread on Passover. R. Yehuda holds the position that the obligation is attached to the object, the bread. He, therefore, ruled that the bread itself must be burned (destroyed). The Sages, however, believe that the obligation is upon the person, the subject, that he may not possess bread on Passover. They, therefore, ruled that one may dispose of their bread any way they choose, so long as it is no longer in their possession (see Saiman 2007, 53–54).

This distinction is interesting but appears unnecessary until one sees its broad explanatory power. The respective rulings of R. Yehuda and the Sages also help explain a related issue in a seemingly unrelated medieval legal discussion. One may not derive any benefit from holy objects which can no longer be utilized for their intended purpose (*Temurah* 7: 4–6). For example, sacrificial meat which became ritually impure is burned, while Torah scrolls which have become worn and unusable are buried. When holy items are burned, one is permitted to benefit from the ashes. When holy items are buried, however, their remains may not be utilized for any purpose (*Temurah,* 34a).

When discussing whether the ashes of bread burned before Passover may be utilized on Passover, Jacob ben Asher, "the Tur," writes that according to R. Yehudah, it would be permissible, but surprisingly, that according to the Sages it would not. The Tur's understanding of how the Sages would rule places their ruling in conflict with the halakhic ruling noted earlier that one may derive a benefit from the ashes of formerly holy items. According to R. Hayyim's analysis, however, the explanation of the Tur is clear, almost obvious. According to R. Yehuda, there is an obligation that the bread be burned. The burning of the bread fulfilled the halakhic obligation, and its ashes thus become permissible. Once one performs that commandment of burning the object (the bread), restrictions on it vanish. According to the Sages, however, there was never a halakhic obligation to burn the bread, only that the person not possess it. The burning was, therefore, not a specific halakhic act, and therefore, its burning does not change the forbidden status of the bread even after it becomes ashes and is no longer recognizable as bread.

Thus, a straightforward clarification of the precise nature of a legal obligation, that is, whether the law refers to an object or an individual's responsibility vis-a-vis that object, can tell us much about the logic of Talmudic Sages and their medieval commentators.

The Ta'amei Ha-mitzvot problem

Whereas Brisker conceptual distinctions, metaphysical commitments, subjective epistemic experience, and Halakhah appear often throughout our discussion of Soloveitchik's philosophy, reference to the *ta'amei ha-mitzvot* question will appear less frequently. However, the *ta'amei ha-mitzvot* problem motivates Soloveitchik's entire philosophical program.

Ta'amei ha-mitzvot is a classic problem in Jewish thought that attempts to formulate explanations or reasons for Biblical commandments.[17] It is a philosophical question in the sense that it looks at the "data" of Judaism, the Halakhah, and goes beyond the demand for mere obedience, to the quest to understand something deeper about each commandment and the nature of the commandments as a whole.

Before talking about reasons for specific commandments, however, it is important to understand that there are not only many answers to the question of what the *ta'amei ha-mitzvot* are but there are also multiple ways of seeing what the question is asking. The most straightforward way of thinking about it is to see the question as asking for the underlying reason behind each commandment. In this sense, the *ta'amei ha-mitzvot* problem asks for an answer to the question of why the Halakhah insists that Jews do or refrain from doing certain actions. For example, the Halakhah mandates that one give charity to the poor. The legal questions concern who counts as poor, how much charity must one give, how often, etc. The philosophical question, however, is: why does the Law require charity? The answer—the *ta'amei ha-mitzvah*—might be given from the perspective of the giver of the law. Perhaps God intended to use the Halakhah to promote a certain kind of society, and charity fits into a scheme of that society. Another kind of answer might be that there is something objectively valuable about charity, so the law demands it of us regardless of its social consequences or what God intended its social consequences to be. Or, the answer might appeal to the nature of all the commandments: perhaps their function is to make Jewish society thrive in some particular way. In that case, charity must fit into that scheme.

Another way of thinking about the question, one closer to Soloveitchik's view, is that it asks what kind of person emerges upon fulfilling a commandment. Does one become better, kinder, wiser, more virtuous, etc.? Instead of looking at the goal of the commandments, we look at the goal of a person and see how each commandment contributes toward this goal or interacts with their motivations.

The discussion about *ta'amei ha-mitzvot* has always been particularly robust when it pertains to laws that appear to have no rationale. For example, the prohibition against wearing *shatnez*, clothing that contains both wool and linen blended together, is the focus of much discussion as it has no apparent logical, ethical, scientific, or social rationale. Nor is there an obvious reason to believe one's personality is molded by not wearing clothing made of *shatnez*.

Philo of Alexandria (ca. 1st CE BCE–1st CE CE), Saadia Gaon (882–942), Maimonides, Naḥmanides (1194–1270), Gersonides (1288–1344), Ḥasdai Crescas (ca. 1340–1410/11), Joseph Albo (1380–1444), Isaac Arama (ca. 1420–1494), Hermann Cohen, and Naḥman Krochmal (1785–1840) are some of the most famous Jewish thinkers to address this problem. Each had his own approach to the question, and each offered unique answers, appealing to a wide range of philosophical ideas, from Aristotelian conceptions of man's purpose to traditional Jewish mysticism.

The *ta'amei ha-mitzvot* problem is philosophically unique. Unlike other questions in Jewish philosophy or the philosophy of religion, such as the problem of evil or the existence of God, it does not stem from a general theological problem which a Jewish thinker can address in a Jewish way by drawing upon and appealing to Jewish sources for the answer (Stern 1998, 1). It is a special problem in *Jewish* philosophy (though similar questions have been asked by philosophers of other religions) as it is not connected to other traditional philosophical questions or traditional questions in Jewish philosophy.

Part of the appeal of this problem for Soloveitchik may be that it is a quintessentially Jewish philosophical question whose answer must be as indigenous to Judaism as is Jewish law. But despite this appeal, it is a question whose canonical answer is rejected both by the legacy of Brisk and by key Hasidic thinkers. Shneur Zalman of Liadi, Hasidic leader and author of *Tanya* (see Chapter 4, Section "*Tanya*"), insists in his book *Torah Or* that wisdom and knowledge can only take us so far and that one follows the commandments because it is the will of God and no more. God's "reasons" trump anything man can say about them (see the passages translated in Batnitzky and Brafman 2018, 57).

The tradition of Brisk, with its sometimes far more abstract and idealized conception of Halakhah, would have a difficult time making sense of the question. Saiman (2018) quotes the following way of understanding the problem from a discussion attributed to R. Ḥayyim:

> One may think that the reason the Torah instituted [the commandments such as charity and performing acts of kindness] is in order for society to function. But in truth, it is the opposite. *Because* there is a commandment not to murder, *therefore* murder leads to destruction. Similarly, because the Torah commanded to give charity, such an act sustains the world …. (205)

On this kind of account, the Halakhah is an end unto itself, not a means to one. We cannot look to social reasons or anything else to explain the commandments. Halakhah, in a sense, must be discussed on its own terms, not philosophical ones (Solomon 1992, 99). Accordingly, Soloveitchik re-interprets the question as asking for the *effect* of the commandments on our conceptual ontology and resulting phenomenology. He wants to understand how the Halakhah literally constructs a world and how the world impacts our understanding of it. Following R. Ḥayyim, Soloveitchik understands the phrase "*ta'amei ha-mitzvot*" more literally, as "the flavor of the mitzvot" (Genack 2018, 37).[18] The construction of the world, its subjective experience (its "taste"), and the connection between the two is the locus of Soloveitchik's philosophical program. Much of his philosophical writing, in one way or another, revolves around this.[19]

On some readings of the *ta'amei ha-mitzvot* problem, there is a sphere of law that is separate from the law itself. Soloveitchik denies this and rewrites the question so that it does not invoke a sphere of law outside the Halakhah. Soloveitchik manages to put together a sophisticated philosophical edifice, elegantly weaving together a number of strands of then-contemporary philosophical thought while simultaneously keeping the entirety of the discourse within the bounds of classical Judaism. He does sophisticated Jewish philosophy without stepping on any halakhic norms. He does not, so to speak, ask about what is above and what is below (*Hagigah* 11b), nor does he inquire into the existence of God or the value of faith. Soloveitchik gives a philosophical analysis, not answers to classical philosophical questions. He offers little in the way of an intellectual defense of a position. Rather, he fits numerous pieces of Jewish thought, Halakhah, history, and texts into a philosophical framework. This framework is a result of responding to the *ta'amei ha-mitzvot* problem in a way that it is not a question but a request for an analysis.

Notes

1　See Carmy (2018, 23–25) on Soloveitchik's use of the history of philosophy.
2　*M'Pi HaShemuah*, Ziegler (1998, 2001, 2004, 2007, 2012, and 2013) collect many of Soloveitchik's halakhic discussions.
3　See, however, the articles collected in Samuelson (1987, §VI).
4　See Solomon (2012, 241) and Boylan (1996, 139) on the relation of Halakhah to *aggada*. A. J. Heschel (1955, 328) criticizes what he calls "pan-halakhism." This has been taken as a critique of Soloveitchik's prioritizing Halakhah over aggadah. Although Heschel criticized Soloveitchik's concept of Halakhic Man in general, it is easy to imagine that Soloveitchik's work nonetheless influenced him. Heschel's 1962/1965/1990 is an extended discussion of two strands of thought in Judaism as reflected in the opposing philosophies of two Talmudic Sages: Rabbi Akiba and Rabbi Ishmael. He may have picked up this theme from his teacher, the historian Heinrich Graetz, who understood Talmud similarly.
5　The philosophical questions surrounding the precise nature of halakhic authority are still quite open. See the essays in Sokol (1992) for some discussion.
6　"Jerusalem" and "Yerushalmi" in the title is a misnomer as Rome then banned Jews from living in Jerusalem.
7　For more on the Geonim, see *Encyclopaedia Judaica* (vol. 7, col 315–324), Lewittes (1987, 111–120), and the article by Gideon Libson in Hecht et al. (1996, 197–250).
8　For a more comprehensive historical overview of Halakhah, see Hecht et al. (1996).
9　Soloveitchik criticizes any religion ("religious liberalism") that places liberal values as its foundation, making it a "handmaiden" to ethical or social norms (*Halakhic Mind*, 88–99).
10　Elon (1975, 13) estimates that (as of 1975) some 300,000 *she'elot u-teshuvot* (responsa) have been written.
11　See, for example, the introductory section "On Halachah and Reform Judaism" in Washofsky (2010): "Reform responsa are 'authoritative' if and only if they are persuasive, to the degree that they convince their readers that this particular answer, this particular application of Torah corresponds to the readers' own conception of Judaism." Washofsky's two-volume work contains seventy-seven *teshuvot* divided into the four traditional halakhic categories: "*Orach Chaim*: Worship, Shabbat, and Festival Observance; *Yoreh Dei-ah*: Ritual Observance; *Even Ha-Ezer*: Personal Status, Marriage, and Family Life; *Choshen Mishpat*: The Life of the Community."
12　"Reconstructing Halakha" https://www.reconstructingjudaism.org/article/reconstructing-halakha.
13　https://therra.org/resolutions-statements-guidelines.php.
14　For more on Soloveitchik and creativity, see later. See also Wurzburger (1997), Schwartz (2007, ch. 11), Kolbrener (2015), and *Maimonides Course* (75f).
15　The lecture can be heard at: https://www.yutorah.org/lectures/lecture.cfm/767722/Rabbi_Joseph_B_Soloveitchik/Gerus_&_Mesorah_-_Part_1.
16　The following summary and example are adapted from Zevin (2007, 33–37). For Soloveitchik's own discussion, see *Eulogy Velvele*. Solomon (1993) is still the

most thorough discussion of the method and the circle of rabbis who created and first employed it. (But see the discussion in Shapiro [1997].) See also Lichtenstein (2000), Ross (2004, 66–68), and Saiman (2007) and (2018, ch. 12).

17 This section is indebted to the Introduction in Stern (1998).

18 David Shatz pointed us to Sacks (2003, 287) who sees *ta'amei ha-mitzvot* similarly.

19 For example, the relationship between *ta'amei ha-mitzvot* and subjectivity and objectivity, as we describe throughout, shows up as a question in a final exam Soloveitchik gave in his Yeshiva University Jewish Philosophy course in the Spring semester of 1936. See: http://text.rcarabbis.org/final-exam-in-jewish-philosophy-of-dr-joseph-soloveitchik-1936/.

4 Soloveitchik's main philosophical writings

What we take to be Soloveitchik's primary contribution to Jewish philosophy is spelled out over a large number of books, articles, and public and university lectures, which can be divided into "foundation," "development," and "personality" texts. This is most easily seen in what is sometimes deemed his early trilogy: *The Halakhic Mind*, *And from There You Shall Seek*, and *Halakhic Man*.[1] *The Halakhic Mind* is his "foundational" work. *And from There You Shall Seek* is an early and important "development" work. *Halakhic Man* (Part 1) is his most important "personality" text.

Let us look at what we mean by each of these three categories before exploring them in depth:

Foundation. The foundation part of his philosophy—the portion of his thought that sets the intellectual foundations and outline—is completely contained in *The Halakhic Mind*. There, Soloveitchik presents a philosophical justification for doing Jewish philosophy after the method for which he will become known. Soloveitchik articulates reasons for abandoning old styles of what we now think of as classical Jewish philosophy and instead advocates approaching Jewish philosophy from a fresh and unique standpoint with a novel methodology using only data indigenous to Judaism.

Development. In the development literature, Soloveitchik describes how to develop the type of religious consciousness possessed by Halakhic Men, the type of people described in his personality works. This can be found most vividly in *Halakhic Man* (Part 2) and in *And from There You Shall Seek*, to an extent in his novella on Talmud and on Maimonides' *Code of Jewish Law*, and his numerous discussions of repentance, prayer, mourning, and other halakhot. We will see how creation and creativity play a central role in developing the Halakhic Mind. "Creation," as Soloveitchik uses the term, refers both to man recreating himself and creating new and original halakhic concepts.

Personality. The personality literature comprises the philosophy for which Soloveitchik is most famous. This material can be found in *Halakhic Man* (Part 1) and "The Lonely Man of Faith." His essays "Catharsis," "Majesty and Humility," and "The Community," among others, paint a more complete picture. This literature tells us how Soloveitchik imagined the ideal Jewish personality—the "finished product," the paradigmatic Halakhic Man, who lives a redeemed halakhic life. When we read his personality sketches, we begin to appreciate Soloveitchik's methodology of interrogating Jewish sources to develop portraits of idealized Jewish personalities.

The essence of the foundation, development, and personality literature can be described by the questions they address. Broadly speaking, the foundational work addresses the questions: Is the world different for halakhic Jews? If so, what does that mean? What shapes a Jewish world, and what methodology should we use to understand the relationship between this world and the religious experience of a Halakhic Man? The development works address the questions: How does one attain a Halakhic Mind? What must one do and how must one live to gain the experiences that a Jewish mind has? The personality works address the question: What is it like to have a Halakhic Mind, and what does that mind look like?

Foundation

The Halakhic Mind: philosophical background

> For were we to analyze the mystery of the God-man relationship as reflected in the Jewish religious consciousness ... it would be necessary that we first gather all objectified data at our disposal: passages in the Holy Writ pertaining to divinity and divine attributes; ... moments of tension between God and man, as in the case of Job; many halakhic problems where certain attitudes of man toward Divinity have found their expression; all forms of cult, liturgy, prayer, Jewish mysticism ... Out of this enormous mass of objectified constructs, the underlying subjective aspects could gradually be reconstructed.
>
> (*Halakhic Mind*, 90–91)

Plato and Aristotle

The history of philosophy, especially as viewed through Soloveitchik's lens, is filled with dualities, dichotomies, and dialectics. Plato and Aristotle are a teacher-student pair often said to be the ancient Greek paradigms of two radically opposed ways of thinking about the nature of the world. They represent an early dichotomy in the history of Western philosophy.

Plato was born in Athens during the period in which the Anshei Knesset Ha-gedolah—the Men of the Great Assembly—were canonizing the Hebrew Bible across the Mediterranean. Plato represents a view that sees the world in which we live as merely a shadow and illusion, while the actual "real world" exists in all its mathematical perfection in a "higher realm," what philosophers sometimes call the Platonic world of "forms." This "higher realm" houses the archetypes of all the objects in the world, especially the perfect version of the Just, the Beautiful, and most important, the Good. On Plato's reckoning, the goal in life is to "ascend" to a higher realm and apprehend the forms. Only in doing so can one grasp the true reality. Since the second century, mystics have been borrowing this approach to reality and incorporating it within their own worldview. As recently as twentieth-century Germany, neo-Kantian philosophers were adapting this approach to suit their philosophical goals.

Aristotle, on the other hand, is usually taken to be the down-to-earth scientist who demands we observe, categorize, and study samples of objects in this world in all their inherent messiness. Aristotle argues against the existence of Platonic forms and believes it is scientifically unimportant to worry about an object's form. We ought rather to understand the world by examining what it gives us and make inferences from what we observe. To understand the world, we must approach it first via our experiences, for that is the only place we can start.

Plato sees our world as inferior to the "real" perfect world, while Aristotle takes this world to be the only reality. The poet Samuel Taylor Coleridge once remarked that everyone is born either an Aristotelian or a Platonist, and he did not think it possible for an Aristotelian to become a Platonist, and he is certain that a Platonist could not become an Aristotelian. This sentiment strikes many thinkers as true. There are simply two different ways of understanding the world. These two figures represent the prototypes for two opposite idealized types of people as exemplified in the history of Western thought. Their opposing views are taken as early examples from Western philosophy of two incompatible but coherent schools of thought. Plato and Aristotle are also paradigmatic cases of individuals with complete and consistent approaches to the world. Their respective philosophical perspectives have come to represent their worldviews, and discrepancies between them are generally attributable to their underlying view of reality.

Rationalism and empiricism

Brevity requires that the above is practically a caricature of Plato's and Aristotle's positions, as is the following discussion of their early modern followers. The post- and neo-Kantians, whom we will have more to say about later, were busy rewriting the history of philosophy. Hegel, Schopenhauer, Kuno Fischer, Ernest Cassirer, Paul Natorp, and others located the origins of modern philosophy with René Descartes (Mercer 2020), and they divided the subsequent philosophers into two schools of thought: rationalism and empiricism. Descartes, Spinoza, and Leibniz are "rationalists"; Locke, Berkeley, and Hume are empiricists. This taxonomy, however oddly gerrymandered it is, was designed to situate Kant in the space they believed he occupied in the history of philosophy. It is the way the history of philosophy would have been presented to Soloveitchik and, to a significant extent, is still presented to philosophy students today.

On the current account, rationalists take scientific truth to be grounded in reason, in *a priori* speculation about the nature of the world. To guarantee our knowledge of science, we must provide a philosophical metaphysical foundation to prop it up. Descartes and Leibniz (1646–1716) hold that science needs philosophical support that only comes from first speculating about the true nature of reality and its Creator. Descartes believes that science requires philosophical argument to show that knowledge itself is possible; hence, his famous "I think, therefore I am" argument. This argument proves that at least one thing exists: oneself. Given that the proof hinges on the fact that Descartes thinks, he can build on it and show that he is in essence a thinking being. He then shows that his innate ability to think provides him with a clear and distinct idea of God. God can then be proven to exist by various *a priori* arguments (especially the "ontological argument") solely requiring reason, akin to mathematical arguments, instead of arguments that depend on observing the material world (like the kind biology uses). Descartes then argues that God is not the kind of being who would allow him to be deceived as he observes the world. Therefore, his scientific observations must be fairly accurate—hence, a rationalist foundation for science and scientific knowledge.

On the other hand, empiricists like John Locke (1632–1704) and David Hume (1711–1776) oppose the idea that philosophy provides a foundation for science. Science, they argue, is grounded only in the material world. That is not to say there is no room for philosophical speculation about science. There is. Philosophy must explain, for example, how humans obtain the kind of knowledge science provides and also its limitations. But scientific knowledge itself is "grounded" in the actual world and not in metaphysical rationalization of the nature of thinking or an idea of God. Empiricists accept scientific findings without needing to offer philosophical arguments justifying the scientific knowledge they obtained.

Though a staunch empiricist himself, Hume grasped the limitations of the empiricist conception of science. Scientific knowledge is grounded in experience. We know all that we do because we have somehow observed or experienced it. But scientific knowledge is more than mere observation. It is, at a minimum, a description of the causes of things. Collecting observations is not science. Science is the enterprise by which we grasp relationships that exist in the natural world: how causation works and how objects interact.

Consider an example fashionable in Hume's time: We observe a billiard ball moving, hear it colliding with a second ball, and then see the second ball move. Relying strictly on these empirical observations, all we can say is that we observed two balls moving, one after the other; hardly a scientifically noteworthy event. When we go beyond our empirical observations and say that ball A *caused* ball B to move, we have offered a scientific assessment of *why* the second ball moved. *That* is interesting science. In arguing this, Hume exposes the limitation of empiricism as an approach to scientific knowledge. How can empiricism possibly give us the scientific knowledge we need to understand our world when it has nothing to say about causes, an essential ingredient of science? Empiricism thus seems unable to provide the kinds of descriptions that science needs.

Hume attempts to rescue both science and empiricism by presenting an alternate way of thinking about causation. We experience causation, he claims, as a psychological phenomenon. When we see events co-occurring often enough, when we notice a "constant conjunction" of events, we call that a cause. When we notice ball B moving after ball A moves and hits it, over and over, we get used to those kinds of events co-occurring and expect this to repeat itself. This expectation is what we call "cause." Nothing more.

Given his version of how empiricists understand causation, it follows that for Hume, science begins with observations. We notice over and over that one event follows another, so we associate the pair of events in our mind and call it a cause. Causation is just successive events that we have observed in the past that we expect to observe repeatedly in nature. We have no way to gain knowledge about whether or not there are actual causes or what they are. So, only in this limited form, both science and empiricism are secure.

Kant

The German philosopher Immanuel Kant (1724–1804) appreciated the motivations behind both rationalist and empiricist schools of thought as well as the powerful criticisms of empiricism raised by Hume. Combining the two schools, Kant explains that scientific knowledge necessarily emerges from the empirical world but is also a product of our rational intuitions, held in the mind, *a priori*. Kant uniquely synthesizes the empiricist and rationalist traditions. He agrees with empiricists that empirical sense-driven experience is the only way to obtain information about the world and addresses Hume's skepticism about our knowledge of causes.

Kant claims that it is a mistake to assume that just because all knowledge *arises from* experience, it is also *grounded* in experience. In other words, although everything we know about the world is derived from our experience of it, our knowledge is rooted in something deeper than mere observation.

Consider causation. We say event A causes event B when we continually see the two events occurring one after the other. But as opposed to Hume, whose theory of science is that all we can know about these events is that they simply always happen together, Kant argues that additional presuppositions must be accepted.

What are these presuppositions? Kant asks us to consider what is happening when we see two billiard balls that are "constantly conjoined" in what we take to be a causal relationship. Ball A moves, touches ball B, and then ball B moves; one event occurs *after* the other. We cannot observe causes between them; we do not observe one event occurring *because of* another. Kant retorts, however, that there are numerous things we cannot observe. For example, we cannot observe the time in which the motion takes place; we merely observe events. We *presuppose* that the events take place within time. Time is not detected by any of our sense organs, nor do we have sensory experience of time independent of events. Human reason *presupposes* the concept of time nonempirically, epistemologically prior to our experience of events.

We also presuppose the concept of space nonempirically; we do not independently experience it. More precisely, all our experiences present themselves to us as existing within space, just as they do in time. Kant thus explicates our sensible representations of objects as general forms of our "pure intuitions of space and time." Kant understands these *a priori* intuitions of the categories of time and space as preconditions for scientific understanding (using the term "a priori" slightly differently than his predecessors). It is only possible to understand objects in the external world if we intuit them as existing in space and time.

Causation is similarly not simply a habit of the mind based on experience, as Hume believed, but rather based on something more fundamental that sensory experience does not provide. In order for something to be an object of experience, Kant argues that we must *presuppose* that it is subject to the network of causal regularities.

Our experiences are thereby organized within a rational framework that cannot come from our experiences alone. The rational framework includes categories of understanding within which we fit our experience of the world. These categories are supplied *a priori* by human understanding and work together with our general intuitions about the sensible world to shape our experience of its structure. Our subjective mind is not independent of the objective world; our experience depends both on the information we get from the senses and the *a priori* framework our mind imposes on that information.

We assume, in other words, that objects of the world exist in space and time, they are organized and amassed in a certain way, and have certain causal relationships to one another. We do not experience this organization; rather, these concepts are supplied by reason, *a priori*, and help us organize our experiences. These concepts provide the lens through which we filter all of our experience. Science involves observing data through the lens of "the forms of our intuitions." Our *a priori* forms of intuition and categories of understanding are thus nonempirical preconditions of knowledge that we use to make sense of what we see in the world. They are templates through which we filter our experiences and make them coherent. Finding these templates is one of Kant's main philosophical goals.

It has been noted that "[s]ince the end of the eighteenth century no non-Jewish philosopher has been more central to Jewish philosophy than Kant" (Franks 2007, 53; and see Batnitzky 2011, 22–23). This applies no less to his influence on Soloveitchik than to such figures as Kant's acquaintance Moses Mendelssohn (1729–1786), Markus Herz (1747–1803), Solomon Maimon (1753–1800), and Hermann Cohen and his followers.

It is certainly reasonable to wonder how Kant's speculation about causation and the structure of experience impacts Jewish philosophy. Soloveitchik borrows two important ideas from Kant. First, Soloveitchik's conception of an *a priori* rational framework, related to the Kantian version as filtered through Hermann Cohen and the neo-Kantians, is used to explain how Halakhic Man interprets his world. We find, for example, Kant's analysis of scientific epistemology echoed in Soloveitchik's claim that "... the Halacha works like a mathematician in an *a priori* world. Its constructs are ideal. *Torah she-be-al-peh* [oral law] does not study reality. It prepares abstract schemata and applies them to the world of the senses" (*Noraos Harav*, 10:85). The "abstract schemata" are analogous to Kant's "forms of intuitions." More closely related to our project, we find Soloveitchik's definition of halakhic a priorism whereby "[t]he Halakhah organizes the realia given by observation into halakhic constructs, or *a priori* schemata, which convert the sensuous data into a halakhic-objective order" (*Emergence Ethical*, 18). Halakhah does not construct its content *a priori* like mathematics does; rather, it is the lens through which we process what we experience of the world.

While for Kant, the scientist's *a priori* framework consists of categories of quality, quantity, modality, and relation (Kant 1902, 61), Halakhic Man's *a priori* framework for interpreting his world consists of a variety of halakhic concepts such as holy (*kadosh*), pure (*tahor*), invalid (*pasul*), and kosher, as well as a variety of halakhic objects and actions such as ritual bath (*mikvah*), *lulav*, document (*shtar*),[2] blessing, prayer time, and sacrifice. Soloveitchik makes extensive use of this analogy with Kantian thought using the Halakhah as the framework that contains the ideal Jews' categories of experience by which they organize their world.

Second, the Kantian preoccupation with the relationship between subjective experience and the objective world pervades Soloveitchik's thinking in ways obvious even to the most superficial readers of his works. But a more nuanced look at Soloveitchik's view of the Kantian *a priori* forms of intuition and the subjective/objective relation demands a closer look at Hermann Cohen, one of Kant's most important commentators.

Hermann Cohen and neo-Kantianism

Kant quickly became a central figure in the history of philosophy, ultimately spawning different schools of interpretation and generations of scholarly study that continues to this day. Early Kant interpretation was influenced by the emerging discipline of psychology. Thinkers began interpreting Kant in psychological rather than philosophical terms. They understood Kant as treating the mind as a natural phenomenon that can be studied like anything else found in nature. They believed that the Kantian tradition is best understood as seeking out psychological mechanisms by which our brain translates the sensations taken in by the senses into a coherent picture of the world. The neo-Kantians interpreted Kant differently.

Hermann Cohen[3]—the principal architect and spokesperson for what came to known as Marburg neo-Kantianism[4]—advocates an understanding of Kant that gives pride of place to *philosophy* that strives to rescue Kantian thought from its psychological interpreters. Epistemology is not psychology, and the neo-Kantians wanted to make sure Kant is understood as concerned with the former, not the latter. In doing so, Cohen argues that Kant is a philosopher interested in exploring the *justification* of metaphysical knowledge about things like God and the soul, and space and time, rather than the psychological motives for our metaphysical beliefs. Kant wants to understand the *evidence* for what is true and false, not the psychological phenomenon of beliefs themselves. The psychological phenomena can be studied as part of the natural world; evidence for facts about metaphysics cannot be studied that way. Kant wants to know about the epistemological statements we make about knowing the world *a priori*, not about the phenomena of the world or the brain itself. This is in Cohen's analysis a logical inquiry, not a scientific one. It is in line with an important distinction made by the philosopher Hermann Lotze (1817–1881), for example, who argues that we must clearly distinguish between science and logic, that is, what philosophers of the time would think of as a distinction between "being" (existence) and "validity" (true in virtue of something's logical form). We often confuse being with validity because we tend to associate what exists with what can be truly stated about something. But this is not the case. The distinction may make more sense if we consider an example from the realm of mathematics. $2 + 3 = 5$ even if there are no 2 s, 3 s, or 5 s; it is true, even if none of the things under discussion (like 2 s) has anything resembling "existence." 2 does not have to exist for it to be true that $2 + 3 = 5$. (There may be two books or two giraffes, but the abstract number 2 in the perfectly true sentence "$2 + 3 = 5$" itself does not exist.) Thus, something can be valid without having to say anything about it existing. The project Cohen attributes to Kant is logical, not physical.

Cohen argues that it only makes sense to talk about physics and metaphysics within the realm of Lotze's logical validity not in the realm of being. Scientific objects thus are really logical constructs shaped by our *a priori* concepts. Accordingly, Cohen was concerned with the logic of how we construct these scientific concepts, or what can be called the "constitution of being."

Later in his career, Cohen would move from defending a philosophical interpretation of Kant to forging a novel philosophical system of his own. The project begins in 1883 with an analysis of mathematical infinitesimals (see Samuelson 1989; Moynahan 2003), which his contemporaries found very problematic (see Schirn 2017, 47–48; Fraenkel 2016, 85), and moves in 1902 to a system of logic, parts of which even his student, Paul Natorp, found obscure. In this project Cohen moves beyond keeping philosophy from becoming an offshoot of psychology; he also tries to keep philosophy away from idealist metaphysics. Idealism treats our awareness of objects as if it were merely an awareness of how objects appear *to us* and not as if we are actually aware of the object itself. For idealists, when someone looks at an object, they are actually looking inward, at a subjective representation of the object. The outside object is real and makes its way into one's subjective consciousness, but one is not directly aware of the object itself. According to idealists, being unaware of the reality external to our mind is a hindrance toward a scientific understanding of the world. Cohen wants to preserve the idea that we are, in some way, directly aware of the outside world.

Cohen defends the Kantian idea that *a priori* structures of human knowledge determine how we perceive objects and acknowledges that the outside world may differ from how we perceive it. Nevertheless, Cohen argues that what matters to us is what we experience through our *a priori* categories of pure thought. (These *a priori* categories are logically prior, and they are not acquired first; we need to understand the categories before we can understand that which we perceive.) Furthermore, while Kant claims that empirical information is the source of knowledge, Cohen argues that *pure thought*—logical categorical thought—is the actual origin of knowledge and that it is the job of philosophy to investigate these categories. Not only is Cohen's primacy of pure thought his central critique of Kant, his student, Paul Natorp (1854–1924), would later argue that it is the view that allows for a scientific philosophy that is not reducible to physiology and psychology. Moreover, and perhaps more surprising, Natorp shows that this view of Cohen also makes room for an independent science of psychology, a feature that will become important to Soloveitchik's future work. Soloveitchik's dissertation is generally occupied with Natorp and Cohen on the notions of pure thought and the constitution of being.

Cohen's first major book on Kant's theory of experience began the neo-Kantian concern for the relations between the subjective and the objective that ultimately came to pervade the Marburg agenda (Natorp 2015). Soloveitchik argues in his dissertation (*Reine Denken*) that Cohen's epistemology does not in itself allow us to grasp reality or provide a scientific understanding of the objects of the world. We have no way, in other words, of correlating the objects in the world with our subjective impressions of those objects. Yet there must be some way we correlate our subjective experience with the objective world. This is one of Soloveitchik's primary disagreements with Cohen's later epistemology.[5] Though the dissertation is about epistemology, the disagreement plays an important role in Soloveitchik's Jewish philosophy, which dedicates much space to the relationship between the "objects of Halakhah" and the subjective experience of them. Soloveitchik's Jewish philosophical reconciliation of the subjective and objective is "a major lifelong concern" (Lichtenstein 2003, 201) influenced by Natorp and others who would describe a method of "reconstructing" the real world from the objects of sensation, which is how an acceptable scientific psychology can be formed.

Natorp's general approach describes consciousness as including a threefold structure: (1) there is a content (that thing of which one is conscious), (2) there is a subject (who is conscious), and (3) there is a relation between the content and the subject of consciousness (Natorp 1912, 24; see Dahlstrom 2015, 242; Luft 2010, 87n23).[6] A few years after this discussion of Natorp's will see Max Scheler pick up this approach and apply it to the philosophy of religion (see Chapter 4, Section "The emergence of phenomenology"). Soloveitchik's program would similarly be to understand (1) the content of the world, shaped by the halakhic concepts, about which one is aware; (2) a Halakhic Man, a subject who perceives that world; and (3) a relationship between the halakhic world and Halakhic Man. More on that shortly.

The Kantian and neo-Kantian concern for the relation between the objective outside world and the subjective inner world is not confined to philosophy. Late-nineteenth and early-twentieth-century Germany was an extremely fertile intellectual period, and Kant's legacy spilled over to many areas of science. During the birth of quantum mechanics, for example, Niels Bohr and Albert Einstein were divided over whether or not it was possible to separate the subjective from the objective. Bohr, because of his commitment to the Principle of Complementarity, believed that the objective world cannot be disentangled from our subjective perceptions; Einstein disagreed. Kant's legacy lives on independently but also through the history of contemporary analytic philosophy, especially the philosophy of science. Much of analytic philosophy is only possible because of the groundwork which Cohen and the neo-Kantian program had laid down.

Cohen's Jewish thought

Because Soloveitchik and so many subsequent Jewish thinkers took various parts of Hermann Cohen's philosophical system seriously in so many ways, we too must look at him somewhat more in depth, this time as an important Jewish thinker and not only in abstraction as the architect of the philosophical edifice that is Marburg neo-Kantianism. We must keep in mind that Cohen is one of the very small group of thinkers whose significant influence on the larger secular community he was a part of is equal to his influence on the history of Jewish thought, and to an extent, it is so only *because* the neo-Kantian cannot really be separated from the Jewish thinker. Beiser (2018, vii) makes the (only slightly controversial) claim that "[i]t is artificial and arbitrary to separate Cohen's philosophical and religious writings, which were inextricably intertwined. The philosophical were the basis for the religious; but the religious were the motivation for the philosophical." Thus, our previous discussion of Cohen, as well as the present one and the ones in Chapter 4, Section "Hermann Cohen on repentance," and Chapter 5, Section "Anti-Zionism," are misleadingly placed apart. They should be seen as a coherent statement of Cohen's view. How did Cohen integrate his role as Kantian scholar with his position as Germany's most prominent philosopher of Judaism, and what features of his thought are so important for Soloveitchik's intellectual development? What about Cohen's legacy is important for Jehiel Jacob Weinberg, Alexander Altmann, Nehemiah Anton Nobel, Gershom Scholem, Franz Rosenzweig, Walter Benjamin, Leo Strauss, and an interesting variety of other Jewish thinkers of his time?

The Cohen family records were destroyed by the Nazis. What remains is his published work and a few biographical details that can be reconstructed from his writing, correspondence, public information, and recollections of people who knew him. We do know that Hermann Jescheskel Cohen was born in 1842 to a poor, traditional Jewish household in Coswig, Germany. His father, Gerson Cohen, had been a cantor and someone with whom he spent much time studying Talmud. At age 15, he entered the Jewish Theological Seminary in Breslau (the intellectual forerunner of the Conservative Jewish institution of the same name currently in New York City), headed by Zacharias Frankel (1810–1875). Frankel espoused "positive-historical" Judaism and the belief that religious faith would be enhanced by studying Judaism via critical and historical methods championed in Leopold Zunz's ideal of the *Wissenschaft des Judentums*. He studied to be a rabbi under many of their eminent faculty including the philologist Jakob Bernays (1824–1881), the historian of philosophy Manuel Joël (1826–1890), and the Jewish historian Heinrich Graetz (1817–1891) for four years before abandoning rabbinical aspirations and finding his passion in philosophy. It is likely he abandoned the seminary because of an interaction with Samson Raphael Hirsch (1808–1888) that made him realize that being a rabbi would not allow him the intellectual independence he desperately needed (Beiser 2018, 15).

He moved on to study at universities in Breslau, Berlin, and Halle. Recognized as a philosophical genius, he ultimately found a position in Marburg which, remarkably for an unconverted Jew, eventually became a full professorship, which lasted for nearly forty years (Cohen 1971, 15ff). At the time of his appointment as professor when he succeeded his mentor Friedrich Lange, who fought greatly on Cohen's behalf, he was among the very few unconverted Jews to hold an academic chair in Germany and the first unconverted professor of philosophy to become an ordinary professor at a recognized university (Beiser 2018, 92). That this could happen was largely due to a brief liberal period toward Jews under Bismarck where they held many civil rights, not just in theory but also in practice.

In 1868, Cohen made his first foray into the Jewish public sphere when he offered a qualified defense of Rudolf Virchow, a Christian politician and historically important nephropathologist who headed a pathology institute and had a reputation for not being anti-Semitic. He was publicly accused of failing to hire a Jewish pathologist. Virchow's argument was that the institute was designed to prepare people for academia, and as of yet no Jew had ever been admitted as a regular professor in pathology. It would be a waste of an opportunity to give the spot to someone who would not make the best use of it. Cohen didn't quite defend Virchow, but he did generally praise him and downplay the significance of the charge against him. Over the course of his remarks, however, he does complain that Virchow had previously hired a Jew who had been baptized, a fact that pains other Jews, who see that they must resort to conversion to be successful (Beiser 2018, 46–49).

In 1869, Cohen delivered a lecture about the Sabbath that eventually became his first substantial Jewish publication. It also marks the beginning of his preoccupation with the relation between the Jewish origins of ethics and social justice and the continuing relevance and import of Judaism. This connection is reflected in most of his subsequent Jewish writing.

In 1880, somewhat early in his Marburg academic career, during a spate of anti-Semitic backlash in Germany, he reentered the public sphere in defense of Judaism when the anti-Semitic historian Heinrich von Treitschke wrote an article advocating Jewish assimilation to German culture and the abandonment of their Jewish way of life. (In that article Cohen's former teacher Heinrich Graetz was singled out, historian-to-historian, with particular vehemence as a primary target.) Treitschke's article was taken to support the views of even the most fanatical anti-Semite. Cohen came to Judaism's defense. Cohen's outspokenness on this matter made him the public spokesperson for German Jewry (Poma 2006, ch. 1). The exchange between Cohen and Treitschke was particularly difficult as Cohen was a fervently patriotic German. He also strongly supported Jewish national assimilation in German society and culture, though simultaneously believing that Judaism had a unique and important mission of promulgating religious monotheism requiring Jews to maintain their religiously distinctive identity. Treitschke would make no such distinction between Jewish nationality and Jewish religion as Cohen insisted upon. Cohen was initially somewhat conciliatory to Treitschke and critical of Graetz, in particular of the latter's religious particularism, favoring instead the idea that Judaism is a universal religion that could blend with German society and culture. By the end of the affair, however, Cohen was more committed than ever to the defense of Judaism.

In 1888, Cohen and a notorious anti-Semite, the foremost Bible scholar of his era, Paul Lagarde, were asked to testify as, essentially, "expert witnesses" in what is believed to be the first legal case involving the defamation of Judaism, the "Fenner Trial." He testified about the relationship between the Talmud and faithful Jews and the Talmud's prescriptions vis-a-vis non-Jews. The testimony was in the context of a trial in which Leo Munk, the Chief Rabbi of Marburg, filed a legal complaint against Ferdinand Fenner for defaming a public religion at a local rally in Marburg by stating that Jews are scoundrels, the Talmud is the supreme authority for the Jews, and it teaches that Jews may cheat and steal from the "*Gojim*." Cohen was defending Judaism and Jews against charges of what now might be called "dual loyalty," wherein Jews' primary allegiance is to the Talmud at the expense of fellow German citizens. The anti-Semitic context was apparent to all, and ultimately the court penalized the defendant for defamation, though the penalty was a mere fortnight in jail and payment of costs. The trial and its aftermath greatly disillusioned Cohen when his university position was suddenly made far less comfortable than it had been before he so publicly defended Judaism (see Beiser 2018, ch. 7.4). Following this incident, the other faculty made a point of standing up and walking out when he entered the faculty lounge, among other slights.

Franz Rosenzweig sees Cohen at this point coming to think of himself as a *ba'al teshuva* of sorts, one who has "returned" to Judaism, and his Jewish identity reasserted itself in various ways (though in the most important senses, he had never really been estranged from Judaism). Cohen, for example, did not keep a kosher home but complained bitterly that his Russian Jewish students did not (Fraenkel 2016, 84). He became less tolerant of baptized Jews. It became somewhat of a convention among some academic Jewish families in Germany that their sons and daughters, upon marrying Christians, would be baptized. At some later point in his life, Cohen refused on principle to enter a home if one of the couple was a Baptized Jew (Fraenkel 2016, 76).

When he retired from teaching in Marburg, he moved to Berlin and taught general and Jewish philosophy at the Academy for the Scientific Study of Judaism. At the time, World War I was erupting, and his friend Paul Natorp accused him of being too preoccupied with Jewish affairs, though he tirelessly fought on behalf of both German and Jewish causes, believing that this will finally be the time that Germans will come to understand the profound inseparability of German and Jewish culture.

Despite his unwavering support of Germany, his colleagues in Marburg perpetrated one last anti-Semitic indignity upon him. When Cohen retired from teaching in 1912 and moved to Berlin, they refused to appoint any of his students, such as Ernst Cassirer, to his now vacant department chair as was then customary in German universities. Instead, they simultaneously slighted his philosophical program and religious dignity by replacing him with a teacher of experimental psychology, the young Erich Rudolf Jaensch, who was then known for his research on memory and later known for his Nazi-supporting views on science and race.

Cohen's 1913 and 1914 lectures in Berlin were published posthumously in 1919 as *Religion of Reason out of the Sources of Judaism*. This, his last book, parallels Kant's *Religion Within the Limits of Reason Alone*, and it shows the vibrancy and rational acceptability of Judaism in the tradition of Abraham Geiger and Leopold Zunz. Within it, Cohen argues—though Kant would not have agreed—that the Judaism of the Bible and Talmud best captures the notion of a Kantian religion of reason (though emphatically Judaism is not the Kantian religion of reason).

The three works that form Cohen's system of philosophy—*Logik der reinen Erkenntnis* (*Logic of Pure Knowledge*), *Ethik des reinen Willens* (*Ethics of Pure Will*), and *Ästhetik des reinen Gefühls* (*Aesthetics of Pure Feeling*)—similarly have their counterparts in three of Kant's philosophy works, *Critique of Pure Reason, Critique of Practical Reason,* and *Critique of Judgment.*

Adapting an idea from the Jewish philosopher Baruch Spinoza (1951, chs. 4–5), Kant had gone so far as to deny that Judaism was a religion in the ethical sense that both he and later Cohen would require of a "real" religion. Kant charged Judaism and Jewish law as being merely a collection of laws that supported a political entity rather than a set of laws that embody a set of ethical precepts to which one adheres out of a sense of doing the right thing.

Kant argued that to Judaism's original political charter was later appended a moral code to make Judaism appear as a religion centered upon ethical feelings, intuition, and duty, that is, a universal religion (Kant 2009, 139; see also Rotenstreich 1984, 62ff, Kaplan 2007a, 209). Judaism, claimed Kant, is problematic as its laws are inherently coercive. While its idea of reward and punishment appears to be this-worldly, it is too particularistic to comprise a universal religion. An ethics-based religion (like Christianity), Kant argued, requires individual autonomy to allow one to freely choose to obey rather than to be coerced by the state. It requires a concept of eternal reward and punishment (which Kant denied Judaism originally possessed) and universality (which, according to Kant, came only with Christianity.)

Cohen, motivated by both political and philosophical concerns, without pointing a finger at Kant, argued that Jews choose to follow Halakhah in the same way that one chooses to do their duty to what is ethical. Following Halakhah is indeed an autonomous act of the will and not a coerced set of practices (a theme Yeshayahu Leibowitz would later make a central part of his thought).

Beyond Cohen's defense of Halakhah as autonomously chosen acts, Cohen contends with Kant's conception of God, which is also in general problematic. Kant thinks we cannot know about entities for which it is impossible for us to have direct experience. So how do we come to our knowledge of God and the soul? With respect to metaphysical objects like these, Kant argues that the *a priori* principles of reason that our mind uses to make sense of the world can also play a role in giving us knowledge of these objects, so long as we understand the role they play as regulative, not constitutive. Meaning, the categories of experience only provide a certain kind of knowledge, namely, knowledge of what we ought to do and how we must conduct our search for knowledge. It does not give the kind of knowledge that tells us what exists and what the world is like (Kant 2009, 138–41).

Cohen assumes that philosophy's job is to understand the logical conditions underlying scientific thought. Philosophy investigates the structure by which people shape what they are given by the real world. It then tries to understand the important role of the mind in "creating" the objects of the world. In this Cohen is following Kant.

Kant, after all, said, "Two things fill the mind with ever new and increasing admiration and reverence … *the starry heavens above me and the moral law within me* … I see them before me and connect them directly with the consciousness of my existence" (Kant 1997, 133). Kant looks no further than his own cognitive structures for the moral law. Kant, like Hume, rejects the traditional proofs for God's existence (i.e., the ontological, teleological, and cosmological arguments). He is responsible for formulating the "moral argument" for God's existence: If reason demands that we believe in a moral law (which it does via the logic of the categorical imperative), it must also demand that we believe in a disinterested ability to dole out happiness (i.e., reward) in proportion to that morality. It must also demand we have a concept of an eternal world in which that happiness is doled out and a soul which can receive that happiness even without our temporally restricted bodies. It is, therefore, necessary to postulate that there is a God that can do this (Kant 1997, 103–10), a soul to which it can be done, and an eternity to do it.

Thus, Cohen's understanding of the nature of religion, like Abraham Geiger's and Kant's, is grounded in ethical theory and his idea of God is grounded in the categories of experience. Like Kant, Cohen looks inward for God. For him, God is a "regulative ideal" that grounds our ethical intuitions and religion of reason is an ideal of pure monotheism. It is the conceptual idea of the total radical otherness of God. It is the idea that God is absolutely different from man. This God, like Maimonides', is very much not anthropomorphic.

Cohen argues that an ideal rational religion (i.e., a "Kantian religion" derived from Kant's understanding of the nature and centrality of reason, as per Kant 2009) emerges from the source material of Judaism, in particular its ethical and legal source material. Cohen thinks Kant's religious prejudices blinded him to the reality that Judaism's approach is religion of reason.

Cohen's "regulative ideal," like Kant's postulated God, lacks the "concreteness" of a personal God; it is another *a priori* category of thought that guides morality. It is a concept that avails itself of Lotze's distinction between existence and validity. It examines religion in terms of whether or not the concept of God is valid, not whether or not He exists. This is a subtle (and perhaps unsustainable) distinction, but it is an attempt to show that we cannot make sense of God's existence, but we can say that the idea of God is a valid one (Beiser 2018, 2ff). God is the core idea through which we filter all the impressions we get from our senses. Not the impressions that tell us what the world is like but rather the impressions that go beyond that, to ethics, to tell us what we *ought* to do and what our goals ought to be. It is a regulative ideal of the kind we will see Halakhah take on in Soloveitchik's system. Halakhah is Soloveitchik's *a priori* lens through which he evaluates his world and uses it to determine his actions.

Like his descriptions of God, Cohen's Jews are idealized as well. He does not describe a historical people who had wandered in the desert but rather philosophizes about the essence of a hypothetical religious community that resembles the Israelites in the Bible. The Bible was not given to us by a historical Moses but rather that Moses represents the paradigm of a religious leader. This approach allows Cohen to understand Judaism from Jewish sources as a religion of reason of a sort that is not present in other religions. Judaism is a rational paradigm of reason that cultivates ethical sensibilities, has prophets whose instructions are grounded in concern for all of humanity in universal terms, and promotes a universal messianism to bring about social justice, as Kant would demand. Judaism is not necessarily the only religion that meets these criteria–in theory; others could too.

Cohen's approach initiated a new and controversial discourse in Jewish thought. Leo Baeck (a student of Cohen whose work in places bears some affinity to Soloveitchik's), Franz Rosenzweig, and many other Jewish thinkers defined their philosophical approach in opposition to, or as a reaction to, Cohen's. In some ways, Soloveitchik did the same. Soloveitchik's approach to philosophy begins by rejecting Cohen's empirical world in favor of the empirical world of Halakhic Man. Soloveitchik does not seek out a universal religion of human values of which Judaism is but an example. Rather, he looks for a particularistic Jewish philosophy not beholden to the views of liberal ethics, secular accounts of social justice, or any form of Christianity.

Cohen died in Berlin just eight years before Soloveitchik's arrival. Many people there, almost certainly many of the Jewish intellectuals, still remembered Cohen when Soloveitchik arrived, and much of the lore, gossip, and stories were being passed around together with his *Religion of Reason*, published soon after his death. Many of the Jewishly significant anecdotes of Cohen's life were probably familiar to Soloveitchik, and Cohen's Jewish thought can be seen as a springboard for his work. It is easy to imagine that in looking for a thesis topic, Soloveitchik would be attracted to the figure and work of Hermann Cohen. Cohen was in a sense both a Jewish and philosophical role model.

Though Soloveitchik drew upon the edifice of Halakhah itself, whereas Cohen drew upon a somewhat select set of Jewish texts and doctrines, their accounts have many interesting connections. As we see later, the role of Soloveitchik's Halakhah parallels Cohen's role for God. Soloveitchik picks up various parts of Cohen's account of Maimonides (see Ravitzky 1986, 171), and there is an important relationship between the way they interpret the two versions of the creation of Adam in the Bible (Cohen 1995, 85ff, cf. Kaplan 2007b, 113, 4n53). Later we shall have an opportunity to talk about atonement, a central theme in Cohen's Jewish philosophical program when we talk about Soloveitchik's concept of repentance, and again when we briefly contrast Cohen's anti-Zionism with Soloveitchik's Zionism. But let us first take a quick look at some philosophical developments that took place in Germany after Cohen, the last bit of background we will need to understand the *Halakhic Mind*.

The emergence of phenomenology

After Kant's death in 1804, German philosophy went through a period of idealistic philosophy dominated by the philosopher G. W. F. Hegel, as well as a period now known as German Classicism and Romanticism. Neo-Kantianism, which generally saw itself in opposition to the metaphysics of idealism (and strove, as Otto Leibmann phrased it in 1865, to "go back to Kant"), flourished in Germany from about 1860 to 1918. After Cohen's death and the German defeat in World War I, neo-Kantianism came increasingly to be seen as a Jewish mode of doing philosophy (as opposed to an Aryan way) and as representing the more conservative values of the German Kaiser State. It nonetheless remained an important mode of German philosophical thought until Natorp's death in 1924 and persisted through 1933, when the Weimar Republic ended, the Nazi party took power and the last neo-Kantians, most of whom were Jewish, were dismissed from their academic positions. Soloveitchik's dissertation, officially accepted in 1932 (though defended two years earlier), was among the last in the tradition of neo-Kantian dissertations published in Germany.

Phenomenology is a post-Kantian movement in that it follows the empiricist-rationalist debate and builds on Kant's attempted reconciliation. The phenomenological movement sprouted in the post-Kantian soil of the interwar years. Natorp's philosophical psychology, which deeply influenced Soloveitchik, paved the way for Edmund Husserl's phenomenology (see Luft 2010). Phenomenology examines the structures of subjective consciousness and how we experience the world from the first-person point of view, in the way we do, because of the kind of beings that we are, the kinds of mental processes we have, and the way the world is presented to us. It asks questions such as: What is it like to experience an object? What is it like to be an individual experiencing the world or parts of it? What is the structure of perception? Can the concept of experience be examined carefully and philosophically?

There are various kinds of experiences, such as remembering, desiring, imagining, feeling emotion, thinking, and, of course, perceiving. Phenomenology develops extensive accounts of how we experience time, space, other people, our own bodily actions, communication, and our everyday activity. The central structure of these forms of experience is that they are directed toward something, real or imagined. Consciousness is an awareness, for example, about an object. Phenomenology is predicated on the idea that experience is directed toward objects of any sort only through or when mediated by particular concepts, ideas, or thoughts. It is these thoughts and concepts that phenomenology examines, in particular those that inform the types of experiences that we have repeatedly, such as seeing a beautiful piece of art, hearing a song, and throwing a ball.

Soloveitchik exploited the new phenomenological method to understand and define Halakhic Man's holistic experience of the world. Chapter 4, Section "Personality," will show how Soloveitchik grappled with the phenomenological experience of Halakhic Man: How do Halakhic Men experience the world when their categories of experience differ greatly from most other people's and also differ from prototypical personalities well described by early psychoanalytic theories?

With the emergence of modern logic and scientific theory, a clear distinction was made between objective facts and their subjective representations.

Various branches of philosophy emerged, one concerned with the objective features of the world that comprise the sciences (the philosophical movement known as logical positivism) and one studying the subjective world. This latter movement is the early psychology as understood by Franz Brentano (1836–1917) (a teacher of Sigmund Freud) in Germany and William James (1842–1910) in the United States. The study of phenomenology involves drawing from both traditions with a combined theory of subjective psychology and objective meaning.

When Soloveitchik was in Berlin, the three most prominent phenomenological philosophers were Martin Heidegger, Edmund Husserl, and Max Scheler. Now somewhat more obscure, in his time however, while Soloveitchik was in Berlin, Scheler was one of the most prominent living philosophers (see Chapter 4, Section "Max Scheler on repentance"). Scheler inaugurated the idea of a philosophical anthropology to counter Heidegger's existential phenomenology of our human type of "being." Soloveitchik was very much among those philosophic youths influenced by Scheler's thought. Soloveitchik cites him often, especially in *Halakhic Mind*, where a debt to him is expressed explicitly (120n62).

Soloveitchik took from Scheler perhaps the very idea of a phenomenological account of religion, an account whose philosophical questions are about the perspective of religion from its practitioners and one that is concerned with the relationship between the spiritual and the nonspiritual as opposed to the relationship of what can be proven to its proof. In an analysis that should look familiar from our discussion of Natorp a few pages back, Scheler is concerned with the phenomenological accounts of three types of material: (1) the *objects* of knowledge, the things we know about; (2) the intentional *act*, the act of knowing itself; and (3) the *relationship* between the subject and object, that is, between the act and the object. Thus, Scheler is concerned with understanding the thing we know about, our act of knowing, and the experience of the relationship between knowing and the thing known (Scheler 1960).

Like Otto, whom we discuss later, Scheler is concerned with the experience of the holy or the divine itself. Soloveitchik, on the other hand, is concerned with Halakhic Man's experience of the halakhic world he creates himself. He will not be concerned with the Absolute; how could he? He is interested in the world.

The aforementioned ideas constitute the main philosophical background relevant for understanding *The Halakhic Mind*.

The Halakhic Mind: context

The Halakhic Mind is (probably) the first book (Rosenak 1996, 279) we possess that Soloveitchik wrote after completing his dissertation in Berlin. It is written during what is sometimes called his "academic period," early in his writing career, and is not intended for a popular audience. Written in the style of what was then cutting-edge German philosophy, it is terse and challenging and presupposes a wealth of philosophical knowledge and sophistication. It has nary a hint of the accessible poetic style that would later come to characterize Soloveitchik's philosophical output. With the exception of the title and the last few pages (i.e., 85–102), the work also has nothing that would indicate that it is a work of Jewish philosophy. It is written for a philosophically mature audience. Correspondingly, our introduction to that book contains a large amount of philosophical background.

The Halakhic Mind dates to about the same time as *Halakhic Man* and *And from There You Shall Seek*. It seems likely that Soloveitchik conceived the idea for this work in the mid-1930s and considered publishing it then. The following exchange most likely applies to *The Halakhic Mind*, whose original proposed title was *Is a Philosophy of Halakhah Possible?* (Kaplan 1987, 143, and see Berkovits 1962, 110). Responding to a request from Rabbi Leo Jung (1892–1987) to submit an article on the *Musar* movement[7] for the *Jewish Library* series, Soloveitchik responded that he would rather write on "'The neo-Kantian conception of subjectivity and objectification of the act and its application to the analysis of the *ta'amei ha-mitzvot* problem.'[8] The interpretation of this central thought of the neo-Kantian philosophy will prove to be of great value for the elucidation of the basic problems of modern Jewish philosophy ... [A]s yet no attempt has been made to evaluate Cohen's theoretical philosophy as a source of modern Jewish thought. My intention is to exploit this latter field for the purpose of enriching our philosophico-religious aspect ..."[9] But this heady project was not to be. Jung apparently rejected Soloveitchik's proposal, and *The Halakhic Mind* (if this is indeed the work Soloveitchik had intended to send to Jung or publish in *Tradition*) would not be published for another forty-seven years.[10]

Soloveitchik's first philosophical work, his dissertation, *Reine Denken*, is about neo-Kantian idealism, specifically the work of Hermann Cohen, some of his students, and Heinrich Maier, a less well-known neo-Kantian who taught in Berlin.[11] Cohen's writings—both philosophical and Jewish—had a profound effect on Soloveitchik's philosophical thinking. *Halakhic Mind* can be seen as a response or alternative to some of Cohen's work. While Cohen derived a "religion of reason" from a subset of Old Testament and rabbinic ethical pronouncements, Soloveitchik derived an authentic Jewish philosophical system from what he saw as the central part of Judaism: Halakhah.

More significantly, instead of treating God himself as an *a priori* category, as Cohen did in treating God as a "regulative ideal," Soloveitchik took something that is very real to the life of the halakhic Jew and made that the reality by which the world is understood. Soloveitchik did not need to postulate or impose a God to make sense of the universe as Cohen did. He put all questions about God's existence to the side, treating them as questions that entered philosophy via sources not indigenously Jewish. Instead, he asked, What is it about reality that shapes the mind of the authentic Jew?

What categories of experience do Jews impose on the world? Soloveitchik's answer is that halakhic Jews look at the world using the categories made familiar to them by Halakhah. Like Kant's categories of space, time, causation, quality, quantity, etc., the Halakhah has its own presuppositions. According to Halakhah, something can be, for example, ritually pure, kosher, private property, forgiven, sanctified, and acquired.

Soloveitchik's answer to the aforementioned questions has a number of advantages over Cohen's. First, it does not make God a human construct, a rational presupposition we use merely to structure part of our reality. Such an answer is too arbitrary. Cohen's approach may make God's existence necessary for living ethically in the world, but God is still a human construct. For Soloveitchik, God is not a human postulate. Second, Soloveitchik argues that a religion or approach to religion that does not prioritize the lived realities of its participants is sterile and accompanied by a host of problems. For example, it encourages a kind of dualism which Soloveitchik believed is historically found in Christianity in which people separate their everyday actions from their spirituality, allowing them to be barbaric in their external practices while maintaining a clean religious conscience internally. On Soloveitchik's account, one's religion is so intrinsic and pervasive that its cognitive structures cannot be separated from one's everyday life. Religious dictates, or Halakhah, is inherent to a Jew's experience and literally shapes the world, worldview, and daily routines.

While the end result of Cohen's work is a picture of a natural "religion of reason" whose intellectual foundation models a rational liberal religion, Soloveitchik's proposed method is to be used to create a philosophy of Judaism that is more authentically Jewish than even the philosophy of Maimonides, which is ultimately derived from non-Jewish Greek and Arab thought. Readers familiar with S. R. Hirsch's work will readily recognize this complaint against Maimonides.[12]

Soloveitchik argues that Maimonides' philosophy, as presented in his *Guide for the Perplexed*, imputes ethical or moral justifications for commandments (*ta'amei ha-mitzvot*) normally assumed to be nonrational (*ḥukim*). Soloveitchik believes such efforts are doubly misguided. First, when not explicitly stated in the Torah (written or oral), we cannot hope to know why a certain commandment was mandated. Second, similar to an argument of Leibowitz (1992, 17–18), when we assign an ethical or moral justification for a commandment, it becomes a mere "handmaiden" to ethical and moral principles, which Halakhah is not.[13]

Soloveitchik, therefore, believes it is mistaken to try to establish why the nonrational commandments were mandated. Instead, he argues, we must take the details of Halakhah as they are and develop a philosophy of Judaism from them. In doing so he seeks to address the *ta'amei ha-mitzvot* problem.

In a eulogy, Jonathan Sacks describes how Soloveitchik contrasted his philosophy of Judaism with that of earlier Jewish philosophy and with the philosophy of A. J. Heschel, who was widely read at the time:

[Soloveitchik] said, "In the past, Jewish philosophy—*machashevet Yisrael*—and halakhah were two different things. They were disconnected." "In truth," he said, "they are only one thing and that one thing is—halakhah." The only way you can think Jewishly and construct a Jewish philosophy, is out of *halakhah.* He gave me one example. He said, "You have read Professor A.J. Heschel's book called *The Sabbath*?" I said, "Yes." He said, "It's a beautiful book, isn't it?" I said, "Yes." And he said, "What does he call Shabbat? —a sanctuary in time. This is an idea of a poet. It's a lovely idea. But what is Shabbat? Shabbat," he said, "is *lamed-tet melakhot*, it is the thirty-nine categories of work and their *toladot*, and it is out of that *halakhah* and not of poetry that you have to construct a theory of Shabbat."

(2003, 286–87)

Some years later he writes:

Rabbi Soloveitchik ... spoke about the need to create a new kind of Jewish thought, based not on philosophical categories but on Halakhah, Jewish law. Law was the lifeblood, the DNA, of Judaism, and it was more than mere regulation of conduct. It was a way of being in the world. Jewish philosophy in the past had based itself on its Western counterpart, and in so doing had failed to express what was unique about Judaism, its focus on the holy deed.

(2011, 90)

This is precisely what Soloveitchik does in his philosophical works. In *The Halakhic Mind*, he lays the foundation for his project by discussing methodology. The actual carrying out of the Jewish philosophy project would emerge in other works. *Halakhic Mind* is an attempt to show how it is possible to do philosophy of religion in a way that is philosophically respectable and simultaneously innately and natively Jewish. This is also his only significant work that is almost wholly (except for the final pages) couched in secular terms.

Soloveitchik argues that much of Jewish philosophy over the years is merely Christian, Muslim, or secular thought in Jewish guise. His own philosophy would be an analysis of, and approach to, the *ta'amei ha-mitzvot* problem, derived from data internal to Judaism. While Soloveitchik uses the sophisticated philosophical machinery of neo-Kantianism as well as a host of other philosophical ideas to help him frame a version of the problem of *ta'amei ha-mitzvot*, he does not use its ideas to solve the problem. The solution lies in the relationship of Halakhah to the Halakhic Man.

The argument of The Halakhic Mind

The Halakhic Mind spells out a new program for Jewish philosophy.[14] The program requires taking Halakhah as the objective data of the real world of lived Judaism. These data serve as the basis for reconstructing an idealized subjective consciousness of an authentic Halakhic Mind.[15],[16] Let us see what this means.

Beginning with a theme that derives from Natorp's thought, *The Halakhic Mind* opens with a discussion of the nature of general philosophical methodology and defends a certain kind of intellectual pluralism[17] that encourages or at least allows for new ways of thinking about philosophy of religion. It argues that like the various sciences which each have their own approaches to knowledge, philosophical knowledge about religion should also be thought of on its own terms. It argues on the grounds that there is a flowering of diversity in the kinds of objects that science recognizes along with a corresponding diversity in how scientists attain knowledge about these kinds of things (*Halakhic Mind*, 4) and concludes that religion, with its own kinds of knowledge, should be granted its own epistemic authority.

Like other thinkers, philosophers approach their topics with certain assumptions about the world and the way we come to know about it. Every now and then, as the sciences develop new ways of understanding the world, philosophers must adjust their assumptions accordingly. Recall that Soloveitchik's intellectual life was molded in an atmosphere of intellectual upheaval to which we in the twenty-first century are only now adjusted. It was beginning to become apparent, for example, that immaterial things like magnetic fields are able to exert force over material objects. The question about whether empty space has a shape was just beginning to be understood, as were questions about the existence and nature of fundamental particles.[18]

Science was in the process of evolving, but philosophy had not kept pace. Typically, philosophers and scientists share a worldview. But around the turn of the twentieth century, philosophers fell behind, in part because philosophers continued to think of science as only physics,[19] even as biology and psychology were making rapid progress understanding their respective domains using newer tools and methods (*Halakhic Mind*, 8ff).

Philosophers cannot always agree about the assumptions they ought to make about the real world. Soloveitchik, accordingly, defends the notion that when philosophers and scientists cannot settle on an approach toward knowledge or reality, it is intellectually acceptable for philosophers to consider a variety of philosophical assumptions to use as background for their own investigations. Philosophers should thereby feel free to propose a philosophy of religion that has its own unique intellectual methodology that is different from science or even other philosophical approaches. In a time when, for example, mathematics, science, and common sense cannot agree on how to think about something as basic as space, there is nothing intellectually untoward about using different methods and assumptions to suit different realms of intellectual inquiry.

Psychology and philosophy understood new things about the world. Physics and chemistry understood old things in new ways and even discovered whole new kinds of objects. Reality itself was not as uniform as had previously been thought. (Light, for example, is now thought of as both matter and as an immaterial wave. Some particles were said to exist but have no mass; objects like fields could causally interact with objects in the world yet themselves not be material objects, etc.[20]) If reality itself was not uniform, science could not insist on a uniform way of *knowing* reality either. An "epistemic pluralism," or a diversity of ways of coming to know the world, emerged. Therefore, a variety of philosophical methods are appropriate and justified for the variety of domains that people study.

Moreover, different domains of inquiry now see one and the same thing from different perspectives. Time, for example, means one thing to the scientist and another to the psychologist. Why then should it not mean a third thing to the philosopher? The moment is thus ripe to take advantage of the emerging methodological pluralism in the disciplines and put it to use in the philosophy of religion (14).

Soloveitchik then reasons (along similar lines as Dilthey) that if there are different ways of thinking about the physical sciences, there should also be a number of valid ways to think about the social sciences, like psychology. He appeals to the fact that both psychology and physics study a variety of *kinds* of things (e.g., material and nonmaterial, perhaps conscious and unconscious). After all, contemporary philosophers (of Soloveitchik's time and to an extent now as well) accept a plurality of interpretations of reality, and many scientists accept that there are a number of ways to understand the very nature of the fundamental pieces of reality.

There is no single accepted interpretation of what the "real world"—physical or social—is made of. Similarly, there are many plausible ways of gaining knowledge about science, philosophy, and the social world. The physical stuff that we take to be real is, additionally, now taken to be real in a number of *kinds* of ways. These two latter facts suggest we should accept that the social and psychological world can also be thought of as a realm made up of a variety of kinds of things.

How does this plurality of ways of understanding impact Soloveitchik's philosophy of religion? For there to be a philosophy of religion, religion must be the kind of thing that is represented or embodied in a person in a certain psychological way, and it must be more than just a set of emotional and sensory reactions to the world. Like scientific epistemology, religious cognition is an intentional and cognitive act. We apprehend something external to us (even if that external object does not necessarily exist) and then mentally process it. Pluralism, as just described, allows religion to have its own legitimate interpretation as to how to obtain knowledge as well as its own understanding of how religion causes people to process external data. Religion, in other words, shapes the way people process the external world, and because of this it should be studied in the same way we would study any physical object that shapes the way we see the world. We must understand religious epistemology because Religious Man is a creature trying to understand the real world.

When processing data from the outside world, these cognitive acts often make use of categories in a way that is unique to a religious thinker.

Consider again the category of time. The physicist, religious thinker, and the psychologist all treat time in different ways. Each of their respective ways is useless to the other thinkers. Time has unique connotations for the religious person that emerge from a way of thinking religiously about the world. The religious person may think of time in terms of the cycle of prayers or festivals, whereas a physicist will be concerned with time as the speed that light travels between objects, and a psychologist is worried about time as something that affects people's moods. For the religious person, the past can be rewritten, say via repentance. Rewriting the past may make little sense in other contexts, but it can be very useful to religion.[21] This also applies to many other familiar categories used in the sciences (*Halakhic Mind*, 49–50).

Thus—and this is a crucial point—philosophers should take their cue from science when constructing an approach to understanding religion. As with science, an approach to religion must begin with objective data. For the scientist, the objective data are facts of the physical world; for the philosopher of religion, the objective data are the facts of religion whose social, ethical, and behavioral components are no less objective than scientific facts.

***

Philosophy of religion is thus justified in exploring a new approach to knowledge and reality.[22] The final step before reaching the core of the argument is then to understand that objective data are contrasted with the subjective world.

Science and its philosophy have been perpetually tasked with trying to explain how subjective beings like ourselves can acquire knowledge about the objective world: how can a being "trapped inside" a human body with human senses know what the outside world is really like without outside data being colored by the fact that one is human? After all, our senses can only provide a small part of the story of reality, and that part is shaped by a multitude of human experiences, prejudices, and idiosyncrasies. The heart of Kantian and neo-Kantian thought involves sorting this all out.

***

With these preliminaries out of the way, we can now think about religious epistemology and its unique issues by describing a two-step process: (1) coordinating objective religious facts with subjective religious experience and (2) reconstructing subjective experiences from the objective data which we have (*Halakhic Mind*, 62).

What does this mean, how do we do this, and what counts as religion's objective data? We begin with an approach now familiar from Natorp and Scheler, by using science as an analogy with religion and consider three "orders" or domains we can study: (1) the subjective, (2) the objective, and (3) the subjective organization that emerges from the objective organization (*Halakhic Mind*, 62).

As we saw earlier, Kant and Cohen disagree on the direction of knowledge: Should we figure out what is objective based on our subjective experience of the world, or should we construe our subjective states in terms of the objectivity of the outside world? In other words, do the facts of our mind determine how we perceive the world, or do the facts of the world determine how our mind ultimately sees it? Kant states the former. Cohen and his school claimed the latter (*Halakhic Mind*, 64).

Soloveitchik sides with Kant here. Consider the "spiritual act" in the philosophy of religion, which typically projects outwardly from subjective to objective. Take the relation of God and man as an example of a spiritual impulse. On the subjective side, man has feelings of love and wrath, immanence, and remoteness from Him, etc. These subjective feelings give rise to judgments and rules. So for example, a judgment one might make given the relations we just mentioned between God and man might be that God exists or that He is merciful. These judgments, in turn, lead to the outward projection: the concrete manifestation. These judgments give expression to concrete rituals. A rule that might emerge from a judgment about God's mercy may be that one shall worship God or pray in a certain way (*Halakhic Mind*, 66–68). More tersely:

Subjective experience → objective judgments → concrete objective manifestations.

For example,

Sense of awe → belief in God's power → ritualized prayer.[23]

In this we see an important relationship between the subjective and objective: subjective experiences give rise to objective norms of behavior. But beside the subjective and objective, we also mentioned a third domain: the subjective organization that emerges from objective organization. What is this? It is the whole system of thought, the whole personality that emerges from combining all the subjective experiences in one's life.

It was always understood that in the physical world, we can understand objective causal relationships and correlate these relationships with the subjective world. Modern psychology strives to understand the relationship between subjective states too. So, symbolically, if D_1, D_2, D_3, ... are objective properties (data) of the world and S_1, S_2, S_3, ... are corresponding subjective properties of individuals (perhaps ideas, philosophical stances, mental categories, and feelings), then we understand that the objective properties are related to (↔) one another as follows:

$$D_1 \leftrightarrow D_2 \leftrightarrow D_3 \ldots$$

This just means that some things in the objective world are related, perhaps causally, to other things in the objective world. We also understand (though Cohen did not) that some of the objective data of the world can be correlated with the subjective properties of individuals:

$$D_1, D_2, D_3 \ldots$$
$$\updownarrow \;\; \updownarrow \;\; \updownarrow \ldots$$
$$S_1, S_2, S_3 \ldots$$

Some bits of objective data correspond to something specific in the mind. The idea or the category of a table may be correlated with the concrete table currently being observed. Modern science also understands that we can talk about how the subjective states of a person are related to one another to form a whole system of thought. So we understand that:

$$S_1 \leftrightarrow S_2 \leftrightarrow S_3.$$

The concept of the table may be correlated in the mind with the memory of the last meal eaten at the table or the price one paid for the table. Understanding this, however, is still not an exact science. We may not always be able to explain exactly how the mind combines all the ideas and forms a coherent whole.

Whereas science (at least since Kant) starts with the series of subjective connections ($S_1 \leftrightarrow S_2 \leftrightarrow S_3$) and attempts to see how the objective data are connected to one another ($D_1 \leftrightarrow D_2 \leftrightarrow D_3$), philosophy of religion, particularly a natively Jewish one, takes this process in reverse (*Halakhic Mind*, 72) and starts with the objective data and attempts to reconstruct subjective experiences from it. Our philosophy of religion takes the data of the world and tries to extrapolate what it is like to perceive that data.

To understand how this is done and understand why this is a Jewish philosophy of religion, we must first understand what comprises Judaism's "objective data" ($D_1, D_2, D_3, \ldots$). For Soloveitchik, the answer is clear. The objective data of Judaism is Halakhah (very broadly construed). The goal of Jewish philosophy is to examine Judaism's objective data, that is, the Halakhah, and to reconstruct from it the *ta'amei ha-mitzvot,* the "taste" of the mitzvot, how Halakhic Man experiences the commandments.

This reconstruction of the subjective from the objective is a complex undertaking. Let us consider the following two scenarios to get a feel for what Soloveitchik is trying to get across. The first is purely hypothetical. (This is our example. Soloveitchik's is about Plato (*Halakhic Mind* 74–75) and is expressed far more tersely.)

1. Say we want to understand a particular primitive religion. We might start by imagining how the religion could have originated. We imagine a primitive man (the "founder") alone one night in the forest. There is an unexpected sound and something brushes against his shoulder. Suddenly a light flashes in the sky. There is a deafening crack and a tree falls, narrowly missing him and blocks his path. This man has an epiphany which engenders within him religious and spiritual feelings and awareness. Perhaps this causes him to imagine angry or capricious gods who need to be placated.

He later tells others about his experience, and a religion is born. These primordial feelings that he experienced are the subjective experiences of the ancient religious founder. We could label these subjective religious experiences as Subjective Experience S_1, Subjective Experience S_2, Subjective Experience S_3... (S_1, S_2, S_3, ...).

But we cannot really know about the subjective religious experiences of the founder(s) of a particular primitive religion. They are long gone. They cannot be questioned. What then can we do to understand the original feelings of awe that inspired the religion? The solution is to examine the limited objective evidence of the religion that remains. We discover data: perhaps we find a stone altar, a pit filled with goat bones, a crude utensil depicting a fallen tree, a knife engraved with a thunderbolt, descendants who have an annual ritual involving loud falling trees, etc.[24] We could label these pieces of objective data as D_1, D_2, D_3, ...

We could then analyze this limited set of objective data (D_1, D_2, D_3, ...) and try to "reconstruct" the subjective experiences the primitive founder may have had. We refer to this reconstructed data as R_1, R_2, R_3, ... These new extrapolated subjective experiences, however, are not identical to the original subjective experiences (S_1, S_2, S_3, ...). At best, they are poor approximations of the original subjective experiences. Nevertheless, this is the best we can do to try to understand the subjective experiences of the practitioners of this primitive religion.

2. Next, consider the case of Judaism for which we have an abundance of objective data. We are not interested in the way any particular founder saw the religion, but rather, we wish to understand the subjective worldview of thoroughly dedicated, religious, and knowledgeable Jews. We want to grasp the Halakhic Mind. We wish to know how it understands the lived experience of Judaism and its values. What is it like to possess such a mind? What is it like to be one of the Jews who was or is part of the process of living or shaping Halakhah (in any of its manifestations)? If we could theoretically determine this set of subjective values and experiences, we might label them (Jewish Subjective) JS_1, JS_2, JS_3, ... But we cannot ask actual halakhic men of the past what subjective religious experience led them to create the myriads of halakhic rulings and shape them as they did. We cannot ask them to describe what it is like to be them. We can no longer ask them about their internal world and worldview. Halakhic Men in their most ideal form are rare, and most are long gone.

What then can we do to understand Judaism and the halakhic worldview? We begin by identifying the objective data of Judaism, the Halakhah. Unlike the primitive religion discussed earlier, the objective data of Judaism, the Halakhah, are very detailed, thorough, and evolved. We could label this set of objective data, for example, the *halakhot*, Jewish texts, ethics literature, and exegesis, as (Jewish Data) JD_1, JD_2, JD_3, ...

We can now take this objective set of data (JD_1, JD_2, JD_3, ...), put it together, and form a system of data ($JD_1 \leftrightarrow JD_2 \leftrightarrow JD_3$ ...) (see Kaplan 1987,

151–54) and use it to "reconstruct" a new subjective set of data which we label (Jewish Reconstructed subjective data) $JR_1, JR_2, JR_3, \ldots$ This set of data can then be put together along the lines of modern psychological theory and be seen as a whole system of subjective consciousness $(JR_1 \leftrightarrow JR_2 \leftrightarrow JR_3 \ldots)$.[25] This description could then be spelled out as a series of personality traits, priorities, ontology, motivations, thoughts, feelings, etc.—in other words the "worldview" of the Halakhic Mind.

Less abstractly, for Judaism, the *mitzvot, mussar,* Talmud, scripture, and law codes form and describe an interconnected halakhic system. One who embodies the system by living a life steeped in its practice and study is led to form judgments about the world, about what exists in it, and how it is configured. The judgments shape what exists, what is important, and how one interacts with the world, and then they in turn give rise to various feelings, impressions, personality characteristics, and conceptual categories, which collectively make up the personality of Halakhic Man. This personality can then be described in the same way that early-twentieth-century personality psychologists described other prototypical personalities such as that of the Aesthetic Man, Economic Man, Political Man, or Theoretical Man. The task of Soloveitchik's Jewish philosophy of religion is to correlate the halakhic system with the subjective consciousness, thereby reconstructing Halakhic Man's personality.

Remember, however, that this reconstructed subjective data, although quite refined, is still only an approximation of the original subjective religious experiences held by authentic personalities of the past (*Halakhic Mind,* 86). Nevertheless, by reconstructing the subjective experience, we have spelled out the *ta'amei ha-mitzvot;* we understand how a Halakhic Man experiences a world ontologically shaped by his Halakhah. We can thus begin to comprehend the worldview of Halakhic Man, the subject of our next section.

Personality

> Man is … involved in an unresolvable contradiction, in an insoluble dialectic, because he is caught like Abraham's ram in a thicket of antinomies and dichotomies. He swings like a pendulum between two poles: the thesis and the antithesis, the affirmation and the negation, identifying himself either with both of them or with neither.
>
> (*Majesty Humility,* 26)

The previous section described somewhat abstractly Soloveitchik's plan for remaking philosophy of religion using Halakhah as the salient feature of Judaism and Jewish life. Now we can begin to understand Soloveitchik's entire philosophical program. Halakhah determines what the world is like. Each aspect of the Halakhah gives rise to an aspect of one's personality by shaping one's attitudes and conceptual worldview. Taken as a whole, all of

Halakhah shapes an entire worldview. Soloveitchik's plan calls for examining the Halakhah; then examining the subjective life of an individual who is a product of studying, following, and creating Halakhah; and finally reconstructing the relationship between the Halakhah and the individual.

In this chapter, we explore the individual. What is Halakhic Man's subjective phenomenological worldview? What is it like to be someone who is the product of a halakhic worldview? In Soloveitchik's most famous work, *Halakhic Man*, we get a sketch of Halakhic Man's personality. An essay called "Catharsis" describes an important key to understanding the essence of the personality. "The Lonely Man of Faith," "Majesty and Humility," and other essays provide Biblical models and justification for Soloveitchik's method. Finally, in the eulogies he delivered, we see pictures of Soloveitchik's contemporaries who embody these personalities. Before we discuss the works themselves, however, some more background is warranted.

Halakhic Man: context

Plato and Aristotle---II

To this day there may be no more sophisticated biography of Plato's mentor, Socrates, than that written by Heinrich Maier (1913), Soloveitchik's doctoral supervisor. Hermann Cohen also placed great weight on Plato's thought. Plato was the subject of Cohen's first substantial publication. It was an attempt to read Kantian philosophy onto Plato's theory of forms. Paul Natorp similarly examined the history of ancient Greek thought for anticipations of neo-Kantianism, as he would subsequently do for Descartes' philosophy. Actually, a number of influential neo-Kantians like Eduard Zeller and Wilhelm Windelband also wrote significant works on Plato and on ancient Greek philosophy.

These considerations justify one more foray into the ancient Greek background of Soloveitchik's thought. Previously, we saw a brief sketch of Plato's and Aristotle's metaphysics; now we turn to their respective ethics. Plato's most famous book, the *Republic,* is arguably the most influential book in the history of philosophy. Among other things, it describes Plato's vision of an ideal political community. The description of this community hinges on the nature of the ideal life for man to lead, arrangement of society, leader, and education. The *Republic* is written as a conversation between Socrates—the main character in most of Plato's dialogues—and a variety of other characters.

The *Republic* is notable as the first book of political philosophy in the West, as well as the first description of a utopia. Part of what comprises a utopian society is its citizens living up to certain ideals. Such ideal citizens are described in various ways throughout the *Republic*. For instance, we see in the character of Socrates, Plato's protagonist, the personality of the ideal philosopher. He is the kind of person who is meant to be in charge of a perfect society because he is both a model citizen and the kind of person who can create and lead citizens in a perfect world. We also see a portrait of the philosopher as someone who loves wisdom and is enthusiastic about learning. We see in the other characters people who should not lead a perfect state because they do not possess the proper personality traits. Cephalus, for example, finds philosophical problems uninteresting. Characters like Thrasymachus should also not rule because the relativism he espouses denies even that there are philosophical problems that political leaders need to consider. We also see character profiles of the tyrant, who is the worst kind of ruler; "the Democratic Man," who is morally only a step above the Tyrant; and the Honor-loving Man, who is a step above that. Each of these characters typifies a person and the function they play in a respective political regime.

Plato creates these characters to make philosophical points about the nature of states and their inhabitants. Soloveitchik similarly uses Biblical characters to typify personalities of ideal human beings or ideal Jews. He also extrapolates from the full corpus of Jewish literature to capture the personality of the ideal halakhic Jew.

Aristotle's view of good and bad gives him a different perspective. Aristotle's ethics involves understanding what it is that generates our value judgments about individuals: What makes us characterize some people as good and others as bad? His answer is what we now assume was typical of ancient Greek thinking—moderation.

In his *Nicomachean Ethics*, Aristotle explains that we praise individuals whose character traits (virtues) are balanced and appropriate (see *Sacred Profane*, 6). Consider Aristotle's example: courage. Courageous people are praiseworthy when they face danger appropriately. There are two incorrect, extreme, and opposing ways to face danger. A person can be rash or impulsive and do foolhardy things in the face of physical danger, doing things about which people are likely to say, "That's a way to get yourself killed!" On the other extreme, one might flee or hide. This may keep one safe but would invoke scorn and accusations of cowardice rather than praise.

Aristotle held that the ideal person is one whose habits routinely have them exhibiting praiseworthy actions: deeds that occupy a middle ground between extremes that are routinely condemned as going too far or not far enough.

Aristotle describes the ideal for many traits including temperance, generosity, magnanimity, ambition, honesty, and friendliness. For each he describes the relevant personality features, the ideal middle, and the extremes that deviate from the ideal. As he does for courage and its extremes—cowardice and rashness—he does for honesty and its extremes—boastfulness and undue humility. So too, for each of the other virtues he describes the extreme excess, the extreme deficiency, and the ideal middle.

Maimonides

Aristotle's portrait of the ideal person was picked up by many philosophers, including the Jewish thinker Maimonides. Not as concerned with what people praise and disparage, Maimonides deals with a more practical question: how can one develop an appropriately virtuous personality?

Maimonides agrees with Aristotle when he says that we ought to habituate ourselves to become an ideal person, but he also wants to know how. Maimonides, therefore, adds a caveat to Aristotle's psychology of habituation. He proposes what can be called a "pendulum" notion of habituation. If one's habits are not as they should be, and one finds oneself tending toward either extreme, one ought to move oneself to the opposite extreme and over time will be pulled toward the middle (*Mishneh Torah, Book of Knowledge, Discernment*, ch. 2, pt. 2).

Plato, Aristotle, and Maimonides all see the holistic personality as central to an individual's ethical composition. They all believe it is vital that we are the right kind of person, and being the right kind of person draws upon specific features of our character. In the case of Aristotle and Aristotelians like Maimonides, the right kind of person is one who properly negotiates the character between the bad extremes and finds an appropriate center.

Tanya

We previously noted Soloveitchik's affinity for *Likutei Amarim* (See Wolfson 2015, Boylan 1996, 139), a book commonly referred to as *Tanya* written by Shneur Zalman of Liadi in 1797. *Tanya* is a text studied by Hasidic Jews in general, and by Lubavitch Hasidim in particular, and Soloveitchik's discussion often seems inspired by it. The first part of the book, subtitled *A Book for Intermediate [People]*, has the "intermediate" person as its central theme. *Tanya* opens with definitions of righteous, wicked, and intermediate people. A righteous person is dominated by his passion for good, a wicked person by his passion for evil, and an intermediate person grapples with both. *Tanya* quotes the Talmudic sage Rabbah declaring himself an intermediate person, to which an incredulous Abbaye wonders what chance anyone else has if the great Rabbah is merely intermediate.

Toward the end of Part One, *Tanya* clarifies that the intermediate person is not actually someone ruled by both his good and wicked passions, but rather, within such a person, there are two "judges" giving conflicting advice as to how they should act. An arbitrator is required to adjudicate their opposing guidance, and God Himself is this arbiter. The intermediate person is the one who sides with his passions for good. Rabbah is said to be an intermediate person because both good and evil are ever present within him, and his evil impulses are suppressed only by his constant prayer (Chapter 13).

The *Tanya*'s psychological drama is spelled out in terminology best appreciated by mystics. The two motivators are the individual's divine and natural souls. Mode of expression notwithstanding, a similar dialectical interplay between conflicting passions requiring some kind of reconciliation is omnipresent in Soloveitchik's work. He, too, envisions the ideal personality as a certain kind of "intermediate person" torn between two poles—two personalities, two sets of passions and constraints. He is a Halakhic Man who successfully grapples with all these conflicting forces in the correct way. When discussing Soloveitchik's essay "Catharsis" and some of his other works in this "Personality" section, we explain his novel theory of Halakhic Man's approach to conflicting personality demands. For Soloveitchik, Halakhic Man differs from other people in that he is *not* one whose character traits navigate a moderate middle road but rather one who struggles with conflicting extreme personality traits in very specific ways. Accepting conflicting impulses from the extremes and dealing with the resultant dialectical tensions are the results of being an ideal halakhic person.

From philosophy to personality psychology

After Thomas Aquinas, Christian morality in the Middle Ages borrowed Aristotelian ethics, and it remained a significant way of thinking about morality until the nineteenth century. Subsequently, John Stuart Mill and Immanuel Kant presented alternate ways of thinking about ethics, founded respectively on utility and rationality. Neither of their two views is relevant to our point except for one detail: both Kant and Mill espoused approaches to ethics that take conduct and actions, and not the Aristotelian concept of a balanced character, as ethically significant. Kant and Mill are more concerned with the *rules* that guide proper conduct and actions rather than the virtues exhibited by the individual.

Nonetheless, character ethics persisted despite the towering and persistent influence of Kant and Mill. Later in the nineteenth century, Arthur Schopenhauer (1788–1860) developed an ethics that moved from virtues and personality traits and focused instead on entire personalities. Like many Christian writers before him, Schopenhauer championed the idea that key figures in Christian history like Jesus and St. Francis of Assisi are to be thought of as having led prototypically enlightened lifestyles. Schopenhauer's ethics accordingly advocated emulating the lives of ideal personalities (Schopenhauer 1969, §§ 68, 70).

Less than a generation later, Friedrich Nietzsche (1844–1900) further developed this line of thinking—though radically differently. He rejected both Kant's and Mill's views of ethics and developed an almost anti-ethics view of morality. Nietzsche argued that the historically accepted view of ethics is detrimental and restrains great men from flourishing. Great men need latitude and freedom to achieve greatness but are held back by systems of oppressive morality imposed upon them by a society of inferiors. Needless to say, such a view did not endear him to thinkers like Cohen or Soloveitchik (*Halakhic Man* 164n147; and see Rynhold and Harris 2018).

Nietzsche's enormously influential "ethics" derived from an analysis of Greek tragedy, from which he distilled two archetypal elements battling for control over humanity: the Apollonian and the Dionysian (after the sons of Zeus in Greek mythology). Apollonius represents reason, and Dionysus represents chaos. Nietzsche, following many eighteenth-century thinkers in aesthetics, science, and literature who talked about "opposing drives," claimed that great art fuses the two ways of affirming life: order and chaos. Thus, for example, Nietzsche claimed that Socrates and Socratic dialectic is problematic because it represents a purely Apollonian point of view and does not exhibit any Dionysian influence. In one way of understanding Nietzsche, man (or an entire culture) needs to embody the opposing personality traits within himself to truly affirm life. If an ethical system suppresses either one, it impedes the emergence of greatness (Nietzsche 1956).

Nietzsche quite frequently uses the idea of human types to represent idealized individuals. His idea of human archetypes, and the idea of competing inner personality struggles, though not Nietzsche's version in particular, worked its way into German Romanticism, early psychoanalytic theory, and even Freudian thought. Additionally, the idea that science and philosophy (and the scientific mind and the philosophical mind) are locked in a kind of struggle can be found throughout Nietzsche's program.

With the rise of modern psychology in the beginning of the twentieth century, the debates over innate ideas, mental structures, and epistemology took on new forms. One emerging school of thought was characterized by characterologies and typologies (see *Halakhic Mind*, 54). These typologies sketched outlines of the basic features, drives, motivations, interests, priorities, and goals of different kinds of personalities.

The German psychologist Carl Jung (1875–1961), a contemporary of Freud, believed, along Kantian lines, that the mind innately houses abstract structures that are given concrete definition when the individual comes into contact with the empirical world. Jung claimed there are mental "forms" common to all humans which we employ to organize our life experiences. This was one of the central themes in academic (as opposed to applied) personality psychology of this period. Psychologists then began to study particular types of individuals and their traits.

Jung's influential 1923 book *Psychological Types* (Jung 1971) traces the history of psychological typology (types of personalities) and categorizes people by their psychological function, the way they perceive the world and how they make decisions. Jung argues that there are eight basic personality types based on the four main functions of consciousness: sensation and intuition, and thinking and feeling. Each of these is modified by one's introversion or extroversion. One's personality is determined by the combination of personality types they manifest and repress.

In 1928, in the same intellectual and cultural milieu, Eduard Spranger published *Types of Men*, which quickly became popular in German intellectual circles. Spranger, working within frameworks outlined by his teacher Wilhelm Dilthey,[26] explained that just as we meticulously classify plants and animals, we must also classify man in a more nuanced and fine-grained manner than simply as a member of the species "man." He proposed a four-step process to scientifically categorize men by their personality types:

(1) isolate a single value/tendency in an individual personality; (2) consider the value/tendency in its pure form and idealize it; (3) understand the relation of this one-sided type to the whole individual; and (4) counterbalance the initial artificiality of the personality type by a process of individualization, which emphasizes specific historical, geographical, and personal circumstances. To understand an individual personality, one must understand the personality traits in their purest form to assess their "type" and then see how they are manifested in actual unique individuals in their individual contexts.

In his book, Spranger analyzes and compares six types of individuals, each of which is defined by a particular value orientation: (1) the Theoretical Type, who only values truth and is driven to impose rational order on the world; (2) the Economic Type, who values money and objects only insofar as they are useful; (3) the Aesthetic Type, who values form and harmony and strives to make life beautiful; (4) the Social Type, who loves people and wants to benefit them; (5) the Political Type, who values power and wishes to gain authority and influence; and (6) the Religious Type, who values unity with the universe and wants to understand his relationship to the cosmos. According to Spranger, these are the different kinds of people in the world. Each person fits into one of these categories. No one, of course, embodies a pure version of any of the above personality types, but everyone has one dominant personality type, which is modulated by the rest of their personality and environment.

Related typologies (as found, e.g., in the works of Gordon Allport) were quite popular in the United States through the 1960s. This method is still popular as the forerunner of the personality types described by such scales as the Myers-Briggs Personality Inventory. Soloveitchik draws heavily on this way of thinking about people in his own work in ways that will become clear shortly.

This approach was common not just in psychology but throughout the social sciences. Spranger's contemporary Max Scheler, whom we discuss further later, thought of personalities not in terms of types but as part of a hierarchy that mimics their sociology. He proposed a hierarchy of values with pleasure on the bottom; then utility, vitality, and culture in the middle; and spiritual values on the top. This hierarchy of values corresponds to his hierarchy of personalities: the saint on the top, the genius in the middle, and the hero and artist at the bottom.

The idea of isolating, identifying, and describing personalities and personality traits is a research project spanning the whole history of Western thought. These specific methods of analysis slid out of fashion around the late 1950s in part due to revulsion for the way these methods were used to advance the race theory advocated in Germany prior to and during World War II by psychologists such as Ernst Kretschmer and the Jaensch brothers (e.g., race psychology used to justify the difference between German and Jewish science[27]). Professional psychologists rarely write along these lines nowadays, though offshoots of this method are still present in popular psychology. Nonetheless, such was the state of the art in philosophy and psychology in pre-war Germany, and these methods are sometimes still fruitfully employed.

Soloveitchik's personality sketches: an overview

Personality sketches, sometimes referred to as "typologies" or "typological sketches"—influenced by the works mentioned earlier—make up the most famous part of Soloveitchik's thought.[28] Each essay of the "personality literature" discussed in this section is unique, and each has its own purpose and motivation. Nonetheless, common themes emerge from all of these works:

1. Most describe two personalities that are opposed to one another such that a single mind cannot coherently embody both of them simultaneously.
2. Each essay claims that neither of the two described personalities by itself is adequate, in important ways.
3. The essays explicitly or implicitly argue that the ideal person draws from both idealized personalities.
4. The halakhic ideal involves living with the tension of opposing personalities without necessarily reconciling or synthesizing them in any familiar way but rather by drawing on the best of both of them.
5. The tension expresses the key to the complete final ideal personality.

In what follows, we examine *Halakhic Man*, "Catharsis," "The Lonely Man of Faith," "Majesty and Humility," "The Community," and eulogies delivered by Soloveitchik. We spell out the opposing personalities that Soloveitchik describes in each work and discuss the nature of the ideal person that emerges from the union. We also describe what emerges from the totality of this literature and in the process see a main goal of Soloveitchik's philosophical project.

Halakhic Man: overview of the book

Halakhic Man is a rich and complex book with layers of nuance, texture, and detail.[29] On its surface, its primary interest is to describe an idealized version of a person whose worldview is shaped by the ontology of the Halakhah. His personality is a unique concatenation of two incompatible personalities, both of which are individually criticized and even scorned. One personality is the "Cognitive Man" type, and the other the "Religious Man" type. Cognitive Man is characterized by an attitude that drives him to understand the empirical quantifiable universe. This is his overwhelming feature. Religious Man, on the other hand, strives to appreciate and connect with the transcendent mystery of the universe. Both these personality types are deficient in important ways. Halakhic Man is a special kind of hybrid who is both meticulously quantitative about the law and simultaneously qualitative about how he relates to the mysterious Unknown. The personalities of Cognitive Man and Religious Man are not naturally compatible, in the same way Spranger claims that no individual can have a personality type that is predominantly Economic and also Aesthetic. Nevertheless, the "hybrid" creative personality of Halakhic Man represents an ideal Jewish person.

The overarching goal of *Halakhic Man* is to define the personality type of Halakhic Man. To accomplish this Soloveitchik:

1. describes the idealized personalities of both Cognitive Man and Religious Man;
2. shows the deficiencies inherent in both Cognitive Man and Religious Man;
3. describes how Halakhic Man embodies personality features of both Cognitive Man and Religious Man but without their respective deficiencies;
4. shows how the study, understanding, and observance of Halakhah shape the worldview of Halakhic Man; and
5. shows how Halakhic Man is no less creative than Cognitive Man in his construction of new and novel halakhic categories and concepts.

We proceed as follows: We first examine Cognitive Man and possible sources for Soloveitchik's description of his personality, then do the same for Religious Man, and finally describe Halakhic Man. In the section after that, we elaborate on Soloveitchik's conception of hybrid personalities and its historical antecedents. We then proceed to Soloveitchik's other personality works.

Halakhic Man is a novel work that sees philosophical value in describing in idealized terms the nature of a specific type of individual. This individual is the hero of *The Halakhic Mind*, the previous work described. *The Halakhic Mind* provides an argument that justifies creating Jewish philosophy that analyzes the relationship between the metaphysically real and objective Halakhah, on the one hand, and the subjective state of the person whose entire psyche is molded by exposure to that Halakhah, on the other. This latter individual is the one Soloveitchik strives to describe in *Halakhic Man*.

Halakhic Man describes the phenomenological outlook of an idealized Halakhic Man by providing a character sketch of his personality. Is Soloveitchik describing any *specific* person in his sketch of Halakhic Man? Many scholars have thought so. Some see self-reflection in *Halakhic Man* (Kaplan 1987, 192); others see a meditation on great Jewish figures of the past, Elijah of Vilna, or Soloveitchik's father, Moshe (Pick 2009), or his grandfather, Ḥayyim of Brisk (Kaplan 1987, 192; Schwartz 2007, 56; Solomon 1993, 49; 2012, 238). Some see a prototypical philosopher of Halakhah

(Brafman 2014, 136), general Lithuanian Brisker Judaism, etc. We believe, more broadly, that Soloveitchik's Halakhic Man can refer not only to all these but also, loosely, to any person with the correct personality features; those whose worldview, in an idealized sense, is shaped by the study, understanding, and observance of Halakhah; and those whose creativity is expressed by constructing novel halakhic categories and concepts. There is no reason to think that because there is an ideal type, every instance of it is identical. A person may have unique personality traits and values, which may not be present in other Halakhic Men. Nonetheless, these values, while not required for a Halakhic Man, certainly do not prevent a person from being one. The specific people to whom Soloveitchik refers in *Halakhic Man* are significant only in that they have stark and vivid (and perhaps extreme) characteristics that he identifies with Halakhic Man.

Throughout, the personality of Halakhic Man is contrasted with other types of individuals who have many enviable traits but are clearly not Halakhic Men.[30] Specifically, we get sketches of prototypical Religious Man (what Soloveitchik calls "*homo religiosus*") and also the idealized Scientific Thinker ("Cognitive Man"). Halakhic Man turns out to be the person who emerges from a distinct halakhic worldview, as two opposing personalities existing together within the same person in a certain manner and context, containing the best of each. Note, however, that we do not receive three full character sketches or personality profiles. Rather, we receive expositions of certain traits that are relevant to our understanding of Halakhic Man. Most of what we receive is of the form: Religious Man strives for X, whereas Cognitive Man is uninterested in X, and vice versa (Munk 1996, 79).

Halakhic Man reflects a dialectical mindset involving two opposing selves: Cognitive Man and Religious Man. As Cognitive Man, he is driven to analyze and quantify the world through the prism of Halakhah. As Religious Man, he is pulled toward the transcendent. These dual personalities, however, are in conflict. Halakhah demands that he focus on the human needs, joys, and suffering of our world, for example, aiding the poor, protecting the widow and orphan, and appreciating food and sexual pleasure.[31] As Religious Man, he is drawn away from the world. As he yearns to leave it all behind and cleave to God, he neither enjoys the earthly pleasures nor is he moved by the plight of the suffering and infirm. He cannot simultaneously be bound to the earth and attached to the heavens.

Unlike Religious Man, who lives a tranquil life surrendered to the transcendent, Halakhic Man's existence is not serene. He is pulled by the deeper mysteries, but he cannot shelter himself in a religious cocoon. Halakhah demands he busy himself with the nitty-gritty of everyday life. He thus lives an existentially lonely, conflicted existence. His mind pulls him in opposite directions. He not only needs to actualize the idealized universe as formulated by Halakhah but he also wants to understand the transcendent mystery of it all. Once he accumulates significant data about his world, he feels compelled to stop worrying about the minutiae of the law and focus on deeper questions: Why is there a world? Why am I here? But the "why" questions are too speculative for a man so enmeshed in the concrete problems of people and law, and so Halakhic Man is once again pulled away from such thinking. And so it goes in an endless dialectical tug of war between probing the elusive mystery of the "why" and the concrete quest for the "what." Ultimately, Halakhic Man is enhanced by such radically opposing views.

Cognitive Man and his origins

What does Soloveitchik mean by "Cognitive Man?" Who is he? What is he like? How does he think? What is his relationship with the world? What motivates him? After whom is he modeled?

The secondary literature on Soloveitchik is replete with speculation and also serious analysis of the model for Cognitive Man. Though we do not defend this, as not much hinges on it, and it is far from our current concern, Cognitive Man can be seen as reflecting the description of the man with the Theoretic Attitude described in Eduard Spranger's book *Types of Men* (Spranger 1928, 109–29), though only loosely. Persuasive arguments, however, have been put forth attempting to show how he is modeled after Hermann Cohen (Kaplan 1973, 45) or at least the image of the person who can be derived from Cohen's epistemological works. Some even see Cognitive Man modeled after Soloveitchik himself. We need not decide this here. The personality described is an idealized one, it need not represent a specific individual, nor must it reflect exactly an individual's philosophy or psychological profile.

Cognitive Man is motivated by one goal: to understand the world as he perceives it. He seeks order, to grasp the laws of nature, and an analysis of necessity in nature. If he cannot quantify, organize, categorize, or otherwise make sense of some phenomenon, he cannot acknowledge its existence. As he imposes order on something, he affirms its reality. Cognitive Man takes this reality to be objective and strives to understand it by sheer force of his reason.

Nature herself encourages this attitude by oftentimes being amenable to analysis and quantification. When nature complies, Cognitive Man takes note: he measures; he categorizes. When nature is mysterious and obscure, Cognitive Man must accept this arena as unknowable. He is not concerned with anything beyond what can be contained by his ability to subsume it under empirical laws and regularities. That is the limit of his comfort zone.

Cognitive Man sees the world through the lens of the *a priori* categories he imposes upon it. Like the scientist, he is constantly trying to determine if and how the objects in the world match the mathematical equations and abstract templates he has presupposed for them. He attempts to be objective and disinterested while occupying himself with intellectual constructions as he coordinates his ideal view of the world with reality. He is unconcerned with transcendence or anything not of this world. He is interested in the "what" of reality, not its "why."

Religious Man and his origins

Cognitive Man is single-mindedly devoted to understanding the quantifiable universe. Some see such an attitude as wholly misguided, missing what is essential or even real about the universe. Among those who criticize Cognitive Man are prototypical "Religious Men," another of Spranger's personality types. Soloveitchik's characterization of Religious Man is far more textured and nuanced than his picture of Cognitive Man. Religious Man is also criticized more. We are given considerably more information about Soloveitchik's inspiration for "Religious Man" than for his Cognitive Man, so we need not rely on Spranger's characterization. Here too, however, various models have been proposed to account for Religious Man's character. Some scholars, for example, have examined the Kantian or Maimonidean roots of this personality (Schwartz 2007). In what follows, we examine other more obvious sources.

Schleiermacher and Otto

Friedrich Schleiermacher (1768–1834) is perhaps the most significant German theologian since Martin Luther. His work influenced most subsequent German theological discussion. *Halakhic Man*'s portrait of Religious Man echoes a central point in Schleiermacher's insistence on a nonrational religion as outlined in his seminal 1799 work *On Religion: Speeches to Its Cultured Despisers*. Schleiermacher, like his contemporary Jakob Friedrich Fries (Fries 1805), believed that religion must be rooted in "intuition and feeling" (1998, 22) as opposed to reason and ritual. Schleiermacher believed Judaism had once been such a proper religion, though traces of that kind of religion are no longer detectable (114) as they have been obscured by Jewish law. Schleiermacher explicitly contrasts his own intuitive and simple pietistic Protestantism with the then dominant German Enlightenment view of Judaism (as presented by the *haskalah*, Jewish Enlightenment) as a religion that was once pure and beautiful but which had "long since degenerated into a code of empty customs and a system of abstract concepts" (99).

Soloveitchik's portrait of Religious Man frequently invokes the idea of the *Mysterium Tremendum*, a term coined by Rudolf Otto (1869–1937), a man who followed Hermann Cohen as professor at Marburg in 1917 and was a colleague there of Paul Natorp. Otto—a German Protestant philosopher, theologian, and comparative religionist very much influenced by Schleiermacher—uses this term to describe our phenomenological experience of God as mysterious and fearful. Religions, primitive through modern, all have as their central feature a concept of mystery, which make them appealing to the human mind. In his influential theological work, *The Idea of the Holy* (Otto 1923), Otto explains that the concept of holy includes both mystery and awe. He refers to the associated feeling as "the Numinous." ("Numinous" is used instead of "holy" as "holy" has taken on connotations of God's moral perfection and moral purity.) The Numinous cannot be directly described only by analogy, similarity, and by what it is not.

For Otto, our religious consciousness, our knowledge of God, is twofold: rational and nonrational. The rational is our *understanding* of God; it is the characteristics we attribute to Him based on our understanding of what God ought to be: omnipotent, omniscient, compassionate, etc. The nonrational is how we *experience* God, as "Numinous." Otto describes the Numinous as best he can using three adjectives: *tremendum* (awesomeness, overpowering might or force, an element of energy or urgency), *mysterium* (mystery, the wholly other); and *fascinans* (fascination).

A central feature of Otto's book, upon which Scheler builds his phenomenological analysis of religion, is the phenomenological analysis of the Numinous experience, that is, how we experience God with feelings of *tremendum*, *mysterium*, and *fascinans*. *Tremendum*, for example, is described as containing the idea that the religious experience involves dread, awe, and urgency. *Mysterium* is described as encompassing the feelings of wonder, mysteriousness, and the experience of the wholly Other. Otto shows that the idea of the religious experience is found in various religions and in different periods, for example, in the Old and New Testaments and in primitive religions. Otto sees in the Hebrew Bible the experience of the Numinous reflected in the Hebrew word *Kadosh*, generally translated as "holy" but literally meaning "set aside" or "wholly Other." Such experience is beyond rationality and transcends categories of space and time.

Otto's focus is on our experience of God, the Numinous. In contrast with Schleiermacher and Barth, Otto is adamant that a successful religion must balance its rational and nonrational elements. If a religion is dominated by either the rational or the nonrational, it is deeply flawed. If dominated by its mystical nonrational aspect, its adherents are prone to self-righteousness, intolerance, and, in extreme cases, holy war. When a religion is dominated by its rational beliefs, there is no mystery, and it is a hollow religion devoid of necessary passion and mystery. A successful religion, argues Otto, must contain both rational and nonrational elements. The experience of God—feeling God's presence—is central to any real religion but is hardly its sole component. Otto also emphasizes the religious importance of our intellectual understanding of God.

Soloveitchik's description of the worldview of Halakhic Man parallels Otto's description of a healthy religion, only much more so. Halakhic Man uses both aspects of his personality, the cognitive and the religious, to understand and experience God. Unlike Otto, however, who offers no systematic plan for encountering God, no road to religious experience, Soloveitchik lays out a three-step process—shaped and guided by Halakhah—which molds Halakhic Man's consciousness and leads him to the highest form of religious communion with God: cleaving to Him (*d'veikut*). Soloveitchik also sees most other religions, especially as compared to Judaism's system of *Halakhah,* as having a severely impoverished relationship with the real world. Otto may pay lip service to the "cognitive" or nonmystical aspect of religions like Christianity, but Soloveitchik is skeptical that they offer solid grounding in the real world.

Otto and Soloveitchik do, however, agree on at least one thing. They both find it difficult to articulate the feeling of the Numinous. Otto points out, following Karl Barth and Emil Brunner,[32] that the religious experience is not a feeling that is easily transferred to others (Otto 1923, 8, 62). Soloveitchik similarly writes that "[w]hile I have succeeded, to a great or small degree, as a teacher and guide in the area of '*gadlut ha-mochin*' [intellectual greatness] ... I have not seen much success in my efforts in the experiential area. I was not able to live together with them, to cleave to them and to transfer to them the warmth of my soul. My words, it seems, have not kindled the divine flame in sensitive hearts."[33] Elsewhere he states, "I am not a bad teacher. However, I cannot transmit my recollections to them. If I want to transmit my experiences, I have to transmit myself, my own heart. How can I merge my soul and personality with my students? It is very difficult. Yet it is exactly what is lacking on the American scene ... This is exactly our greatest need in the United States—to feel and experience God's Presence."[34] This difficulty in transmitting experience, that Otto by way of Schleiermacher describes, is part of Religious Man's personality. Overcoming this difficulty is part of Halakhic Man's challenge. (The discussion of the eulogies later expounds further on Soloveitchik's attitude toward the transmission of religious experience.)

William James

William James also appears to have influenced the description of Religious Man. James is one of the founders of American psychology and a central philosopher of the American Pragmatist school. In 1902, he penned a now classic study of the psychology of religion in his book *The Varieties of Religious Experience* (James 2004). There James describes a number of characters and psychological types, mostly of religious people, each of which manifests and embodies religious experience differently. For example, he describes the Mystic (328–371), the Saint (230–86), and the personality for whom religion is about being Healthy-Minded (78–118). He describes Hybrid character types (151–70) and Rationalist types. He does this as a contribution to the study of religious personality types (James 2004, 104). As opposed to the dominant way of doing philosophy or religion, by offering an argument in support of a thesis, James chose to simply take reports of spiritual and religious experience at face value and see what could be gleaned from them about religious consciousness and experience.

James marshals a host of empirical testimony, frequently quoting at length from reports of mystical experiences. Though he acknowledges experiences from traditions as diverse as Yoga, Sufism, Buddhism, and the spectrum of Christianity, the Jewish mystical experience is absent from this work save for a brief quote from Philo (414).[35] Soloveitchik in a sense rectifies this. In a passage that parallels one of James', he inserts an autobiographical aside that would seem as germane to James' study as any other: "There are times at night when I feel as if someone [the Divine Presence] is standing behind me, bending himself to look over my shoulder to peer into the Talmudic text at the topic I am studying at that moment" (Rakeffet-Rothkoff 1999, 2:189, and see *On Repentance*, 303).[36] Or: "The moment I returned home I would rush to my room, fall on my knees and pray fervently. God, in those moments, appeared not as the exalted, majestic King, but rather as a humble, close friend, brother, father: in such moments of black despair, He was not far from me; He was right there in the dark room; I felt His warm hand, [so to speak], on my shoulder, I hugged His knees [so to speak]. He was with me in the narrow confines of a small room, taking up no space at all" (*Majesty Humility,* 33). Like James' work, Soloveitchik's is peppered with vignettes illustrating the religious experiences he struggles so hard to describe.

Though the Religious Man component of Halakhic Man is indispensable, alone it is problematic. Much of Soloveitchik's criticism of Religious Man comes from the fact that for Religious Man, religion is a subjective experience.[37] Soloveitchik is very uncomfortable with this one-dimensional personality. Thus, the works of Schleiermacher, Otto, James, and others are generally cited critically in the description of Religious Man.

Religious Man (homo religiosus)

Spranger provides two extreme models of Religious Man. In one model, Religious Man views the physical world as inconsequential, and he thus withdraws from it to contemplate and take comfort in the Divine. In another model, Religious Man sees everything in the world as a product of God, and thus everything is significant and worthy of his attention. Spranger acknowledges that most Religious Men fall somewhere between these extreme models. Scheler later provides a more nuanced typology of Religious Men. Soloveitchik, when describing Religious Man, appears to use Spranger's former model of Religious Man, a model all too familiar in history—the Religious Man absorbed in his own spirituality but deaf to the cries of the oppressed and blind to the evil of the wicked.

Soloveitchik's sketch of Religious Man draws heavily on the portraits derived from Schleiermacher, Otto, James, and early phenomenologists like Husserl.[38] We obtain not only a more comprehensive picture of Religious Man than we get of Cognitive Man but also a much less flattering one. It has even been suggested that we are to think of Halakhic Man as solely Cognitive Man (Schwartz 2007). Much of what we hear about Religious Man is that he lacks some vital stabilizing elements to keep him in check morally and spiritually: stabilizing factors that would prevent self-absorption, barbarism, and spiritual sterility. It is also worth stressing again that here "Religious Man" is what Soloveitchik calls *homo religiosus*—a type of person solely guided by a certain kind of spiritual mindset. He is not describing a practicing Jew or a practicing member of any particular religion.

The picture we get of Religious Man is not a pretty one. While Cognitive Man may be spiritually austere, his very humanity is not fatally flawed. He does not ignore the world and its problems. The same cannot be said, however, for Religious Man.

Religious Man and Cognitive Man think differently and have different priorities. They have different categories of experience. They see the world through different lenses. Religious Man revels in mystery and is fascinated by it. He sees mystery everywhere, even in order, which he takes to be the biggest mystery of all! The mystery itself is the goal, not a prod to seek deeper understanding. Religious Man wants to understand nature, but knowledge itself is still the greatest mystery.

Religious Man's world is multilayered. He looks at the universe and searches for another beyond it. The world we live in is but a pale reflection of the one he seeks. This is a sentiment familiar in different guises to readers of Plato, Philo, Spinoza, Kant, many Christians, Arabs, phenomenologists, and idealists. Religious Man does not merely seek a world beyond this earthly one but *requires* of himself to break free of the bonds of the reality of this world and ascend to a higher one, to a world that is wholly good and eternal. Sometimes he does this by rejecting this world, and other times by embracing it. Different religious and moral systems represent intermediate positions on this spectrum. In all cases, Religious Man longs for a refined and purified existence beyond the bounds of concrete reality where he can overcome the limits of his body and embrace a higher reality.

Religious Man does not desire to partake of this world. It is a mere transitional stage for him, and he has no desire to bring the transcendent down here. He would rather flee from this world than fix it. He lives only for the world to come. He treats the supernal reality as a refuge. He experiences no transcendence in the everyday affairs of this world.

Religious Man's ontology reflects his personality. Unlike Cognitive Man, he sees the world subjectively, blurring forms and their boundaries, merging the higher realm with the lower, the corporeal with the spiritual.

Religious Man is terrified by mystery in the world, yet at the same time drawn to it. He is trapped between the poles of love and fear, between fascination and repulsion, and this causes him spiritual anguish. The more he examines the world and the more he knows, the more he is in the dark. Religious Man is both aware of his lowliness and his greatness, of his nothingness and his infinite nature, but he cannot reconcile them. He strives to merge his personality with the Infinite's and has no aspirations to individualism apart from the Eternal.[39]

Religious Man loathes physicality. He prefers the realm of the spirit and has no interest in sanctifying this world. For him, even religious rituals—nonrational religious acts—are designed to lift man out of this reality. He has a constant need to abandon this world for a better one.

Halakhic Man

The sketches of Cognitive Man and Religious Man are profiles of very different personalities. They present opposing personalities, yet both have some admirable qualities. More significant, however, is what Soloveitchik finds problematic about each: Cognitive Man lacks a spiritual existence, while Religious Man is so focused on the transcendent reality, he forgets the needs of his fellow creatures and is liable to forsake his responsibilities toward them.

And so, Soloveitchik tells us, the ideal Halakhic Man is a paradoxical hybrid who draws from both personalities, however incompatible they are, and has a unified "dialectical" personality. He is ideal *because* his two sides must perpetually fight for dominance within him yet work together to form a unified whole. This is how Halakhic Man emerges from the dialectical struggle of competing ideals.

How can Halakhic Man's personality be described? Like Cognitive Man, Halakhic Man is keenly interested in reality but not out of curiosity or existential dread. He does not feel duty bound to redeem mankind from the physical reality of everyday existence. Rather, Halakhic Man sees reality through his *a priori* conception of the world but not in the same way as Cognitive Man. Halakhic Man's conception of the world is given to him by the Halakhah, not physics. Whereas Cognitive Man's categories are set by the likes of relativity theory, space, time symmetry, and the periodic table and his *a priori* conception of the universe involves notions of space, time, and causation, Halakhic Man's categories are set by the holidays, tort law, marriage law, etc., and his *a priori* conception of the universe is set by the rules and priorities of the halakhic system.

This is not to say that Halakhic Man is born knowing Halakhah. Halakhah is no more innate for Halakhic Man than quantum mechanics is for a physicist. Rather, to be Halakhic Man is to be a person whose categories of experience are halakhic categories because that is how they have been shaped. To be Halakhic Man is to be someone who uses halakhic categories to experience the world rather than the categories of economics, art, sociology, or anything else. Neither Halakhic Man nor the scientist can help but see the world the way they do. In other words, Halakhic Man is not someone who has knowledge of Halakhah *a priori*, but rather, his knowledge of the world is halakhic, just as a mathematician's knowledge of the world is seen through a mathematical lens, so to speak.

Halakhic Man lives for this world, not the next. He sees death as inimical to religious life because one cannot follow the law once he is dead. Halakhah is thus not concerned with it. The next world is for reward, but to be rewarded is to be passive. In the next world, there is no opportunity for change, creativity, or accomplishment. It is, therefore, no place for the strivings of Halakhic Man.

But Halakhic Man *is* concerned with transcendence. Though his image of the world resembles Cognitive Man's, and he is occupied with coordinating his halakhic view of the world with the world itself, he is only content if he also establishes a connection with something greater.

Halakhic Man's approach, however, is unique. Unlike Religious Man who works his way from this world into the next, Halakhic Man starts out in a higher realm and ends down here. Halakhic Man yearns to bring the transcendent down to earth and fix the world. Instead of focusing on heaven, his religion directs his gaze onto actual people.

Thus, the Halakhah reverses the spiritual direction. Halakhah occupies itself with the lower realm and does not try to raise the world up high but rather to bring the higher realm down to our material world. While Religious Man ascends to God, Halakhic Man brings Godliness down to our world. Holiness for the Halakhic Man is not a separate realm distinct from our reality. Man brings God down into this world, which, for Halakhic Man, consists of a real biological life lived according to Halakhah. For Halakhic Man, the infinite God is brought into the finite world.

What Halakhic Man gets from Cognitive Man is an appreciation for Jewish law as a quantitative science. Halakhah seeks to quantify the laws. Halakhic epistemology requires an understanding of quantitative concepts. The tendency of Halakhah is to translate the qualitative features of religious subjectivity—the content of the religious man's consciousness—into firm quantities and actions.

Halakhah makes religion objective. It gives us clear, precise, and authoritative rules; it gives form to amorphous religious feelings. It translates subjective religious feelings into concrete objectivity just as a physicist translates qualitative perceptions, like light and sound, into quantitative mathematical relationships. Halakhah thus objectifies the subjective religious feelings by introducing external acts into the world of religion. It also seeks to structure the corresponding part of man's spirit. The Halakhah counteracts the subjective spirit of Religious Man.

Halakhic Man's worldview subordinates the world to religious performance. His ontology is a handmaiden to the normative, even in a case in which the norm is not real or attainable.[40] In other words, the way he understands the nature of the world is modeled after how he thinks the world ought to be. The *a priori* conception of Halakhah shapes his very world.

While his cognition is directed toward the fulfillment of the Halakhah, his focus is on determining the Halakhah. In that sense, Halakhic Man resembles Religious Man; they both hear religious imperatives echoing from every aspect of creation. But while Religious Man must overcome his bodily sensibilities to accept a higher law, for Halakhic Man the law applies even to his bodily functions. Halakhic Man does not lead a dual existence—physical and spiritual—one of which he must overcome.

Like Cognitive Man, Halakhic Man values objectivity, lawfulness, crisp boundaries, clear statutes, and judgments over subjectivity or vagueness. Halakhic Man knows there is a clear separation between a majestic creature such as himself and a lowly beast. He knows this because the Halakhah tells him so. God connected man to Himself via Halakhah, and that is how man is both lowly and infinitely great. Religious Man is troubled by the fact that he is simultaneously lowly and also great, that he is nothing and infinite. He cannot readily harmonize these competing self-conceptions of lowly creature, on the one hand, and as someone connected to a Creator, on the other. Halakhic Man, as we will see later (Chapter 4, Section "The Day of Atonement: greatness, insignificance, and repentance"), finds this unproblematic.

Halakhic Man neither fears the physical world nor does he find it foreign. He comes prepared with his *a priori* categories by which to organize and tame it. Even the prospect of death does not frighten him as he can think of death in objective halakhic terms; it is not personal. Halakhic Man rules over death by making it into something he understands; to know something is to have dominion over it.

Though he does not shun the world, Halakhic Man does not overindulge in it either. He is solemn, living life with a dignified, well-balanced personality. Halakhah is his constant guide, determining the time, place, and method for joy, sorrow, and dread.

Halakhic Man does not attempt to deny his individuality by merging with the Infinite. Instead, he approaches the world actively and autonomously. His autonomy is so great that he surpasses the prophets and, so to speak, even God Himself, who must defer to man-made decisions of halakhic courts (*Halakhic Man*, 81).[41] Man is created with the ability to create, innovate, and change, especially in the halakhic realm; something angels cannot do. Man's intellect can grow and create worlds.

Halakhic Man can achieve the ecstatic joy of Religious Man but only as a result of understanding Halakhah *a priori*, applying it to the world, and putting its pieces together. Cognition, in other words, precedes rapture.

Both Kant and Cohen use reason as the justification for their respective ethics and religious outlooks. Halakhic Man does not. His is not a religion of reason, nor does he use reason to derive the rules that guide his actions. Rather, he considers his norms and obligations to man and to God from the perspective of an ideal world of Halakhah which recognizes no distinction between reality and its norms or obligations.

Halakhic Man is sparing in his recitation of psalms and hymns; that is not his kind of religion. His Creator studies the Law, and Halakhic Man serves Him by doing the same. His study of Halakhah is not a means to some end but is an end in itself—the most fundamental end. Even cleaving to God Himself is not the fundamental end. The end is nothing but the Halakhah itself.

Socrates claims that virtue is a form of knowledge (*Meno* 87e–89a). Similarly, Halakhic Man only recognizes those with knowledge of the Torah as pious. He only counts as God-fearing those who cognize halakhic truth. He will not sacrifice his truth for any goal, no matter how lofty. He will thus not bend the law stringently or leniently even for the noblest of reasons. His ultimate goal is to realize the ideal Halakhah in the real world. This goal keeps Halakhic Man honest, impartial, and apolitical. It forces him to embrace justice and righteousness, no matter how inconvenient or unpopular. The dualism that allows some members of some religions to ignore genuine injustice while simultaneously acting solemn with their God is completely foreign to Halakhic Man, whose gaze is steadily fixed on the concrete reality of the world and its inhabitants. Halakhic Man's ritual is not designed to lift man out of this physical reality. Rather, the service of God involves implementing Halakhah in this world.

Halakhic Man is the unique and ideal Jewish personality. Such a person, completely unfamiliar to the literature of personality psychology, is molded by the categories embedded in Jewish law, texts, and tradition. He experiences the world in a particular way and, in turn, participates in shaping its evolution.

Christian (and liberal Jewish) types, as depicted in the psychological works discussed earlier, claim to express what is universal in religion. But this literature assumes a Christian way of thinking about the religious inner life of man. Soloveitchik believes that Christian existence molds Christians in a way radically different from the way Jewish existence molds Jews. The prototypical view of "religious man" in the literature of psychology and philosophy of religion does not represent the traditional Jewish religious experience.[42]

In Chapter 6, on interfaith dialogue, we explore Soloveitchik's view of the broad gulf that exists between Judaism and other religions. He thought their worldviews were fully incommensurate to the point where even meaningful theological communication is impossible. Let us now turn, however, to the way Soloveitchik sees the internal tension between Cognitive Man and Religious Man.

"Catharsis": a methodological interlude

> God appears in two different guises, in two mutually exclusive roles. At Sinai, He revealed Himself as an old teacher full of love and understanding. At the Red Sea He appeared as a mighty warrior. The same God who forbade working an ox on Shabbat killed the Egyptians' horses.
>
> (*Aseret ha-Dibrot*, 115)

All of Soloveitchik's written works and public speeches dealing with hálakhic and Biblical personalities trade in dialectical opposites. Halakhic Man, as we just saw, however abstractly, embodies opposing personalities in tension. In the following sections, we will see how Soloveitchik understands a few different kinds of "dialectical personalities"; more specifically, the Biblical characters of Adam, Abraham, Jacob, and others. The opposing personality traits embodied by Halakhic Men manifest themselves in a variety of ways. We observe one part of a halakhic personality loving God and another fearing him. We see one part approaching God and another fleeing. One sees religion in terms of reason and another revelation; one is free, another completely subjugated to God; one individualistic, another communal; one advances toward God, another retreats; one seeks autonomy, another to surrender himself to God. Soloveitchik takes these traits to be halakhically mandated and engendered for two reasons. First, because Halakhah itself pushes us in opposing directions, which we will see in Chapter 4, Section "Development." Second, because God Himself manifests dualities of actions. As the epigram earlier shows, God is a loving teacher; God is a mighty warrior;[43] He reveals, He conceals; He is merciful, He is just; He made one covenant with the Israelites in Egypt and a different one at Sinai. Even the Halakhah itself is sometimes tender and at other times a harsh disciplinarian.

The fact that Soloveitchik sees God Himself as combining opposing natures is reflected in his understanding of Halakhah. Consider the case of *peshara*, judicial compromise. The Talmud describes a debate between Rabbi Eliezer ben Rabbi Yossi HaGlili and Rabbi Yohanan over whether a court is permitted to enact a compromise between two litigants or whether the court must decide according to the letter of the law. The law sides with Rabbi Yohanan that compromise is both permissible and meritorious, as he believes it achieves both truth and peace (*emet* and *shalom*). Soloveitchik too is sympathetic with the view. He explains further that when compromise is achieved, God Himself is present, for "he too combines *tzedakah u-mishpat*, *emet* and *chesed* [righteousness and justice, and truth and mercy], without which we, as individuals, and we, as a collective society, could not survive."[44]

Elsewhere, Soloveitchik, expanding on a Maimonidean use of the mystical concept of *shefa*, Divine Emanation, concludes that

> *Shefa*, then, refers to a unity of two existences that are incommensurate. It enables one kind of existence to participate in an alien kind of existence. These two kinds of existences logically cannot form one order; yet they do, and this unity between them exists.
>
> We can now see that *shefa* and *hesed* [mercy] are two sides of the same coin. God's *hesed* means that He lets others share in His existence though there is an ontic gap between Him and them. God and the world form one order, though they are incommensurate. Indeed, God's unity and providence demand that He and the world, despite their incommensurability, form one order of existence.
>
> (*Maimonides Course*, 177)

Soloveitchik's essay "Catharsis" is a defense and explanation of this picture of God, Jews, and Halakhah. The essay, though typical of Soloveitchik's speeches, also contains his most overt exposition of the nature of the dialectical tension unifying opposing archetypal personalities. It also expresses most clearly the nature of the tension. "Catharsis" defends and describes the necessity of this tension and explains how the tension itself has a cathartic effect that is religiously mandated. The tension is one in which the individual is never content nor comfortable. Neither aspect of the personality is ever fully dominant; there is always a pull from the opposite side. Just as an individual is about to embrace one side of his personality, he is pulled from the opposite side and enticed to abandon the first. The dialectical tension Soloveitchik expresses manifests itself as a mighty struggle to reach the goal that appears to be of supreme importance to one side of a dialectical personality—and then, at the last moment, abandoning that goal and embracing the ideals of the other side. Sometimes the struggle is resolved, but more often it goes on indefinitely. It is this struggle and not its resolution that Halakhah mandates for a human to achieve their full worth.

Hegel, Marx, Kierkegaard, and Barth

Recall our discussion of Nietzsche's analysis of the Apollonian and Dionysian in man from Chapter 4, Section "From philosophy to personality psychology." The cultural phenomenon known as German Romanticism stressed the idea of opposing natural forces in areas as diverse as art and science. The idea of a dialectic, a process governed by opposite tendencies, was common in nineteenth-century German thought and is one of the central legacies of German Idealism. Soloveitchik himself traces the roots of dialectical thinking back to the pre-Socratic philosopher Heraclitus (ca. 535–475 BCE), and we note that it has appeared repeatedly in thinkers as diverse as Maimonides and J. G. Fichte (1762–1814). What will be important for any discussion of Soloveitchik's work is his notion of the dialectical nature of man, an idea that has meant different things to different thinkers.

Some interpreters see Kant's view of man as dialectical: his *Groundwork of the Metaphysics of Morals* sees man's desire to manifest himself simultaneously as a holy being and also as a human standing in the way of that manifestation. Kant reconciles this dilemma of his twofold self by appealing to what he thinks is the twofold nature of man: the phenomenal self and the noumenal self—the self of perception and the self of the way man really is. The phenomenal self is the human part. This part is in contrast to and falls short of man's self-understanding of his other way of seeing himself, as a *real*, noumenal, being.

The most famous discussions of philosophical dialectic is attributed to the post-Kantian G. W. F. Hegel (1770–1831). We now think of a "Hegelian dialectic," as it is often called (borrowing terminology from Kant), as a process of change. The process begins with a starting point, called a "thesis." This thesis contains within it the seeds of a response called an "antithesis," which emerges from it and in turn generates a "synthesis," a new middle position arising to alleviate the tension between the original thesis and the new antithesis.

Hegel[45] used all these terms somewhat abstractly. Initially he was making an ontological point about the nature of existence. He would also adapt this mode of dialectical thinking to explain world history. The nineteenth-century radical German-Jewish philosopher Karl Marx (1818–1883) also adapted Hegel's idea to demonstrate how history plays out concretely on the world socio-political stage. Marx popularized the idea that the Hegelian dialectic describes a mechanism of social change. Whatever state the world is in socioeconomically is called its "thesis." Perhaps the society in question is capitalist. Capitalism is the thesis. But (for Marx and Hegel) each thesis contains the seed of a mechanism for a change to oppose the thesis, or status quo. Perhaps communism begins to gain currency because capitalism is not working well. This mechanism for change is the "antithesis." In cases like this, the thesis and antithesis clash, say in a revolution, and a "synthesis," say socialism, emerges out of the revolution. This synthesis is then a new socioeconomic state. It is the new thesis, and the cycle continues. Thus, a dialectical account acts as a historical explanation of world events.[46] Now, regardless of whether or not this is the way history actually works, Marx's example shows how thinkers adapted the idea of Hegelian dialectics to describe a process of opposing ideas and situations interacting in certain ways to generate new ones.

Halakhic Man, too, on a very surface reading of the text, describes a kind of synthesis arising out of the tension between Cognitive Man and its "antithesis," Religious Man. Soloveitchik emphatically points out, however, that Halakhic Man is no synthesis of Cognitive Man and Religious Man,[47] nor is he a compromise between the two personalities, nor the product of one personality turning into the other and then forming a synthesis with the original.

A thesis, antithesis, and its subsequent synthesis are all intellectually comfortable positions to occupy, at least for a while. They represent stable ideas. A thesis is the status quo. An antithesis represents the fact that the status quo is untenable and is also a new position. A synthesis is the new status quo. As Soloveitchik sees it, there is nothing comfortable about being a Halakhic Man. Cognitive Man, Religious Man, and all of Spranger's personality types are all mentally comfortable people. Each has an intellectual outlook that guides the answers to all their questions and gives them a consistent worldview free of contradiction and paradox. Each personality provides a stable set of categories of experience. Soloveitchik's ideal people, as reflected in his personality works, are not like this. They all live with tension, conflict, and in constant pursuit of a satisfaction they know they can never obtain. Soloveitchik frequently rejects[48] the approach of thinkers like William James (1995) who explicitly tout the "religion of the happy minded," as such a take on religion is antithetical to ideal Judaism (*Sacred Profane*, 5). The beauty of religion is in its tension, not its serenity (6).

Rather, Soloveitchik's position is explicitly related less to Hegel's concept of dialectic (*Majesty Humility*, 26) and more to the conceptions of the Danish theologian Søren Kierkegaard (1813–1855), Ludwig Feuerbach (1804–1872), and Franz Overbeck (1837–1905).[49] Kierkegaard is generally regarded as founding religious existentialism. Like Hermann Cohen and some existentialists, such as Nietzsche and Tolstoy, Kierkegaard saw the goal of life as becoming an "individual," as opposed to being a mere member of a group. Kierkegaard believed that in his day there were three obstacles standing in the way of people becoming individuals: the popular press, which thought for people; the State Church, which believed for people; and Hegelian philosophy, which chose for people. Kierkegaard believed that Hegelian dialectical synthesis takes difficult "either/or" choices that people must contend with and transforms them into "and" positions that people are comfortable with. For Kierkegaard, the struggle to have incompatible positions makes one an individual, whereas Hegelian compromise makes one conform. More concretely, whereas Hegel thinks that the idea of God can be understood rationally, Kierkegaard thinks of God as higher than logic, or beyond it. For Kierkegaard, the belief in God may require being comfortable with irreconcilable opposites in a way that would have been familiar to proponents of the German proto-romantic *Sturm und Drang* movement, which stressed movement in emotional extremes. His is the kind of unresolvable dialectic that one must simply accept.

The Swiss theologian Karl Barth (1886–1968) used Kierkegaard's sense of religious dialectic in his own work. Barth was a country pastor turned academic, first teaching in Göttingen, then Münster, then Bonn until, in 1935, he was forced to leave for Basel, Switzerland, after refusing to sign an unqualified loyalty oath to Hitler. He attracted a significant following, and his works were very popular and widely known among theologians. "Barthian theology," or "Crisis Theology" eventually became known as "Dialectical Theology." It is an approach to religion that emerged from Kierkegaardian dialectics though (as Paul Tillich later explained) it is actually a way of thinking more in terms of paradox than dialectic. Barth saw no need for dialectical synthesis or reconciliation. God needs no synthesis.

Barth pushed back against both neo-Kantian and liberal doctrines. In his widely read *Epistle to the Romans*, Barth (1933) argues that religion is not to be identified with ethics, as Kant and the neo-Kantians had it. Barth also opposed liberal humanistic Christianity that subordinates religion to one fashionable humanitarian philosophy or another, just as Soloveitchik would later reject any doctrine, idea, or fad that is not indigenous to Judaism to ground his philosophy.

Barth argues that God is wholly separate from the world of sin and transcends the human realm. God is so apart from man that man cannot even approach Him. God, instead, must approach man, which He does through revelation.[50]This view is inspired by Feuerbach's notion of the "I and Thou" (later adapted by Martin Buber), which stresses the great gulf between God and man. Man is not searching for God. How can he? God is too remote to be the object of man's worship. Rather God is the eternal Thou, the quintessential Other who addresses man through revelation. Barth insists on the fundamental incompatibility between such opposing realities as sacred and profane, the temporality of man and the eternity of God, the sovereignty of God and the freedom of man, the immanent and the transcendent.

Dialectical theology employs paradoxical concepts such as the impossible possibility, the absolute transcendence of God in contrast with the self-disclosure of God, faith as a gift and yet an act, eternity entering time, etc. It uses these pairs of opposing concepts to teach that the only way to really appreciate the kind of thinking appropriate to describe the relationship between God and man is "dialectically." Dialectical thinking involves thinking in question and answer form such that each answer generates a new question. It especially involves thinking in terms of both sides of an irre- concilable paradox simultaneously. For Kierkegaard, the dialectic can be apprehended as the tension that exists when God is revealed as he is con- cealed or in a sin not being known until it is forgiven. For Barth, finite man cannot grasp the whole of the infinite nature of revelation of God in in- dividual statements. Instead, he must embrace all sides of each of God's revelations, however paradoxical and contradictory they are. In the end, a complete synthesis of such opposites is impossible. All opposing positions must simply be accepted.

Barth's followers include Emil Brunner, Friedrich Gogartin, Rudolf Bultmann, and Eduard Thurneysen, all prominent names in Protestant theological circles in the 1930s. Barth also came to have significant influence over thinkers like Martin Buber, Franz Rosenzweig, Paul Tillich, Dietrich Bonhoffer, Reinhold Neibur, and Jacques Ellul.

Soloveitchik[51] will have a somewhat different approach to the God-man relationship in *AFTYSS*, but there is certainly a resemblance to Barth's. The two thinkers had much in common.[52] Barth attacked the liberal Christian tendency to situate the divine in the realm of the ethical or the subjective. Soloveitchik attacked liberal Judaism (and Christianity) for the same reason. Barth was opposed to liberal Protestant innovations just as Soloveitchik was opposed to liberal Jewish ones. Both were opposed to religious tendencies that subordinate their respective religious values to humanistic ones. Both avoided invoking "feeling" as a basis for religion. Neither was bothered by the new Biblical criticism though each for their own reasons. Most significant for us is their common approach to forms of dialectical theology. Barth exploits the idea that there are opposing ten- dencies in the universe that manifest themselves in the God-man relation- ship. Soloveitchik's phenomenological view exploits the idea that Halakhah causes man to experience these opposing tendencies. Neither thinks that the opposing positions can be in any way reconciled. Barth thinks the tension can be apprehended and is the source for theological Christianity. Soloveitchik thinks the tension makes up Halakhic Man's reality.

Soloveitchik thus adapts the idea of dialectic to suit his own purposes. Let us next see how he describes and defends his view of Halakhah's mandated dialectical movements in his essay "Catharsis."

"Catharsis"

The main thesis of "Catharsis" is that Halakhah demands catharsis—not the familiar kind where one purges one's feelings but rather a catharsis that comes from certain kinds of intellectual realizations.[53] Specifically, Soloveitchik holds that for the sake of halakhically mandated personal fulfillment, one must realize and accept specific tensions that are part of a fulfilled Jewish life.

In a standard "Brisker method" move, Soloveitchik describes situations that appear similar on the surface but lead in opposite directions. The confusion is resolved when we understand that the original similarity is merely superficial in light of conceptual clarification (ḥakirah). In the short essay "Catharsis," Soloveitchik clarifies the concept of "strength." "Strength" can be used to refer to opposite traits, depending on context. The two kinds of strength are implicit in the two different Hebrew words that can be used to denote strength: *koaḥ* and *gevurah*. Soloveitchik tells us that humans are imbued with both *koaḥ* and *gevurah*, and the *koaḥ* in humans is locked in a dialectical struggle with human *gevurah*.

Koaḥ, Soloveitchik argues, implies physical strength possessed by both man and beast, whereas *gevurah* is the capacity to attain victory and is unique to humans. *Gevurah* implies not physical strength, but rather heroism, or action undertaken contrary to human logic. The Biblical Jacob used *gevurah* as he fought against the angel (*Genesis* 32:25–30) and is also manifested in the Jewish people throughout the generations as they engaged in an "absurd" struggle for survival.

Heroism using physical strength is aesthetic and fleeting. In contrast, *gevurah* is contemplative, hushed, and mute. *Gevurah* is an enduring way of life. It demands withdrawal at the proper moment, just as Jacob withdrew after he defeated his antagonist, a professional warrior. In the Biblical account, Jacob fought the angel but eventually let him go instead of slaying him. That is heroism.

Elsewhere (*Five Addresses*, 106) in a parallel discussion about *koaḥ* and *gevurah*, Soloveitchik wonders, "Why actually did Jacob have to fight?" What did Jacob achieve in his struggle? After all, there was no real outcome: no spoils, no conquest. Jacob seemed to gain nothing from his encounter with the adversary. Soloveitchik answers that "the struggle itself sanctifies." That is the kind of struggle born of *gevurah*.

Further on, Soloveitchik expounds on the concept of a "Hebrew," as in "Abraham the Hebrew," so called because Abraham came over to the other side of the river (the words *ivri* and *evr*, "a Hebrew" and "side," are etymologically related). Why, asks Soloveitchik, is Abraham's crossing the river such a significant feature of who he is?[54] Soloveitchik explains that the designation "a Hebrew" symbolizes what it is to be a Jew. "A Jew does not live on one side of the river, but on both, at the same time" (116). To be a Jew is not to take one side but to take both.[55]

Halakhah demands that we purge or purify ourselves and attain catharsis. How? By taking both sides and engaging in a dialectical movement—we boldly push forward and then humbly retreat. Like Jacob, we must not "consummate" our victory. We must act in a manner expressing a certain frustrating tension involving indulgence and self-denial. After accepting defeat, we may once again resume our forward march to victory. We must do this at every level of our existence: carnal, emotional, intellectual, and moral-religious.

We must always be ready to admit defeat in our religious life. If one has not redeemed his religious life, he may become self-righteous, insensitive, and even destructive. On the long journey of life, at some point one must reach the absurd stage at which one finds oneself bankrupt and forlorn. Man spends time feeling extremely close to God, a feeling punctuated by long interludes in which God feels extremely remote. There are long periods of despair, punctuated by brief moments of ecstasy. The long periods when God's face is hidden (*hester panim*) is when the catharsis takes place. The catharsis is an endless cycle in which the myriad opposing sides of Halakhic Man's personality, such as his Cognitive side and Religious side, oscillate and vie for dominance. Just as one personality dominates, the other asserts itself in an endless internal struggle that fashions a special personality.

Soloveitchik suggests that the "charismatic personality" overcomes such dichotomous aspects of their personalities to a certain extent and moves toward a kind of synthesis that finds completion in the messianic era (*Emergence Ethical*, 190–92). In the here and now, this struggle, this cathartic discomfort, and not the mere features of his personality, is the essence of Halakhic Man.

The Lonely Man of Faith

> I am lonely because, in my humble inadequate way, I am a man of faith for whom to be means to believe, and who substituted "credo" for "cogito" in the time-honored Cartesian maxim.
>
> (TLMOF, 3)

Once we understand the general strategy, we are prepared to see Soloveitchik's most well-worked-out example of the "halakhic mandate" for understanding man in the dialectical fashion he does. In this case, the halakhic mandate comes from the fact that God Himself describes man in the manner of Halakhic Man. He does so in the beginning of *Genesis*, the first book of the Hebrew Bible. Soloveitchik shows that the Biblical Adam has two distinct personalities, both of which contribute to his full personality. Neither personality dominates, nor is there a merger of personalities. Adam is a unique blend of two incompatible personality types. He draws on the best part of each and vacillates in manifesting them.

Inspired by the parallels in the essays, many commentators are intrigued by the ways *Halakhic Man* differs from "The Lonely Man of Faith." Even the casual reader will spot numerous differences in tone, style, emphasis, and message. *Halakhic Man* was originally written and published in Hebrew, TLMOF in English, a fact that, at least for some, indicates different intended recipients and whose respective intended audiences account for their different ways of thinking about idealized halakhic personalities (see Kaplan 1984–1985, 337ff; Hartman 2001, 99–101; Schwartz 2007, 12ff for discussion). Some see Soloveitchik's own inner struggle between his Lithuanian Brisker self, inherited from his ancestors, reflected in *Halakhic Man*, while his true emotional Ḥasidic self is exhibited in TLMOF (Singer and Sokol 1982). Others argue that *Halakhic Man*'s personality sketch is exclusively and apologetically Jewish, while the sketch in TLMOF contains a more universal message (Hartman 2001, 101–4). Yet another commentator sees a completed conceptual synthesis of two personalities in *Halakhic Man* while the one in TLMOF faces an infinite and hence impossible-to-complete task (Turner 2014, 300). Soloveitchik may be highlighting the differences between an ideal Halakhic Person and an Ideal Person. Perhaps in TLMOF Soloveitchik is constrained by the limited source material of a few verses in *Genesis*, whereas in *Halakhic Man* he is free to draw upon a wide range of established scholarly tradition with regard to the nature of Cognitive Man, Religious Man, and his own personal internal phenomenological conception of a halakhic personality. All the suggestions ring true to some degree, and while we do not adjudicate the reason for the shift of style here, we hope the readers will look to all the personality essays for themselves and speculate about the nature of their real difference.[56] Here, however, we wish to emphasize what all the personality essays have in common. We look first at some background, and then at TLMOF, the next personality essay.

Two passages from the book of Genesis

> *Genesis*, Chapter 1: (26) And God (*Elohim*) said: "Let us make man in our image, after our likeness; and let them have dominion over the fish of the sea, and over the fowl of the air, and over the cattle, and over all the earth, and over every creeping thing that creepeth upon the earth." (27) So God (*Elohim*) created man in His own image, in the image of God (*Elohim*) created He him, male and female created He them (28). And God (*Elohim*) blessed them and God (*Elohim*) said unto them, "be fruitful, and multiply, and fill the earth and subdue it, and have dominion over the fish of the sea, over the fowl of the heaven, and over the beasts, and over all the earth."

Genesis, Chapter 2: (7) And the eternal God (*Tetragrammaton-Elohim*[57]) formed the man of the dust of the ground and breathed into his nostrils the breath of life and man became a living soul. (8) And the eternal God (*Tetragrammaton-Elohim*) planted a garden eastward in Eden ... (15) And the eternal God (*Tetragrammaton-Elohim*) took the man and placed him in the Garden of Eden to serve it and to keep it.

Two Adams

The book of *Genesis* repeats the story of the creation of Adam (man), first in Chapter 1 and then again in Chapter 2. The differences between the two accounts are striking. In the first version, Elohim creates and in the second it is *Tetragrammaton-Elohim*; in the first, man is created in the image of God while nothing is said about how his body was formed, and in the second, he is fashioned of the dust of the earth and God breathes into his nostrils the breath of life; in the first, he is tasked with having dominion over the earth, and in the second, he is there to serve it; in the first, Adam is created male and female, and in the second, he is created as man alone and Eve appears later as a helpmate. Further reflection reveals more differences between these two passages.

Students and Bible scholars have been trying to understand the rationale for the strange repetition of the story at least since Philo Judaeus, a Jewish philosopher who predates the Talmud and perhaps even the canonization of the Hebrew Bible. Why repeat this story in two consecutive chapters? Why are there significant differences between the two chapters, and what can we learn from them? Philo interprets this repetition in Platonic terms, claiming that the first version of the story presents the creation of an idealized human, whereas the second version presents a more earthly version of a human (Philo, *On the Creation,* 19).

Soloveitchik points out early in the essay (11) that there is a standard rabbinic answer, originating in ancient hermeneutical works such as the Midrash. Traditionally, when a story is told that invokes Elohim, the "generic" name for God, we interpret that story as reflecting a God that rules in nature. He judges the participants strictly, as if acting according to fixed natural law. But when a story is told invoking the Tetragrammaton, the "proper" name of God, we are to assume a personal God who is acting mercifully rather than judging according to the strict letter of the law. In the language of the sages, seeing that man could not exist if God were perpetually judging him by the strict letter of the law (represented originally by Elohim), God also judges mercifully (represented by the Tetragrammaton). This rationale is used over and over again in religious writings to explain perplexing bits of scripture (see references in 11n*). Soloveitchik himself uses it often, for example, when discussing the binding of Isaac and the Ten Commandments (see, e.g., *Aseret ha-Dibrot*).

In nineteenth-century Germany, an almost exact contemporary of Hermann Cohen—the Protestant Bible scholar Julius Wellhausen (1844–1918)—articulated (Wellhausen 1885) what is now known as the "documentary hypothesis."

Roughly, his widely influential claim is that the document we now know as the Pentateuch (the first five books of the Hebrew Bible: *Genesis, Exodus, Leviticus, Numbers,* and *Deuteronomy*) was originally four separate source documents (and also some smaller ones):

> "J" refers to the Jahwist (Tetragrammaton) source because the Tetragrammaton name within this source was known by humans from the very beginning of its Creation story. The narrator refers to God as Tetragrammaton and never as Elohim (although people in the story do.) The J text comprises about half of *Genesis* and half of *Exodus*;

> "E" refers to the Elohist source because the Tetragrammaton name within this source was not known until God revealed it to Moses at the bush on the Mountain of God (Exodus 3:15). Until then God was referred to as El or generically as Elohim (God). The E text comprises about half of *Genesis* and half of *Exodus*;

> "P" refers to the Priestly source. In this source God revealed His Tetragrammaton name to Moses in Egypt (Exodus 6:3). This source comprises much of *Leviticus* and pieces of the other books;

> "D," refers to the Deuteronomist source which is exclusively in *Deuteronomy* and which takes up almost its entire book.[58]

> "R" refers to the redactors who edited the Pentateuch into the format we currently possess.

Much of the evidence for this style of thinking about the Bible is internal to the Bible itself, for example, varying literary styles, repetitions, and usage of different divine names.

When presented compellingly, such a theory[59] challenges more traditional views of the creation of the Hebrew Bible. On the one hand, it provides a natural explanation of how the text was written and there is much internal evidence to support such a theory. On the other hand, it flies in the face of the traditional account of the text as divinely dictated or inspired, thereby undermining Jewish religious self-understanding. Solomon Schechter went so far as to call such Bible criticism "higher antisemitism." Hermann Cohen, however, was very much influenced by Wellhausen and his approach,[60] and in Soloveitchik's time, in Berlin, this hypothesis posed a powerful challenge to traditional theories of the Bible.[61] It was quite widely discussed in intellectual circles and particularly by Orthodox Jewish intellectuals such as Issac Breuer and D. T. Hoffman at the Berlin Hildesheimer Rabbinical Seminary, before Soloveitchik's arrival, and Jehiel Jacob Weinberg while Soloveitchik was in Berlin (Solomon 2012, 243).

In some sense, Soloveitchik's essay "The Lonely Man of Faith" can be seen as a reaction to this kind of Biblical criticism (Levenson 1994, 102n6,

Ross 2015), though responding to Wellhausen is hardly its main purpose (Batnitzky 2011, 61).[62] In a recurring theme (e.g., *Adam Eve* and *Nature Man*), in TLMOF Soloveitchik provides us with a novel model for how to not be bothered by biblical criticism. This at once provides a defense of his larger philosophical program by showcasing the Biblical (i.e., halakhic) precedent for his approach. TLMOF is a poetic *midrash* (Bible exegesis), if you will, in which Soloveitchik shows that the two accounts of Adam in *Genesis* are not different versions of the same event but rather descriptions of two aspects of man (or at least a certain kind of Man), which Soloveitchik refers to as Adam the First (Adam I) and Adam the Second (Adam II). What to critics is proof of multiple Biblical authors are to Soloveitchik two condensed personality sketches reflecting two aspects of man, both of which are sanctioned and willed by God.[63] What to Bible critics demonstrate the human hand in Biblical authorship is to Soloveitchik a meditation on the loneliness inherent in a life of faith.

Soloveitchik takes the two versions of the creation story to be telling us about two personality types, which together make one an ideal man of faith. Soloveitchik unpacks each of the two versions of the creation of Adam and extracts a personality sketch from each. He calls Adam the First "Majestic Man" whose purpose is rooted in the pragmatism of this world. Adam the Second is "Covenant Man," whose purpose is rooted in a covenant in which God and Adam are partners and both play integral roles. Adam the First is dignified; Adam the Second is redeemed. Both are necessary personality components of an ideal person. Together they explain how one may indeed be a lonely man of faith.[64]

How vs. why

Soloveitchik tells us that the two descriptions of Adam in the book of *Genesis* differ because they describe two different personality types. Adam the First is a creative being. He is intelligent, capable of confronting the outside world, and inquiring into its complex workings. He is tasked with subduing nature and has the intellectual resources to do so. But he is not interested in ethics or metaphysics, only the practical question: "How does the cosmos function?" He only inquires to further his control over nature. In dominating nature, he attains the dignity of being human, as opposed to a helpless brute whose environment controls him. This dignity involves imitating his Creator by copying His work though not necessarily understanding it.

Since an orderly existence is a dignified existence, Adam the First also creates aesthetic and legal norms. Not concerned with metaphysical truth, these norms instead conform to his sense of beauty and order, nothing more.

Adam the Second, on the other hand, is also intrigued by the cosmos, but his personality impels him to ask very different kinds of questions. Instead of "How?" he asks "Why?" "What?" and "Who?" Why did the world come into existence? What is the purpose of the world? Who is He that shadows me but disappears every time I turn?

Adam the Second does not seek out God in quantifiable laws of nature but rather in an irresistible fascination with a beautiful qualitative world. He takes in the world with a childlike naiveté without imposing his own structure of mathematical-type laws upon it. Adam the Second lives in close union with God, his very existence intertwined with his awareness of the Creator.

Though they employ different strategies, both Adams are equally provoked by the mystery of existence and have identical motivations: to be human as God commanded them to be. Their diverse methods are not the product of different goals but rather the result of differing interpretive approaches to a common goal.

Dignity vs. redemption (discussion of TLMOF)

While Adam the First pursues dignity by eschewing a natural existence and mastering his environment, Adam the Second seeks redemption. What is the difference? Dignity is found in relation to others, in the outward gesture that allows the inner self to be expressed. Only those who communicate with others in word and action are dignified. The silent Anonymous Person is not dignified. Adam the First, who seeks dignity, was created with Eve in a society and has the tools to socially interact within it to lead a dignified life.

Adam the First exists in a natural community, which he is impelled to join to accomplish his goals as social contract theorists understand them. Adam the First joins a community for practical reasons, not because he is somehow incomplete when alone. By himself, Adam the First is alone but not lonely. His natural community is there to help him accomplish tasks, not enhance his existential situation. Adam the First does not need redemption, nor does he need to be completed. Sometimes he needs assistance. He is charged by God to act with others, not exist with them.

Adam the Second can be a member of a community, yet still be lonely. To understand how, consider the basic distinction between dignity and redemption. Redemption is an awareness of one's own situation; it is a mode of being which is inherently different from being unredeemed. One can be completely alone and still be redeemed. One who is redeemed knows that his existence is worthwhile and rooted in something stable and unchanging. Dignity, on the other hand, is not an awareness of self, nor can it be manifested without others.

Redemption cannot be attained by controlling one's environment but only by controlling oneself. A dignified man conquers; redemption, however, comes from recoiling in the face of a Higher Truer being.

When Adam the Second discovers his humanity, he feels defeated. The self-awareness he feels when seeking redemption brings about an awareness of his own incompatibility with others. He realizes his separation from his environment.

Pragmatic vs. covenantal community

To be redeemed, one must do something that leads to the discovery of a companion with whom one can uniquely form a community. One must sacrifice, surrender, and retreat to find companionship.

Adam the First does not have to sacrifice to form the utilitarian community he needs. Adam the Second's community, however, is one of communication and communion, both sacrificial gestures. This latter community is born of crisis and distress and reached full fruition in the covenant between God and Abraham as described in *Genesis* (cf. *Community* §5).

The covenantal faith community is a state where one cannot share of oneself, nor is it a community that can be experienced by others. In this community one is lonely. The loneliness is inherent, and thus, Adam the Second must quest for a new kind of community, not merely the pragmatic one of Adam the First.

Adam the First's community is a community of interests; Adam the Second is involved in a community of commitments born in distress and defeat with three participants: I, thou, and He: Adam the Second, his community, and the God that binds them. Adam the First managed to find the female by himself; Adam the Second was introduced to his companion, Eve, by God. Together the latter two form an existential community molded by sacrificial action and suffering, with God as a partner in that community. God's infinite nature joins man's finitude in forging a unified community.

The covenant answers Adam the Second's questions. He sees God in His handiwork. But the handiwork presents an equivocal message. On the one hand, God is visible; on the other hand, remote. That is why God introduces himself to Adam the Second with his proper Name (the Tetragrammaton), symbolizing a more intimate meeting than could be implied by the descriptive name "Elohim," God-as-source-of-cosmic-dynamics, which sufficed for Adam the First.

The covenantal relationship created between Adam the Second, Eve, and God is established by God revealing Himself and man preparing for and accepting the revelation. The revelation creates a "prophetic community," and man's response creates a "prayer community." Combined, this is the covenantal community, so called because (a) both prophecy and prayer can only be understood in terms of a covenant within a community; (b) both communities involve I, thou, and He. Anything the prophet gets from God is public and goes from He to I to you. Similarly, prayer from I to He must include you. (c) When forming, both communities freely take on ethical obligations. Prophecy and prayer are then the same, except in prophecy God speaks to man, and in prayer, man speaks to God.

Man cannot reveal himself to his fellow man without joining him in covenantal prayer and moral action. Yet God is necessary to bridge the communication gap between the private languages of people within the covenantal community.

Adam the Second is insecure because he is aware of the shortness of his existence. Adam the First is only aware of the present. Adam the Second is aware of the past and future in which he does not exist. But the covenantal relationship of Adam the Second uses God and the *mesorah*—the community of the chain of tradition[65]—to connect man to the past and the future.

The dialectic

The man of faith is lonely because he does not have an existential partner. He finds redemption in a covenantal faith community by aligning his finite existence with God's infinite existence. He becomes a revealed-to man, that is, someone who has partaken in the Divine revelation. But even after joining the faith community, complete redemption is still impossible. He continuously goes back and forth between the faith community and the pragmatic community of Adam I. Such oscillating is the goal of Halakhah: to connect this-world existence to the covenantal community in such a way that man is never fully comfortable in either.

The Biblical dialectic explains how Adam the First, the dignified man out to subdue the world, and Adam the Second, the lonely man of faith, are actually one individual confronting himself. Man is destined to perpetually oscillate between the community where his ontological loneliness is cared for and the community where he materially succeeds without rooting himself in either.

The contemporary Western religious person only identifies with the pragmatic Adam I and thus fails to acknowledge his own true needs. Only Divine sanction can give his moral norms permanence, worth, or redemption. The man of faith has needs that are not pragmatic. His commitment to his covenant is not logical, and he does not utilize the same categories of thought as does the scientific man. His commitment to God encompasses both his rational and nonrational existence; it involves the logic of his mind, heart, will, and more.

The faith experience requires a message unfamiliar to a pragmatic society; it requires a message of surrender and defeat, not triumph and conquest. And this is exactly what modern man rejects. Western man cannot surrender himself unconditionally. He demands reciprocity from God in a way foreign to the mechanics of faith.

The dialectical personality of the Biblical Elisha

In the closing chapter of "The Lonely Man of Faith" (103–6), Soloveitchik provides us with a short but moving personality sketch of the Biblical Elisha in whom Adam I and Adam II vie for dominance.

Originally, the personality of Majestic Man (Adam I) was in the fore. "He [Elisha] was the son of a prosperous farmer, a man of property, whose interests were centered around this-worldly, material goods such as crops, livestock, and market prices. His objective was economic success, his aspiration—material wealth" (103).

While so engaged in his majestic endeavors, Elijah passed by and cast his mantle upon Elisha, and in an instant he was transformed. "He was initiated into a new spiritual universe ... a new vision of redemptive covenantal reality incommensurate with the old vision ... He bade farewell to father and mother and departed from their home for good" (104–5). Covenantal Man (Adam II) was now in the fore. Yet even so, Elisha faced disappointment and failure. "Many times he felt disenchanted and frustrated because his words were scornfully rejected ... Elisha was indeed lonely, but in his loneliness he met the Lonely One" (105).

Elisha's vying personalities gave him no rest. "Later, when he achieved the pinnacle of faith and arrived at the outer boundaries of human commitment, he came back to society as a participant in state affairs, as an advisor of kings, and a teacher of the majestic community" (105). Majestic Man once again emerged.

So the cycle continues. In great people personalities compete for dominance. Each personality comes to the fore as required by time and place. Struggling with such a dialectical personality makes one not only conflicted and lonely but also redeemed and great.

"The Community"

"The Lonely Man of Faith" looks at man from the perspective of two possible communities in which he can exist—the one that cares for his ontological loneliness and the one that cares for his material needs. The essay explains the dialectical struggle that takes place within a modern Person of Faith who can never fully identify with either of the communities in which he exists. In Soloveitchik's essay, "The Community," he asks an even deeper question about the nature of humankind. He engages an old subject at the heart of political theory by raising the question of the individual and the community. To political philosophers (remember, Soloveitchik initially studied political science), this question is at the heart of the debate over what is central when considering an ideal political situation: the rights and needs of an individual or those of the community (cf. Brunner 1941, 293–307).

Soloveitchik is asking a related metaphysical question. Which entity is *ontologically* prior, the individual or the community? What are the fundamental units of society: individuals who comprise the society, or the community which is comprised of individuals? In what can initially sound like a mere question of semantics, Soloveitchik inquires whether there are individuals in the world who, when put together, comprise a collection called a community, or whether there are communities in the world that, upon close examination, can be said to be made up of pieces called individuals.

Aristotle's *Politics* (1253a28) famously holds that the community is ontologically prior to the individual, almost as a person is to a cell from his body. In both cases, the latter cannot survive without the former. People, Aristotle argues, are by nature political animals. Anyone living apart from society is either a beast or a god. In modern times, collective identity, responsibility, and the social good are tied to the idea that society is prior to the individual. In the past few hundred years, however, thinkers have again considered the individual to be ontologically central. People are sometimes said to have a drive for individualism or independence from political authority. This attitude has been accompanied by the rise of libertarianism, modern liberalism, and individual rights.

Although this position is often identified with Aristotle, Hermann Cohen reads a related view into Plato. Cohen's ethics argues that humans, as ethical beings, are not natural beings but political beings (Beiser 2018, 182f, 229f). Ethical beings only exist in the context of the state.

In Soloveitchik's time, the view of the ontological priority of the community over the individual perhaps saw its fullest expression in the work of Max Scheler who argued that not only is the community metaphysically prior to the individual but the community is also known by individuals *a priori*. In a phenomenological analysis of how we become aware of other people, Scheler asserts that an individual on a desert island would be aware of an emotional emptiness that would appear when he performed certain conscious acts. Knowledge of others would appear in the sphere of this emptiness (Scheler 1973, 521).

What, for Scheler, constitutes a "community," as opposed to any of a variety of kinds of collections of people? A community is composed of people who understand themselves to constitute such a community. When the individuals understand themselves and one another in the context of their community and they understand the collective goals and traditions of the community, they thereby understand the "essence" of the community and thereby constitute it.

Scheler explores the different ways that individuals have shared feelings and the different types of communities that people form and the different types of collective actions the communities perform. In the context of these communities, individuals perform social actions: actions that require the acceptance of the one it is directed at, such as requests or promises, which are only meaningful if the one who receives the request is in a position to consider it or the recipient of a promise can believe it. Scheler explicitly contrasts these other-directed actions with self-directed actions such as introspection, self-respect, or self-discipline. Individuals act and express themselves both as individuals and as members of a community (Scheler 1973, 519ff).

We see Soloveitchik similarly distinguishing between different types of communities and individual and collective action.

One of the founders of modern social science, the French Jewish sociologist Émile Durkheim (1858–1917) thought of *Homo Sapiens* as *Homo Duplex*, Man with Two Natures: one individual, one collective. In contrast with Soloveitchik, Durkheim thinks of the collective as the realm of the sacred and the individual as the realm of the profane. For sociologists, this debate centers on the analysis of human behavior: is it possible to analyze collective behavior as a natural phenomenon, or can we only make sense of individual actions? For political theorists one stake in this debate involves doling out of rights. Should more rights be assigned to the individual, or should we assign rights with an eye toward the collective good? For Soloveitchik, however, the question is ontological; it is about the fundamental categories of existence as well as people's responsibilities.

After World War I, Max Scheler argued for an integrated world culture in which the nations of the world reconcile their natural differences and peacefully coexist. In parallel, he sought the same for man who must integrate themselves as individuals prior to ending war between nations. Man was understood as analogous or as similar in structure to the state.[66]

Similarly, in *On Repentance* Soloveitchik makes clear that as far as Halakhah is concerned, both individuals and the community exist on an ontological par. He explains that the individual is an entity unto himself with legal obligations and standing; so is the community. On one way of looking at it, there are three kinds of entities that can offer sacrifices in the Holy Temple in Jerusalem: individuals, groups, and the community of Israel (*Knesset Yisrael*).[67] The community of Israel is not identical to the group containing all the Jews. Even if all Jews got together and paid for an animal to be sacrificed, it is not a "communal sacrifice." Repentance is similar. Sometimes an individual must repent for an action; sometimes a group and sometimes the community as a collective, separate from, and above its individual members must repent. Hence, Judaism recognizes three ontological categories.

"The Community" is a novel way to think about this dialectic within a single personality. The two contrasted personalities in this essay are (1) the human as a whole Autonomous Individual and (2) the human as a mere piece of a Community. How does Judaism, that is, Halakhah, understand humankind?[68]

It should not surprise us to discover that on such a central question, Soloveitchik argues that Judaism sees mankind as inherently both an autonomous individual and a piece of a community, locked in a certain kind of dialectical struggle. The experiences of being alone and being together are *jointly* basic elements of the Jewish self. On the one hand, a person is a complete being whose primary existence is within themselves. On the other hand, the person is a piece of a community whose main identity lies in the community of which they are a part.

In one sense (and there seem to be Nietzschean sentiments working here), being a lone individual is a necessary feature of being an ideal Jew. One can only be original and creative while alone and set apart from others and society; a social person tends to imitate and emulate those within their society; he borrows what others have created. Solitary Man is a rebel, a hero, who can set himself apart and rebuke others who are wrong and unfair. On the other hand (and this is the response to Nietzscheanism), Man is not only a protester but also an affirmer. Ideally, he is a part of the community as a teacher and leader. Thus, to fully realize himself, Man must be both alone and above the community and also a member of a community.

Halakhah claims that a community is formed with words, what J. L. Austin called a "speech act" (Austin 1962) and Max Scheler called a "social act" (Scheler 1973). By greeting one another, people form a community with their words. They recognize each other's worth. They declare that the other person is not expendable.[69] This causes them to take responsibility for one another in a way that is manifested in a community of prayer, which emerges with the experience of responsibility. Jewish prayer is almost exclusively formulated in the plural—we pray on behalf of the community.[70] A community of charity is similarly construed. This prayer-charity community is a teaching community centered on adults and children who hear stories that recapitulate events in Jewish history and situate the Jews as a people therein.

As always, man is locked in an inner dialectical struggle. The ideal Jew is at once a whole individual and also a mere piece of the community. Halakhah forces Man to actualize himself by having a dual view of his own personality—the part that is formed in prayer, teaching, and charity, on the one hand, and the part that stands apart to rebuke the wrongdoer on the other—never fully accepting either role completely.[71]

Lest we think that Soloveitchik saw Halakhic Man, the Lonely Man of Faith, or any of the other "dialectical individuals" as mere theoretical entities, we note how he also saw such personality clashes embodied in real people he knew. Some of those individuals make up the subject of our next section.

The eulogies

In Hebrew and Yiddish, the word *machatunim* denotes the relationship between the sets of parents of a married couple. When Soloveitchik's daughter Atarah married Isadore Twersky, Isadore's parents, Rabbi Meshulam Zusha Twersky and Rebbitzin[72] Rebecca Twersky, became Joseph and Tonya Soloveitchik's *machatunim*. Soloveitchik's *machutin*, Rabbi Twersky, was a Rebbe, the leader of a small Hasidic sect originating in the Ukraine.[73]

In Judaism, as part of the mourning ritual, it is customary to deliver a eulogy on the thirtieth day after a prominent person dies. When his *machatunim* passed away, Soloveitchik delivered a eulogy.[74] Our interest in these eulogies lies in the fact that they exhibit Soloveitchik's standard philosophical approach but with a twist. In the eulogies, Soloveitchik sketches the personalities of real people as opposed to the idealized portraits we have seen until now. In *Halakhic Man*, we saw a phenomenological picture of a theoretical person locked in a dialectical struggle between his "cognitive" and "religious" personalities. The analysis of the two Adams exhibits the Biblical roots of such an approach. "The Community" is a brief analysis of one aspect of an internal dialectical struggle with roots in political theory. In the eulogies, the dialectical method is applied to real people. Soloveitchik could not give a phenomenological account of what it is like to be any of these people. However, he looks at people he knew well and describes them in terms that fit his way of thinking about halakhic Jews as dialectical beings.

The eulogies add a novel dimension to the dialectical approach, one that will lead us into the next section. They show us another side of Halakhic Men. We see how they are part of the Jewish chain of tradition, the *mesorah*. This transmission of the tradition from one generation to the next is achieved when Halakhic Man, or a "covenantal community" of Halakhic People, is educated by opposing forces, both individually and communally.

Even Soloveitchik's explanation of the purpose of eulogies exhibits a dialectical character. He notes that a eulogy serves two purposes: to make people weep and to tell the life story of the deceased. The former reason speaks to the heart; the latter to the mind. In the former the mourners express grief and achieve a catharsis; in the latter they bid farewell. Soloveitchik delivered six eulogies that have subsequently been published (some only partially), all of which are discussed later.

In the eulogy for the Rebbitzin, we learn that a complete individual Halakhic Man needs both a masculine and a feminine influence as part of his education. The former inculcates knowledge; the latter wisdom and warmth. In the eulogy for the Talne Rebbe, we see similarly that a community requires two kinds of educators, one for mass education and leadership and the other for the serious teaching of the law to the next generation of individual leaders.

We learn related lessons from the eulogies for Soloveitchik's uncle R. Velvele, Zev Gold, and Ḥayyim Ozer Grodzinski. The connection between the education of the Jewish people and the transmission of the tradition is most explicit, however, in the eulogy for Ḥayyim Heller.

The Rebbitzin of Talne

The "Tribute to the Rebbitzin of Talne" contains a character sketch, or at least part of one, and another approach to understanding a whole individual as a function of two ideal types situated in one individual in a specific way. In this case, the whole person is one who inherits, embodies, and transmits the two separate chains of the *mesorah*, the halakhic tradition from the revelation at Sinai to the present. Both start at Sinai, but one is transmitted through the community of fathers who teach texts, morals, and discipline. The other chain comes from the community of mothers who teach Halakhah as a lived experience and not merely an intellectual exercise. Everyone must be both a pupil and a teacher in this chain. Everyone is part of a society that links the present with the past and future.

The character sketch here is not nearly as comprehensive as the one in

Halakhic Man or as descriptive as that of "The Lonely Man of Faith." It outlines a woman with three qualities: (1) Wisdom, which includes innate intelligence, accumulated knowledge, and intellectual curiosity; (2) Greatness, which involves staying quiet while leading a household, staying calm in the face of crisis and adversity, and being humble yet aware of her own strength. As necessary, she complies but also makes others do her bidding; and (3) Dignity. She is a leader in the sense that she can compel others to do the right thing. She is a spiritual aristocrat yet not petty. She has a sense of inner pride, tolerates pain and suffering, ignores coarseness and vulgarity, commands respect, and leads without intending to.

We do not know if Soloveitchik had anyone in particular in mind when writing *Halakhic Man*. There is only a description in the abstract of what the personality of a Halakhic Man is like. Here (undoubtedly constrained in style by the demands of the genre and occasion), Soloveitchik begins with a specific person, the Rebbitzin of Talne and provides a sketch of her personality. The job of the ideal male is a transmitter of texts and information. The description of an ideal female is someone who can give over the important feminine contribution to Jewish life: an appreciation for reality itself.[75]

The father's role is to teach his child how to read, comprehend, analyze, conceptualize, classify, infer, and apply. His role is an intellectual-moral one that shapes the child's qualitative side. The mother's role is to convey by example the practical everyday rituals of Judaism as expressed at home on each weekday, on Sabbath, and on festivals. "The fathers *knew* much about the Shabbat; the mothers *lived* the Shabbat, experienced her presence, and perceived her beauty and splendor" (77, emphasis in original). A great woman spiritually resembles the dialectical personality of Biblical women. She is humble and shy yet has an indomitable will and an unshakeable determination. She is simple but tenacious, meek yet fearless.

Soloveitchik sees the relation between man and woman in the same way he sees the relation between an individual and the community. Though there is no reason to think that women cannot be as much of "Halakhic Men" as men, Soloveitchik writes here that the masculine and feminine play complementary roles in forging the next generation of Halakhic Men. Mother and father working together are able to instill the proper values for the child to have the necessary qualities to live a life with the tension that makes them Halakhic Men. In the absence of both the proper masculine and proper feminine influence, one will not have the right components in his personality to become a Halakhic Man.[76]

Elsewhere Soloveitchik writes (*Yemey Zikkaron*, 32–34) that the student-teacher relationship reaches its pinnacle when it embodies a male-female relationship as well as a female-male relationship. When a teacher implants information in his students, the teacher plays the active (male) role, and the students play the passive (female) role. However, when a student questions his teacher and ignites a spark within him, their roles are reversed. The student then plays the active (male) role, while the teacher, internalizing the student's challenge, plays the passive (female) role.[77]

The Talne Rebbe

Rebbitzin Twersky's husband is also eulogized, but in the speech delivered for him, we find Soloveitchik talking about the transmission of the tradition slightly differently. He distinguishes two kinds of teachers necessary in a covenantal community: the King Teacher and the Saint Teacher. These are two equally important transmitters of tradition. Soloveitchik thinks of the Talne Rebbe together with the Biblical high priest Aaron, as Saint Teachers, in contrast with Aaron's brother Moses, Moses Maimonides, the Vilna Gaon, and Hayyim of Brisk who were King teachers. What is the difference between a Saint Teacher and a King Teacher?

The teachers differ in their methodologies, approaches, and in the media they employ (*Eulogy Rebbe*, 75). The King Teacher teaches Halakhah. He teaches how to read and understand texts, reconcile opposing views, analyze, systematize, and infer. He teaches words, how they are communicated, and how they form law. He prioritizes truth over love, speaks to the mind, and only to those few whose intellects are capable of understanding and contributing to his abstract scientific mode of analysis. He rebukes the sinner and is angered by injustice. He is lonely.

The Saint Teacher, however, is not focused on the tangible words that make the law, but rather on the invisible soul of the Torah. His job is to draw man into the unity of God's word and human existence (75). He speaks to the heart. He teaches how to celebrate victory and experience grief. He communicates to his students something which Soloveitchik himself frequently lamentes he is unable to: the feeling that the law is supposed to engender. The Saint Teacher is a gregarious teacher of the entire community. His teaching is "exoteric, democratic, understandable and accessible to both the simpleton and philosopher" (78). He prioritizes kindness over truth, is saddened by sin, and perplexed by injustice.

This distinction between the Saint Teacher and the King Teacher echoes a debate that raged during the inception of the Hasidic movement in the eighteenth century. The rabbinic elite, as they are known, opposed the formation of the Hasidic movement on many grounds, but one in particular was the role of rabbis. Rabbis like Elijah of Vilna wanted rabbinic hegemony and power to remain with the great scholars, the "*talmidei ha-khamim*." Hasidism was a populist movement, in contrast to the distinctly nonpopulist mitnagdic (anti-Hasidic) movement. The Hasidic movement emphasized the role of the *tzadik* over that of the *talmid hakham*. The *tzadik* is a holy person, who must be knowledgeable in Jewish law and Talmud, but whose primary role is to encourage piety and holiness and concentrate on spreading it through the community. The anti-Hasidic (mitnagdic) ideal of rabbinic leadership is the aloof scholar whose authority in matters of

Halakhah is absolute. With ideas that evoke fragments of his early bio-graphy, Soloveitchik explains that both kinds of leaders are necessary for a halakhic covenantal community: the kind that has many students and promotes communal piety and the kind that has few students and fosters their individual intellectual development and encourages their leadership potential.

Other Jewish leaders

The chain of the halakhic tradition and the sets of opposing forces necessary to sustain it are the focus of most of Soloveitchik's eulogies. The people he eulogized were those he considered to be great teachers and leaders of the Jewish people.

In the eulogy for his uncle R. Yitzḥak Zev (Velvele) Soloveitchik (1886–1959), the "Brisker Rav," Soloveitchik distinguishes between what he calls the Rosh Hashanah and Yom Kippur personality types. Both Rosh Hashanah, the Jewish New Year and Yom Kippur, the Jewish Day of Atonement are sacred days on the Jewish calendar. However, Rosh Hashanah is associated with God's public revelation, whereas Yom Kippur is associated with private divine revelation. The paradigm of the Rosh Hashanah Man is Aaron, the Biblical High Priest. The paradigm of the Yom Kippur Man is his brother Moses. Both personalities are necessary in a community that strives to perpetuate God's covenant and the Halakhah. As a pair, they are similar to the Saint Teacher and King Teacher, but they play different roles in trans-mitting the tradition. Yitzḥak Zev, who died on Yom Kippur, is identified with the prophet Moses, the Yom Kippur Man. He was a more private person—less accessible to the community than the priest—and his accom-plishments are less widely appreciated and understood. But his role is just as necessary as that of as public a personality like Aaron the Priest (Saks 1999).[78]

The eulogy for Zev (Wolf) Gold (1889–1956), the founder of Yeshiva Torah VoDaath in Brooklyn and a leader of the Mizrahi movement, is si-milarly tied to the Jewish calendar. Soloveitchik speaks of his leadership style by describing the Sabbath and Festival Man and contrasts him with the Rosh Chodesh Man. On Sabbath and festivals, one can walk down the street of any Jewish neighborhood and know that it is a Sabbath or a festival day. People dress differently, congregate differently, and greet one another dif-ferently than they do on other days. Rosh Chodesh, however, the day that marks the new lunar month, has few outward signs indicating the specialness of the day. It is a more private holiday, just as Gold's leadership style was more private, less heralded, and nonostentatious. Zev Gold was a proto-typical Rosh Chodesh Man.

Soloveitchik also eulogized Ḥayyim Ozer Grodzinski (1863–1940), a communal leader of pre-war Lithuanian Jewry and member of the Brisker circle, and praised both his scholarship and leadership. Soloveitchik employs an analogy with two of the vestments worn by Temple era High Priests—the *tzitz* and the *ḥoshen*, the headband and the breastplate. The former was worn on the head near the mind, and the latter on the chest, near the heart. Soloveitchik says that Grodzinski is one of those rare individuals who possessed the greatness associated with both mind and heart. The *tzitz* symbolizes his deep and vast knowledge of the Halakhah, while the *ḥoshen* represents his love and commitment to the Jewish people.

Ḥayyim Heller, the subject of our final discussion of Soloveitchik's eulogies, is also unique as a Jewish educator. As Soloveitchik's mentor and colleague, Heller was himself a true link in the chain of tradition. Heller too is presented in terms of opposing learning styles and also in terms of embodying opposite personality traits.

The eulogy presents a number of dichotomies. First, it compares two styles of learning. The first style is extended, systematic, and lengthy. It involves moving from problem to problem until a topic is exhausted and the truth is revealed. The other style, Heller's, is concentrated, brief, and short. He works intuitively to come up with confident, correct halakhic conclusions.

Soloveitchik speaks of the difference between the Adult and the Child personalities. The Mature Adult personality cannot approach God. He may be smart, knowledgeable, experienced, sober, and businesslike, but if he is too clever, too practical, or too jaded, he cannot be great. Only a child, with naiveté, curiosity, playfulness, enthusiasm, eagerness, and spiritual restlessness who hopes, dreams, and yearns for beautiful and elevated things can shed tears and pour out his soul to the Almighty.

Soloveitchik notes that his grandfather, Ḥayyim Brisker, was both a great abstract thinker with an "iron discipline" and also a Child. Similarly, his father, Moshe, was a genius and a Child. And, like Soloveitchik's grandfather, Ḥayyim Heller was both. He united intellectual greatness and innocence of heart (cf. *Ahavat ha-Torah*, 182f). He possessed unusual knowledge and the "delightful simplicity of a small boy." He embodied that strange polarity that characterizes authentic Judaism (*Eulogy Heller*, 62–65).

Summary: personality sketches—"Majesty and Humility"

When discussing Biblical personalities and when describing great people he knew, Soloveitchik continually returns to the theme of opposing dialectical personalities. In *Yemey Zikkaron* (78–80) he compares his two grandfathers to Joseph and Judah. Elsewhere he speaks of the Biblical Esther, a proxy for ideal womankind, as the perfect reconciliation between the Ideal Adult and the Ideal Child. An adult needs guile, cunning, maturity, and experience. A child needs hope, naiveté, and feeling. Esther could only accomplish her "Purim miracle" using both aspects of her personality, while Mordechai (an "adult") is constitutionally unable to design a successful plan (*Insights Esther*).

In the essay "Majesty and Humility," Soloveitchik considers the dialectical nature of the ideal person in the person of Adam, the first man. When considering the dust from which Adam was created, the Biblical commentator quotes two Midrashic homilies. The first has God gathering this dust from the four corners of the earth, and the second has God fashioning Adam from the dust of a particular spot of earth—the spot of the future site of the Holy Temple's altar. The allusion is that on the one hand, Man is a cosmic being—intellectually, experientially, and in his very ability to wander. On the other hand, he is rooted in one spot; he is here-minded and wants to stay on his plot of land. Both Men search for God. Cosmic Man sees God in the infinity of creation, while Origin-minded Man experiences God in His closeness to man. In times of joy and ecstasy, man experiences God in the majesty of infinity. In times of sorrow, man experiences God in the humility of the infinitely small. Halakhah acknowledges the morality of victory and triumph and also the pain of withdrawal and retreat. Man is created to both strive for victory and to accept defeat.[79]

In *Vision and Leadership* we find well-developed personality sketches portraying the dialectical nature of both Joseph (1–69) (and to a lesser extent of the Pharaoh under whom he served) and Moses (70–222). Joseph exhibits not only saintliness but also the dialectically opposing attributes of pragmatism and vision, strength and ambivalence, and "inspiration and precision, fantasy and practicality, vision and a distinct awareness of an unalterable reality, poetic sweep and scientific accuracy" (5–8, 22). Pharaoh similarly exhibits pragmatism and vision (20–27). Moses the Midianite, who is cynical of the Children of Israel and tries to forget them, struggled internally with the younger, more optimistic Moses. Ultimately the younger Moses prevails (75–78). In a posthumous essay "The Crisis of Human Finitude," Job is contrasted with Ecclesiastes (*OOTW* 152–56) to similar effect.

Halakhic Man is pulled by opposing needs to know and to understand. He also experiences the gamut of dialectical tensions. He feels conflicted, and this is his greatest asset. He thrives on the inner turmoil constantly created by the opposing drives. Soloveitchik describes in great detail the two conflicting sides that make up each aspect of an ideal Jewish personality. He describes the nature of the tension itself and how the two elements interact to produce that novel personality that is the essence of Halakhic Man. Just as there are many aspects of Halakhah, so too is Halakhic Man multifaceted. But there is more to Soloveitchik's thought than describing Halakhic Man and justifying the idea that doing so is a Jewish approach to the philosophy of religion. There is a practical question which we alluded to in our discussion of Maimonides. How does one become a Halakhic Man? What is the relationship between Halakhah itself and the various manifestations we just saw of Halakhic Man? That is the subject of our next section.

Development

In Exodus (30:7) we read: "... every morning when Aaron[80] fixes the candelabra he shall cause the incense to ascend." These were the two duties of the high priest. Kindling the *menora* (the candelabra) symbolizes light, knowledge, clarity of concept, and depth of analysis. In short, it symbolizes the halakhic mitzvah performance. The incense reflects the mysterium in creation, the human being reaching out for *d'veikut* [connection] with God Who is the source of all existence. It symbolizes the colorful, subjective, religious emotion.

The Torah thus says coordinate the two, the incense with the candelabra, the subjective with the objective, the experience with the deed, the passion with the performance, the romance with the outer discipline. First (in the mitzvah of *tzitzit*) comes "and you shall look upon them," a deed performance, and then, only then, will the recollection of the mitzvot, the experience, come.

(*First Rebellion*, 109)

In this section we complete our discussion of Soloveitchik's main philosophical program. In the "Foundation" section, we spelled out Soloveitchik's vision of a new Jewish philosophy, one grounded in Halakhah whose aim is to reconstruct and understand the Halakhic Mind from the data of the Halakhah. In the "Personality" section, we described the unique dialectical personality of Halakhic Man, which emerges from his understanding and application of Halakhah.

In this "Development" section, we bridge the gap between the objective metaphysics of the Halakhah and the subjective epistemological mind. We describe the causal process going from Halakhah to personality, the relationship between the objective and the subjective, the former giving rise to the latter. We will see how Halakhah molds and creates the personality and consciousness of Halakhic Man. The resultant personality contains aspects of both Cognitive Man and Religious Man, as well as a full range of conflicting emotions and values including joy and sadness, majesty and humility, a compulsion to both approach and retreat from God, and love and fear Him, among many other emotions. We will see how Halakhah creates Halakhic Men by setting their ontological categories of experience, by defining the objects of their world, and by mandating actions that evoke emotional and spiritual experiences. This process only happens in this way for those people for whom halakhic categories are meaningful. The halakhic personality that emerges is a rich and conflicted one. By grappling with the tensions of these opposing forces, the greatness of Halakhic Man emerges.

And from There You Shall Seek

The act of a Mitzvah and the fulfillment of a Mitzvah

In the quotation that opens this section, Soloveitchik discusses two mitzvot (commandments) performed daily in the holy temple: lighting the menorah and burning incense.[81] Soloveitchik takes this pair of commandments as symbolic of something much broader: the objective act of performing a commandment and the subjective experience arising from its fulfillment.[82] Light, in the Bible (as for Plato), is often a metaphor for knowledge, clarity, and depth of analysis (i.e., everything needed to establish the correct format of a *mitzvah*). Thus, lighting the menorah represents the objective act, the performance of a *mitzvah*. Incense, in all its swirling amorphousness, represents the mystery within creation and human beings reaching out to God. The burning of incense represents the subjective and perhaps mystical or emotional experience of a mitzvah. These two duties of the High Priest together symbolize for Soloveitchik the entirety of a mitzvah: the objective act and the subjective experience.

In the above quotation, Soloveitchik uses a pair of *mitzvot* to illustrate the objective act and the subjective experience.[83] However, Soloveitchik more commonly discusses the objective and subjective components of a single commandment, such as his discussion of the commandment to wear ritual fringes.[84] Soloveitchik often points out that the subjective experience of a mitzvah, its fulfillment (*kiyyum ha-mitzvah*), usually happens concurrently with the objective act (*ma'aseh ha-mitzvah* or *pe'ulat ha-mitzvah*), but sometimes, in certain "experiential" commandments, it does not (see Kaplan 1987, 193ff).

For example, the objective act of repenting (the *ma'aseh ha-mitzvah*) includes confessing one's sins. The subjective experience, however, the fulfillment of the mitzvah (*kiyyum ha-mitzvah),* occurs as one has the intellectual and emotional experience of regretting his sin and undertaking never to do it again.[85] The act of the mitzvah and its fulfillment take place at different moments. Or, another example, "the obligatory recitation of the Shema [prayer] is strictly a physical verbal performance, but its fulfillment is internal ("*ba-lev,*" literally, "in the heart") ..." (*First Rebellion*, 107). And again, in discussing the Passover *seder*, Soloveitchik notes that we are "enjoined not only to praise and give gratitude, but also to break forth into spontaneous song ... The Jew's heart is overflowing with feelings of joy and thanksgiving ... he cannot repress this authentic need to express his gratitude to the Holy One, Blessed be He" (*Nine Aspects*, 39). With other mitzvot, however, such as holding the *luluv* and *etrog* (the "four species") on Sukkot, the act of the mitzvah and the fulfillment of the mitzvah happen simultaneously as one lifts them up. The commandment to eat the matzah on Passover is similarly fulfilled when one eats the matzah.

Whether we consider the above pair of commandments, lighting the menorah and burning the incense, or whether we consider an individual commandment such as *tzitzit*, it becomes clear that for Soloveitchik, the objective act of fulfilling a commandment and the subjective experience of the person performing it work in tandem to actualize the commandment and help mold one's halakhic consciousness. Commandments are possible because of the legal categories that make them make sense. Performing *mitzvot* gives rise to epiphanies, revelations, realizations, emotions, experiences, and feelings toward God that work with Halakhic Man's *a priori* categories to create a Halakhic Mind.

Soloveitchik expresses this pithily in a discussion of the Biblical Korah:

> [T]here are two parallel religious orders in Judaism, the objective and the subjective. Judaism ... consists of two facets: x) the Divine discipline, call it *Shulchan Aruch*, Halacha, or any other name, y) and the great romance between finitude and infinity, between God and man. These two different experiences are inseparably united. The deed without the experience is an incomplete act, an imperfect gesture.
>
> (*Noraos Harav*, Vol 10, 89–90)

Halakhic Man's personality has aspects of both Cognitive Man, the scientist, and Religious Man, the spiritual person. How does the Halakhic experience shape each of these parts of Halakhic Man's personality? We begin with a brief discussion of Rudolf Otto's understanding of the religious experience.

Rudolf Otto

The theologian Rudolf Otto's book *The Idea of the Holy* helped shape Soloveitchik's conception of Religious Man (as described in *Halakhic Man*). His work significantly informs our conception of the phenomenology of Religious Man, that is, the subjective experience of what it is like to be him but tells us nothing about how to bring about a religious experience that constitutes the ultimate phenomenology. Rather, Otto presupposes we have such religious experiences:

> The reader is invited to direct his mind to a moment of deeply-felt religious experience, as little as possible qualified by other forms of consciousness. Whoever cannot do this, whoever knows no such moments in his experience, is requested to read no further; for it is not easy to discuss questions of religious psychology with one who can recollect the emotions of his adolescence, the discomforts of indigestion, or, say, social feelings, but cannot recall any intrinsically religious feelings.
>
> (Otto 1923, 8)

Although many people have religious feelings or experiences, many do not, and Otto's phenomenology of religion has nothing to say about the latter group of people. So how can an experience that is not shared by all committed religious people be part of a lived day-to-day religion? It is hardly democratic or even meritocratic. How "spiritually elite" must one be to have such experiences? In what way must one be elite? On Otto's conception, one has either had an experience of the Numinous or one has not. Why is Otto's religion so unfair as to deny the central feature of his religious understanding to so many people on the basis of the fact that they have simply not been lucky enough to be graced with it? Moreover, how does the experience of the Numinous (Chapter 4, Section "Schleiermacher and Otto") even come about? What connection does the feeling have with religion? By what criteria can we judge such an experience to be religiously meaningful or authentic? Even further, the experience of the Numinous is not a constant experience. It is a random, occasional, and fleeting experience. How can that be a central part of one's religious life?

Soloveitchik's understanding of the nature, function, and influence of Halakhah answers all these questions. An effective and authentic religious experience comes about via the proper fulfillment of the Halakhah. One does not merely *have* religious feelings or experiences. Halakhah *causes* them. Some of the feelings are temporary and give rise to other feelings; some are temporary and motivate actions, while some things that Halakhah generates are not feelings but personality dispositions.

This understanding of the function and nature of the Halakhah, first and foremost, explains the relationship between Halakhah, on one hand, and the phenomenology, worldview, and psychological profile of Halakhic Man, on the other. Second, it is Soloveitchik's response to what he took to be a general misperception in theologians like Otto, Schleiermacher, and many others, who perceived Jewish law as an ossified legal code, devoid of spirituality, long gone stale a thousand years before. Schleiermacher's conception—which was likely absorbed from his counterparts in the Jewish Enlightenment, the *haskalah*—is particularly wrongheaded but in a way that is difficult to grasp from outside the halakhic system.

Consider the rabbinic approach to prayer from the perspective of a Western religion, say a typical branch of mainstream Christianity. Imagine one sets out to write the definitive treatise on prayer. Certainly in the eyes of a Western theologian, what would likely be foremost on the author's mind is a God-directed interaction stemming from inner spiritual drives that manifest themselves in man's primary mode of self-expression—language. The treatise would describe feelings and emotions, clinging to and entreating a Being with whom one is seeking a special relationship. One expects to read, in some manner, about the longing for communion with God and the personal relationship with Him that prayer brings about.

But when one looks at the classical source on Jewish prayer—the Talmudic tractate *Berakhot* (or most any standard Jewish discussion of prayer)—one finds mostly technical details: lengthy analyses of chronological minutiae used to determine precise times for prayer, extensive legalistic discussion about the precise phrasing of prayers, the number of blessings before and after the *Shema* prayer, which prayers are said seated versus standing, which direction to face when praying, etc. One encounters nary a word about longing for communion with God. One finds little about the subjective feelings that motivate prayer toward the One to Whom prayer is directed.[86] What then can the system of halakhic prayer say to the

Western thinker who cannot fathom the purpose of such an account of prayer or what the prayer actually does for the individual praying? Moreover, how can such a legalistic prayer system respond to the Western charge that Jewish prayer is merely part of an antiquated monotonous ritual provoking no religious sentiment?

In his account of Halakhah as the vector for religious experiences, Soloveitchik combats both the notion that technical details of Halakhah are all there is to a Halakhic Person and that the technical details themselves offer little spiritual advancement.

Characterizing Halakhah as the means by which one's personality develops also acts as a counterweight to Otto's characterization of Christianity (as opposed to Judaism) as the pinnacle of religious sophistication and development. Otto understands Christianity as superior to other religions in that it is best at balancing the rational and the nonrational aspects necessary for a religion. Otto dedicates a portion of his book to show how Christianity is the perfection of the Old Testament approach to the transcendence of the Holy. Ancient Judaism, by contrast, on Otto's account (like on Schleiermacher's), kept man feeling crushed and sinful due to God's wrath, remoteness, and distance.

Soloveitchik sharply disagrees with Otto's characterization of Judaism as having too distant a God and with his assessment of Christianity's supposed superiority. Soloveitchik charges Otto's picture of Christianity (the Christian Religious Man) as exhibiting an exaggerated preoccupation with the nonrational and the Divine, which leaves the door open to unapologetic toleration of barbarism by his fellow religionists.[87] In Soloveitchik's thinking, Halakhic Man's focus on the concrete situation of this world is far superior, in part, because he could never be in the position of Christian Religious Man who excuses his own blind eye to cruelty by explaining that his gaze is on a loftier plane of experience.[88]

In this way Soloveitchik—in responding to what he takes to be Otto's misperceptions of Judaism—outlines a clear account of the role of Halakhah in the life of the halakhic Jew and simultaneously responds to various Protestant philosophical views as well (Borowitz 1983, 238).[89]

Cognitive and religious aspects of Halakhic Man

Recall that Halakhic Man's personality contains aspects of both Cognitive Man and Religious Man. Through study and application of Halakhah, Halakhic Man develops those aspects of himself that resemble Cognitive Man's personality and uses his mental faculties to search for God in the universe. The God that man finds through his understanding of the cosmos, however, is insufficient. His understanding alone is insufficient to achieve an authentic religious experience of the Numinous. Here Halakhah comes to his rescue. By studying and applying the Halakhah, he develops his intellectual side, and by recreating the ever-unfolding event of revelation, it sets Halakhic Man on a spiritual journey—from revelation, to imitating God, to cleaving to Him. Cleaving, the culminating step in the quest toward God, is the ongoing overarching religious experience that is unique to Halakhic Man. His religious experiences, the essence of his personality, emerge from the totality of Halakhah.

Categories: Halakhah molds the cognitive aspects of Halakhic Man

How does Halakhah develop the traits normally associated with a scientist or mathematician in a Halakhic Man's personality? To rephrase, how does Halakhah create the Cognitive Man part of Halakhic Man's personality?

A mathematician or a scientist imagines a purely ideal feature of reality, for example, that the area of a circle is equivalent to pi times the radius of the circle squared ($a = \pi r^2$). Using this *a priori* conception of the nature of circles combined with other relevant concepts, he correlates his imagined ideal of the world with the actual world to determine whether and how the real phenomenon he observes (the area of an actual measured circle in the real world) corresponds to his imagined ideal construct (the area of the circle as calculated by his mathematical formula). Like mathematicians, scientists also look at the world and check, for example, if liquids freeze at the predicted temperature, if the environment changes as his models predict, if light travels at the theoretically proposed speed, if planets revolve at the predicted orbit, etc. Cognitive Man is constantly looking at the world and correlating it with his pre-established theoretical version.

Halakhic Man operates similarly. He has fixed statutes, principles, and categories of experience given to him by the Halakhah to serve as his *a priori* concepts, just as the scientist has mathematical equations. He uses halakhic categories to experience and assess reality. When he encounters a specific phenomenon in the actual world, he correlates it with the *a priori* concepts of Halakhah. Soloveitchik articulates this in the following example:

> When halakhic man approaches a real spring [of water], he gazes at it and carefully examines its nature. He possesses, *a priori*, ideal principles and precepts which establish the character of the spring as a halakhic construct, and he uses the statutes for the purpose of determining normative law: does the real spring correspond to the requirements of the ideal Halakhah or not?
>
> (*Halakhic Man*, 20)

In this case, certain configurations of water = a *mikvah* (ritual bath). This conception of the ontology of the world descends from the legacy of the Briskers who claim, for example, that water halakhically unfit for a mikvah is just *not water* (Saiman 2018, 206). Using a *mikvah* under certain circumstances alters the legal status of objects in particular ways. Under the proper conditions for example, it can render an impure item pure. Other examples are not difficult to come by. A gathering of ten people who meet certain requirements is a quorum, a *minyan*. Halakhic man is constantly comparing gatherings of people to his *a priori* concept of *minyan*. He will ask himself if some group he encounters comprise a proper *minyan*. Certain articles of clothing require *tzitzit*, ritual fringes. Halakhic Man looks at clothing and instinctively evaluates whether or not they meet his *a priori* concept of a garment.

Throughout his speeches and essays, Soloveitchik provides numerous examples of halakhically set constructs and categories, for example, sanctity of land, sanctity of boundaries, all the inhabitants of a land (*Five Addresses*, 94), the Land of Israel which we possess by virtue of our forefathers (*On Repentance*, 103–4, 278), long and short versions of blessings (*Eulogy Heller*), *min-be-meno* (foods of the same type that mix), *biryah* (creature, living entity), *mum* (defect) (*Emergence Ethical*, 18, 20, 22), etc. These categories get fixed as structures in Halakhic Man. It is in his constant comparison of the real world with the *a priori* categories in his mind that Halakhic Man's task resembles that of Cognitive Man who is constantly comparing his own constructs and predetermined formulae with the physical world he observes.[90]

For the scientist, new discoveries require new concepts. Consider force, energy, matter, black hole, space, light, sound, lepton, simultaneity, string, epigenetics, species, mirror neurons, universe, and numerous other scientific phenomena that have recently been discovered. These all became integrated into the scientist's conceptual scheme for which she attempts to find correlating physical phenomena. For the Halakhic Man, new events and situations force a comparable creation of new halakhic categories. The State of Israel, for example, forced the creation of new categories, as there had never been a halakhically acknowledged Jewish government in a state that was not governed by halakhic principles. This forced Halakhic Men to become creative and devise new halakhic categories that would become part of the conceptual scheme for all subsequent generations of Halakhic Men.

This creation of concepts and the constant comparison of the world to the conceptual constructs in his head are what mold the cognitive consciousness of Halakhic Man.

Emotions: Halakhah molds the religious aspects of Halakhic Man

The study and practice of Halakhah forces one to see the world as Cognitive Man does, but can it also affect him spiritually? Can it also give rise to characteristics associated with Religious Man? We do not associate spirituality with Cognitive Man. Why then should we associate it with Halakhic Man? How does objective Halakhah mold Halakhic Man's subjective religious experience and consciousness in a way consistent with the best character traits of Religious Man?

We will answer this latter question in two ways on two levels. First, we will look to one of Soloveitchik's early works, *And From There You Shall*

Seek, where we find a very general answer to the question of how Halakhah molds and develops Halakhic Man's spiritual consciousness. We will see that Soloveitchik believes that when man is at his most vulnerable and open to change, when he is demoralized by his sins, mourning for a close relative, and when he is at his lowest spiritual level and when he feels morally, religiously, and emotionally bankrupt, the stage is set for him to discover God and return to Him (*On Repentance*, 133). When man properly proceeds through the halakhic regimen prescribed for such times, he develops the spiritual connection with his Creator that is unique to a Halakhic Man.

Moreover, Soloveitchik believes that each and every Halakhah is described by halakhic categories that their adherents can't but help to embody. Also, when the halakhot are performed properly, they each give rise to specific feelings, emotions, drives, goals, aspirations, and personality features within the Halakhic mind. We give examples of these later. Cumulatively the halakhot shape the personality of Halakhic Man; they define Halakhic Man.

And from There You Shall Seek: context

Soloveitchik tells us that *And from There You Shall Seek*[91] is about one of the most complicated problems in the philosophy of religion. It is about change, growth, and metamorphosis in religious life (*Halakhic Mind*, 130n98). It is in this work where " … I trace out the portrait of the character of the halakhic man in terms of his inner world, his obligation and his desire to run towards the Holy One Blessed be He" (*CCC*, 321), noting also that it is a spiritual autobiography—it " …is myself, it's my own experiences" (Holzer 2009a, 49).[92]

The essay's title *And from There You Shall Seek* is only two words in Hebrew, *U-Vikashtem mi-Sham*, and is taken from *Deuteronomy* (4:29). Its basic message states that when a person seeking God loses all hope, it is precisely at that moment that he feels God beckoning him, giving him the opportunity to find his way back. It is from there that man seeks God.

In broad terms the essay's two main themes are (in what we label "Part 1") to explain the role Halakhah plays in man's successful search for God and ("Part 2") to explain how Halakhah molds Halakhic Man's religious consciousness. As Shalom Carmy put it, Soloveitchik "undertook, in *U-Vikashtem miSham*, to map the phenomenology of man's encounter with God, with his starting point the fundamental datum of man who is confronted by revealed law …" (Carmy 1997a, 22). It does this over the course of twenty chapters[93] that can be grouped into an introduction, Part 1, Part 2, and a summary.

The introduction (Chapter 1) sets the stage with a metaphorical reading of *Song of Songs* in which man searches for God who reveals Himself, only to once again hide. Part 1 (chs. 2–14) describes a process whereby man successfully searches for God by ascending three successive layers of transcendence:

(a) Revelation (chs. 2–5), (b) Imitating God (chs. 6–10), and (c) Cleaving to God (chs. 11–14).[94] By studying, practicing, and creating Halakhah, man re-creates the event of revelation, that is, he recreates the Halakhah as given by God at Sinai. Imitating God, which is a biblically mandated commandment, enables man, ultimately, to cleave to God. Part 2 (chs. 15–19) describes how, having recreated the event of revelation by the study and practice of Halakhah, Halakhah, in turn, creates Halakhic Man's unique consciousness in three ways: via the intellectual process of deciding and developing Halakhah (Chapter 15); by elevating and sanctifying man's bodily functions, which makes them part of the halakhic experience (chs. 15–16); and finally, by re-enacting the original halakhic experience in the form of one generation teaching Torah to the next, recreating the original revelation at Sinai (chs. 17–19). The summary (Chapter 20) recapitulates Part 1.[95]

Part 1 uses Halakhah in a broad sense to include not only actual Jewish Laws such as imitating God and cleaving to Him but also Jewish norms and ideas borrowed from *midrash* (homily), mysticism (*kabbalah*), liturgy, etc. (cf. Chapter 3, Section "Torah study"). Part 2, however, (especially Chapters 15–16) speaks of Halakhah in a narrower sense to refer to the minutiae of Jewish Law: what Jews may eat, how and when to engage in sexual intimacy, etc. We begin with Part 1 to understand how one achieves the highest level of spirituality which culminates in cleaving to God.

And from There You Shall Seek: Part 1

LEVEL 1: REVELATION

In the "Personality" section, we discussed how Halakhic Man is a dialectical personality—a unique composite of Cognitive Man and Religious Man. We explained how these personalities clash with one another and how it is specifically this tension that makes Halakhic Man what he or she is. Although Part 1 of *And from There You Shall Seek* focuses on the search for God, we will show how Soloveitchik describes conflicting emotions and drives within Man (e.g., the need to approach God and retreat from Him; loving and fearing God; the experiences of love and awe) as he goes through each of the three layers of spiritual transcendence.[96] We will also show that it is specifically the conflict within each pair that helps develop Halakhic Man's personality.

Halakhic Man uses both the "cognitive" and "spiritual" aspects of his personality to search for God. Which one of these methods is ultimately successful in discovering Him? Soloveitchik argues that the rational scientific search for God (the natural religious experience) alone is inadequate. Searching for God in the beauty and orderliness of the universe will not reveal God. Arguments using categories resulting from our finite, contingent, temporal existence will not work to prove truths about the Eternal. We cannot make inferences from finitude to infinity, from temporality to eternity, or from physical to transcendent. Also, yearning for God through reality does not imbue man with faith. Merely observing the universe and searching for God within it cannot redeem man from his faults or give him happiness and purpose. Such rational cosmic religiosity devolves into pantheism, a mere step from atheism.[97] Man needs something more than his scientific side; he must also use his spiritual side, the revelational religious experience, to discover God. It is only then that man successfully develops a personal relationship with his Creator.

Contrary to Descartes' assumption (see Chapter 4, Section "Rationalism and empiricism"), consciousness of the world and self does not involve logical demonstrations or proofs. We know we exist and that the world exists without needing proof. So, too, with our consciousness of the Divine. If there is a world, if anything at all is real, then there is a God who is the foundation and origin of everything that exists. If there is a self, then there is a living personal God who fills our consciousness. The religious sensibility does not offer decisive proofs, draw inferences, or make deductions. It senses and experiences God in its innermost consciousness. There is a Barthian dialectical quality to the process of encountering God's presence.

In moments of inspiration, people hear the sound of the Lord. It is a powerful experience but an ephemeral one. Man uses his intellect to search for God, but when he reaches the limits of his intellect, he becomes alarmed and retreats. This is the crisis point at which God reveals Himself from beyond time and space.

> God revealed himself to Adam when he had sunk into the deep mire of the original sin ... The Israelites leave Egypt—as slaves ... who have not yet rid themselves of the filth of servitude ... —and God reveals himself ... They sin with the golden calf ... and the Holy One, Blessed Be He, comes down in a cloud from the heavenly plains and stands with Moses.
> (*AFTYSS*, 30)

Revelation is not a reply to man's quest or his longing. Man does not and cannot know when or why God will reveal himself. God surprises man. When man's desire to search has ended, when his heart is dulled and his soul frozen, God emerges from His isolation and reveals Himself to man (30).

When God reveals Himself, it is not to impart scientific knowledge but to command him and give him the responsibility for keeping the laws and statutes. God commands Jews to follow a unique way of life without explaining why or for what purpose. When man seeks God, he wants God to enlighten him about the universe and the essence and fate of man. But instead of finding the Hidden Intellect, he encounters the Inscrutable Will. Instead of revealing the secrets of creation, it demands unlimited discipline and absolute submission. "The Infinite, all powerful Will places man in a state of subjugation from which there is no release" (35).

The faith that comes with this first stage of revelation is available to everyone, not just to a spiritual elite. It emerges from fulfilling the commandments. Distinctions in intellectual or spiritual capacity are irrelevant. But although religion is democratic and open to everyone, it does allow an individual to ascend in his spirituality and have a unique religious experience. Everyone can fulfill the commandments. Only the elite, however, can rise above the Lord's congregation and fulfill the Halakhah, through deep comprehensive study of Torah (58–60).

Man searches for God. When he is at his lowest and has lost all hope, God reveals Himself. In so doing God does not explain the mysteries of the universe but rather offers man His commandments and asks man to submit to His will (35). This level of divine revelation is the first layer of religious consciousness and is available to everyone.

LEVEL 2: IMITATION

Once people have had a revelation of God, they can move on to the next stage and experience what generations of philosophers and theologians have called *imitatio Dei*, imitating God—one of Judaism's 613 commandments.[98] To reach this level of religious experience, man's religious consciousness must mature. He must move from a relationship with God that entails *love and fear*—a relationship of revelation attained by following commandments—to a more sophisticated relationship of *love and awe*. Man thus progresses to the next level of religious awareness by imitating God's attributes.

In both these relationships, there are moments when man approaches God and moments when man retreats. Both the approach and the retreat are religious experiences. The way Soloveitchik expresses this is reminiscent of what kabbalists call *ratzo va-shov*, "back and forth" or more literally "ran and returned." *Ratzo va-shov* is based on a phrase from *Ezekiel* 1:14 where the Prophet Ezekiel describes the "vision of the chariot" with "… the creatures … dashing *back and forth* like flashes of lightning." In Kabbalistic terminology *ratzo* is often the desire to break out of the "vessel," to leave one's physical body, to ascend and cleave to God, followed by *shuv*, the realization that fulfillment is accomplished only when one descends back to the physical world and worships God here below as he is meant to do. At this stage, Soloveitchik presents his understanding of approach to and flight from God.

When man is in the love/fear relationship with God, he approaches God to escape his fear of death and retreats from Him when he fears being punished for his sins. At this stage fear is the overriding motive.

Man lives with the existential fear of knowing he will ultimately die. He thus imagines God as a safe refuge in which he will be liberated from his suffering. Both his terror of death and his need to escape it draw him toward God. At that moment he experiences God's manifestation as a merciful Being, what the sages call "*midat ha-rahamim*" (47–49).

Sometimes God appears as an awesome and terrifying Judge, One Who demands subordination, self-sacrifice, and the fulfillment of His commandments. God punishes people who violate His law. At that moment, people experience God as a Judge, what the sages called *"midat ha-din"* (49–50). Recall that Soloveitchik, like numerous Jewish thinkers before him, repeatedly returns to God's dual nature, sometimes manifesting justice and at other times mercy. The experience of mercy and justice parallels the pragmatic need for a pleasant this-worldly existences, on the one hand, and the ability to sacrifice of oneself for God, on the other. God is the ultimate dialectical being, and similarly man, if he follows the Halakhah, dually manifests himself.

God's mercifulness causes man to love and approach Him. His justice causes man to fear and retreat from Him. Both the approach toward God and the retreat are religious experiences (51–53).

Trust in God, as expressed in the expectation of reward, and fear of God as expressed in the dread of punishment, are both necessary for religious consciousness, as is the desire to run toward Him and to flee Him. Halakhah restrains man with the promise of reward and punishment; it both frightens and reassures him (52).

The expectation of reward and punishment is crucial to religious consciousness. Limiting the religious experience to its spiritual aspect leads to the elimination of its grandeur and influence; one who has no fear has not subordinated himself to God. On the contrary, without fear one might imagine himself manipulating God for his personal everyday needs (54).

Though one must fear God prior to loving Him, God also wants man to worship him with joy. If man's sole experience of God is fear, his religious life is flawed and his service incomplete. On the other hand, if man ignores his obligation to the world and withdraws from it, he compromises his religious experience. Halakhah demands that man act within his community and take part in the development of the world (55–56).

How does a relationship to God transition from one involving love and fear to one involving love and awe? On the surface layer of our awareness, there is a dichotomy between our quest for God and our awareness of Him. On this surface layer, we seek reward and fear punishment. Below the surface, however, the desire for reward and the fear of punishment are transformed into love and awe (91–93).

Man begins to understand that not only did God create the world but also He encompasses everything. He is the continuous Force within it, and without God there is no world. With this clarity of understanding, man's experience of longing and fear transforms into an experience of love and awe. He seeks no reward, his love for God becomes unconditional, and he is willing to give up his life to share in the Essence of Being (61–63).

Awe is different from fear. Fear is instinctive and caused by the sense of an outside threat. A religion that focuses only on fear deteriorates into a religion of magic and superstition. Fear is incompatible with love, but awe is not (67).

In what can also be seen as an instance of *ratzo va-shov,* Soloveitchik describes the dialectical emotions of love of God and being in awe of Him. Man oscillates between being pulled toward God (love) and recoiling from Him (awe). Man runs toward God, for how can he distance himself from God and live? He retreats from God, for how is it possible to attach oneself to an all-consuming God? This running toward God and fleeing from Him, caused by love and awe, writes Soloveitchik, is the most magnificent form of worship (69).

Even as man endeavors to surrender himself to the Divine will, he desires the freedom to do what he believes is right. If man would truly cleave to God and accept His Will fully and unconditionally, he would attain absolute freedom from social pressures and human desires. Being unsuccessful in fully realizing this ideal, man instead tries to imitate God. It is an admission of failure, as if to say, "Even though I cannot cleave to Him, perhaps I may be able to imitate Him" (75–76).

Man imitates God's attributes by being merciful, slow to anger, charitable, etc. By internalizing and imitating these values, man convinces himself that he is acting with moral freedom. As he is struck by awe, however, he remembers his eternal subjugation to God. He oscillates between divine decree and individual creativity, between spontaneity and reverence for the revelational commands.

Imitating God is thus a step beyond experiencing revelation, but is not the ideal, not the highest spiritual plain. Man can reach higher. He can cling to God (81).

LEVEL 3: CLEAVING TO GOD

How is imitating God a stepping stone toward the ultimate spiritual level of cleaving to Him, to *d'veikut?*[99] In the first layer of religious consciousness, revelation, man experiences God through *love and fear* (cf. *Tanya* 8a). God is experienced as both a King and a Lover (*Maimonides Course,* 233). In the second layer, imitating God, man experiences Him through *love and awe.* In the final layer, cleaving, man experiences God through *pure love.* At this level, the repeating cycle of advancing out of love and recoiling out of dread, going back and forth, is transformed by man's absolute love for God, to an advance with no retreat—simply cleaving to Him.[100]

What does Soloveitchik mean by cleaving? Let us begin with what it is not. Cleaving is not merging. Judaism does not acknowledge man uniting with God but rather cleaving to Him. He does not deny his own essence and merge with God but rather affirms his essence and attaches it to God. Man comes closer to God when his life is filled with goals, initiatives, and actions so long as he does not imagine his own prideful, insolent independence (87–88).

While mystics understand God as an all-consuming fire which consumes man when he unites with Him, Halakhah understands cleaving as mandating that one should cleave to Torah scholars and others who live lives of value and elevation. Man is elevated when he joins with a like-minded community of those serving God. Contemplation without deeds and actions does not redeem man. He must fulfill the Halakhah, which is the most fundamental element in the realization of man's religious mission (88–89).

The reason for revelation is not that man be absolutely subservient or fearful but rather that he be totally redeemed (92). The main motive for God's revelation is His infinite love for His creatures and His desire for man to live a complete, meaningful, and redeemed existence (89).

Cleaving to God according to Halakhah entails mastering His knowledge, that is, the knowledge of Halakhah, and imitating His unity of *thought*, *will*, and *action*. Not only must we *master* the Halakhah (thought) but we must *commit* ourselves to its observance (will) and follow through with *acts* of lovingkindness, justice, and righteousness (actions) (93).

When thought leads to will, and will is transformed into action, the thinking, desiring, and achieving individual arrives at the level of cleaving to God. To know Him is to be a man of God with aspirations and achievements, in whom study and practice, knowledge and will, are blended together in a unified spiritual whole. God's word is His thought, His will, and His action. By imitating Him, we become like Him.

***

It is in this way that the Halakhah guides man, using conflicting drives and emotions toward spiritual transcendence that culminates in *d'veikot*, cleaving to God. Elsewhere Soloveitchik tells us that cleaving to God is the unique personal subjective aspect of a mitzvah (*First Rebellion*, 106). It is the part of the commandment that in a sense emerges, but is distinct from, the performance of the commandments themselves. But how exactly does this happen?

The epistemology and metaphysics of cleaving   Since cleaving to God is the ultimate achievement in becoming a Halakhic Man, we need to understand the nature of the cleaving process. What is the metaphysical and epistemological nature of cleaving to God? What are the mechanics of the cleaving process? How does one cleave? How many parts are there when two independent objects cleave to one another? Does it involve some kind of cognition or understanding? How does the study, knowledge, and fulfillment of Halakhah cause one to reach the point of cleaving to God (93–99)?

When we speak of knowledge or of knowing something, we imply that there are two entities: a knower and something to be known: a subject and an object. This is true even about self-knowledge. When we say one has self-knowledge, we consider a person to be thinking of herself in two ways: as subject and as object.

When we say, however, that God knows Himself or that God has knowledge of any sort, there is no distinction between Subject and Object (i.e., God and what God knows) for that would destroy His perfect Unity. God and His knowledge are One. Also, in light of God's uniqueness, when we speak about God and His world, there too is no distinction between Subject and Object. God is the One and the Only, since everything exists within Him. Two things follow from this: first that as far as God's self-understanding is concerned, there is no distinction between Subject and Object, and second that God does not understand the world as an independent finite world but as part of Himself.[101]

Now, since God is one with his knowledge and God is one with His world, the result is that when there is knowledge, there is cognitive unity between the subject and the object. When one grasps the essence of a Halakhah, one thus unites his knowledge with God. That is when the process of cleaving to God begins. The one difference between God's cognition and man's is that God's cognition is continuous while man's starts and stops.

Echoing Kant, Dilthey, Scheler, and others, Soloveitchik sees cognition as a metaphysical act of joining the knower to that which can be known (Munk 1996, ch. 1, 1999, 119). The world is both the object of God's knowledge and human knowledge. By knowing the word of God, that is, the Halakhah, the individual knows the Creator and cleaves to Him. Man must, however, also imitate God in the sense that His Thought, Will, and Action are one. To cleave to God, one must imitate Him: he must know His commandments (thought), desire to obey them (will), and actually perform them (action).[102]

Soloveitchik writes in the summary of *AFTYSS* (Chapter 20) that "[a]ctive participation in the work of reconstructing the content of revelation is the goal of Judaism as it wends its way through three levels of transcendent consciousness." Reconstructing the content of revelation means determining the primordial Halakhah. How does one do this? By studying and analyzing Halakhah and by performing its dictates, one puts oneself on the path toward the highest spiritual level.

Having established on a *macro* level how studying Halakhah and acting according to its strictures cause man to cleave to God and ascend to the highest spiritual level, Soloveitchik proceeds (chs. 15–19) to show how Halakhah, on a *micro* level, develops man's spiritual aspects—how man develops the personality traits associated with Religious Man.

And from There You Shall Seek: Part 2

Part 2 of *And from There You Shall Seek* studies the inner world of Halakhic Man from a different perspective. Part 1 is primarily concerned with Halakhah's role, broadly construed, and man's desire and obligation to connect with God. In the following discussion of Part 2, Soloveitchik focuses on specific functions of Halakhah that help develop the inner world of Halakhic Man. He does this in three different ways. The first paragraph of Chapter 15 (107) summarizes Soloveitchik's approach:

Judaism's aspiration to raise human consciousness to the level of spiritual consciousness, a level which combines the natural human aspiration for God with revelational faith, is manifested in three ways: (1) the rule of the intellect; (2) the elevation of the body; (3) the perpetuity of God's word.

To clarify, Judaism develops man's spirituality: (1) by having the human mind reconstruct the Halakhah as it was revealed at Sinai; (2) by regulating bodily functions such as eating and procreation; and (3) by equating one generation transmitting Torah to the next, with the original revelation of the Oral Torah at Sinai, making it accessible to all subsequent generations, even to those which did not physically stand at Sinai.

THE ROLE OF THE INTELLECT

In *Halakhic Man* and other works, Soloveitchik explains how the study of Torah is an intellectual activity analogous to the activity performed by a scientist. Whatever the role of the scientist analogy is in other works, here its function is to show how the study of Torah develops Halakhic Man's consciousness.

Studying the Torah is a cognitive function like any other intellectual activity. While Torah was revealed at Sinai it is up to the scholar to derive new ideas from old ones and to create new and original halakhic concepts and methods. The only authority in deciding Halakhah is reason, and while there can be no change or reform within Halakhah, there is unlimited opportunity for creativity and innovation.

For Soloveitchik, it is clear that those who disparage Judaism and say that the Halakhah has become fossilized have never properly studied a page of Talmud nor partaken in the creativity and innovation of doing Halakhah. The sweep and scope of its deductive creative thought, its analytic acuity, its subtlety of abstraction, and its systemic consistency are at least the equal of other abstract and precise intellectual disciplines. This is the first way that Halakhah shapes and transforms man's inner world (107–10).

ELEVATING THE BODY

Soloveitchik argues that *halakhot,* which pertain to mundane bodily functions—those which dictate what we may eat, when and how we may be sexually intimate, etc.—are precisely those which imbue us with holiness. Halakhah aims to sanctify man's body, refine the bestial aspects of human life, and raise them to the level of divine service. This process does not take place through denial and deprivation but by stamping the natural aspects of human existence with direction and purpose. Halakhah does not forbid the pleasures of this world, nor does it demand asceticism. It enjoins man to take pleasure in the glory and splendor of creation but in a refined, measured, and purified manner.

The animalistic behavior of eating, upon which man's life depends, has been refined by Halakhah into a religious ritual and elevated moral act. When someone eats sacrificial meat, he also feeds strangers, orphans, and widows. Such eating constitutes not only religious worship but also an act of social morality, including needy people in the circle of one's enjoyment.[103]

In the eyes of Halakhah, eating in the presence of God is a higher priority than prayer. This eating is not a mysterious symbolic form of worship. It is the ordinary eating that man enjoys and with which he satisfies his hunger. Even wine, the symbol of licentiousness and drunkenness, is transformed into the (halakhic construct of the) cup over which blessings are recited.

While Greek thought attempts to give the dinner table (the *symposium*[104]) the character of an intellectual gathering devoted to philosophical discussion, Judaism refuses to do this; it dedicates the dinner table not to human intellectual matters but to divine matters—to discussions of the Torah received from God. When man eats properly, in accordance with the requirements of Halakhah, he is eating before God.

Neither Greek philosophy nor Christianity grasped the moral and metaphysical aspects of sexual intimacy. Only Halakhah gives this act a solid basis in religious life. The commandment to be "fruitful and multiply" (*Genesis* 1:28) is the first in the Torah. The same Halakhah that forbids sexual intimacy when the wife is menstruating also imposes a duty upon man to have periodic relations with his wife out of love and affection. Halakhah established the concept of "intimacy which fulfills a commandment."

Man worships his Creator with his body: via eating and sexual activity, for example, and therein lies the greatness of Halakhah. By sanctifying the body, it creates a unified man who worships God with his spirit and his body, elevates the beast within him, and contributes to the development of his inner spiritual life (110–21).

THE PERPETUITY OF GOD'S WORD

Halakhah molds man's character and consciousness via study and sanctification of the body. But there is a final component: transmission of Halakhah. Not only is man a link in the transmission of the Halakhah, but when he transmits the Torah to the next generation, he reenacts the revelation at Sinai—the central experience of Jewish history.

Revelation never ends. The revelation of the Holy Presence (*shekhinah*) at Sinai flows as waves over the course of time. The perpetuation of the revelation involves the transmission and receiving of the Oral Torah from generation to generation. This act is not merely a matter of teachers or parents telling their children about the Halakhah. It is the joining together of all generations with the original revelation at Sinai.

A master of the Halakhah sees himself not only as a transmitter of the Halakhah but also, in a sense, as though his words were emanating from Sinai. The individual and the community come together through an act of historical identification with the past and the future. Halakhic Man is united with all generations of Jews, and he understands himself as such (139–48).

We thus understand how the broad character of Halakhic Man is fashioned via the roles of his intellect, his bodily functions, and as a transmitter of Halakhah. Many details, however, remain to be filled in. What is the *specific* connection between each individual Halakhah and the individual unit of Halakhic Man's personality? To understand this, we must now leave our discussion of *And from There You Shall Seek* and examine Soloveitchik's treatment of individual commandments. While he did not discuss every commandment, we can extrapolate lessons from the commandments he did discuss in depth. We focus on three: mourning, repentance, and prayer.

Mourning develops Halakhic consciousness: Out of the Whirlwind

People speak about religious experiences today, trying to stimulate religious experiences with drugs ... But one cannot get a religious experience—that is, a Jewish religious experience—without utilizing the materials of Halakhah. There can be no philosophy of science or nature unless one is an expert in the fields of physics, chemistry and biology ... So, too, it is impossible for one to philosophize about Judaism ... without having the Halakhah at his fingertips (*OOTW*, 9, 10).

Halakhah shapes Halakhic Man's religious consciousness on multiple levels. On the macro level, as we saw in a somewhat abstract discussion of *And from There You Shall Seek*, the halakhic life helps one ascend through three levels of religious consciousness: on the first level, man encounters God's revelation; on the second, he imitates God, and finally on the highest level, he cleaves to Him, *d'veikut*. For Soloveitchik, at a certain point Halakhic Man's personality itself, via its understanding of Halakhah, cleaves to God.

We also saw that on a micro level, individual halakhot such as eating and sexual intimacy help elevate Halakhic Man's religious psyche and shape his halakhic categories. These examples, however, are rather limited. We, therefore, now turn our attention to other writings and lectures by Soloveitchik, to examine how other halakhot—specifically repentance, prayer, and mourning—concretely shape particular aspects of Halakhic Man's religious consciousness.[105]

There are many individual *halakhot* about which Soloveitchik left an extensive legacy regarding their details, their levels of meaning, and the relationship between the laws and the consciousness of Halakhic Man. He subjected them to intense scrutiny, allowing us to extract a clear picture of his understanding of the relationship between the act of the Halakhah (i.e., the performance of the commandment) and the cognitive, psychological, and spiritual experience it evokes in a Halakhic Man. As Soloveitchik understands it, the halakhic and phenomenological are intimately related, and the goal of Jewish philosophy is to understand that relationship, in essence, to reconstruct one from the other. When reading Soloveitchik, we must pay careful attention to the experiences that each commandment is said to evoke. In so doing, we are rewarded with a deep understanding of this core aspect of Soloveitchik's Jewish philosophy.

Mourning shapes religious consciousness

Ritual halakhic mourning thoroughly dominates one's life during the period following the death of a relative.[106] It is a topic whose laws and philosophical import preoccupied Soloveitchik for long periods of his life especially following the deaths of his father and his wife. For Soloveitchik, mourning and repentance are two successive steps of a single process. When a person is in a state of mourning, he is also motivated to repent. "The aching heart is a contrite heart, and a contrite heart is, of course, an atoning heart" (*OOTW*, 5). In a sense, mourning can be viewed as the first step leading to repentance, individual providence, and prophecy.

Two types of mourning

Halakhah recognizes two types of mourning, each with its own stages and styles of grief. The first type of mourning, "individual mourning," follows the loss of a close relative; one mourns a personal loss. The second type of mourning, "historical mourning," is when the Jewish people as a whole collectively mourn for a historical calamity that occurred in the distant past. Halakhah dictates what a mourner should do and how he should feel while simultaneously being cognizant of the emotions and feelings swirling in his mind. This is true for both kinds of mourning (*OOTW*, 9–30).

Individual Mourning (*Avelut Hadashah*). When a close relative dies, Halakhah acknowledges two distinct stages of grief: *aninut* and *avelut*. The period of *aninut* starts at the time of the death of the relative and ends when the deceased is buried. During this stage, Halakhah relieves the mourner of any obligations to perform positive commandments—except, of course, for the obligation of burying the deceased. The exemption from performing other commandments is based on the halakhic principle that one who is involved in one commandment (here, burying the deceased) is relieved of simultaneously being obligated to perform other commandments.

There is, however, another reason why a mourner is exempt from positive commandments: Halakhah recognizes that one is not in a proper state of mind to perform them. It is at this point when a man cannot but help ask the quintessential existential question: "If death is the final destiny of men, if everything human terminates in the narrow, dark grave, then why be a man at all?" (*OOTW*, 2). The obligation to perform commandments is associated with people who are preoccupied with life and not with one who has just encountered death. During this stage, Halakhah encourages people to experience their dark emotions. They must act like human beings. They must cry, weep, despair, grieve, and mourn. They feel as if they are alone and cut off from God.

The *kaddish* prayer recited by the mourner after the burial marks the turning point from *aninut* to *avelut*. At this stage, Halakhah demands an about-face and insists that man is capable of mastering not only his deeds but also his emotions. Halakhah, which was tolerant of man's dark emotions during *aninut,* commands him now to disengage from his black mood and re-engage with the community as his grief slowly recedes (*OOTW*, 1–8).

This re-engagement is well scripted to gradually pull the mourner back into communal life. First the seven-day period—the *shiva*—occurs where the mourner is surrounded by family, friends, and members of his community. This is followed by the *shloshim*—the thirty-day period in which mourners may not marry or attend communal festive meals, and, in a public display of mourning, men do not shave or get their hair cut. In the following ten or eleven months, while most acts of mourning are eliminated, the mourner continues to engage with the community and recites the mourner's *kaddish* prayer in the synagogue. The dead are still remembered throughout a mourner's lifetime on the anniversary of the deaths and on holidays in which the *yizkor* prayer is recited.

Historical Mourning (Avelut Yeshanah). Historical mourning involves the Jewish community collectively mourning for a calamity (e.g., the destruction of the Temple) that befell the Jewish people in the distant past. Soloveitchik points out that the laws of individual mourning and those of historical mourning are very different. In individual mourning, Halakhah guides the mourner through a series of ever-decreasing stages of mourning and grief. The first seven days are the most extreme, followed by the first thirty days which are less so, and finally, the balance of the year which is the least restrictive. Halakhah thereby reflects the reality of human nature. As time passes, the tragedy recedes from memory, and so too does the emotional pain. Halakhah thus decreases the mourning rituals as time passes.

In the case of historical mourning, however, the process is reversed. There is no spontaneous reaction to the historical event; it happened a long time ago. It is, therefore, necessary for Halakhah to build up the community's sensitivity to the historic tragedy. In the case of commemorating the destruction of the Holy Temple in Jerusalem, the annual mourning begins with the period of "the three weeks," which has the fewest halakhic rituals and restrictions, followed by the first day of the month of Av, followed by the week in which the Ninth of Av (Tisha B'Av) occurs, and finally, the most extreme mourning, which takes place on the Ninth of Av itself.

The laws of mourning work in opposite directions for the two types of mourning to account for the differing psychological realities. In a period of "historical mourning," Halakhah guides a person through successive stages of *increased* mourning. In "individual mourning" Halakhah guides a person through successive stages of *decreased* mourning. *Halakhah* shapes not only man's actions but also his emotions and his religious consciousness surrounding tragic events. Deviation from proper halakhic mourning or excessive mourning is explicitly forbidden regardless of the level of personal grief. Halakhah would view that as engendering an illegitimate psychological state. One's mind would not be in harmony with the halakhic norm.

The most interesting and important scientific work in circulation on the nature of mourning in Soloveitchik's time would have been Sigmund Freud's *Mourning and Melancholia*. Published in 1917, it anticipates what we now think of as clinical depression. It compares, and importantly, contrasts grief, as a response to the loss of something or someone beloved, with melancholic depression. Freud explains that mourning is a healthy process that one consciously passes through and cannot be subverted. Melancholia on the other hand is pathological; it is not a result of a loss or a loss that the melancholic can easily identify. Melancholics often turn inward and blame themselves for their grief. Soloveitchik similarly sees mourning as a halkhically sanctioned healthy process but believes that in the same way that the halakhic ritual of individual mourning is so similar to the privations of Yom Kippur, the halakhic phenomenological instinct is to turn inward, to experience guilt, to understand that death is a consequence of human imperfection, and that we often do not appreciate things—man or God— until it is gone from our lives. This mindset engenders feelings of guilt and compels one to repent.

In both private and communal mourning, the halakhic mourner's task is to ask oneself what the experience of mourning teaches the mourner. Halakhic mourning makes demands on the mourner that impact the psychological condition. The process of mourning—both the natural experiences and the shape they take on once they are guided by Halakhah—should cause one to experience certain emotions. They should give rise, for example, to fear and anxiety; they should inspire one to repent (connecting repentance and mourning). For Soloveitchik, it is these emotions of fear and anxiety, the sense that we accept the tragedy, etc., that are the proper *kiyyum hamitzvah*. The *fulfillment* of mourning, as opposed to the *act* of mourning, begins with the feeling of loneliness and grief and culminates with the desire to repent. Without these emotions and drives, halakhic mourning is incomplete; it was not done properly. We next turn to repentance to see its function in Halakhic Man's consciousness.

Repentance develops Halakhic consciousness: On Repentance

Soloveitchik's thoughts on repentance are scattered throughout his works and are elaborated upon in *Halakhic Man* (Part 2, ch. III), in a collection of his reconstructed lectures contained in *On Repentance,* as well as in other smaller works. We digress first for a brief discussion of earlier characterizations of repentance which Soloveitchik was well aware of and from which he drew in his own account of the nature of repentance and in the phenomenological consequences that repentance has for the development of Halakhic Man.

Hermann Cohen on repentance

Jewish sources from the Bible to contemporary popular works contain extensive discussion of the nature, form, and purpose of atonement, or repentance. The most prominent Jewish source is certainly Maimonides' *Laws of Repentance* from his *Mishneh Torah,* and to a lesser extent his *Guide to the Perplexed*, though other medieval sources, such as Bachya ibn Paquda's *Duties of the Heart,* are important as well. Another classic source is *Sha'arei Teshuva,* by Rabbenu Yona of Girona (d. 1264), one of Maimonides' contemporaries who, according to legend, wrote this book as penance for his role in the Maimonidean controversies. This latter book is a detailed analysis of the means and mechanics of repentance. Although Soloveitchik disagrees with the book on important points, he draws upon it, as he does from a wide range of classic Jewish literature. He also draws on nonrabbinic sources in his analysis of repentance. Two of the most interesting nontraditional sources from which Soloveitchik draws and makes quite creative use are Hermann Cohen's *Religion of Reason* and Max Scheler's essay "Repentance and Rebirth."

As mentioned earlier, Hermann Cohen's philosophical work wielded considerable influence over Soloveitchik.[107] Cohen dedicates a number of essays and Chapter XI of *Religion of Reason* to the concept of repentance. One of Cohen's main aims is to argue for the political right of Jews, as Germans, to remain Jewish and religiously separate but simultaneously culturally integrated into the larger German society. To do this he must explain Judaism's contribution to German civilization and to the universal religion of reason of which, he believed, Judaism is a prime example.

The chapter of Cohen's book that deals with repentance is a linchpin for his thesis and plays a pivotal role in the rest of his analysis of Judaism as a religion of reason. Cohen attempts to understand the nature of sin and in course, the nature of the individual sinner. The discussion is pivotal because sin and forgiveness are important transformative experiences that turn man from a mere individual into an "I," an autonomous, reborn, moral, and rational creature in control of his destiny. This creature is not a mere biological member of the human species, but rather one who has transcended his own individuality and is, in essence, a part of humanity, not merely a sociological creature who merely interacts with other individuals.[108] For Cohen, the goal of ethics is the dissolution of the individual. The individual is biological and isolated (178). Repentance for Cohen—though not for Maimonides—is to liberate man from sin and transform him from a mere individual to an "I" to a point where he is master of himself and no longer subject to fate (194). This is something that only repentance can accomplish (187).

Cohen argues that repentance is a process that begins with remorse, followed by a confession of guilt and casting away sin, and culminates in the creation of a new spirit, a new "I" (203). This new "I" is characterized by its infinite all-pervasive nature and purpose that must be fulfilled by man alone and not by God (198). It also involves repenting for one's sinful life as a whole and not merely for specific sins (205). The self-purification (*tahara*) and the self-sanctification (*kedusha*) of repentance must be performed by man but be directed toward God alone, who provides forgiveness and pardon (*seliḥa u-meḥila*).

Recall from our earlier discussion (Chapter 4, Section "Hermann Cohen and neo-Kantianism") that Cohen defends the Kantian idea that religion of reason is a religion not of law but of ethics, and Judaism is an example, *par excellence*, of such a religion. It is for this reason that Cohen claims that on Yom Kippur, one repents publicly only for violating moral prohibitions (219). Moreover, one only repents with and for the community, because this is how one goes from being biological and isolated to transcending one's own individuality and destiny. One goes from merely interacting with others to being integrated into a whole community by internalizing responsibility for the collective. In this, an individual acknowledges suffering as God's providence, forcing the former to recognize the pure monotheistic nature of the Latter. The individual recognizes, in accordance with religion of reason, the ethical nature of God.

For Cohen, repentance is a core point of monotheism. Without it, man cannot become self-sanctified and consequently fulfill his purpose on earth. For Soloveitchik too, repentance is pivotal to the creation of a Halakhic Man. It is a vital stepping stone to the highest level of service to God: prophecy.

Max Scheler on repentance

Max Scheler's (1874–1928) influence on the history of philosophy in general and on Soloveitchik in particular is still underappreciated largely due to Nazi repression. As an anti-fascist with two Jewish parents, his works were suppressed between 1933 and 1945 and his reputation never recovered.[109] But in Soloveitchik's time, he was well known. The philosopher William Barrett recalls a conversation with Hannah Arendt in which she described the powerful influence Scheler had on the philosophic youth of Germany in the 1920s (Kelly 1977, 8).

We have already had an opportunity to speak about Scheler's phenomenology of religion (Chapter 4, Section "The emergence of phenomenology") and his political philosophy (Chapter 4, Section "The Community"). In "Repentance and Rebirth" (in Scheler 1987), a 1921 essay in vogue when Soloveitchik was in Berlin, Scheler addresses the nature of repentance. In part, the essay argues for rejecting certain characterizations of repentance. He rejects Nietzsche's view, for example, that repentance is a kind of inner deception whereby one tells oneself that he could have initially refrained from the sin, which now puts him in the position of being unable to endure the image of himself as having committed the sin in the first place (91) (see Rynhold and Harris 2018, ch. 5). Another view that Scheler rejects is that repentance is a form of self-punishment for having done something bad.

Scheler charges that then recent philosophers almost invariably saw repentance as a negative act, highly uneconomical, superfluous, pointless, and senseless (90, 93). Scheler rejects three other "modern views" of repentance: the "fear-theory"—a kind of wish that one hadn't done something which is precipitated by his fear of punishment; the "hangover theory"—a state of depression or moral hangover when the aftereffects have proven harmful and unpleasant; and finally, repentance as a "psychological malady." These rejected explanations view repentance as spiritual deadweight and self-deception (93) that are supposed to leave the penitent spiritually where he was, pre-sin.

Scheler instead sees repentance as the way the soul heals itself. In religion it is the mechanism through which God endows man with the ability to return whenever he strays (94). The consequence of every act in a person's life is fully actualized only after the person has lived his entire life. Therefore, so long as he is alive a penitent can redirect the negative effects of his past evil actions (95). Everything in our past might

> still be genuinely altered in its *meaning* and *worth* ... every event of our past remains *indeterminate* in significance and *incomplete* in value until it has yielded *all* its potential effects ... Therefore, the extent and nature of the effects that every part of our past may exercise upon the sense of our life lie still within our power at *every* moment of our life ... Even this "senseless" attempt alters the unalterable and places the regretted conduct or attitude in a new relation within the totality of one's life, setting it to work in a new direction (95–97, *emphasis* in the original).

If a person does something bad and later repents, he is no longer the same person who committed the original act. True repentance—when a person acknowledges his past sin and undertakes to act differently—burns away a person's previous inclinations and desires for evil and builds the person anew. From its inception, repentance contains the blueprint of a new man with a new heart (104). Repentance "cannot drive out of the world the external natural reality of the deed and its causal consequences ... All that stays in the world. But it can totally kill and extinguish the *reactive* effect of the deed within the human soul" (113). Such genuine repentance puts an individual in an even better place than he would have been had he never sinned.

Scheler's views, or variants of them, are represented in some of the most interesting parts of Soloveitchik's lectures and writings on repentance. Changing the projection and the consequences of one's past sins and recreating oneself through repentance are major motifs in both Scheler's and Soloveitchik's thought on repentance.[110] Though Soloveitchik believes that future acts dominate the past, while Scheler (like proponents of the Mussar movement) seems to think that the present rules over the past, both of them are uncomfortable thinking of time as immutable in the way physicists typically do. The role of repentance is crucial to religious thought, and Soloveitchik views it as the first step in the development of Halakhic Man's personality. It is part of a chain of events leading to individual providence, which can ultimately raise a person to the spiritual heights required of prophets.

Repentance shapes Halakhic consciousness

Throughout his works and lectures, Soloveitchik repeatedly discusses repentance, especially in his annual lectures delivered from 1962 to 1974 during the Ten Days of Repentance between Rosh Hashanah and Yom Kippur.[111]

In typical Brisker fashion, Soloveitchik distinguishes between two types of repentance derived from Maimonides' conflicting statements. In one instance Maimonides writes that when one repents, the person must verbalize the sin; in another instance he writes that one need not do so.

Soloveitchik claims that Religious Man, for whom repentance serves to merely divest him from the legal/semantic category of a wicked person (*rasha*), has no need to verbalize his sin. If one is wicked and repents, the individual is no longer considered a wicked person. Hence, the statement in the Talmud that declares that if a woman accepts a betrothal from a man who says "be betrothed to me on the condition that I am righteous," they are in fact betrothed regardless of how wicked he actually is, because he might have had thoughts of repentance in his heart (*Halakhic Man*, 110ff).

On the other hand, for Halakhic Man, repentance requires what philosophers call a "speech act" (Austin 1962). Soloveitchik claims that this verbal act is a separate function of repentance. This part of halakhic repentance is the first step in a three-stage process (i.e., repentance, individual providence, and prophecy) that shapes religious consciousness and creates a new I.[112]

STAGE 1—REPENTANCE (*HALAKHIC MAN* 2:3)

The Talmud states that when a person repents, his past sins are transformed into meritorious acts (*Yoma* 86b; *Halakhic Man,* 116). It also states (*Berakhot* 34b) that a penitent is on a higher spiritual level than one who never sinned. By what metaphysical magic is a sin transformed into a meritorious act? A sin, after all, unleashes a series of unfortunate events. For example, if a man were to be unfaithful to his wife, it could unleash a chain of events leading to the breakdown of his marriage and cause pain to many people.

By what mechanism does such a sin, upon repentance, metamorphize into a meritorious act? Can repentance undo all the damage the sin wrought? Also, why do the sages claim a penitent to be spiritually superior to one who never sinned? We would think, *prima facie*, that at best a sin and subsequent repentance would cancel one another out, like removing a stain from a shirt, leaving the individual at best in the same place as one who never sinned. We would not think that the penitent would be better.

Soloveitchik explains that when a man repents, he alters the trajectory of the chain of events which would have flowed from his sin. If a man is unfaithful to his wife, his marriage would likely disintegrate. If he were to fully repent, however, he would change the chain of cause and effect put in motion by his sin, his family life could be rebuilt. By repenting, a person causes a different series of events to flow from the original sin. He has thus changed the nature of the original sin, and having done so, he has re-created himself as a very different person; he constructed a new I who is superior to his former self.

When a person realizes he has sinned, he has the opportunity to develop religiously through a process that starts with repentance (*teshuvah*), is followed by individual providence (divine supervision of an individual; *hashgahah peratit*), and leads ultimately to a level associated with prophecy (*nevuah*).

When Religious Man (e.g., a Christian Religious Man) sins, he is depressed. He mourns for the yesterdays that can never be changed, and repentance is but a shield against punishment. Halakhic Man, however, neither weeps nor despairs. He repents as an act of self-recreation. He regrets the past and resolves to act differently in the future. He severs himself from his previous I and becomes a new I.[113]

Repentance consists of (1) reflecting upon the past and separating out that which is living from that which is dead; (2) developing a vision of the future in which one distinguishes between a future that is already present (i.e., a future he could expect if he does not repent) and one that has not as yet been "created"; and (3) examining the cause located in the past in light of the future, determining its direction and destination.

Past, present, and future in this sense unite. The past joins with the future and are both reflected in the present. Past sins can engender future *mitzvot* which in turn transform the past sins.

The idea of the future reigning over the past does not make much sense in physics, where we generally assume causes precede their effects. But in this context, a different logic is in play. (Recall Soloveitchik's epistemic pluralism [Chapter 4, Section "The argument of *The Halakhic Mind*"] in which different domains may use their own internal logics and methodologies.) Great men utilize their past sins to achieve admirable goals. "In the place where repentant sinners stand, even the wholly righteous cannot stand" (*Berakhot,* 34b; Maimonides *Law of Repentance,* 7:4).

STAGE 2—INDIVIDUAL PROVIDENCE (*HALAKHIC MAN*, 2:5)

Aristotle (and Plato in a different way) understood the objects in the world in terms of the combined abstract forms of things and the matter that actually makes them up. He believed that form, that is, a universal idea, is real and makes up an authentic existence. Matter (and by extension an individual person) does not attain the level of authentic existence but is only an image of the universal idea (form). Halakhah, however, proclaims that an individual (matter) can achieve authentic existence and immortality. How does Maimonides reconcile Aristotle's view with Halakhah?

To explain both immortality and divine providence, Maimonides places man in a special category. Divine providence and immortality for all species other than man apply only to the universal (form) but not to the particular individual (matter). For man, however, it depends. If an individual is passive, then his divine providence is only a general type of providence provided for him as a member of the species man. If a man is active and a creator, then his existence is in the arena of "form." His intellect transcends his "matter," and he achieves individual immortality and divine providence commensurate with his actions.

Whether or not a person attains divine providence and immortality is a decision the individual must make. If his actions are deemed worthy by God, he becomes a man of God in all its splendor, and he cleaves to the absolute Infinity and the glorious "divine overflow" (*shefa*). If he is unworthy, he ends up as just one more example of the biological species, man.

Achieving Divine providence is a commandment and is the stage that follows repentance. Man is obligated to broaden the scope and strengthen the intensity of the individual providence that watches over him. When a person creates (or re-creates) himself, ceases to be a mere member of species man, and becomes a man of God, he has fulfilled this commandment.

STAGE 3—PROPHECY (*HALAKHIC MAN* 2:6)

The principle of prophecy as an article of faith requires one to believe that prophecy is real, that is, that God causes men to prophesize. It also demands of man that he aspire to the rank of a prophet, even though prophecy is solely dependent on Divine grace. When a person reaches the peak—prophecy—he has fulfilled his task as a creator and becomes a different type of person. (See *I Sam.* 10:6, *"And the spirit of the Lord will come upon thee, and thou shalt prophesy with them, and shalt be turned into another man."*)

Put in somewhat medieval Aristotelian terms, once a man actualizes the universal form, that is, he connects himself to the "intellect of God," he acquires a particular form (*tzurah*) (as opposed to being mere raw undifferentiated matter [*homer*]).[114] He then achieves an individual mode of existence (*hashgahah peratit*), a unique personality, and an active and creative spirit. He leaves behind the general domain of being a mere member of the human species and enters his own personal domain as an individual.

Through repentance, man recreates himself anew and raises his religious consciousness from that of a sinner to one who is worthy of divine providence. By excelling in his service to God, he further elevates himself to the level of a prophet.

While this appears to be a spiritual account of repentance, and indeed it is, it is also a psychological and phenomenological account. Prophecy is not merely an ability or an event but also a state of mind. While prophecy is something bequeathed by God, it is not something *merely* bequeathed by God. The individual must undertake the proper mental preparation. The same holds true for divine providence and creativity. These are complex modes of thinking, categorizing, and reflecting on the world and are all part of the personality of Halakhic Man. When one repents, he is in a new frame of mind. His mind is open and configured differently than it previously had been. It is in a state in which it could never have been without repentance. Repentance is thus a prime example of how Halakhah shapes the Halakhic Mind. Let us now turn to another part of Halakhah which shapes a worldview: prayer.

Prayer develops Halakhic consciousness: "Thoughts on Prayer"

Published together with the first (Hebrew) printing of *And from There You Shall Seek* is a small essay in which Soloveitchik puts forth a prototype of a detailed halakhic, philosophical, and phenomenological analysis of a specific commandment: prayer. It illustrates how Soloveitchik understands the relationship between the proper performance of a religious commandment and the effect it has on the Halakhic Mind.

In the essay, "Thoughts on Prayer," Soloveitchik uses "prayer" to refer primarily to the weekday *Amidah* prayer, also known as the *Shemoneh Esreh* or "eighteen" benedictions, as recited by observant Jews three times daily: morning, afternoon, and night.[115] The morning and afternoon *Amidah* prayers are in lieu of or correspond to the twice-daily sacrifice in the Temple, which in turn are reminiscent of the Binding of Isaac. The prayer is comprised of a string of blessings. While the first three and the last three blessings of the *Amidah* are common to all prayer services throughout the year, the inner blessing(s) vary in number and content from weekday to Sabbath to holidays.

Soloveitchik understands the essence of prayer as worship of the heart, as words directed toward God that reflect our inner subjective experience. When prayer does not reflect what is in our heart, it is not meaningful. Prayer is stormy and full of doubts, as it is rooted in the dialectic nature of man. It reflects man's opposing emotions and feelings which move from heights to valleys to heights.

Soloveitchik struggles to understand how someone can approach a transcendent God and petition for his personal needs, something done repeatedly during prayer. He offers three justifications: The first is a philosophical/psychological explanation. It is impossible to exist without the ability to express one's inner feelings. Second, a historical reason: there is a precedent for prayer from the patriarchs and matriarchs. Finally, a Halakhic reason: prayer is a proxy for the twice-daily sacrifices that had been offered in the Holy Temple in Jerusalem.

Prayer is not just an aspect of life; rather, all of life is entwined with it. Worship of the heart is continuous with the way we live our lives. Our actions must parallel the righteousness and sincerity of our prayers; otherwise, our prayers are worthless.

Prayer parallels the dialectical character of the religious experience. As we saw in *And from There You Shall Seek*, man loves God and fears Him; man yearns and retreats. As man recites the first three blessings of the *Amidah* prayer, his dialectical experiences are awakened. In the first blessing known as "Fathers,"[116] he feels joy as he envisions God's loving-kindness (*hesed*). From the first generation to the last, God partners with lowly man and listens to his entreaties. In an instant, fully cognizant of the dialectic that permeates man's approach to prayer, the mood changes from love to dread, terror, fear, and insignificance, as man moves from the "Fathers" blessing to the second blessing of "Strength."[117] Reciting this next blessing, the worshipper feels empty and worthless. God is all powerful, and man is weak. Man cannot even provide for his own needs. He turns toward God and lays his prayers before Him as a slave before his master. He is prepared to ask God for unearned loving-kindness. When he encounters the third blessing, "Holiness of God,"[118] he is filled with dread; he is prepared to give himself over fully to God. The prayer thus reflects the full range of Halakhic Man's psychological existence.

Toward the end of the *Amidah* (the *Avodah,* i.e., the 17th blessing), we ask God to accept our prayers as a fire offering. In the plain sense, the prayer applies to the fire offerings brought in the Temple. The fire offering was a sacrifice that stayed on the altar until it was completely burnt. Soloveitchik notes, however, that the *Avodah* blessing can also be referring to the fire offerings inherent in our daily prayers. Meaning, God created the universe and commanded Jews to observe His laws. In violating the laws, one forfeits the right to exist. In the Temple, when Jews sinned, they would bring a sacrifice. Watching the animal being slaughtered would invoke within the sinner a subjective phenomenological experience of forfeiting his life. Although God had outlawed human sacrifice, the concept remains. When we recite the *Avodah* blessing, we ought to imagine that we are ready to give up our very life for God.[119]

The Binding of Isaac was the ultimate and most perfect subjective experience of sacrificing for God. Once Isaac was bound on the altar, Abraham experienced the requisite subjective feeling, and there was no need for Isaac to be slaughtered. Abraham had already internalized his willingness to do so. The actual killing of Isaac would have been super-fluous. Jewish sages express this most perfect subjective experience of Abraham when they wrote, "[Isaac's] ashes are viewed as if they lay piled on the Altar" (*Torat Kohanim, Parashat Be-Hukkotai*, 8:8).

The Binding of Isaac, the Temple offerings, and prayer (*tefillah*) all evoke the same subjective experience: everything in the universe was created by God, we live at His mercy, and we are ready to sacrifice for Him—even life itself.

The Day of Atonement: greatness, insignificance, and repentance

In the previous section, "Thoughts on Prayer," we described how the daily *Amidah* prayer helps shape Halakhic Man's consciousness by evoking a range of contradictory feelings toward God. In this section, we see how the specific *Amidah* prayer recited on the Day of Atonement similarly helps develop Halakhic Man's religious consciousness.

When a prototypical Religious Man considers his place in the cosmos, his self-esteem is pulled in opposing directions. On the one hand, he feels in-significant and worthless: What is mortal man in relation to God's mighty universe? He is mindful of the verses, "When I behold thy heavens, the work of thy fingers, the moon and the stars, which thou hast ordained; what is man, that thou art mindful of him? and the son of man, that thou visitest him?" (Psalms, 8:4–5).

On the other hand, Religious Man feels proud and exalted when he re-minds himself of the elevated role assigned to him by God: "Yet thou hast made him a little lower than the angels, and thou dost crown him with glory and honour. Thou makest him to have dominion over the works of thy hands; thou hast put all things under his feet" (Psalms, 8:6–7).

Religious Man is thus torn and unable to resolve the tension between his insignificance and his greatness. Is he worthless, or is he but a bit lower than the angels? How should he perceive himself? How should he feel?

Halakhic Man, like Religious Man, also grapples with this tension. During *Ne'ilah*, the final *Amidah* prayer of the Day of Atonement, Halakhic Man confesses his insignificance and worthlessness:

> What are we? What is our life? What is our kindness? What is our righteousness? What is our salvation? What is our strength? What is our might? What can we say before you Hashem, our God and the God of our forefathers—are not all the heroes like nothing before you, the famous as if they had never existed, the wise as if devoid of wisdom, and the perceptive as if devoid of intelligence? For most of their deeds are desolate and the days of their lives are empty before you. The preeminence of man over beast is nonexistent, for all is vain.

Yet immediately afterward, the prayer highlights man's greatness:

> You set man apart from the beginning and You considered him worthy to stand before You, for who can tell You what to do, and if he is righteous what can he give you?

Like Religious Man, Halakhic Man is torn. God had set him up for greatness, expecting man to stand before Him and serve Him. Yet man also knows that he is all too human. He has sinned and is unworthy of God's grace. How can he stand before God? How can he have any self-respect? But unlike Religious Man who cannot reconcile this tension, Halakhic Man can and does because Halakhah comes to his rescue. Yes, he sinned, but the halakhot of repentance point his way back. He is commanded to regret his sins and repent. Halakhah assures him that God will forgive him and that he will once again be worthy to stand before God and serve Him. The *Ne'ilah* prayer continues:

> Now you gave us Hashem, our God, with love this Day of Atonement, a deadline, pardon and forgiveness for all our iniquities, so that we can withdraw our hands from oppression and return to You, to carry out the decrees of Your will, wholeheartedly.

Halakhic Man grapples with his halakhically ordained conflicting feelings of greatness and insignificance. He knows that God had set man aside for greatness. He also knows that his sins made him unworthy to stand before God. The conflict gives him no rest. How can he resolve this tension? The Halakhah points a way out of his quagmire. The fasting and the prayers of the Day of Atonement (the acts of the mitzvah) encourage introspection and repentance (the subjective fulfillment of the mitzvah) as highlighted in our prayer. With true repentance, man recreates himself and becomes a new person who is once again worthy to stand before God and serve him (*Halakhic Man*, 66–72). Prayer and repentance thus synergistically combine to shape the consciousness of Halakhic Man.

Having repented, Halakhic Man's tension is resolved. Nonetheless, this is not the beginning of a serene existence. Halakhah demands that he go on with the nitty-gritty of his this-worldly life. This in turn will likely cause him to once again stumble and sin. The dialectical tension of greatness and insignificance will then resurface, and the endless cycle continues.

Prayer develops Halakhic consciousness: "On Seating and Sanctification"

Soloveitchik has much more to say about prayer than he addresses in the essay just discussed. Prayer is a fairly extensive lifestyle commitment from the perspective of one who follows Jewish law. Like repentance, and mourning, which we previously addressed, prayer consumes much energy and elicits a transformative human experience. Prayer for Jews is communal. It requires an ongoing commitment to a certain routine. Much of one's life must be scheduled around prayers and their timetables. Halakhic prayer involves an extensive prayer regimen with numerous rules, regulations, times, rituals, etc. and also engenders certain feelings, but only when done properly. Why is meticulous attention to the very many specific details of the Halakhah so important to religious consciousness? How can a mind distinguish between following all the details precisely and not? How can a small ontological change in reality determine whether or not one will develop the right kind of mind? Let us look to one of Soloveitchik's smaller essays, written in his capacity as a leader of Orthodox Jewry.

An active debate among American Orthodox rabbis in the 1950s prompted severe comments from Soloveitchik. The debate was over the configuration of synagogues. The traditional Orthodox halakhic view, and Soloveitchik's, was that a synagogue must have a physical partition that separates the section in which men are seated from that in which women are seated. The trend at the time was for "liberal congregations" to erect synagogues without partitions that allowed for "mixed pews" seating men and women together.[120]

Soloveitchik's most significant response on this topic was an essay first appearing in Yiddish and subsequently in English as "On Seating and Sanctification." His essay is relevant for us in the present context because he offers a brief account of the impact prayer has on one's personality. In the process he offers a threefold defense of his position against mixed seating in the synagogue while criticizing the liberal Jewish approach to Halakhah. Whereas synagogues traditionally seated men and women separately, modern liberal synagogues seat them together in the familiar manner of the pews in Christian churches. Soloveitchik's legal view was as emphatic as it was traditional. He held that the Halakhah prohibits one from even entering a synagogue with pews that seat men and women together. He went so far as to advise Jews to stay home on the High Holidays and not hear the sounding of the *shofar*, the main event and key halakhic obligation of the Rosh Hashanah service, rather than enter a liberal synagogue.[121] As we saw him do with prayer itself, Soloveitchik offers legal, historical, and philosophical reasons to justify his staunch position.[122] (1) Halakhah forbids such a seating arrangement. (2) Mixed seating is a vestige of primitive Christianity and is foreign to Judaism. The separation of the sexes dates back to, and is derived from, the configuration of the Holy Temple in Jerusalem, which had separate courtyards for men and women. Moreover, when primitive Christianity was still in hiding and had not yet distinguished itself from Judaism, finding oneself in a service that had the sexes seated together was a sure sign that one was praying with a deviant sect even if they were otherwise trying to conceal their identity. And finally (3) praying with family contradicts the spirit of Jewish prayer. Prayer requires man to feel lonely, that he can rely only on God, to feel withdrawn from the rest of the world. It requires distance from the security and frivolity that comes from praying with family.

Soloveitchik insists that one will have the proper phenomenological experience only when prayer is conducted according to halakhic guidelines. One will manifest the characteristics of Halakhic Man only when one prays in the manner that Halakhic Men have been praying throughout Jewish history. If one prays properly and in the proper setting, following the precise halakhic requirements, one will experience the feeling of aloneness and separateness that prayer engenders. The technical details of the act of the Halakhah cannot be separated from the experience that comes about from the act of the commandment. Changing the seating arrangement in a synagogue will give rise to the wrong psychological experience. One will not achieve what the Halakhah is grooming one for unless every detail is correct. One can develop a Halakhic Mind only if the individual follows the details of Halakhah.

A widely circulated, though perhaps apocryphal, story (Meiselman 1998, 9–10) makes a related point. A woman approached Soloveitchik asking if it is halakhically permissible for her to wear a *tallit* in the synagogue during the prayer services; she wanted to wear the ritual prayer shawl which Halakhah requires only be worn by men.

Soloveitchik recommended that she proceed slowly and wear the *tallit* but without the required *tzitzit*, the ritual fringes comprising the essential part of the *tallit*. In other words, he instructed her to wear something that was not a *tallit* at all but only bore a superficial resemblance to one. He then asked her to report back a few weeks later and relate her experience.

When she returned some weeks later, she reported on the deep spiritual nature of her religious experience while wearing the nonkosher *tallit*. Soloveitchik then pointed out that her magnificent experience had been caused not by something with religious significance but by something that had no halakhic validity at all. It was an object that men were technically forbidden to wear. Her experience was therefore unrelated to Halakhah and halakhically irrelevant.[123]

A moral we derive from this anecdote is that for Soloveitchik, there is an intrinsic connection between meticulously following Halakhah and the religious experience it engenders. Each Halakhah gives rise to a particular experience when performed correctly and adds a very specific piece to the consciousness and personality of Halakhic Man. If done right, each Halakhah that is properly fulfilled produces a feeling that is part of a halakhic phenomenological context. If there is no ensuing experience, that constitutes proof that the Halakhah is not being performed correctly. If there is an experience with no halakhic counterpart, that is evidence that the experience is not related to the authentic experience of Halakhic Man.

***

The interconnected discussions of mourning, repentance, and prayer discussed previously all bring out Soloveitchik's understanding of the nature of

Jewish law and the phenomenology it gives rise to. When combined with his larger approach to Jewish philosophy, they account for how he sees the relationship between man and Halakhah, subjective and objective, phenomenology and ontology. The laws are objective; the feelings they engender and categories they shape are subjective. Understanding the relationship between the two is the task of working out the *ta'amei ha-mitzvot* problem.

Repentance, prayer, and mourning are just some examples of halakhot whose observance impacts the worldview of Halakhic Man. We emphasized those which are well represented in Soloveitchik's published work (see Blidstein 1989, 293; Kaplan 2007b, 80ff.). Reuven Ziegler compiled a list of halakhot that Soloveitchik discusses in this manner. It includes "fasting and blowing the Shofar in times of crisis, reciting the Shema, retelling the Exodus, charity, shofar, Hallel, taking the four species, Torah study, and Torah reading" (quoted in Shatz 2008a, 181; see also the discussion in Kaplan 1987, 148, 159ff). What applies to these should hold for all the other halakhot.

The phenomenological experience of Halakhic Man is the sum total of the experiences, each of which is caused by specific halakhic actions undertaken and understood properly. It is only by studying, understanding, and following Halakhah in all its detail that one becomes the type of person whose *a priori* mental categories are halakhic categories. It is only by using the halakhic categories to fully encounter the world that one can interact with it as Halakhic Men must.

A final note: on the religious experience

There is an aspect of Soloveitchik's philosophical project whose subtlety makes it easy to overlook. We alluded to it previously, but it is worth highlighting: we must not disregard the prominence Soloveitchik affords—at least on a surface reading—to a certain kind of spirituality.

Soloveitchik's reconceptualization of Jewish philosophy of religion is to correlate the objective Halakhah with corresponding subjective experiences that come about from interacting with it. Recall that Halakhah affects Halakhic Man in two basic ways. First, the study and creation of Halakhah create in his mind an interconnected web of concepts through which he sees and understands the objects of the world. Second, the practice of Halakhah (i.e., performing the mitzvot) evokes conflicting (dialectical) thoughts, feelings, and emotions, including a wide variety of God-directed emotions and feelings (Kaplan 2007a, 81) such as love for God, fear of Him, being in awe of God, feeling alternately great and insignificant before Him, and feeling simultaneously remote from God and near Him.

All of these—the concepts, emotions, and the God-directed experiences—have their origin in the objective Halakhah. Considering only the religious (i.e., God-directed) emotions for a moment, we note that Soloveitchik reflects on them in various ways: as the subjective part of the Halakhah, as the fulfillment of the mitzvah, and as a natural function of observing commandments. These experiences go hand in hand with their re-spective objective halakhic counterparts—the act of the mitzvah— and give rise to the proper fulfillment of the mitzvah. Curiously, although Soloveitchik often expresses the idea that Halakhic Man has intense God-directed feelings, he never clearly articulates the notion of Halakhic Man's "spiritual side," although we do get a sense of it from his depiction of the Religious Man aspect of Halakhic Man's personality.

Soloveitchik notes that the generic Religious Man is spiritual. But it is unclear where Religious Man's spirituality comes from or what its origins are. How does one achieve spirituality? Moreover, what does it mean for Halakhic Man to be spiritual? For universal Religious Man, spirituality is something he feels, but there is nothing that guarantees that these feeling are contingent on being ethical or on the fulfillment of an action mandated by God. Although spiritual feeling may arise from a mindset directed toward God, these feelings are not necessarily contingent upon doing anything mandated by Him. Soloveitchik wants a way to show how spiritual feelings are connected to spirituality.

Spirituality, as understood in our culture and also by theologians like Schleiermacher and Otto, can come about spontaneously or be brought on artificially. It is precisely this definition of spirituality that Soloveitchik finds foreign and from which he takes great pains to distance himself:

> People speak about religious experiences today, trying to stimulate religious experiences with drugs ... But one cannot get a religious experience—that is, a Jewish religious experience—without utilizing the materials of Halakhah. (*OOTW*, 9)

Halakhic Man's religious experience is meaningful only when it is brought on by a halakhic act. For Halakhic Men, and by extension for all observant Jews, the religious experience cannot be divorced from the divine imperative. When it is, it becomes idolatrous (*Noraos Harav* 10:92).

The importance and centrality of the religious experience to Soloveitchik's philosophy of Judaism must be stressed. For Soloveitchik, performance of the mitzvot evokes a variety of conflicting emotions and feelings directed toward God, and these experiences are integral and central to the mitzvot. Hence, the refrain among some Jews and non-Jewish theologians that "Judaism is only concerned with obeying the law," implying that belief or intent is hardly in-tegral to Jewish religious life, is clearly repudiated. For Soloveitchik, the re-ligious experience is and must be an integral part of the mitzvot.

It would be a mistake, however, to say that the fact that a Halakhah evokes a religious experience makes the *purpose* of the mitzvah the religious experience. Recall Soloveitchik's criticism of Maimonides' attempt to assign ethical considerations as the basis for the nonrational commandments. Soloveitchik argues that if ethics is the purpose of the mitzvot, then we have made the mitzvot secondary to ethical considerations, which they are not.

Ethics would then be the highest ideal in Judaism and not the word of God. To Soloveitchik, this is absurd.[124] So too with regard to the religious experience. While Soloveitchik makes the religious experience an integral and central part of the mitzvot, he certainly does not make it the purpose of the mitzvot. The mitzvot are not secondary to ethical considerations and neither are they secondary to the religious experience, "no matter how redemptive it is ... no matter how therapeutic it is, no matter how substantial its impact upon the total personality of man. The point of departure must always be the objective external act ..." (*Noraos Harav* 10:90–91).

Summary of Soloveitchik's philosophy of religion

We can now take stock and summarize Soloveitchik's entire program and put it all together to see his big picture clearly. We use the notation from the "Foundation" section and a sampling from our discussion of the way Soloveitchik applies it.

$JD_1, JD_2, JD_3 ...$ Commandments such as prayer, mourning, repentance, *tzitzit*, etc. and their associated halakhic concepts

are independent objective data of Judaism (halakhot) which form an interconnected system such that

$JD_1 \leftrightarrow JD_2 \leftrightarrow JD_3 ...$ laws of prayer, mourning, repentance, *tzitzit*, etc. are all related to one another within the halakhic system.

This system is correlated with the subjective personality of a halakhic adherent as follows:

$JD_1 \leftrightarrow JD_2 \leftrightarrow JD_3 ...$ Halakhic mourning entails that halakhic concepts of death,
$\updownarrow$ $\updownarrow$ $\updownarrow ...$ mourning, proper burial, etc. became fixed as *a priori*
$JR_1, \quad JR_2, \quad JR_3 ...$ categories of experience and also gives rise to the emotions of fear, anxiety, and estrangement from God. Repentance reorganizes our concept of time; engenders feelings of both greatness and insignificance; takes us closer to God, to a level of prophetic revelation; makes us creative; and re-creates us as a person; prayer entails categories of time of prayer and proper number of blessings as well as feelings of aloneness and separateness, love, and dread. Each and every Halakhah engenders a particular ontology and gives rise to particular feelings and emotions.

An ideal Halakhic Man's personality is the interconnected parts of his individual subjective experiences that come from Halakhah and can be described as:

$JR_1 \leftrightarrow JR_2 \leftrightarrow JR_3 \ldots$ one who feels both great and insignificant, love and terror, fear and anxiety, lonely and communal, and who has a myriad of conflicting subjective psychological phenomenological experiences which all interact in one consciousness.

The person described previously will end up cleaving to God and having meaningful and profound religious experiences. He will also be conflicted in ways that emerge from the competing subjective demands, transformations, ontological commitments, and changes engendered by understanding and practicing Halakhah. The conflicts arise because some of the subjective personality traits and intuitive *a priori* categories are mutually incompatible.

Notes

1 That these works comprise one unit, see, e.g., Kaplan (2007a, 211); Johnston (1999, 16).
2 See "Otiyot Niknot b'mesirah" in *Shi'urim Abba*, vol. I, 260–79 on "document" as a halakhic category. See also Solomon (1993, 138) and Schwartz (2007, 293f) for its meaning to the circle of Brisk.
3 Munk (1992, 1996) first noted the relevance of Cohen's thought for Soloveitchik's *Halakhic Mind*. Beiser (2018) is a broad intellectual biography to which this section and the next is greatly indebted. See Poma (2007) for the relation of Cohen's Jewish work to Kant, and Seeskin (1997).
4 Following the influence of philosophers like Hermann von Helmholtz, Kuno Fischer (with whom Cohen would have a falling out), Otto Liebmann, Schopenhauer, Eduard Zeller (who treated Cohen quite improperly early in his academic career), J. F. Fries, Friedrich Lange, and others, a number of philosophers influenced by Kant began rejecting the speculative philosophy known as "absolute idealism," perhaps most closely associated with philosophers like Hegel. The various neo-Kantianisms coalesced into a number of schools, one first around the University of Marburg and another around Baden-Württemberg, in Freiburg, Heidelberg, and Strassburg. These two main schools had different goals for Kant scholarship. Marburg neo-Kantianism, most closely identified with Hermann Cohen, Paul Natorp, and Ernest Cassirer, focused on philosophy's role in grounding empirical inquiry. Baden neo-Kantianism most closely associated with Wilhelm Windelband, Heinrich Rikert, and Emil Lask focused on ethics and aesthetics (axiology) and necessity and universality.
5 See Schwartz (2007, 44–53) for an analysis of Soloveitchik's rejection of Marburg idealism.
6 Noam Chomsky, the founder of modern linguistics, argues the main contribution of linguistics will be toward understanding mental processes. He proposes a strikingly similar program for a psychological science of language. The psychologist has three tasks: (1) discovering the innate schema of language in the *mind,* (2) study the *environmental* simulations that triggers the schema, and (3) find what it means to say that the stimulus *correlates* with what we hypothesize is the innate schema (Chomsky 1968, 88–89).
7 A Jewish ethical movement that arose in nineteenth-century Lithuania among non-Hasidic Orthodox Jews, most closely identified with Yisroel Salanter.
8 The title *Halakhic Mind* is not Soloveitchik's; it was invented by its publisher. See Zelcer and Zelcer (2017) for discussion of this title.

9 Letter from Soloveitchik to Jung in *CCC* (271–72).
10 Though the essay was advertised as early as 1962 (together with other writings he never published), it appeared as *The Halakhic Mind* in 1986, the year Soloveitchik retired from teaching when illness had begun to take its toll. The book was published from an untitled manuscript that was certainly not edited to Soloveitchik's usual standards. Though the book is structurally sound, typographical errors and anomalies abound. For example, there is a strange partial reference (p. 122n66) to a dissertation published in 1971 even though the book claims to have been unchanged from its original 1944 writing. See Mark Zelcer's "Errata for R. Joseph B. Soloveitchik's *The Halakhic Mind*" available at www. Hakirah.org/vol23ZelcerMErrataTheHalakhicMind.pdf.
11 Maier was one of Soloveitchik's dissertation sponsors, as well as the University of Berlin instructor of the introduction to philosophy course attended by M. M. Schneerson.
12 See, e.g., Hirsch (1969, letter 18) and Sacks (2011, 217–18). A. J. Heschel (1996, 156) raised similar concerns.
13 There are also some senses in which Soloveitchik elides the differences between *hukim* and *mishpatim*. See Aharon Zeigler here: https://www.torahmusings.com/ 2018/02/chukim-mishpatim-no-difference/.
14 Earlier works on *Halakhic Mind* (whose interpretation we often diverge with) include Spero (2009, chs. 4 and 5), Kolbrener (1997), Sacks (1997), Kaplan (2007a), Schwartz (2007, ch. 2), Cohen (2008), Rynhold (2012–2013), and Brafman (2014, ch. 2).
15 The phrase "halakhic mind" does not appear in all of Soloveitchik's works. (Thanks to Lawrence Kaplan for pointing this out to us.) We, however, use the phrase "Halakhic Mind" to refer to the mental state, mental life, personality, or consciousness of a person steeped in the Halakhah in a way which will become evident throughout our discussion. We use the phrase for consistency with the literature and the existing book title, though "halakhic consciousness," "religious consciousness," or some similar phrase may be truer to Soloveitchik's style and intention.
16 Compare Leibowitz (1992, 135ff): "While in the middle ages religious thought and scientific thought met on a common plane, today points of contact between them can be found, if at all, only in the restricted area of the cognitive elements of religion ..."
17 Cf. Natorp (2015, 164). See Johnston (1999) for discussion, especially for the relationship to James (1912). See also Hyatt (2014) for a discussion of the various notions of pluralism in Soloveitchik's work.
18 Soloveitchik's discussion, in a sense, anticipates or at least alludes to the events that typify part of what is known as the Forman Thesis (Forman, 1971). Paul Forman argued that the achievements in new areas of science in Weimar Germany starting in the 1920s were born of the hostile, intellectual climate that simultaneously rejected the Weimar state as illegitimate and also rejected the classical Newtonian view of causality, materialism, and determinism in formulating quantum mechanics. Soloveitchik who was in Germany for a good part of this revolution picked up on the intellectual turmoil and exploited the fact that not only was there dissatisfaction with traditional scientific categories but there are also whole realms of science and nature to which they do not apply.
19 To a great extent, this did not drastically change until the 1980s.
20 It was in this same period that the controversy about the nature of numbers and mathematics was in full swing, with formalism, intuitionism, and logicism all competing for dominance, just as relativism, emotivism, realism, and nihilism were competing in ethics.

21 Soloveitchik elaborates on this theme in various contexts. See in the section on "Development." See also Kaplan (1987, 180ff) and Woolf (2012).

22 Turner (2010, 45) argues that Soloveitchik's justification for religion to use a new approach to knowledge and reality could also be used to justify different approaches by other religions and even by other Jewish religious denominations.

23 Cf. *Worship Heart*, 3.

24 Note the affinity of this style of analysis with the *Völkerpsychologie* that Hermann Cohen made use of in his analysis of some religious concepts.

25 This can be expressed more tersely as follows: the raw data of Halakhah are:

$$JD_1, JD_2, JD_3. \ldots$$

which forms the connected halakhic system:

$$JD_1 \leftrightarrow JD_2 \leftrightarrow JD_3 \ldots$$

which can be used to reconstruct the subjective data as

such:
$$JD_1 \leftrightarrow JD_2 \leftrightarrow JD_3 \ldots$$
$$\updownarrow \quad \updownarrow \quad \updownarrow \ldots$$
$$JR_1, \quad JR_2, \quad JR_3 \ldots$$

to get a whole system: $JR_1 \leftrightarrow JR_2 \leftrightarrow JR_3 \ldots$ which is a description of the Halakhic Mind that shows a Halakhic Man's subjective mental states and describes how they are connected to one another.

26 Spranger's broad psychological approach was based on Dilthey's critique of "analytical psychology." Dilthey, one of the pioneers of modern social scientific thinking who apparently influenced Soloveitchik, made a distinction more important to the Baden neo-Kantians and separated psychology off as a "human science" as opposed to a physical or biological science. Doing so thereby allows individuals to be analyzed from the standpoint of their complete mental structures and also in terms of the relationships between the objects of their minds in a way consistent with Soloveitchik's method described here. See Dilthey (1977, 1979, esp. 87–97, 133–54). See Rynhold (2003, 2005) for discussion.

27 Considering personality typologies as belonging to all members of a people shows up throughout the history of science in writers as varied as Plato, Aristotle, the Hippocratic treatises, Said al-Andalusi, Kant, and Scheler. To appreciate how this manifested itself in the intellectual *zeitgeist* of Soloveitchik's time, we note the following example: In 1893, the eminent mathematician Felix Klein gave a lecture in the United States in which he speculated that different races (the Teutons as opposed to the Latin and Hebrew peoples) have different mathematical intuitions (Klein 1911). He developed this theme in a seminar on the psychology of mathematics in 1910–1911. The lectures heavily influenced the young Erich Jaensch, who would go on to write a number of books on racial personality types that were extremely influential in Nazi Germany, including one specifically on mathematics. His books correlate ethnicities with mathematical and scientific proclivities and abilities. Oswald Spengler's 1917 influential *Decline of the West* also contains a chapter that correlates mathematical (and scientific) styles with races. In 1923, the mathematicians Theodor Vahlen and Ludwig

Bieberbach (one of M. M. Schneerson's mathematics teachers in 1928), both sympathetic with Nazism, co-founded a mathematics journal that similarly advocated for the idea that different mathematical styles were correlated with different races. The mathematicians Udo Wegner, Oswald Teichmüller, Eva Magner, and Cl. H. Tietjen all defended similar ideas. By 1933, the psychologist Carl Jung took these differences for granted (see, for example, his Foreword to the December 1933 issue of the *Zentralblatt fur Psychotherapie* whose editorship he had just taken over). In 1935, German physicists and Nobel laureates Philipp Lenard and Johannes Stark were dismissing Einsteinian physics as "Jewish physics" in prestigeous international scientific journals like *Nature* in a way that soon became commonplace throughout Nazi Germany (see Segal 2003 for context).

28 See, e.g., Borowitz (1966) and Lyčka (1995).

29 There is extensive secondary literature on *Halakhic Man*. See Shatz (2008a, 2018) for bibliographic material, summary, and discussion.

30 The translator's Preface to *Halakhic Man* (VII) points out that this work may be seen as a counterpart to Leo Baeck's essay "Romantic Religion." Walter Kaufmann, Baeck's translator, also points out that one of Baeck's favorite idioms was "*Es ist ein zwiefaches* (sic) (Baeck 1958, 8)," loosely, "it has a twofold nature." This expression accurately describes Baeck's treatment of "classic" and "romantic" religion, or the tension between "mystery" and "commandment," and other distinctions Baeck made. Soloveitchik similarly can be said to have this idea as a recurring theme pervading his work.

31 Cf. Leibowitz (1992, 12ff).

32 See Brill (2006, 265). Brill (2010a, 129) quotes Barth's *Church Dogmatics* saying that one who is not a Christian cannot hope to understand Christianity.

33 *Ahavat Ha-Torah*, 420; translation based on Lichtenstein (1996, 55). See also *On Repentance*, 133–34 and Ziegler (2012, 100–03).

34 Rakeffet-Rothkoff (1999, 2:169, 170); *Ahavat ha-Torah;* see also Soloveitchik's lament over the disappearance of the Erev-Shabbos Man in *On Repentance* (88–89n). Lichtenstein (1996, 55) relates the following anecdote: "After his wife's death in 1967 [Soloveitchik] initiated intensive [lectures] for [students] who would come to Brookline to learn during the summer. One day (ca. 1969–1970), he stunned the group by announcing that, inasmuch as he found them spiritually desiccated, he would now, in addition to the regular shiurim on the [section of Talmud], learn the *Likutei Torah* [a work of ethics] of the *Ba'al haTanya* with them; and he started, the following day, with the section on [I am my beloved's and my beloved is mine]. 'But,' he confided to [Lichtenstein] subsequently, 'It didn't really help.'"

35 Zeitlin's (1913, 205–35) essay on the phenomenology of religion similarly bemoans James' overlooking Judaism.

36 Compare with James (2004, 73). "Sometimes as I go to church, I sit down, join in the service, and before I go out I feel as if God was with me, right side of me, singing and reading the Psalms with me .... And then again I feel as if I could sit beside him, and put my arms around him. Kiss him ..." See also *On Repentance*, 142.

37 Leo Baeck's 1922 essay "Romantic Religion" (in Baeck 1958) advances a similar criticism and similarly ties it to Christianity (see also the translator's Preface to *Halakhic Man*, VII).

38 Soloveitchik understands Religious Man similar to the way he understands Husserlian phenomenological reduction. He believes that Religious Man's subjective perspective on the world lets him ignore or even cause human suffering because he is so focused on his own personal spirituality. He also points

out that the most celebrated philosophers of the third Reich were students of Husserl (see *Halakhic Mind*, 53). Presumably Soloveitchik sees Husserl's reduction—as a reaction to Natorp's reconstruction—as a defense of philosophical subjectivity, just as he sees Schleiermacher and Otto's Protestant defense of religious Subjectivity—as a reaction to Jewish Halakhic objective thinking. Soloveitchik thinks both the Protestant thinkers and the Husserlian phenomenologists are missing a key ingredient. (See also Schwartz 2007, 22–25.)

39 This theme can be seen as having antecedents in Kierkegaard's discussion of Abraham's particular actions involving the binding of Isaac being reconciled with the universal ethical (see Kierkegaard 1985, Problemata I).

40 Note how counterintuitive this is. One would think that the normative is subordinate to ontology. That is, as Hume might put it, what *ought* to be the case has to work within the parameters set by reality, what *is*. For Halakhic Man, the opposite is the case. The halakhic *ought* determines the reality of what *is*. See also *Maimonides Course*, 179. See Roth (1989, 204–5) for discussion.

41 Cf. the widely discussed Talmudic story of the oven of Akhnai in *Bava Metzia* 59a–b.

42 Soloveitchik on a few occasions denigrates liberal Protestantism and liberal Judaism as being primitive and naive in their description of the religious experience as inducing tranquility, comfort, and peace of mind. For Soloveitchik, the religious experience is complex, rigorous, dialectical, and tortuous (*Halakhic Man* 139n4). He also strongly criticizes Christian Religious Man (*homo religiosus*) who turns a blind eye toward real-life problems of this world to seek transcendence in a higher realm (*Halakhic Man* 1: viii). These criticisms appear to be too broad. Perhaps the former criticism is understandable given what he took to be at stake in the battle over the future of American Judaism and the latter criticism as an outgrowth of the historical Jewish experience with (European) Christianity. Critical work is necessary to evaluate these and his other criticisms. It is worth noting that Soloveitchik takes issue with such Protestant thinkers as Otto and Barth, though he does not directly engage polemically against liberal Jewish thinkers like Heschel or Buber. (See also Chapter 4, Section "Rudolf Otto.")

43 Similar conflicting imagery of God is also found in the *Anim Zemirot* prayer recited on the Sabbath: "Aged on judgement day and youthful on the day of battle."

44 Aharon Ziegler at https://www.torahmusings.com/2017/01/power-peshara-compromise/.

45 This interpretation of Hegel is currently out of favor, though he was often understood this way (see, e.g., the neo-Kantian philosopher Windelband 1892, 465–66). It was probably how Soloveitchik would have understood him. It was likely presented as such to make sense of the neo-Kantian position of rationalism as the thesis, empiricism as the antithesis, and Kant as the synthesis. Though inaccurate, nothing about Soloveitchik's argument (or ours) hinges on whether or not Hegel himself held the view commonly attributed to him. Hegel's actual, less appreciated, central view is that some concepts can only be understood in terms of their opposites: up and down, infinite and finite, one and many, general and particular, essence and existence, union and separation, etc.; one of each pair only makes sense because of the other.

46 Hegelian philosophy of history spawned an extensive debate among nineteenth-century Jewish intellectuals. Hegel claims that Judaism is a religion of transcendence stunted in an adolescent phase of historical development. He also claims that Judaism posits an absolute dichotomy between God and man and that the dichotomy is only overcome by Christianity's bridge in God's

incarnation in human form. Jewish historians like Heinrich Graetz and philosophers of history like Nachman Krochmal explicitly reject parts of Hegel's philosophy of history though generally in the service of promoting an alternative picture of Jewish law and its history (Batnitzky 2011, 43ff).

47 *Halakhic Man*, 3–4. See also *Majesty and Humility*, 25. Shatz (2008a), however, notes that *Halakhic Man* (4) claims that "[out] of the contradiction and antinomies there emerges a radiant, holy personality whose soul has been purified in the furnace of struggle and opposition and redeemed in the fires of the torments of spiritual disharmony... The deep split of the soul prior to its being united may, at times, raise a man to a rank of perfection ...," which "suggest that, in the Hegelian fashion the Thesis and Antithesis which coexist in the *ish ha-Halakhah* blend in a higher Synthesis" (189). He notes, however, that this is contrary to the above-cited stance from *Majesty and Humility* in which Soloveitchik "... denies that these tendencies are ever reconciled" (190).

48 Most famously in *Halakhic Man* (fn. 4, 141–42). Cf. a 1972 interview with A. J. Heschel: https://www.youtube.com/watch?v=FEXK9xcRCho, 18:20–20:30.

49 Soloveitchik (like many others) traces the origins of dialectical thought in theology to Kierkegaard (see *Halakhic Man*, 139n4, and cf. *Halakhic Mind*, 3). See also Ziegler (2012).

50 Barth's (1935) collection of sermons *God's Search for Man* reflects this. Incidentally, one need look no further than the titles to see the influence on A. J. Heschel's (1955) *God in Search of Man*.

51 See Brill (2006, 265ff; 2010, 118–21, 129–33).

52 Barth clearly occupied Soloveitchik's thought as he was writing his early works. Barth's influence can most easily be seen in part I of *AFTYSS*. But note that Barth and dialectical theology are mentioned in the opening passages of *Halakhic Mind* and *Halakhic Man*.

53 An extended discussion of *Catharsis* can be found in Ziegler (2012, ch. 2).

54 For more on Soloveitchik on the Biblical Abraham, see Blidstein (2015).

55 In that context, Soloveitchik is talking about being both religious and also a member of a secular state. He insists that the State of Israel not sacrifice one for the other.

56 See also Ravitzky (1986) and Koltun-Fromm (2012).

57 The four letter name for God in conjunction with Elohim.

58 Our description of J, E, P, and D is based on Friedman (2017, 45–49). Friedman also argues that E, P, and D are Levite sources, while J is not.

59 Today there are a number of competing theories of Bible criticism on offer, some more closely related to Wellhausen's than others.

60 See Kaplan (2000, 200–02) for some points of convergence and divergence between Cohen and Wellhausen.

61 Maimonides rules, "There are three who deny the Torah: One who says that the Torah is not from God—even a single verse, even a single word—if he says Moshe stated it on his own, he is a denier of the Torah ..." (*MT: Hilkhot Teshuvah* 3:8).

62 While the challenges of Bible criticism did not clearly influence Soloveitchik's philosophy (though he sometimes alludes to it, e.g., *Emergence Ethical* 170n, 193), it did motivate some of his practical decisions. He opposed, for instance, Orthodox involvement in the Jewish Publication Society's first English Bible translation. He felt that as a Conservative institution, their motivation was to bring Bible translation in line with higher Bible criticism, archaeology, and contemporary philology, and not to infuse the English translation with traditional Jewish thought (*CCC*, 110). See Chapter 7, Section "Soloveitchik and Biblical criticism" for further discussion.

63 In a novel twist on Soloveitchik's approach, the journalist David Brooks has adapted Soloveitchik's conception of the two Adams as those that embody two competing sets of virtues: those that one puts on their resumes and those that are put in eulogies. He refers to this frequently, especially in Brooks (2015). Kaplan (2010b) discusses how TLMOF has been used by various modern Orthodox thinkers. Rosenberg (2012) is another interesting use.

64 Brill (2010b, 122) traces the characterization of Adam I and Adam II as Majestic Man and Covenantal Man, respectively, to Karl Barth who himself inherited this distinction. (See, however, Blidstein 2012, 73–75, who sees sharp distinctions between Barth and Soloveitchik in their interpretation of the Biblical narratives of Adam.) Of particular interest is a statement in Barth's *Church Dogmatics* (vol. 3, pt. 1, 240): "La Peyrère, the author of a book about the pre-Adamites which appeared in 1655 … was thus basically on the right track when he propounded the theory that *Genesis* 1 tells the story of the natural, pagan man, and Genesis 2 that of the Jew, i.e., the man of the history of salvation."

65 "Mesorah," an important theme in Soloveitchik's thinking, here refers to the chain of transmission of the law from God to Moses at Sinai down to the present time. This is a central rabbinic concept that substantiates the legitimacy of the law. The Mishnaic tractate *Avot* begins: "Moses received the Torah from Sinai and transmitted it to Joshua, and Joshua to the Elders, and the Elders to the Prophets, and the Prophets transmitted it to the Men of the Great Assembly." Sherira Gaon's *Epistle*, written in the tenth century, gives a detailed account of the individuals who are said to have transmitted the tradition from Moses to his own time. Maimonides' introduction to *Mishneh Torah* lists forty generations of the transmission from Rav Ashi, an early editor of the Talmud, back to Moses.

66 Plato similarly saw the harmony of states. See Pappas and Zelcer (2013).

67 Herskowitz (2015) argues that some of Soloveitchik's understanding of Knesset Yisrael is best understood in light of the German idea of the *volk* as found in Johann Gottlieb Fichte, Martin Heidegger, and others. Fishman (1996) sees the distinction between Soloveitchik's "groups" and Knesset Yisrael as the same distinction made by German sociologists talking about *Gemeinschaft* and *Gesellschaft*.

68 Compare this to Hermann Cohen, who sees the question of the individual versus society as a question of ethics, not ontology: "The dissolution of the individual is the highest triumph of ethics. The ethical individual, as an isolated single being having the basis of his life in metabolism, disappears, to be resurrected in the I of the state and, by means of the confederation of states, in mankind. This is the climax ethics can achieve for the human individual. The prophets of social morality, in their messianic monotheism, join in the achievement of this climax" (Cohen 1995, 178). See also the discussion on 215ff where Cohen, like Soloveitchik, considers this issue in the context of its role in repentance. See *On Repentance* (97–125).

69 Emmanuel Levinas, the Jewish philosopher and Soloveitchik's contemporary, often speaks in similar terms.

70 Hermann Cohen also took as important the fact that much of the Yom Kippur confession is in the plural: "We trespassed, we acted treacherously, we have stolen, we have slandered …" This is all said regardless of whether or not the individual has committed the specific sin. For Cohen, this is the model of how atonement works and ultimately how Jews take responsibility for one another and even for the whole world.

71 Cf. Leibowitz (1992, ch. 8) who reaches a related conclusion via a very different route.

72 The title "Rebbitzin" denotes the wife of a rabbi or a pious woman who is great in her own right.

73 A brief account of the Twerskys can be found in Biale et al. (2018, 641).

74 These eulogies are distinct from the annual Yahrzeit lectures delivered on the anniversary of his father's passing, which were largely centered on Halakhah and Aggadah. See Fox (1996) for a discussion of the import of the eulogies and Kanarfogel (2018, 77–79) for a discussion of R. Michael Bernstein's eulogy.

75 This is expressed more abstractly in *Shnei Sugei*. See also Kaplan (2013) for discussion.

76 In *Five Addresses* (ch. 2, §4) Soloveitchik argues similarly that a person must contain both male and female characteristics. Man must be an active creator but also a humble and passive recipient; he must be a master and a disciple.

77 In the same chapter (*Yemey Zikkaron*, 34–37), Soloveitchik explains that the God-man relationship is also both male-female and female-male. As Creator, He is active, and man, the beneficiary of Creation, is passive. However, for God to be manifested as dwelling among us (*Shekhinah*), God is passive, while man's performance of the mitzvot is the active manifestation of *Shekhinah*.

78 An interesting note on Soloveitchik's state of mind while delivering this eulogy can be found in *OOTW* (133).

79 "Majesty and Humility" may be Soloveitchik's most Kierkegaardian essay (*pace* Oppenheim 1998). There are strong parallels between the tension Soloveitchik describes between the Cosmic Man and the Origin-minded Man, and the paradox Kierkegaard describes involving the knight of faith and the tragic hero (inspired by the Biblical Abraham). See Kierkegaard (1985, Problemata II).

80 This corrects for an error in the text.

81 Maimonides, *Mishneh Torah, Sefer Avodah, Hilkhot Temidin u-Musafin*, the fifth and sixth item in its introductory list and the corresponding chapter 3:1 and 3:10.

82 This is perhaps Soloveitchik's most famous halakhic innovation (*hiddush*). See Kaplan (2013, 93n54) for references to discussion.

83 In *Noraos Harav* (10:96) we find, however, that these two commandments together are also considered a mitzvah. "The burning of the incense and the lighting of the lamps has been merged by the *Torah* into one *Mitzvah*. A separate kiyum is obtained … by lighting the candles almost simultaneously with the burning of the incense." Cf. *Vision and Leadership* (205–6).

84 In addition to the objective and subjective components of *tzitzit* quoted earlier (*First Rebellion*, 109), Soloveitchik also speaks about how the white fringes signify "clarity, distinctiveness, and openness," how they denote "rationality, simplicity and truthfulness …" while the blue fringes are associated with "distance and inapproachability … Whatever we cannot reach, whatever is outside our control, whatever suggests mystery …" (*Vision and Leadership*, 188).

85 See Sztuden (2010, 2011, 2012) for a detailed discussion of *ma'aseh ha-mitzvah* and *kiyyum ha-mitzva,* especially as they relate to the mitzvot of rejoicing on festivals and mourning for a recently deceased relative. Soloveitchik explains that these two mitzvot are incompatible and one therefore does not mourn for a deceased relative on the festivals. Sztuden analyzes why these two mitzvot are incompatible in light of Soloveitchik's position that dialectical or conflicting emotions do coexist in the performance of other mitzvot such as prayer.

86 Adapted from Hartman (1989, 252ff). See Solomon (1993, 230) for the possible inspiration for this example in Hayyim Soloveitchik. It expresses the same sentiment as the first quote from Sacks in Chapter 4, Section "The Halakhic Mind: context." Cf. Leibowitz (1992, 16–17, 31–32).

87 Hermann Cohen criticized Christianity for the same reason (see Beiser 2018, 219, 284). In *Maimonides Course*, Soloveitchik also addresses Henri Bergson's

criticism that "the Jew gets lost in a maze of laws and norms where he can never discover God" (211). Soloveitchik responds that "[p]erhaps the Jew's experience of God is less direct than the Gentile's. The question is: What is more important—a disciplined life, ruled by ethical laws, or a foggy mystical experience, devoid of any impact of the religious norm? It is clear that the former is far better, even if the experience of God in such a life is more remote ... the direct experience of God in itself is not redeeming. It can degenerate into barbarism, can exist in combination with cruelty and the unleashing of the worst animal instincts. Only the objective norm is redeeming. Balaam was close to God and was still a satanic figure ... Cruelty and mysticism went hand in hand in Catholicism" (212–13). Cf. Leibowitz (1992, 24).

88 Soloveitchik further criticizes Christianity, e.g., in *Emergence Ethical*, where he charges it with not understanding the nature of man.

89 Despite the profound influence of Martin Luther's anti-Semitism on subsequent German Protestantism and Protestant theology, it does not appear in either Otto's or Schleiermacher's views. Otto, who for obvious theological reasons had no sympathy with Hermann Cohen's view of Judaism as a religion of reason, was a longtime close friend of people of many religious groups, including (among others) the Orthodox Jewish mathematician Abraham Fraenkel, who eulogized Otto in the Hebrew newspaper *Haaretz* (3/7/37). Otto told Fraenkel that his central religious views were inspired by a Yom Kippur spent in a synagogue in North Africa (Fraenkel 2016, 152).

90 For a slightly different formulation of Soloveitchik's concept of the *a priori* categories of Halakhah, see Kaplan (1987, 154–57). For critique, see Agus (1954, 39), Shihor (1978, 149), and Solomon (2012) whose reading differs considerably from ours.

91 Soloveitchik also refers to this work as "The Revealed Halakhah and the Hidden Love of God" (*CCC*, 321).

92 Shalom Carmy quotes Soloveitchik saying "old-time *Gedolim* [sages] refrained from talking about themselves, but that the disconnection of modern man from living exemplars of religious existence has made self-revelation an educational necessity" (Carmy 1997a, 31n22).

93 The chapter grouping is slightly but inconsequentially different in the original Hebrew version.

94 The Editor's Introduction to *Maimonides Course* 55n38 points out that in his lectures on Maimonides, Soloveitchik's argument moves from *devekut* to *imitatio* in accordance with the order in the *Guide* and in the *Book of Commandments*, while in *AFTYSS*, as discussed in our text, he follows the lead of *Mishneh Torah* and proceeds from *imitatio* to *devekut*.

95 The original Hebrew manuscript of *AFTYSS* is lost, and perhaps certain clues to Soloveitchik's intention lost with it. However, it is striking that only what we call "Part 1" is summarized at the end. "Part 2" may be a later addition or an afterthought.

96 Schwartz (2012) is a thorough sophisticated analysis of *AFTYSS*.

97 The charge of pantheism—the idea that God and the Universe are one and the same—perpetually follows Spinoza. It is also a *bete noire* of quite a few subsequent German Jewish philosophers including Hermann Cohen.

98 Soloveitchik derives this as a Biblical commandment from the phrase *vehalakhta be-derakhov* in *Deut.* 28:9. See also Hartman (2001, 81–88). See *Minyan ha-Mitzvot le-ha-Rambam, z"l*, positive commandment 8.

99 "*D'veikut*" is a word of biblical origin that describes the concept of "clinging" (*Gen* 2:24). The word is frequently used in Kabbalistic and Hasidic discourse to describe the ideal relationship between man and God.

100 In *Maimonides Course* (237), Soloveitchik states, however, that the love/fear tension will only be resolved at the end of days. See Zelcer (2017, 43–46) for a discussion of differences between *AFTYSS* and *Maimonides Course*.

101 Ravitzky (1986) addresses Soloveitchik's use of Maimonides' thought as distinguished from his own. In a 1964 talk (see above ch. 2, n8), Soloveitchik claims that the *Tanya* (with which he states the *Nefesh HaHayyim* was largely in agreement) was the earliest "who dared to quote" Maimonides' *Guide* (on this issue) and made the problem of the unity of the knower and the known central to its project. He says Hayyim Brisker also addressed it (though not in those words). See Lustiger (2016–2017) for discussion.

102 See the Editor's Introduction to *Maimonides Course*, 33n25ff for historical notes on this Maimonidean view and see Munk (1999).

103 See also *Seder Meal*, 163.

104 An ancient Greek *symposium*, at least as Plato's dialogue *Symposium* and the archaeological record has preserved it, is a ritualized meal which typically involved food, wine, entertainment, intellectual discussion, and sometimes sex.

105 See the essay "The Redemption of Death" in *OOTW* for a related analysis of *parah adumah*.

106 For Soloveitchik on mourning, see Wolowelsky (1996), Blidstein (2012, 121–38), and Rynhold (2005, 63ff).

107 Our discussion of repentance is in many places indebted to Kaplan (2006), especially for its analysis of Soloveitchik, Cohen, Isaac Blaser, Maimonides, Rabbenu Yona, and Scheler's views. See there for more details on some of the subjects covered here. See also Batnitzky (2011, 57–64), Turner (2014), and Beiser (2018, ch. 9.3).

108 See Cohen (1995, 186–87, 193), and note 68 above.

109 Blau (1997), Kaplan (2006), Schwartz (2007, 298–301), and Rynhold and Harris (2018, ch. 5) discuss Max Scheler's influence upon Soloveitchik's concept of repentance. Blau also notes Scheler's importance for Alexander Altmann (Scheler was the subject of Altmann's dissertation), Joseph Wohlgemuth, and Jehiel Jacob Weinberg. Ozar (2016) spells out the relationship between some of Scheler's work and part of *Emergence Ethical*. See Kelly (1977) for an overview of Scheler's thought.

110 While both Scheler and Soloveitchik describe how current actions can change the trajectory of past sins, Goldman (1996, 180–88) explains how they differ with respect to attaining the will to repent. According to Scheler, the path to repentance starts by examining past sins. Only by regretting these sins does a person attain the will to repent. According to Soloveitchik, however, the ability to repent comes about when a person starts to see the present—his place in the world—as part of a continuum which started at Creation and which continues into the infinite future. Only then does he attain the ability to repent and recreate himself as a new person.

111 Soloveitchik's work on repentance can be found, among other places in: Part II of *Halakhic Man*, *Sacred Profane*, and *On Repentance*.

112 See Rynhold (2005, 65–70).

113 There is some affinity between what Cohen and Soloveitchik would call "creating a new I" and what L. A. Paul has called a "transformative experience" (Paul 2016). An analysis of repentance along these lines would be interesting. Similarly, recent research on the psychology of personal identity (Strohminger and Nichols 2014) suggests that when people make significant moral changes in their personality, we stop identifying them as the same person and think of them as new individuals.

114 See the Editor's Introduction to *Maimonides Course* 40n29, 65ff Supplement to Note 29 for analysis and critique of the Maimonidean and Maimonic contexts of this idea.

115 For more on Soloveitchik on prayer see, e.g., *Worship Heart, On Repentance*, e.g., 71ff, Hartman (2001, 2003), Amaru (2005), Kaplan (2007a), Rynhold (2012–13), and Schwartz (2019).

116 "Blessed are You, Lord our God and God of our fathers, God of Abraham, God of Isaac, and God of Jacob; the great, mighty and revered God, God Most High, who does kindness and creates all, who remembers the kindness of the patriarchs and will bring a redeemer to their children's children for His name's sake, in love. King, Helper, Savior and Shield! Blessed are You, Lord, the Shield of Abraham."

117 "You are eternally mighty, Lord. You give life to the dead, You have great power to save. You make the wind blow and the rain fall. (In summer: You bring the dew.) You sustain the living with kindness, you revive the dead with great mercy. You support the fallen, heal the sick, and free captives, and keep faith with those who sleep in the dust. Who is like You, Mighty One, and who resembles you, King who slays and gives life, and makes salvation flourish! You are faithful to revive the dead. Blessed are You, Lord, who revives the dead."

118 "You are holy, and Your name is holy, and holy ones praise You daily. Blessed are You, Lord, the holy God."

119 "Be pleased, Lord our God, with Your people Israel and with their prayers. Restore the service to the inner sanctuary of Your Temple, and receive in love and favor the fire-offerings of Israel and their prayers. May the service of Your people Israel always be acceptable to You. And let our eyes behold Your merciful return to Zion. Blessed are You, Lord, who restores His Presence to Zion."

120 Despite Soloveitchik's uncompromising position, it was not always put into practice. Marc Angel and Avi Weiss write ("And you shall love the proselyte," *Jerusalem Post*, 4/22/14) "Back in the '60's and '70's, many Orthodox rabbis ordained at Yeshiva University (YU) served in mixed-seating shuls ... Soloveitchik felt that in certain communities, YU rabbis should serve because the shuls might one day construct a *mehitza*."

121 Although Soloveitchik's position was that synagogues must have a *physical barrier* separating men and women (*mehitza*), the recommendation regarding not hearing the shofar pertains only to synagogues that do not *segregate* men and women. Synagogues that segregate the sexes, but have no physical barrier, do not fall under this (Kaplan 1999a, 308, 9n21).

122 Soloveitchik may have adapted this approach in part from Hermann Cohen's approach to philosophical questions that were both philosophical and historical/genealogical (though not in any Nietzschean sense). This is Cohen's *Volkerpsychologie* (see Beiser 2018, 166ff). Blidstein (2012, 37–62) and Kaplan (2013, 83–89) discuss three other English language responsa Soloveitchik wrote that make use of "axiological premises" and "philosophico-historical" considerations as part of the process of working out a halakhic issue. Specifically, see Soloveitchik's letters regarding an interfaith chapel at Cornell University, placing found children in Jewish welfare agencies, and on drafting Orthodox rabbis for the U.S. Armed Forces Chaplaincy (*CCC* 3–10, 11–22, 23–60). The latter responsa, where he ruled that Yeshiva University may go ahead with a plan to have a draft lottery to provide chaplains for the U.S. military, is particularly interesting for understanding Soloveitchik's approach to making halakhic decisions. It is also usefully contrasted with the passage written by Yisrael Meir Kagen (the "Chofetz Hayyim") on a related topic. See the excerpt translated in Batnitzky and Brafman (2018, 82–83).

123 Soloveitchik specifically talks about the feelings associated with *tzitzit* in *First Rebellion*. See also (Besdin 1989, ch. 2).
124 Michael Wyschogrod (1983, xv, 191–97), a student of Soloveitchik, argues the same point, though for different reasons. See Statman (1996), Carmy (1997b), and Spero (2009, ch. 3) for general discussion of Soloveitchik and the relationship between Halakhah and ethics.

5 Zionism

Background

Chapter 4 showed how a large amount of Soloveitchik's writing on philosophy comprises a unified and complete philosophical program. We discussed his justification for and description of a new type of Jewish philosophy: his methodology for reconstructing the mind of Halakhic Man from the data of halakhah; a typological description of this Halakhic Man; and finally, how living, breathing, real Halakhic Men are formed by the Halakhah.

Having laid out and explained Soloveitchik's broad philosophical project, we note that not all of his writing fits neatly into this tripartite structure. Some of his other works are purely halakhic, some Talmudic scholarship, and some philosophical. Though they are outside what we think of as his central philosophical project, they all utilize one or more of his methods: an adherence to Brisker methodology, a penchant for dialectical thinking, analytical distinctions, and precise analyses of relevant concepts. They all contribute to the timeless intergenerational discussions of current and future Jews who value the Halakhah.

Two important topics which go beyond his main philosophical program are his writings on Zionism and his stance on interfaith dialogue. Soloveitchik's thoughts on these topics were written as responses to the "needs of the hour" what the Sages might refer to as *hora'at sha'ah*. We are not suggesting that Soloveitchik saw these views as applicable only for a particular moment in history, only that the need to address these issues arose from contingent historical events, and not broader timeless philosophical considerations.

Following World War II, the Holocaust loomed large in the consciousness of two major religions. For Judaism it highlighted as never before, the need for a Jewish homeland. For Catholicism it was an ethical wake-up call to reexamine its attitude toward the Jewish people. As Jews became ever more focused on a Jewish homeland and subsequently on the State of Israel, Soloveitchik found it necessary to rethink and explain his attitude toward Zionism and to outline his and his coreligionist's obligations toward the Jewish State. As the Catholic Church in the 1960s began to reexamine its stance toward the Jewish people, circumstances compelled Soloveitchik to formulate and publish his view of the way Jews may and may not interact with theologians of other religions. In this chapter and the next we discuss these topics.

***

More than any other issue, except perhaps the position he held at Yeshiva University, it was Soloveitchik's Zionism which created deep rifts between himself and his family, friends, and coreligionists. It caused him to be revered and beloved by some and also loathed and reviled by others. What was it about his Zionism that elicited such strong reactions from those within his religious milieu? Let us begin with some background.

Zion. The etymology of the word "Zion" is uncertain. It may mean a rock or a stronghold. Originally it referred to a hilltop near Jerusalem. In the Bible (*2 Samuel* 5:7), Zion is a fortress conquered by King David which became known as the City of David. During Biblical times, it also signified the Temple Mount and by extension the city of Jerusalem. The word has subsequently been used in Jewish liturgy, literature, poetry, and thought to refer to the entirety of the Land of Israel.

Zionism. Since the late nineteenth century, the term "Zionism" began to be used to refer to the Jewish nationalist movement that had as its goal the creation of a Jewish state in the historical Land of Israel. The term was coined by Nathan Birnbaum in 1890 to refer to the establishment of a national and political organization as a forerunner to a Jewish homeland. Theodor Herzl, a secular Jew motivated by European anti-Semitism, infused political Zionism with a practical urgency, leading in 1897 to the First Zionist Congress. He is usually considered the founder of modern Zionism. In his diary on September 3, 1897, Herzl wrote prophetically, "At Basel I founded the Jewish State ... In five years perhaps, and certainly in fifty years, everyone will perceive it."

Religious Zionism. Parallel to political Zionism, observant Jews developed a religious and theological Zionism. Religious Zionists generally view Zionism and the establishment of an autonomous Jewish State as God-inspired, beneficial to the Jewish people, and infused with religious significance. Some religious Zionists view the establishment of the State of Israel in messianic terms. They see it as a forerunner or harbinger to the coming of the Messiah and a messianic era. Other religious Zionists see the founding of the state in theological but nonmessianic terms, viewing it as having religious significance but not necessarily presaging the coming of the Messiah.

Yitzhak Yaakov Reines (1839–1915), an original member of the Hovevei Zion politico-religious movement, did not speak of Zionism in messianic terms. He coined the phrase *Merkaz Ruḥani* ("spiritual center," abbreviated as *Mizrachi*) and founded the Mizrachi religious Zionists, a movement that fused religion and labor. Soloveitchik would ultimately adopt a Zionism that is likewise nonmessianic. While he viewed the State of Israel as a divine gift and its establishment as miraculous, he did not see it necessarily as a harbinger of the messianic era (Holzer 2009a, 216–17).

Jewish messianic Zionism, which views the return to the Land of Israel in terms of its role in the ultimate destiny of the Jewish people (i.e., in eschatological terms), was presented most forcefully by Abraham Isaac Kook (1865–1935) and by his son Zvi Yehudah Kook (1891–1982). With the formation of the chief rabbinate in 1921, A. I. Kook became its first Ashkenazi chief rabbi, and in 1924, he set up the school now known as the Merkaz ha-Rav Yeshiva with a decidedly pro-Zionist orientation. Following the 1967 Six Day War, when Israel found itself in control of a much greater part of Biblical Israel, Z. Y. Kook took this to be the fulfillment of messianic prophecies and advocated forcefully for Jewish settlement in all areas under Israel's control.

With the establishment of the State of Israel in 1948 and the original Zionist ideal fulfilled, Zionism took on a new meaning. Instead of championing for the establishment of a Jewish state, Zionists now called on Jews to make *aliyah*—to immigrate to Israel—and advocate for its political, economic, cultural, and military support.

While "Zionism" is a modern term, the longing to return to the Land of Israel is ancient. It dates back to the destruction of the First Temple (ca. 586 BCE) and finds its voice in the Bible, most sublimely perhaps in Psalms 126 and 137. Similarly, with the destruction of the Second Temple in 70 CE and the end of the Second Jewish Commonwealth[1] came the thrice-daily *Amidah* prayer replete with entreaties for the return of God's presence to Zion and Jerusalem.

Anti-Zionism

Despite the historic yearning of the Jewish people for their homeland, Jewish anti-Zionism is ancient and enduring.

Ancient anti-Zionism. The hesitation among Jews to leave the diaspora and return to their homeland was already present during the time of the prophet Ezra when, with the permission of the Persian emperor Cyrus, the Jews began to re-establish a presence in the Land of Israel and rebuild the Temple in Jerusalem around 530 BCE. Many Jews at that time remained in Babylon (approximately in present-day Iraq), and a Jewish population continued to flourish there during the entire Second Jewish Commonwealth and indeed until the twentieth century.

The reluctance of many Jews to return to their homeland during the Second Jewish Commonwealth caused some Jews in the Land of Israel to resent the expatriates. R. Zeira (ca. 220–90 CE), a first- or second-generation Talmudic Sage (*Amorah*), left Babylon for the Land of Israel. Presumably his dialect and dress made him easily identifiable as a Babylonian. A midrash (*Song of Songs Rabbah.* 8:11) relates what happened when he arrived in the Land of Israel:

> R. Zeira went to the market to purchase food. He told the shopkeeper, "Weigh me a nice portion." The shopkeeper answered, "Babylonian,

shouldn't you leave? Your forefathers destroyed the Temple." R. Zeira replied, "Are my forefathers different than his?"

R. Zeira went to the house of study where he heard R. Shiela preach [expounding on the verse]: "*If she be a wall* (*Song of Songs*, 8:9): Had the Jews ascended from exile as a wall [i.e., *en masse*] the Temple would not have been destroyed a second time." R. Zeira reflected, "That ignoramus taught me well."

R. Zeira's ancestors refused to return to Israel in a gesture that was interpreted by many Jews of the period as spurning the Jewish homeland in Zion.

Modern anti-Zionism. Modern Jewish anti-Zionism takes many forms: political, philosophical, cultural, ethical, and religious. Many Jews believe it unpatriotic and perhaps treasonous to support a country other than the one in which they live. For example, during the period of the German Enlightenment, in a reply to the Lutheran Bible scholar Johann David Michaelis—who had argued that Jews not be granted civil rights in Germany because of their loyalty to the ancient Land of Israel (what today we might refer to as a charge of "dual loyalty")—Moses Mendelssohn (1729–1786) wrote the following:

[O]ur Talmudic sages had the foresight to emphasize again and again the prohibition to return to Palestine on our own. They made it unmistakably clear that we must not take even a single step preparatory to return to Palestine, and a subsequent restoration of our nation there, unless and until the great miracles and extraordinary signs promised us in Scripture were to occur. And they substantiated that prohibition by citing the somewhat mystical yet truly captivating verses of the Song of Songs (2:7, 3:5) *I adjure you, O daughters of Jerusalem, By the gazelles, and by the hinds of the field, That ye awaken not, nor stir up love, Until it please.*
(Mendelssohn 1975, 85)

We cannot know whether Mendelssohn wrote this out of what we might call a sincere anti-Zionist conviction or as a polemical retort to Michaelis, but it was likely a point that resonated with enough Jews of his time.

Some Jews oppose Zionism for different reasons. Some believe it is their mission to be a "light unto the nations," a task that can only be accomplished while scattered among them. A century after Mendelssohn, also in Germany, Hermann Cohen understands the function of the Jewish people is to spread the ideas of monotheism, the universality of man, and the need to perfect the world. This can only be achieved when Jews are dispersed throughout the world, not when segregated in ghettos or their own country. For Cohen, Zionism is not only imperfect but also a retreat from the Jewish mission (Cohen 1995, ch. XIII; see also Fraenkel 2016, 84). Cohen, in an unusual step, went even further and argues that the Jewish mission is to suffer for the sins of the world. Cohen argues that the Christian interpretation of the famous "suffering servant" passage in Isaiah 53 is mistaken and it is the Jews themselves who are the suffering servant of Israel, not Jesus (Cohen 1919, 313). Jews suffer for the sins of the other nations. Cohen is criticizing Christians (and Zionists) for not acknowledging the Jews' proper place.[2] Zionists, Cohen argues, want Jews to be like everyone else. In a well-known remark reminiscent of one Nietzsche once made of Englishmen, Cohen commented about Zionists that "the fellows just want to be happy." Gershom Scholem, who polemically engaged with Cohen's anti-Zionism and believed he was generally naive (which Cohen certainly was, in hindsight), would later say that this was the most profound statement an opponent ever made about the movement.

Across the Atlantic, the early American Reform Movement similarly opposed Zionism. In 1885, it adopted the Pittsburgh Platform, which disavowed the Jewish aspiration for a national homeland:

> We consider ourselves no longer a nation, but a religious community, and therefore expect neither a return to Palestine, nor a sacrificial worship under the sons of Aaron, nor the restoration of any of the laws concerning the Jewish state.[3]

With the advent of their Columbus Platform in 1937 and the subsequent founding of the State of Israel in 1948, the Reform movement began to express large-scale support for the Jewish State.[4]

Many Orthodox Jews, especially among ultra-Orthodox (now known as ḥaredi) communities, of the kind from which Soloveitchik hailed, believe, like Mendelssohn, that when God is ready, he will send the Messiah to return the Jewish people to their homeland. They believe that Jews must not use mass settlement or political and military means to do the Messiah's job. When a political initiative is led by secular, nonbelieving Jews, it is all the more reason for Orthodox opposition.

Ḥayyim Elazar Shapira, known as the Munkaczer Rebbe (1872–1937), was among the most prominent Ḥasidic leaders of Hungarian Jewry in his era and was one of the first to make a detailed religious case against modern Zionism.[5] The Land of Israel, according to Shapira, manifests direct divine revelation as well as satanic evil; it is under the direct governance of the *ein sof*, the Infinite One, and yet it is also a gateway to hell. The Zionists' foothold in the land is a manifestation of the destructive forces that have always existed within the holiness (Ravitzky 1998, 74). The Land of Israel has an extra degree of holiness, and therefore, those who live there and violate the commandments are subject to extra punishment. "The evil forces excite God's anger and fury; they are most powerful in the Land of Israel, particularly in Jerusalem. For Satan has his foothold in this very place" (Shapira, *Divrei Torah*, vol. 6, §25, cited in Ravitzky 1998, 75). It is, therefore, a place for an ideal Jew, but not for an average one. Any human attempt to collectively bring Jews to the Land of Israel represents a usurpation of the Messiah's role and an attempt to force the end of days. "One may not rely on any natural effort or on material salvation by human labor. One should not expect redemption from any source other than God" (Shapira, *Kuntres Divrei Kodesh*, cited in Ravitzky 1998, 69).

An even more virulent anti-Zionism was laid out by the Jerusalem rabbi Isaiah Asher Zelig Margaliot (d. 1969) of the *Edah Haredit* ("Community of the God-fearing"), an organization he founded along with Rabbis Isaac Diskin and Hayyim Sonnenfeld in response to the establishment of the Chief Rabbinate in Eretz Israel (Fenton 1994; Ravitzky 2005, 283–84). The *Edah Haredit* is the forerunner of the modern *Neturei Karta* sect in Jerusalem, which to this day openly sympathizes with the national enemies of the State of Israel. Margaliot condemned not only Zionism but also questioned the very Jewishness of Zionists. He divided Jews into two categories: those worthy of being called "Israel" and the "mixed multitude (*eirev rav*)," a reference to the group of dissenters who, according to Midrash, left Egypt with the Israelites and ultimately instigated worshipping the Golden Calf. He claims that members of the modern mixed multitude, that is, the Zionists, don't even have Jewish souls and assert that there is an unbridgeable gap between the two groups that even repentance cannot repair. Repentance only works to repair souls that are "rooted in holiness." Zionists, according to Margaliot, will be destroyed when the Messiah arrives. (We will see shortly that Soloveitchik in this context, possibly in response, strongly repudiated the notion that any Jew is beyond redemption.)

As opposed to the more mystical cases of Shapira and Margaliot, the halakhic case for Orthodox anti-Zionism is laid out in greatest detail by Joel Teitelbaum (1887–1979), the Satmar Rebbe, in his various works, and in particular in the first essay of his 1961 *va-Yo'el Moshe: Ma'amar Shalosh Shevuot (And Moshe Consented: An Essay on the Three Oaths)*. Teitelbaum opens his essay by asserting that the sin of Zionism brought on the Holocaust (5, 7)[6], a now standard ultra-Orthodox refrain, first made by the Hazon Ish (Kaplan 1992, 72). Teitelbaum adds that if we were to take all the sins of the Jewish people and put them on one side of a scale and put the Zionist State on the other side, the Zionist State would outweigh all the other sins (11). He also adds parenthetically (in what has become an anti-Semitic canard) that the Zionists themselves were complicit in the Holocaust, believing that the mass slaughter of Jews would make it easier to achieve their goals of statehood, presumably by engendering world sympathy and support (7).

Teitelbaum bases his halakhic case against Zionism on a passage from the Babylonian Talmud in which God adjures three oaths—two upon Israel and one upon the nations of the world.

[How does] R. Zeira [reconcile his intent to go to the Land of Israel with the verse, *I adjure you, O maidens of Jerusalem, by gazelles or by hinds of*

the field: do not wake or arouse Love until it please! (Song of Songs 2:7)?
According to R. Zeira] the verse only prohibits Israelites from going up
to the Land of Israel as a wall [i.e., *en masse*] ...

[According to] R. Zeira [what is the purpose of the second reference to an
oath?] It is necessary to support the statement of R. Yosi b. R. Hanina
who says that the purpose of the three oaths are: that the Israelites not go
up like a wall; that the Holy One Blessed is He, adjured the Israelites not
to rebel against the nations; and that the Holy One Blessed is He, adjured
the nations not to oppress the Israelites excessively ....

(B. Ketubbot, 111a, authors' translation)

Many ultra-Orthodox anti-Zionists (and others, like Mendelssohn above)
understand these oaths as barring Jews from returning to the Land of Israel
en masse before the arrival of the Messiah. Other ultra-Orthodox Jews, who
do not view Zionism as a specifically halakhic problem, are against Zionism
because it was an initiative of secular Jews who championed ideals that are
against the values of the Torah.

Anti-anti-Zionist rejoinders

In our discussion of *Five Addresses* further on in this chapter, we return to
the criticism of religious Zionism that Soloveitchik did apparently take
seriously: that Israel was built mostly by secular Jews who had no respect for
the Halakhah. Curiously, Soloveitchik spent little effort addressing the alleged "halakhic problem of Zionism." Perhaps he did not view the "three
oaths" as a serious halakhic issue, or perhaps he left this task for others to
work out.

Menachem M. Kasher published his encyclopedic, *The Great Era* (1968),
not only defending Zionism but also strongly advocating for it. A much
smaller work of note was published by Shlomo Chaim Aviner in 1980 de-
tailing thirteen halakhic reasons why the "three oaths text" is not a halakhic
problem for Zionism. Briefly they are as follows: (1) The prohibition is not
applicable when the nations of the world permit Jews to return to the Land
of Israel. (2) When God, as revealed through history, sees fit for the Jews to
return to their homeland, the prohibition is annulled. (3) When the nations
of the world do not uphold their oath, the oaths upon the Jews are annulled.
(4) Aliyah, emigration in stages, is not considered *"en masse."* (5) The
prohibition against ascending *en masse* applies only to the Jews living in
Babylon. (6) The prohibition was only for a thousand years. (7) The oath
prohibits only the rebuilding of the Temple. (8) When there is a dire necessity, the prohibition is annulled. (9) The prohibition was not the unan-
imous opinion in the Talmud. (10) The author of the statements regarding
the oaths, R. Zeira, changed his position. (11) Although Isaac de Leon in his
Megillat Esther[7] rules that there is a halakhic prohibition against going to

the land of Israel *en masse*, many halakhic authorities, including Nachmanides, disagree. (12) The oaths are Divine decrees, not prohibitions (Aviner 1980).

The most significant and widely regarded response to the problem, however, is that (13) the entire Talmudic passage regarding the three oaths is homiletical (*aggadic*) and so has no legal force.

Soloveitchik's changing attitude toward Zionism

Soloveitchik understood how the idea of a Jewish state could be foreign to a Halakhic Man. His grandfather Hayyim Soloveitchik was fiercely anti-Zionist.[8] In the eulogy for his uncle, Soloveitchik explained that R. Velvele had no halakhic framework within which to fit the category of a Jewish state created by secular Jews.[9] One's halakhic ontology shapes one's worldview, and if one's ontology does not contain a secular Jewish state, Soloveitchik reasons, one cannot be a halakhic supporter of modern Zionism.[10]

Soloveitchik himself, however, did develop a religious conceptual framework within which a Halakhic Man could understand the role of secular Jews in the creation of a modern Jewish state. Soloveitchik saw all Jews, secular and religious, united in a community of *fate*. When a Jew is persecuted in one area, all Jews suffer. When Jews return to their homeland, all Jews—religious and not—participate in its rebuilding. Only Jews who accept and practice the Halakhah, however, are part of a community of *faith*.

Soloveitchik was not always an outspoken Zionist. As a young adult, he heard about how his father was mistreated at Tachkemoni, a Zionist school affiliated with Mizrachi. He also witnessed how his father was mocked within their community for heading the Talmud studies department at that school.

Soloveitchik had a high regard for the Lithuanian-born Rabbi Eliezer Silver (1882–1968).[11] In 1937, Silver led the American delegation to the last European Agudah conference and received a mandate to establish Agudah in the United States.[12] Soloveitchik was appointed to head its national executive committee and was chosen as a member of the newly formed American Council of Torah Sages (Rakeffet-Rothkoff 1999, 1:52). One of Agudah's core values was its opposition to secular Zionism.

In an address delivered in 1939, however, Soloveitchik publicly declared his support for political Zionism (Farber 2020, 131–32). When he learned of the horrific destruction of European Jewry, his support for political Zionism became passionate.

> In the midst of a night of the terrors of Majdanek, Treblinka, and Buchenwald; in a night of gas chambers and crematoria; in a night of total divine self-concealment; in a night ruled by the devil of doubt and destruction who sought to sweep the Lover from her own tent into the Catholic Church; in a night of continuous searching for the Beloved—on

that very night the Beloved appeared. The Almighty, who was hiding in his splendid *sanctum*, suddenly appeared and began to beckon at the tent of the Lover, who tossed and turned on her bed beset by convulsions and the agonies of hell.

(*KDD*, 31)

Soloveitchik viewed the State of Israel as a necessary correction for the horrors that befell the Jewish people during the Holocaust. In his essay, "The Six Knocks" Soloveitchik describes six post-Holocaust events in which God reached out to the Jewish people, most of which revolved around the creation of the Jewish State.

When the full extent of the destruction of European Jewry became known, he became an ardent proponent of religious Zionism. He joined Mizrachi and subsequently no longer felt welcome by Agudah. Nonetheless, he remained a passionate Zionist the rest of his life.

Similarly, he ultimately came to change a stance he held regarding secular (nonreligious) Jews. Soloveitchik was initially skeptical of any prospect of genuine cooperation between religious and secular Jews (*Halakhah Aggadah*, Kaplan 1999b, 2013, 66ff). Roughly concurrent with his new stance on Zionism came a rethinking of his position on how religious Jews should take a considerably softer approach toward their secular brethren.

Wurzburger (1996) argues that Soloveitchik's Zionism was based on his philosophical understanding of Judaism. Jews must study Torah, but they must also use technology and advanced science (111–12). Jewish efforts should not be applied exclusively to spiritual perfection; they must also be used to achieve communal interests—which includes reclaiming the Land of Israel, building its infrastructure, and protecting its security (112–15). Soloveitchik also insists that the Torah is not a guide for achieving metaphysical heights but rather a guide for living in the here and now. Only by being ethical, by participating in the welfare of the community do we become godly (114). We must not leave the physical world behind and try to elevate ourselves to God's world. Rather, working with the community and doing acts of loving-kindness bring godliness down to this world. Soloveitchik, following the example of his grandfather, Hayyim of Brisk—who collected money on Yom Kippur (an act generally forbidden) to save a nonreligious Jew—believed that all Jews must work together and take responsibility for one another (118). And thus, for Soloveitchik, Zionism entails working with all Jews—secular and religious—to rebuild the Land of Israel and take responsibility for its security.

The nature of Soloveitchik's Zionism

A non-Messianic Zionism. Soloveitchik did not generally attach Messianic significance to the State of Israel.[13] He did not view its establishment as the ultimate redemption and did not consider it, in the words of the rabbinic phrase, the "beginning of the flowering of our redemption."[14] As a practical matter, he was also unsure "how long the State of Israel would be around, surrounded by a string of hostile forces" (Holzer 2009a, 179).

Neither did Soloveitchik glorify the State excessively (Holzer 2009a, 179; *CCC*, 164) and put it above all else. The only loyalty for a Jew is to God and His Torah. If the State of Israel helps in this obligation, Soloveitchik writes, he will devote his body and soul to it. But if the State interferes, he will not (*On Repentance*, 224).

Soloveitchik believed that it is abominably pagan and folly to consider statehood as the highest achievement and the most precious possession of the Jewish people. A state is a relative good and not an absolute one (Holzer 2009a, 179, 215). To say that Judaism has existed throughout the ages solely to establish the State of Israel is sheer madness. Like Yeshayahu Leibowitz, Soloveitchik believed that equating Judaism with statehood is blasphemy (Holzer 2009a, 179).

Halakhah. Soloveitchik considered the founding of the State of Israel, in and of itself, of nominal halakhic significance. The potential for fulfilling numerous commandments that pertain to the Land of Israel, such as tithing, and the obligation to settle the land, do however, make it halakhically significant.[15]must not lose sight of a law

Among religious Zionists, the status of Israeli holidays has always been controversial. Adding a new religious holiday is no small matter. Doing so inevitably requires a halakhic framework with halakhic concepts. On Israel's Independence Day, which is a national secular holiday in Israel, but considered a religious holiday by some religious Zionists, he would permit the *shliah tzibur*, the leader of prayers in a congregation, to recite the holiday prayer *Hallel* without a blessing. Saying a blessing with *Hallel* would imbue the prayer with halakhic significance. It would require Israel's Independence Day to fit into a halakhic category of a certain sort. Soloveitchik would participate in its recitation, provided it was clear that they were not reciting it to fulfill a halakhic obligation (Holzer 2009a, 196–98). The day was thereby marked as special by the liturgy but not as a religious holiday on par with, say, Passover or Hanukkah.

Nonetheless, his concern for the halakhic value of the State of Israel was broad. Even his attitude toward mere symbols of the State was shaped by the Halakhah:

> Judaism negates ritual connection with physical things. Nonetheless, we must not lose sight of a law in *Shulḥan Arukh* to the effect that: One who has been killed by non-Jews is buried in his clothes, so that his blood may be seen and avenged, as it is written "I will hold the (heathen) innocent, but not in regard to the blood which they have shed" (*Joel* 4:21). In other words, the clothes of a Jew acquire a certain sanctity when spattered with the blood of a martyr. How much more is this so of the blue and white flag, which has been immersed in the blood of thousands of young Jews who fell in the War of Independence defending

the country and the population (religious and irreligious alike; the enemy did not differentiate between them.) It has a spark of sanctity that flows from devotion and self-sacrifice. We are all enjoined to honor the flag and treat it with respect.

(*Five Addresses*, 139)

Religion and state. Liberal democracies separate church and state. Religious freedom and freedom from religious persecution is a right its citizens take for granted. In some of these countries, like the United States, the barrier between church and state is practically absolute. The government not only is forbidden from enacting religiously coercive legislation but it is also barred from providing funding for religious purposes. In other liberal democracies, the barriers between church and state are less absolute. While religious coercion is usually prohibited, some governments recognize the religions of its various citizens and allocate monies toward the support of their respective institutions.

The State of Israel is an example of the latter. It guarantees its citizens freedom of religion, but its Ministry of Religious Affairs recognizes and funds religious institutions. Moreover, it decides who is a Jew, and it supervises religious rituals such as marriage and divorce without any provision for civil channels. The government has also enshrined certain cultural aspects of Judaism into law, which give the State of Israel a Jewish character. These include requiring kosher food in the military and at government functions and the nationalization of Jewish religious holidays. There is also a commitment to maintaining the "status quo" regarding Sabbath observance. On a national level, nonessential projects and services are prohibited on the Sabbath, and many municipalities also enforce a Sabbath ban against public transportation (see Chapter 3, Section "In the state of Israel").

The subject of religious coercion by the government on the population had been a delicate one in the early days of the State of Israel and still is. Secular Israeli Jews often feel that the religious political parties are attempting to legislate a religious agenda that would limit their freedom. From time to time there are public demonstrations and even slowdowns and strikes protesting against perceived encroachment over the lives of nonreligious citizens. Israeli political parties often have religious coercion as a primary agenda item on their platforms.

Soloveitchik was ambivalent about legislating religious practices in the State of Israel. On the one hand, he urged the Mizrachi Party to work politically to establish and enhance religious institutions. On the other hand, he was against any type of religious coercion by the state.

Although Soloveitchik's Zionism is mostly non-Messianic, he argues that if the State of Israel is a fulfillment of the prophetic vision, and a vehicle toward complete redemption, then religion must be an integral part of the state. From a pragmatic perspective, he argued that a state with religious legislation helps counter accusations of dual loyalty directed at diaspora Jews. Loyalty to Israel could then be interpreted as religious rather than nationalistic. Also, religious commonality strengthens ties between Jews in the diaspora and those in Israel. Soloveitchik also believed that state-sanctioned cultural, educational, and spiritual projects would convince secular Jews that Judaism can add meaning to their lives.

In practice, however, Soloveitchik often advised Mizrahi not to advocate for religious legislation that could be viewed by nonreligious Jews as interfering in their lives. Holzer quotes Soloveitchik unambiguously against legislating religious observance:

> I am the one who opposes fully ... the whole business of legislating religion in [the Land of Israel]. To me it is ridiculous, it will obtain the reverse effect. You cannot make a Jew pious or observant by having a police force ... To me, Mizrachi is committing the most terrible historical mistake. We should instead devote all our energies to an educational campaign, to display the beauty of *yahadus* [Judaism], to show the people that we have a comprehensive philosophy, and make them come out of their free will ....
>
> (Holzer 2009b, 142–44)

Nonphilosophical. Soloveitchik's attachment to the State of Israel and its religious institutions was deep and visceral. His talks and publications on Zionism bear few marks of prior philosophical influence and connection to earlier political thinkers. Though Soloveitchik studied political science with some well-respected professors and refers to politico-philosophical concepts such as the social contract theory in other contexts (e.g., *TLMOF*, 28n*, 30n*, n†), there is little indication that his understanding of Zionism drew from that tradition. There is no discussion of Divine Right Theory, the Treaty of Westphalia, Plato's ideal state, Aristotle's notion of the state's role in the good life, Augustine's City of God, Hobbes's state of nature, Locke's theory of democracy, Rousseau's notion of slavery in society, Mendelssohn's *Jerusalem*, or any of the other usual suspects in the realm of political philosophy. Moreover, he is not clearly responding or reacting to Jewish anti-Zionists or non-Zionists like Hermann Cohen or Mendelssohn, or any other historical or contemporary anti-Zionist. In our exposition below, however, we note but a few possible points of contact and philosophical avenues that may illuminate Soloveitchik's thinking.

Zionist activities and its price

Soloveitchik's support for the State of Israel was vocal, and he encouraged Jews to help build its religious institutions. As part of his Zionist activities, Soloveitchik served as Honorary President of the Religious Zionists of America and Honorary President of the Mizrachi-Hapoel Mizrachi World Organization. He was involved in fundraising on behalf of institutions in Israel and was for many years the featured speaker at the Mizrachi annual convention in the United States. This is despite the fact that he had turned down the position of chief rabbi of the State of Israel in 1961 (see Chapter 2, Section "Declining the Chief Rabbinate").

There is a romantic greatness to Soloveitchik not usually noted.[16] From his perspective, he sacrificed his legacy and destiny for his ideals.[17] Soloveitchik hailed from a distinguished lineage of Lithuanian ultra-Orthodox leaders, most of whom looked askance (or likely would have) at anyone championing Zionism or secular education (see, e.g., Dunner and Myers 2015), both of which he openly advocated.[18] Soloveitchik's grand-father, Ḥayyim of Brisk, as mentioned, was unambiguously against secular Zionism. This was also true for the majority of Soloveitchik's peers, the ultra-Orthodox (ḥaredi) elite.

By affiliating with Mizrachi, Soloveitchik wrote himself out of the re-ligious culture into which he was born. Speaking in the third person and using his alter ego, the Biblical Joseph,[19] Soloveitchik spoke of the trauma caused by his decision to leave Agudah and align himself with religious Zionism:

> We must be clear about this: It was not a pleasant experience to be far from the Tribes of God, from the great ones of the generations—from "Levi" ... To be separated from his outstanding brothers, ostracized, as it were, not only by "part of the Sanhedrin" but by the majority of them, was a tragedy to Joseph. They drove "Joseph" from the [intimate Jewish houses of prayer], forced him out of the rabbinate, and expelled him from the society of Torah scholars. They humiliated him everywhere.
>
> (*Five Addresses*, 25–26)

> I was not born into a Zionist household. My parents' ancestors, my father's house, my teachers and colleagues were far from the Mizrachi religious Zionists ... I built an altar upon which I sacrificed sleepless nights, doubts and reservations. Regardless, the years of the Hitlerian Holocaust, the establishment of the State of Israel, and the accomplishment of Mizrachi in the land of Israel, convinced me of the correctness of our movement's path. The altar still stands today, with smoke rising from the sacrifice upon it ... Jews like me ... are required to sacrifice on this altar their peace of mind, as well as their social relationships and friendships.
>
> (*Five Addresses*, 35–36)

Why did Soloveitchik become a Zionist? There appear to be two overriding reasons. (1) He saw the return of the Jews to their homeland as a powerful refutation of the Catholic Church's claim that God had abandoned the Jewish people[20] and (2) during the Holocaust, the Jews in America failed to forcefully protest what was happening to the Jews of Europe. Soloveitchik was determined not to repeat this mistake. He would not remain passive as the Jews in Israel were threatened by their neighboring Arab states (Rakeffet-Rothkoff 1999, 2:156; *KDD* 77–80).

Two of Soloveitchik's well-known works explore his stance on Zionism. In *Kol Dodi Dofek*, Soloveitchik makes a passionate case for religious Zionism. In his *Five Addresses,* he focuses on religious Zionism but with an emphasis on the goals and accomplishments of the Mizrachi movement.

Kol Dodi Dofek (1956)

> I was asleep, but my heart was wakeful. Hark, my beloved knocks! "Let me in, my own, my darling, my faultless dove!" ... I had taken off my robe—was I to don it again? I had bathed my feet—was I to soil them again? My beloved took his hand off the latch, and my heart was stirred for him. I rose to let in my beloved ... I opened the door for my beloved, but my beloved had turned and gone.
>
> (*Song of Songs,* 5:2–5)

Why do the wicked prosper while the righteous suffer? This is perhaps one of the oldest and most baffling theological problems. Soloveitchik tells us that we can grapple with this question from two very different vantage points: from the perspective of the Man of Fate or from that of a Man of Destiny.[21]

A Man of Fate is passive, a mere object. Things happen to him. He bemoans the evil that befalls him and the cruelty he suffers. Against his will he is born; against his will he dies; and between those defining moments, he suffers. A Man of Fate is plagued by an insoluble question: why does evil come upon me? For this question, there truly is no answer. He cannot hope to see or understand the world from God's perspective.

The Man of Destiny, however, does not ask "why," but rather he turns to the Halakhah which instructs him on *what* he ought to do and how he ought to act when evil occurs (Sokol 1999). Halakhah demands he examine his deeds and change his actions. He must empathize with those who suffer, feel their pain, and work within the community to help them. He must bring the Man of Destiny to the fore and change from a passive object to an active subject.

The problem of evil is a classic theological problem that asks how God's existence or at least God's goodness can be reconciled with the evil in the universe. The Biblical book of *Job* is an early discussion of that problem. The Talmud addresses the problem in various places, especially as concerned with the martyrdom of Rabbi Akiba (see Urbach 1975, 444–48). Soloveitchik opens the essay with a discussion of the problem in general and moves to the more specific case of Job's suffering. The real subject of the essay, however, is the more recent and greater evil, the Holocaust. What are we to do in the wake of the destruction of European Jewry, and what is our responsibility to the newly established State of Israel?

Turning again to Halakhah, Soloveitchik argues that when God presents us with an opportunity, especially one brought about in miraculous circumstances, we must not tarry. Halakhah demands we take immediate action. The title of this essay, *Kol Dodi Dofek*, or *Hark, My Beloved Knocks*, is a warning that God is beckoning us and we dare not waste time. God, who had been concealing himself during the Holocaust, is now knocking at our door, beckoning us back to our ancestral homeland. Jews must rise to the challenge, empathize with their coreligionists in Israel, and help them during this precarious time.

Kol Dodi Dofek lays out with verve and eloquence Soloveitchik's defense of Zionism and the importance of the State of Israel. It contains four main themes: the suffering of the righteous;[22] the wondrous events surrounding the establishment of the State of Israel; the two covenants with the Jewish people, one of fate and the other of destiny; and the obligation of Jewish religious Zionists toward the State of Israel.

Kol Dodi Dofek is not a halakhic defense of Zionism. Soloveitchik never wrote one. Rather, it is an intellectual and emotional appeal for Jewish people—especially observant ones—to support the then nascent Jewish State.

Describing the "six knocks," Soloveitchik explains that in 1948, as the Jewish people were beset by convulsions and the agonies of hell, the Almighty, who had been hiding, began to beckon at the tent of the Lover, and the State of Israel was born. These six knocks were as follows:

1. The rebirth of the Jewish State.
2. Israel's military victory over its neighbors in 1948.
3. The shattering of the Christian theological claim that the separation of the Jewish people from their land is proof that Biblical promises relating to Zion and Jerusalem refer allegorically to Christianity and the Christian Church.
4. The return of many secular Jews to religious belief and practice.
5. The lesson to the nations of the world that Jewish blood can no longer be shed freely.
6. The Jewish State as an ever-ready sanctuary for persecuted Jews anywhere in the world.

With a sense of guilt for not having done enough to save European Jewry during the Holocaust, Soloveitchik was determined to do more to protect the security of the State of Israel:

> We all sinned by our silence in the face of the murder of millions ... When I say "we" I mean all of us: including myself, the members of rabbinic and lay organizations both Orthodox and secular, and Jewish political organizations of all persuasions ... In the crisis that the land of Israel is [at present] passing through, Providence is again testing us.
>
> (*KDD*, 78)

All Jews, especially observant ones, must become actively involved in the defense of Israel and help build its institutions in a way that reflects Torah values.

When discussing the problem of theodicy, we explained Soloveitchik's view that one can choose to be either a passive Man of Fate or an active Man of Destiny.[23] Soloveitchik takes this a step further and explains that the Fate/Destiny dichotomy holds true on a national level as well. The Covenant of Destiny that God concluded with the Israelites at Sinai included only those who follow the Halakhah. The earlier Covenant of Fate that God concluded with the Israelites in Egypt, however, included all Jews, whether observant of Halakhah or not.[24] All Jews are united in the Covenant of Fate concluded in Egypt. When one Jew suffers, all Jews feel the pain. When called upon by the Divine, all types of Jews, knowingly or unknowingly, play a halakhic role in rebuilding the Land of Israel. Soloveitchik has thus established a halakhic justification for a Jewish State founded and built mostly by nonobservant Jews.

Although Soloveitchik viewed the creation of the State of Israel as a positive and important event, he did not view it in eschatological, end-of-days, terms. He did, however, see the rebirth of the Jewish State as reflecting a shift in God's will, so to speak, from *hester panim*, concealing Himself, to *kol dodi dofek*, God openly beckoning the Jewish people. With His new involvement, however, come corresponding opportunities and responsibilities for the Jewish people.

Soloveitchik sees both God reaching out and the possibility of missing our opportunity reflected metaphorically in the biblical *Song of Songs*, the very same book that anti-Zionist religious Jews had used to make their argument against Zionism and the Jewish State (Schacter 2006, 55).

KDD in Israeli religious-Zionist consciousness. Schwartz (2006) writes that because he was a great sage and a religious Zionist, Soloveitchik's *Kol Dodi Dofek* was diligently studied in Zionist Yeshivot in Israel, but that its anti-metaphysical (non-Messianic) ideas were not internalized. It was the Messianic views of A. I. Kook, his son (see above), and their students that sparked the imagination of religious Zionists.

This situation, however, has since changed. *Kol Dodi Dofek* is now "making its way to the center of consciousness in Zionist yeshivot. The latent call to abandon metaphysics and to return to 'real' existence is shaping the lives of many religious-Zionists." Schwartz concludes, "[We] can safely say that this work [*Kol Dodi Dofek*] has become the unofficial manifest[o] of the next generation of religious-Zionism. If, in the past, Rav Kook and his circle were setting the tone of religious-Zionism single-handedly, today R. Soloveitchik's approach is becoming a real alternative" (69).

The Rav speaks: five addresses

Between 1962 and 1967, Soloveitchik delivered five speeches in Yiddish (at the time still the *lingua franca* of Jewish religious discourse) to the annual gathering of the Mizrachi movement in the United States. These were published in English as *The Rav Speaks: Five Addresses*. While *Kol Dodi*

Dofek is Soloveitchik's most passionate argument for Zionism and the State of Israel, much rich detail is added in the *Five Addresses*. However, while the subject of *Kol Dodi Dofek* is the State of Israel, in the *Five Addresses* it is the Mizrachi movement, even as the purpose of Mizrachi is to support Israel and advocate for its religious institutions.

Broadly speaking, Soloveitchik's goals for the *Five Addresses* were to spell out the principles of the Mizrachi movement, review its successes and failures, discuss the challenges facing the religious Zionist community in Israel, and get American Orthodox Jews to actively support the Mizrachi movement.

Unstated but implicit in the *Five Addresses* is another crucial goal: making the State of Israel visible and meaningful to Halakhic Men. Recall that Halakhic Man processes the world through his *a priori* halakhic constructs. When he sees a stream of water, Halakhic Man perceives it via the halakhot of *mikvah*, a ritual bath. Similarly, with the State of Israel. Are there halakhic parameters through which Halakhic Man can find significance in a non-Messianic Jewish State established mostly by nonhalakhic Jews? If not, the State of Israel is invisible and irrelevant to Halakhic Man. Throughout the *Five Addresses*, Soloveitchik goes to great lengths to define (i.e., construct, create) halakhic categories that make the State of Israel meaningful to Halakhic Men. We discuss some of these in detail, including the concept of modern conquest of the Land of Israel and the concept of covenants of the Jewish people with God, especially as both of these involve nonobservant Jews.

Let us examine the principles of the religious Zionist movement and some of its accomplishments from Soloveitchik's perspective.

The three principles of the religious Zionist movement. In the *Five Addresses*, Soloveitchik addressed audiences of religious Zionist Jews. He was under no illusions that his speeches would cause anti-Zionists to change their mind and support Israel. That was not his goal there. A religious Zionist Jew, however, axiomatically accepts a number of principles. If one does not accept these principles, the Mizrachi ideology is meaningless to them. What are these principles? The first is the conviction that the foundation and existence of the State of Israel are a miraculous event of immense importance. The second principle is the belief that the Torah is meant to be observed, realized, and fully lived in every place and at all times: within every social, economic, and cultural framework, in every technological circumstance and every political condition—in both the diaspora and in the Jewish State. Finally, the third principal of Mizrachi is that the sanctity of a Jew can never be voided. Though one may be sunk deeply in the mire of sin, in coarseness and in materialism, the soul of man burns within him. It is forbidden to negate the power of repentance. Every Jew can repent.

Each of these three principles is challenged by segments of the anti-Zionist ultra-Orthodox community. For example, Joel Teitelbaum argued that there is nothing miraculous about the founding of the State of Israel, and, on the contrary, the entire endeavor was inspired by Satan. The second principle, that Torah is made to be actualized within every social, economic, and cultural framework, is implicitly rejected by ultra-Orthodox segments that keep their communities within virtual religious ghettos cut off from the values of society. Finally, as previously discussed regarding the mystical case for religious anti-Zionism, the concept that every Jew can be redeemed is rejected by segments of the Edah Haredit/Neturei Karta, who view Zionists as spiritual descendants of the worshippers of the Golden Calf whose souls are rooted in impurity and thus beyond spiritual redemption. Soloveitchik understands that these segments of ultra-Orthodox Jews will not be convinced by any of his arguments because they reject the underlying principles of modern religious Zionism.

The successes of the religious Zionist movement. The religious Zionist movement has many accomplishments. It saved the honor of religious Jewry by helping to build the land and establish the Jewish State. It established a network of religious schools. It preserved the sanctity of the family by preventing the profanation of the priesthood and by not performing marriages between Jews and non-Jews. They preserved the Sabbath by passing by-laws in the municipalities. They fought the "who is a Jew battle"[25] and prevented apostates and monks from being classified as Jews. Finally, they established the rabbinate, which is Mizrachi's crowning success.[26]

Biblical personalities

Throughout his philosophical writing, Soloveitchik consistently explores typological personality sketches such as we saw when looking at Halakhic Man. He also employs a kind of dialectical reasoning, examining an issue from contradictory points of view. In the *Five Addresses,* instances of these methods abound. We find personality sketches, for example, of the Biblical characters Abraham, Sarah, Joseph, Rebekah, and Isaac, although none of these are developed to the extent that are Halakhic Man or the Biblical Adam in *Halakhic Man* or "The Lonely Man of Faith," respectively. Even more prevalent is Soloveitchik's dialectical reasoning, which permeates all the *Five Addresses.* He explores the relationship between opposing concepts such as sword/book, stranger/resident, male/female, *koah/gevurah,* hiding/conquering, field/tent, and wisdom/understanding. A survey of some of these dichotomies might be instructive.

Sword/Book. Modern secular man believes in both the power of the sword—the political-economic foundation of society—and in the power of the books of science to bring total redemption. Similarly, the secular population of the State of Israel possesses boundless faith in the power of the sword and in the power of their secular books.

The task of Mizrachi is to bestow upon the population of Israel not merely the book but the Book of books, to sanctify the secular and to bring about the redemption of the soul. To achieve this, Mizrachi must use the power of both the sword—political leadership and policy making—and the book, creating religious institutions.

Stranger/Resident. Like Abraham, the religious Zionist must remember that in the State of Israel, he is both a stranger and a resident. As a religious Zionist, he is a resident and part of the general community. He engages in business and speaks the language of the land. He takes part in its social-economic institutions and serves in the army. He works in the laboratories and endeavors to overcome illness. He produces and develops the country and is a resident in the fullest sense of the word. As a religious Zionist, he is also a stranger. He belongs to a community that is foreign to the secular culture. His community is full of altars and sacrifices, a world of Torah, of loving kindness, of sanctity and purity, with which the secular culture cannot identify.

So, too, is the State of Israel both a stranger and a resident among the other nations. We are a nation like all other nations, and yet we are a nation that dwells apart.

Male/Female. As we have seen in our discussion of the Talne Rebbitzin's eulogy above (Chapter 4, Section "The Rebbitzin of Talne"), man must encapsulate both male and female aspects, active creator and passive recipient, and master and disciple. All people have the power of the soul: good qualities and feelings which they can share with others to influence them. No one is impervious to the influence of the Master who created the world, and every Jew can be saved.

Man can be a male, creator of worlds. He also has the ability to humble himself, to be a female, passive, before the creative influence of the Creator. When he believes this, he has the power to bring people back to the fold. Eventually, all will humble themselves before the Great Master when He finally appears.

Ko'aḥ/Gevurah. In another distinction we have already seen in our discussion of "Catharsis," there are two Hebrew words for strength. *Ko'ah* refers to power, ability, and physical strength. *Gevurah* refers to heroism. *Gevurah* was on display in 1948 when Israel battled her stronger and more numerous enemies.

Historically, the existence of the Jewish people has been heroic; it has exhibited *gevurah*: it followed Halakhah, it observed the Sabbath, and it educated its children in Torah. Today, too (i.e., 1962–1967), Mizrachi's representatives in the Knesset are not powerful. Their financial resources are meager, yet they carry on the struggle to transform Israel from a secular state into a sacred, heroic country.

Hiding/Conquering. There are two ways to attain sanctity: by hiding behind a wall (i.e., in a virtual ghetto) or by going out into the world and "conquering" it. Mizrachi must emulate both these models. It must engage fully with the modern world, and it must also create institutions and environments in which Jews can study Torah and live by their ideals.

Field/Tent. Rebekah of the Bible insisted that Jacob receive the blessings from his father, Isaac. She knew that if Esau would be the only one who knows how to hunt and be "a man of the field," that is, to go out in the world, or its contemporary equivalent, be a scientist, farmer, or politician, then Jacob has no future. Rebekah explained to Jacob that the field need not be a place of impurity but can, in all its manifestations, be beautiful and glorious. It is easier to remain in the tent (i.e., the yeshiva, study hall) and hold the Talmud with both hands, but when historical circumstances demand it, Jews must be ready, on the one hand, to engage with the world and, with the other, hold the Talmud.

Halakhic categories

The above distinctions are characteristic of the Brisker method of halakhic analysis. An idea Soloveitchik picked up from something Hermann Cohen stresses is the creative role of the subject in creating the objects of experience. The subject does not create objects but only the concepts of the objects. The individual creates the concepts *a priori*, and those concepts are the lenses through which experience is filtered. Similarly, the creative goal of Halakhic Man is to literally create novel halakhic categories or concepts. These categories then become part of the mental apparatus of Halakhic Man. They are his *a priori* categories by which he understands and interprets the physical world.

The State of Israel and its novelty posed special challenges and opportunities for constructing halakhic categories.[27] The challenges emerge because Judaism was suddenly confronted with a novel entity: a modern Jewish but secular nation-state that seems to have genuine halakhic significance. How is Halakhic Man to make sense of such a novelty? Halakhic Man must thus fashion novel halakhic categories with which to confront the world. Soloveitchik explicitly mentions a few of these categories that must be created in light of the new reality of the State of Israel: *sanctity of land, sanctity of boundaries, all the inhabitants of the land.*

Let us now consider two others which Soloveitchik works out in the *Five Addresses*. The first pertains to the legitimacy and sanctity of the modern conquest of the Land of Israel—as was accomplished mostly by secular Jews. In the second, Soloveitchik explains that while secular Zionists do not currently accept the covenant made with God at Sinai, nevertheless, their identification with the State of Israel includes them in the covenant God made with Abraham.[28] Let us examine the two halakhic categories in more detail.

The concept of land acquisition. The nature of a legitimate and legal transaction is one that is generally carefully spelled out in many systems of law. Jewish law is no exception. To acquire something, one must perform an act of *kinyan*, an action that finalizes one's taking possession of an object. Different kinds of objects require different kinds of *kinyanim*. For example, one takes possession of real estate in a different manner than one would take possession of a horse.

To personally acquire the Land of Israel, Abraham performed a *kinyan*, an act of taking legal possession of the land—he traversed its length and width. But to acquire it for all subsequent generations, he also needed to sacrifice for God. His trials and tribulations, which culminated in the binding of Isaac and the burial of Sarah in the Cave of Machpelah, acquired the Land of Israel for all generations.

Soloveitchik understands that the entire Shivat Zion movement (the "return to Zion movement"), which was comprised of both secular and religious Jews, took possession of the Land of Israel: "Hundreds of thousands of dunams of land were [bought], trees were planted, and swamps and marshes were transformed into blooming settlements; they built houses, founded cities, developed industry, built roads and so on" (20). All parties, from religious Zionists to (secular left-wing parties) Mapai and Mapam, built altars and offered sacrifices to God. "The sacrifice of the Jew is always favorably received by God, even if one who offers the sacrifice does not admit Divine purpose."[29] The Arab bullet and the Arab knife did not distinguish between Hebron Yeshiva students and left-wing kibbutzniks. "Therefore we believe that our enemies will in no way be able to undo the second acquisition, effected via altars and sacrifices, and that the land of Israel will remain ours for eternity" (22). Thus, even if the acquisition (from God) was not done with the intention to legally take possession of the land in a legitimate halakhic fashion, the transaction is nonetheless effective. Soloveitchik saw in the collective sacrifice of the entire movement, both its secular and religious members, a case for the legitimate religious acquisition of the land for eternity. Hence, the novel halakhic category of "land acquisition."

The dual concepts of covenant. Halakhah recognizes the category of a "covenant," or a binding agreement between two parties. Jewish tradition discusses two covenants that God made with the Jewish people: the first with the patriarch Abraham and the second with the Jewish people collectively at Sinai. The original covenant with Abraham was intertwined with the land. The second covenant at Sinai was independent of the land. Soloveitchik cites the medieval commentator Rashi, saying that the original covenant with Abraham was not invalidated by the introduction of a new covenant at Sinai. The original covenant with its promise of the land is eternal. An observant Jew who lives in Israel is thus sanctified by two covenants: the covenant made with Abraham and the covenant at Sinai.

Modern religious Jews who today live outside of Israel do not share in the sanctity of the covenant of Abraham. One can be fully observant and yet not participate in the sanctity of the covenant with Abraham when one does not identify with the covenant of Abraham and connect himself to all Jews.

Modern Jews, Soloveitchik notes, unfortunately identify more closely with Western society and less so with their coreligionists. The only way they can retain their bond with the Jewish people is through the State of Israel.

The very fact that Israel is isolated internationally, that the vast majority of Klal Yisrael [the Jewish people] is sympathetic towards her and ready to suffer all manner of charges against her by Jew-haters;

the fact that we identify with the State and see all who oppose it as Jew-haters ... sanctifies us with the sanctity of the Patriarchs. (150)

Secular Jews in Israel who identify with the Land of Israel and sacrifice for it are thus included in the covenant God made with Abraham. This covenant is thus a novel part of the mental life of Halakhic Man, as is the category of land acquisition.

Notes

1 See B. *Berakhot* 28b and B. *Megillah* 17b, which provide two time frames for the establishment of the *Amidah*: by 120 Elders (i.e., during the early part of the Second Temple era); and during the reign of Rabban Gamliel II of Yavneh (ca. 80–110 CE). See also *Yerushalmi, Berakho*t 2:4, 4d. There is a rich literature on this problem. See, e.g., Zelcer (2012).
2 See Batnitzky (2011, 53–57).
3 "Reform Judaism," *Encyclopaedia Judaica*. vol. 14, col. 26 (Jerusalem: Keter, 1972).
4 Ibid., col. 27.
5 See Inbari (2016) for historical and sociological overview of ultra-Orthodox anti-Zionism in its formative years.
6 Reference is to the original printing in Teitelbaum 1961. There is a partial translation in Batnitzky and Brafman (2018, 155–59).
7 *Megilat Esther* is a commentary on Maimonides' *Book of Commandments.* The stated prohibition to ascend *en masse* is in his appendix "Commandments that the Rav [Maimonides] Forgot to Include in the Positive Commandments, According to Nahmanides," Mitzvah 4. Attributed to Isaac de Leon but now generally believed to have been written by Isaac Leon Ben Eliezer ibn Zur.
8 Ḥayyim Soloveitchik was a well-known opponent of Zionism. As an illustration, a well-attested anecdote has him telling a young Raphael Zalman Levine in 1915 that it is preferable to donate spare money to a church rather than to Keren Kayemet l'Yisrael, a fund to purchase land in Palestine for Jews. See Bezalel Naor's "The Religious-Zionist Manifesto of Rabbi Yehudah Leib Don Yahya" at https://seforimblog.com/2019/06/the-religious-zionist-manifesto-of-rabbi-yehudah-leib-don-yahya/#_ftn2.
9 On Soloveitchik and the problem of a Jewish state created by secular Jews, see below and the discussion in Kaplan (2013, 66f). Cf. Leibowitz (1992, 164).
10 Meiselman (1998, 8) uses this eulogy to downplay Soloveitchik's Zionism: "[T]he Rav said that whereas a secular government in Israel does not fit into any halakhic categories, it is religiously irrelevant. This was not just a formulation of his uncle's position, but it was his as well. This is the essential theme of his essay *Kol Dodi Dofek*, in which he states clearly that the importance of the State of Israel has to be evaluated in exclusively pragmatic terms. There is no intrinsic value to that which has no halakhic meaning." Krauss (2000) responds. Quoting *Five Addresses* (137–38) he writes, "[W]e [*Mizrachi*] were the first to explain that the establishment of the State has halakhic significance, since by its means we shall be able to fulfill the *mitzvah* of possessing and settling it. We said, this *mitzvah* is fulfilled not only by building up the country economically, but also by our sovereignty there. The existence of the State of Israel and the fact that Jews and not Englishmen determine *aliya*; that Jews and not Arabs are the political masters in the country; and that a Jewish government, police force and army exists, is the

greatest possible fulfillment of the *mitzvah* of settling in *Eretz Yisrael*" (29–30). Krauss (31) further quotes the same work "[T]here is nothing in Israel's history in vain; and if on the Friday, fifth of *Iyyar* 5708, God said: 'Let there be a State of Israel', His words are not in vain ..." (171).

11 Silver was ordained by Ḥayyim Ozer Grodzinski in 1906; immigrated to the United States in 1907; lived first in New York; and accepted rabbinical positions in Harrisburg, then Springfield, Massachusetts, in 1925, and then in Cincinnati, ca. 1931. He was extremely active in the Union of Orthodox Rabbis in the United States and Canada and the Agudah movement in the United States where he spearheaded efforts to rescue Jewish scholars from Europe during World War II.

12 "The Gaon R. Y. D. Soloveitchik's arrival at the Agudath Israel convention in Cincinnati made a big impression ... especially when it was announced that this gaon [sage] became a member of Agudah and was appointed as head of the national executive committee ... Recently there was a gathering of the executive committee of Agudath Israel in New York. At this gathering ha-Rav R. Y. D. ha-Levi Soloveitchik from Boston participated ..." (*Ha-Pardes*, October 1940, 14(7), 28).

13 Schwartz (1996, 129) notes that Soloveitchik's approach to Zionism mirrors Y. Y. Reines' in two significant ways: The modern Jewish Zionist awaking arose due to anti-Semitism and persecution; current Zionism is not in itself nor is it a prelude to eschatological (messianic) times. See also Shatz (2015, esp. 295–98), Shatz (2018, 189), and Singer and Sokol (1982, 253).

14 David Holzer, who served as Soloveitchik's *shamash* (personal assistant) over a period of six years and recorded many of their conversations, once asked him: "*Is there any validity to hakamas ha'medinah as far as geulah or shivas tzion is concerned?*" Soloveitchik replied: "No. *Yimay ha'Moshiach?* No. Since it contributed greatly to the survival of our people it is very important. This [in] itself is important. But all this stupidity——*aschalta d'geulah, geulah*–I am against it" (Holzer 2009a, 216–17).

15 See also Kaplan (1999a, 300–301) and Lyčka (1995b), but see the discussion below of *Five Addresses*.

16 Sokol (2010) is one exception who notes that the role of the individual hero going against the accepted norms of his culture is a standard feature of German Romanticism, which influenced Soloveitchik.

17 See, e.g., Moshe Stern's (the "Debreciner Rav," 1914–1997) *Be'er Moshe*, nos. 3 and 6, pp 11, 17, who rules that it is prohibited to study with or read the books of one who teaches at Yeshiva University lest realizing his (presumably Soloveitchik's) great erudition in Torah, he will assume that he determined it is permissible to be a Zionist.

18 Soloveitchik was not the first one in his family to be sympathetic with Zionism. The Netziv, Rabbi Naftali Tzvi Yehuda Berlin, Soloveitchik's great-great-grandfather did so before him.

19 In *Five Addresses* Soloveitchik remarks, "I prefer to speak about myself rather than others" (34), and "For he who joined Mizrachi was virtually excluded from his birthplace, and ostracized from his spiritual paternal home" (25). Also, "The Rav spoke of Mizrahi, but we can read it as applying to him ..." (Genack 1998, 211); "It seems to me that autobiographical echoes can be heard in the Rav's words when he refers to the type Joseph the Righteous ..." (Wurzburger 1984, 56). Mayer Twersky sees Soloveitchik's usage of Joseph as referring to the Mizrachi movement (Genack 1998, 119).

20 In *KDD*, Soloveitchik writes, "[T]he Beloved also began to knock on the door of the tent of theology, and *possibly this is the strongest beckoning* ... the theological arguments of Christian theologians to the effect that the Holy One has taken

away from the Community of Israel its right to the Land of Israel, and that all of the biblical promises relating to Zion and Jerusalem now refer in an allegorical sense to Christianity and the Christian Church, were all publicly shown to be false, baseless contentions by the establishment of the State of Israel" (33–34, *emphasis* added).

21 Much has been written about *Kol Dodi Dofek*. The Fall 2006 issue of *Tradition* 39(3) is dedicated to the essay and is a good entry into the secondary literature.

22 The problem of evil and suffering is also the central focus of a few of the essays in *OOTW*, especially "A Halakhic Approach to Suffering" and "Out of the Whirlwind." Soloveitchik has been taken to have various responses to the problem of evil. Sokol (1999) focuses on the notion of a "halakhic response" and clarifies what that could mean. Goldschmidt (2014), focusing on a particular passage in *KDD*, categorizes Soloveitchik's theodicy with other soul-making theodicies as does Lang (2007). See Rotenstreich (1984, 65–68) for a discussion of Kant and Hermann Cohen on the problem of evil and Batnitzky (2011, 62) on Cohen and Soloveitchik. See also Shatz (2002, 2013) and Millen (2004).

23 Blidstein (2012, 68) sees this distinction originally in Martin Buber's distinction between a people and a nation.

24 Blidstein (2012, 65–66) explains that the enslavement of the Israelites in Egypt parallels the Holocaust: in both cases the Jews are objects and are united in a Covenant of Fate imposed upon them by others. Similarly, we would argue that the establishment of the State of Israel parallels the revelation at Sinai. At Sinai all Israelites became united in a covenant of faith. So too in the struggle for the modern State of Israel, all types of Jews—secular and observant—were united in a covenant of faith by fulfilling the will of God (whether knowingly or unknowingly) and working together to establish and rebuild the Land of Israel. See also *Vision and Leadership* (71) in which Soloveitchik compares the *hester panim* of the Holocaust to that of the bondage in Egypt.

25 Almost since the state's inception, and given the centrality of Israel's Law of Return to the state's identity, there has been significant controversy over the question of who is considered Jewish. The definition used by Orthodox Jews is that a Jew is someone born of a Jewish mother or one who converts via a traditional Jewish court and has not converted to another religion. However, other Jewish denominations and some Israelis have argued for a broader definition that includes, say, those with Jewish fathers and non-Jewish mothers, or those who have converted to Judaism via a non-Orthodox court, or even those born Jewish and converted to another religion. Because of the importance of the issue, Soloveitchik praises Mizrahi for their efforts in pressuring the Israeli government to retain the traditional definition.

26 C.f. the Section *Religion and State* above.

27 See also Kaplan (1999a, 302–3); Lichtenstein (1996, 47).

28 Similarly, in *KDD* (51–63) Soloveitchik develops this theme and explains that all Jews, secular and religious, are united in a shared Covenant of Fate. As Ziegler (2012, 275) comments, "Between the charged poles of the Holocaust and the State of Israel, one of its most innovative and important ideas—finding a place within a religious framework for secular Jewish identity—often gets lost."

29 In a letter dated 1984, Shakh (1990, 37), a significant Israeli ultra-Orthodox leader, objects to Soloveitchik's characterization of the sacrifices by secular Jews as religiously significant: "I wonder how he [Soloveitchik] forgot what any young student knows: 'Why was the land lost? Because they abandoned My Torah and did not observe My mitzvot.' Surely those [secular Jews] who deny the fundamental and uproot bodies of Torah; who raise their sons and daughters not to know what Shabbat is, or Yom Kippur, or Passover … is this building the land,

or is this its destruction? Is this building an altar or destroying an altar? There are explicit sections in the Torah, 'If they follow in my ways' ... And if one sees a certain era in which the moment smiles, and evil-doers accomplish (lit., build), there is some reason for this, who knows the ways of God? The Holy One Blessed is He, bears the sins until they accumulate. Each day we need great grace from God for we are still but one sheep among seventy wolves who seek to swallow us ...."

6 Interfaith dialogue

Introduction

Readers familiar with Soloveitchik's work and legacy are likely aware of the controversy he often generated as the leader of a sizable Jewish community. When he first arrived in the United States, he fought the kosher meat industry and established nontraditional institutions like the Maimonides co-educational Jewish day school. His presence at the modern Orthodox Yeshiva University and his stance on Zionism all brought him into conflict with many of his contemporaries, from the community with which he once strongly identified.

This chapter discusses "Confrontation," an essay containing Soloveitchik's controversial statement on interfaith dialogue. As was the case with his stance on Zionism, an attack on his position on interreligious conversation was almost inevitable. The issue arose from historical circumstances, and Soloveitchik, in his capacity as a Jewish leader, took a principled stance. Interestingly, however, in this case the opposition came, not from traditionalists, with whom he was only somewhat in sync, but largely from the Orthodox "left" and even from non-Jews.

Also interesting, while many were opposed to his presence at Yeshiva University and his stance on religious Zionism, they engaged in little reasoned polemic or debate. Opposition, certainly. Genuine dialogue or discussion, rarely. For that matter, his philosophy too, the subject of our fourth chapter, has had an unusual reception. To date, there has been extensive discussion and even much criticism but few evaluations of Soloveitchik's core philosophical program and none which insist that it is wrong or misguided in its essence (cf. Brafman 2014; 37). There are questions about the real nature of Halakhic Man, the consistency of *Halakhic Man* with "The Lonely Man of Faith," the consistency of Soloveitchik with traditional Jewish thought, the appropriateness of secular studies, etc., but there is little that comprehensively challenges his whole program of a new approach to Jewish philosophy and the *ta'amei ha-mitzvot* problem.

Part of the reason is that his philosophical program is less well understood and also that there are few practical consequences of buying into his philosophical approach. There are, however, many challenges to his position in his essay "Confrontation" than one might expect given the quarters from which they come. Soloveitchik's stance on interfaith dialogue generated significant responses by thoughtful people, some of whom, one would suspect, would otherwise generally agree with him on matters of religious concern. In this chapter, we summarize Soloveitchik's essay and his position on interfaith dialogue. In addition, we give the reader a feel for the *shakla ve-tarya*, the philosophical give-and-take of the ensuing discussion surrounding this subject. We also note a number of interpretations of the essay and then briefly recapitulate the debate that followed. We hope this exhibits a scholarly debate by intellectuals who believe they are engaged in what a Talmudist might call a *maḥloket le-shem Shamayyim*, a good faith debate for the sake of Heaven.

Background to Soloveitchik's approach

"Confrontation" was published in 1964 but written a few years earlier. In the essay, Soloveitchik repeatedly uses the term "incommensurate" to describe the relationship between two different religions. The word "incommensurate" literally means "having no common measure." This refers to an instance, say in mathematics, when there is no common unit that can be used to measure two magnitudes. The word is now commonly associated by philosophers and historians of science with Thomas Kuhn's 1962 book, *The Structure of Scientific Revolutions*. In it, Kuhn describes what happens when scientific worldviews, or paradigms, shift; for example, from treating Earth as the center of the universe to seeing it as revolving around the Sun, or shifting from a Newtonian absolutist view of the universe to an Einsteinian relativistic one.

These are no simple matters. A Newtonian scientist at the beginning of the twentieth century, for example, could not merely add some information provided by Einstein to his store of physical knowledge and then become an "Einsteinian physicist." One cannot merely add some information about the universe to one's store of scientific information and then understand the new system. The concepts of space, time, motion, speed, simultaneity, light, energy, force, and mass all take on completely different meanings in the new interpretation of the laws of nature. One's whole idea of the universe and the concepts used to describe its significant components must shift. The two ways of describing the universe—the Newtonian and the Einsteinian—have no common vocabulary. They use the same words, but the words refer to different concepts.

The positions are incommensurable. Because theories are integrated wholes, one cannot compare one to another. One cannot subscribe to part of one theory and part of the other. The older scientists and the newer ones do not speak the same language. They do not communicate scientifically. There is no common frame of reference in which to do so. Scientific change is more than just learning something new; it is about changing one's worldview in a particular area of inquiry. More relevantly, when scientific change happens, there is no point where the older scientists and the younger scientists understand one another. They cannot argue or debate with one another. One either accepts the new version as correct because it answers the questions being asked or sticks with the old version of the theory.

Perhaps not as explicitly, this is roughly how Soloveitchik appears to have viewed the nature of religions as well: two religions are incommensurable as they have no common theological vocabulary or measure to use as a basis for dialogue. They cannot communicate and cannot answer each other's questions. They cannot debate. There is just not enough they share to be able to interact constructively on a theological level.

One way of looking at the nature of the incommensurability of scientific theories is as an extension of Ludwig Wittgenstein's later philosophy of language. Where Kuhn contributed significantly to the end of the positivist era of philosophy of science, Wittgenstein was the inspiration for the beginning.

While Soloveitchik was in Berlin, Wittgenstein was in Cambridge discussing new philosophical ideas that emerged from his 1921 *Tractatus Logico-Philosophicus*. One of the core questions in early philosophy of language is: what does it mean for a word to mean something? In solving the problems of logic, which was a central goal, philosophers of that period believed they had to fully understand what language is. To understand language, they had to know what it means for a word to have a meaning. John Locke can be said to have argued that words are there to "mean" whatever ideas they correspond to in the mind of the speaker. When I say the word "coffee mug," I mean that idea in my head of a coffee mug. So when I say the words to you, you get the same idea in your head and you come to "know what I mean." Modern philosophy of language, starting with Gottlob Frege (1980), the inventor of modern logic, starts with the assumption that the meaning of a word involves objects in the world. Thus, Frege believed that when I say "coffee mug," I mean an object on the table (and a bit more—the sense—that need not concern us here) and that when you understand what I mean, it is because we now realize we are both talking about the same object on the table.

Though Wittgenstein was in many ways intellectually indebted to Frege, by the time of his death in 1951, his ideas had undergone some significant evolution, especially his ideas about language and meaning. Wittgenstein argued in *Philosophical Investigations*, a posthumous text which is perhaps the most influential philosophy book of the twentieth century, that a word's meaning is not the object but rather lies in the way words function to make the world intelligible to us. As Wittgenstein puts it, "[T]he meaning of a word is its use in the language" (Wittgenstein 1958, §41). A word means something to the extent that it fits into the whole of a language. But we are not to look at language word by word; rather, we are to look at larger groups of words like sentences which take their significance from the larger context of human action, "to imagine a language is to imagine a form of life" (ibid. §19). Different forms of life engage in what Wittgenstein called "different language games," using different concepts and breaking up the world in different ways. Those who have different "forms of life" cannot communicate as their languages, which include the way they understand the objects in their world, are incommensurable.

This linguistic incommensurability applies to religion too. In a set of lectures published after his death (and after the publication of "Confrontation"), Wittgenstein (1966) argues that believers and nonbelievers are playing different language games. Their views are incommensurate. When they discuss religious matters, they do not merely disagree; they are simply talking past one another, using the same words but with different meanings. They are not communicating. Hilary Putnam (2008), a contemporary Jewish philosopher, sees this part of Wittgensteinian thought also running through Rosenzweig, Buber, and Levinas—the three most significant Jewish philosophers in the post-Kantian tradition (see Zelcer 2009). Max Scheler is likely Soloveitchik's inspiration for this position. Scheler argues along the same lines as Wittgenstein in claiming that science and philosophy are incommensurate; they have little to say to one another. One cannot be used to judge or criticize the other (Scheler 1980, 78).

This theme runs throughout Soloveitchik's work, though perhaps in a more familiar Kantian sense. We have already seen that Soloveitchik takes religions to be imposing a category scheme upon those who adhere to them. Judaism and Halakhic Man understands the world through the lens of its own ontology, through the specific categories that the Halakhah imposes upon him. All worldviews impose an ontology on those who hold them, including Christianity and other religions. Two people with different category schemes can only talk past each other, not with each other. Since every religious category is tied into the worldview of its religion, one cannot communicate across religions without imposing one's categorical conception on the other. Soloveitchik could not oppose such an imposition more strongly. He would not have Christianity imposing its category scheme on his religion, and he had no interest in imposing Judaism's on Christianity.

Background to the question of interfaith dialogue

Letters written in the 1950s show Soloveitchik's approach toward interfaith dialogue (Kaplan 2013, 76), but it was not until 1960, when the Catholic Church sought to reform its dogma, that his views became a matter of public interest and discussion.[1] When the Church realized that millennia of contempt and hatred toward the Jewish people had contributed to the Holocaust, the Catholic Church began an internal discussion on modernizing its dogma, specifically its attitude toward the Jews.

In June 1960 during Vatican Council II, Augustin Cardinal Bea, president of the ecumenical council, desiring coordinated input from the Jewish community, turned to Nahum Goldmann, president of the World Jewish Congress (WJC). In response, Goldmann called a meeting to which he invited rabbis representing Orthodox, Conservative, and Reform Judaism. Soloveitchik, who then served as chairman of the Halacha Committee of the RCA,[2] was invited to represent the Orthodox viewpoint.

No one, including Soloveitchik, could predict what the outcome of this Catholic soul-searching might be. Some felt that the Church might demand or at least expect that the Jews, being part of the minority faith community, make concessions that would compromise Judaism. Fearing there would be some who would be overeager to do so, Soloveitchik insisted that Jews make no concessions that would compromise any of their tenets:

> [W]e certainly have not been authorized by our history, sanctified by the martyrdom of millions, to even hint to another faith community that we are mentally ready to revise historical attitudes, to trade favors pertaining to fundamental matters of faith, and to reconcile "some" differences. Such a suggestion would be nothing but a betrayal of our great traditions and heritage and would, furthermore, produce no practical benefits.
>
> ("Confrontation," 25)

The only way to command the respect of the Catholic Church, Soloveitchik argues, was to insist that it accept and respect Jewish religious faith exactly as it is:

> We cannot command the respect of our confronters by displaying a servile attitude. Only a candid, frank and unequivocal policy reflecting unconditional commitment to our God, a sense of dignity, pride and inner joy in being what we are ... will impress the peers of the other faith community among whom we have both adversaries and friends.
>
> ("Confrontation," 25)

In an interview[3] with *HaDoar*, a Hebrew weekly, Soloveitchik outlined four reasons why it is improper for Jews to participate in the Ecumenical Council:

1. The Church's role is to proselytize Jews.
2. Some Jews might view the participation of Jewish leaders at the Vatican Council as their acceptance of Church doctrine.
3. Jews ought not suggest to Catholics what they should change in their liturgy. Soloveitchik felt that "[t]he Church is within her rights to interpret our history in her own theological-dogmatic terms" (Sklarin 2009, 367).
4. The Church might demand reciprocity from Jews to similarly amend its own religious texts. Indeed, "Cardinal Ruffini insisted that if the Church would make emendations to its liturgy, the Jews would be expected to

delete certain anti-Christian passages from the Talmud ..." (Sklarin 2009, 382n82).[4]

Soloveitchik was so insistent that Jews not attend the ecumenical council that he threatened to pull Mizrahi out of the World Zionist Organization if Nahum Goldmann sent a delegation to the Vatican Council (*CCC*, xxxv). Goldmann conceded to Soloveitchik's demand and informed Bea that WJC would not send an official representation to the Vatican.

"Confrontation" is Soloveitchik's halakhic/philosophical explanation and justification of his stance on interfaith discourse. It would not be published for another three years after it was written but has invited controversy ever since.[5]

Confrontation

"Confrontation" lays out Soloveitchik's thinking about how to engage with other faith communities and more importantly how not to. It begins in a surprising but familiar way by speaking first of three "confrontations": of man with the physical world of men; with other men; and finally of one faith community, Judaism, with another, specifically Christianity. Again familiarly, Soloveitchik's argument opposing interfaith religious dialogue is threefold: historical, philosophical, and doctrinal.[6]

The essay (Part 1, Chapters 1 and 2) describes how the Biblical account of creation portrays man in three progressive levels of development. These levels represent different stages of the development of man in all generations. (They also closely parallel Kierkegaard's theory of stages toward individuality. Kierkegaard equates becoming an individual with the progression from an aesthetic personality (as symbolized by Don Juan), to a moral one (as symbolized by Socrates), and finally to a religious level of being (as symbolized by Abraham) (Kierkegaard 1987).)

In Soloveitchik's first stage (illustrated using *Genesis*, 2:5–7), man is a "non-confronted" being who sees himself on a continuum with nature. His conscience is not challenged by any imperative. He recognizes neither a command from without nor the moral "ought" from within. "Man ... determined by biological immediacy and mechanical necessity, knows of no responsibility, no opposition, no fear, and no dichotomy, and hence is free from carrying the load of humanity." He is unaware of his uniqueness as man or that he has been summoned by God to rise to greatness. His goal is to attain unlimited aesthetic pleasure.

In the second stage (Part 1, Chapters 3 and 4), man, disillusioned with the mere pursuit of aesthetic pleasure yet confronted by his insatiable quest for aesthetic pleasure, stops and gazes upon his environment. He sees himself as a singular, unfree, restricted person who at the same time is free, uniquely endowed, and capable of rising above his environment. Examining his station in the world, he finds himself beset by fears and loneliness. "Having been taken out of a state of complacency and optimistic naïveté, he finds the intimate relationship between him and the order of facticity ending in tension and conflict" (13).

In the third stage (Part 1, Chapter 5), man is again confronted by an Other, but this time he does not view the Other with a sense of superiority, but as an equal. Two individuals, a man and wife (Adam and Eve), forge a "community" when they begin to communicate with one another. They share a common destiny but they are simultaneously two distinct individuals with different needs, perspectives, and unbridgeable gaps between them. As we shall soon see, it is these gaps that are the main point in Soloveitchik's philosophical case against interreligious dialogue.

Part 2 of the essay explains that a faith community other than one's own puts man in the position of being "doubly confronted." Jews bear a double load: to act as dignified individuals as part of the universal human experience and also to act as sanctified people as part of a covenantal community. These dual confrontations, the universal and the covenantal, allow for communication only if, unlike in the past, both parties enjoy equal rights and full religious freedom, and importantly, only if they are coordinating on matters of universal human concern and not particular theology.[7]

Being uncertain of the outcome of the ecumenical council, Soloveitchik wrote wearily, "We are not ready for a meeting with another faith community in which we shall become an object of observation, judgment and evaluation, even though the community of the many may then condescendingly display a sense of compassion with the community of the few and advise the many not to harm or persecute the few" ("Confrontation," 21). In a period in which Jews still had not yet fully recovered from the trauma of the Holocaust or appreciated the renewal that was the State of Israel, Soloveitchik did not seek or want Christian pity, however generous or well intentioned.

Laying out his idea on how interfaith dialogue can achieve favorable results, Soloveitchik insisted on four conditions. First, Jews are to be understood as an independent faith community, as a religion endowed with intrinsic worth. Judaism must be viewed against its own meta-historical backdrop and not in relation to the framework of another faith community (see also Spiegel 1964). Second, the language used by one religion to express its own faith is not to be foisted upon the other community, something Soloveitchik thought, like Wittgenstein, was impossible without misrepresenting at least one of the communities. Third, Judaism must refrain from suggesting to Christians how they should change their rituals or amend their texts. Fourth, Jews must not trade favors with Christianity which would involve amending any part of Judaism (21–25).[8] Interfaith dialogue is, however, possible if Jews instruct their representatives to work with other faith communities to achieve universal nontheological goals.[9]

The aforementioned conditions, especially the second one, which insists on the incommensurability of interreligious discourse, represent Soloveitchik's argument against religious dialogue. A historical argument is also evident from these conditions: Jews, having been unjustly mistreated by the Church for millennia, were never in a position to participate fully with other religions in spiritual matters. History, therefore, does not authorize Jews to make concessions to others, or even revise Jewish historical attitudes solely to reconcile "some" historical differences.

In an open letter published as an Addendum to "Confrontation" in the *Rabbinical Council of America Record* (*Interfaith Relationships*),[10] Soloveitchik laid out his final thoughts on the matter. The Jewish religious tradition, explains Soloveitchik, expresses itself both universally and particularly. Jews are concerned with the problems affecting the common destiny of man and are opposed to a philosophy of isolation. Jews, however, are also a distinct faith community with a unique commitment, a singular relationship to God, and a specific way of life. In areas of universal concern, Jews welcome an exchange of ideas and expressions with other faith communities. These include issues of war and peace, poverty, freedom, moral values, the threat of secularism, civil rights, etc. In the areas of faith, religious law, doctrine, and ritual, however, Jews are guided by distinctive concerns, ideals, and commitments. Love and dedication to God are personal and intimate and must not be debated or discussed with members of other faiths.

In 1964, in an open letter in the *Rabbinical Council of America Record* (*Interfaith Relationships*; *CCC,* 259–61), Soloveitchik enumerates ten topics in which dialogue with the Christian faith community would not be proper:

1. Judaic monotheism and the Christian idea of Trinity
2. The Messianic idea in Judaism and Christianity
3. The Jewish attitude toward Jesus
4. The concept of Covenant in Judaism and Christianity
5. The Eucharist mass and Jewish prayer service
6. The Holy Ghost and prophetic inspiration
7. Isaiah and Christianity
8. The Priest and the Rabbi
9. Sacrifice and Eucharist
10. The Church and the Synagogue——their sanctity and metaphysical nature, etc.

Soloveitchik believed that theological dialogue, debate, or symposium with other faith communities is not only futile but also damaging to the best interest of both communities.

Interfaith dialogue post Vatican Council II: Feinstein and Soloveitchik

After World War II, Moshe Feinstein was one of the foremost decisors of Orthodox religious law in the United States. In his book of responsa, *Iggerot*

Moshe (YD, 3:43), there are two letters regarding interfaith dialogue. The first, dated March 1, 1967, is in response to a question posed by Dober (Bernard) Lander, who in 1971 would go on to found Touro College. The second is a letter to Soloveitchik dated March 21, 1967 (translated in Brill 2012, 94).

Lander told Feinstein that he had agreed to attend an interfaith conference that was about to be held in New York on March 3, 1967. In attendance would be Catholic and Protestant clergy, as well as rabbis of the Synagogue Council of America and the Rabbinical Council of America (RCA). Lander assured Feinstein that he would only be speaking about social matters which have nothing to do with religion. He wanted to hear from Feinstein whether it was permissible to attend.

Feinstein's response to Lander was unequivocal. He could not attend this interfaith conference nor any other interfaith conference, even if his intent was to speak only about social issues.[11] In the letter to Soloveitchik, his reasoning was straightforward: the intention of the Christian attendees was to convert Jews. Lander followed Feinstein's ruling and withdrew as a participant at the interfaith conference in New York.

After having learned, presumably through his communication with Lander and others, that members of the RCA were planning to attend the March 3 conference, and that perhaps many more would attend the even larger interfaith conference to be held in Boston the following May, Feinstein sent a letter to Soloveitchik (who was then the head of RCA) urging him to join with him in prohibiting rabbinic participation in interfaith dialogues. Accompanying the letter to Soloveitchik was a suggested text that Feinstein wanted Soloveitchik to cosign:

> In regard to the ecumenism that came about through the plans of the Christian leaders whose intent is to cause apostasy, God forbid; which through the workings of Satan successfully convinced even some rabbis to join with priests in established committees in every area and also at conventions in this country and in Europe; we therefore make it known that it is clearly and strictly forbidden to form joint committees of rabbis and priests, or to attend conventions, no matter where, not in Boston nor in any other place, not in this country nor any other country, even to discuss worldly issues that do not pertain to faith and religion, no matter the excuses or rationalizations. Similarly it is forbidden to help the ecumenism in any way for this causes apostasy even if this is not the intent. We are therefore signing to make this prohibition known to all rabbis who observe the religion of our holy Torah, who stand at the breach on this day, the Fast of Esther 1967.
>
> (*Iggerot Moshe*, YD, 3:43)

The date on the letter is important; it is the day that Soloveitchik's wife, Tonya, passed away. Feinstein must have felt strongly about this issue. He penned this letter to Soloveitchik knowing his wife was gravely ill: "I know your preoccupation these days, may God have mercy, but it is for the honor of Heaven ... I am therefore certain that you will ignore your pain and preoccupation and immediately sign that it is forbidden and send it back to me. Your very dear friend and relative concludes and wishes you a double blessing for a full recovery."

We have no response to Feinstein's request, and apparently Soloveitchik never cosigned the above prohibition. We do, however, have a letter Soloveitchik wrote shortly thereafter on April 12, 1967, to Rabbi Pesach Levovitz, then president of the RCA. At this point Soloveitchik had long since formulated his response to Vatican Council II, in particular, and to interfaith dialogue, in general. As we have seen earlier, his response was well thought out and meticulously documented. On the other hand, his relative, Rabbi Feinstein, who was then the leading ultra-Orthodox rabbi in the United States, had sent him a personal letter asking him to join in opposing any type of interfaith dialogue.

Soloveitchik was forced to walk a thin line. While reiterating that dialogue between religions about social issues is permitted, he decided, nevertheless, in accordance with Feinstein's entreaty concerning the upcoming conference in Boston that "... I request the Executive Committee of the Rabbinical Council of America to refrain from participating in, sponsoring or endorsing the interreligious conference on conscience to be held in Boston during May." (Note that he asked only the Executive Committee not to participate.) Soloveitchik's rationale for urging the Executive Committee not to attend this conference could be viewed as a bit forced.

> My objection to participation in this conference is not so much based on the list of topics which are to be discussed, since the vast majority of those belong within the sphere of social morality, but on the unfortunate manner in which this conference has been arranged and publicized. The impression has been conveyed that Orthodoxy has revised its attitude toward ecumenism and plunged into the mainstream of dialoguing and debating the most delicate and intimate theological ideas, which will neither contribute to mutual understanding of the Jew and non-Jew nor toward the promoting and strengthening of the religious cause in general ... It is, therefore, incumbent upon us to be cautious and careful, even as regards problems of social morality, not to become unintentionally involved in the type of dialogue which is presently in vogue.
>
> (*CCC*, 267–68)

Soloveitchik went along with Feinstein and urged the RCA Executive Committee not to participate in the Boston interfaith conference, but he would not repudiate his well-thought-out position that interfaith dialogue—when it deals with social issues—is not only permissible but potentially very beneficial.

Afterword

The essay and Soloveitchik's stance on interfaith relationships were received and interpreted in different ways by different people. First, it has been noted that "Confrontation" was not written in the style or language of rabbinic discourse. It is not in Hebrew, does not cite rabbinic sources, and does not contain the word *assur*, or prohibited (Korn 2005, 2010, 412). Nonetheless, many in Soloveitchik's community chose to see his essay, especially the terse "Addendum," as a halakhic ruling. It was thus a binding religious decision to which his disciples and followers were required to adhere. For them it was not merely a piece of philosophical speculation or religious rhetoric. It meant that they were barred from engaging in religious discussion with members of another religion, especially with Christians.

This was not seen by Soloveitchik's peers or followers as a particularly radical position as Judaism's relationships with other faiths and religions have often been fraught with coercion, mistrust, and suspicion. Yeshayahu Leibowitz (1992, chs. 26, 27) wrote a number of essays in the 1960s whose upshot was also that the nature of Christianity makes interreligious dialogue impossible. Solidifying a ban on certain kinds of interfaith dialogue might not have been expected, but it was not shocking. It was, in some ways, similar to Feinstein's position (*Iggerot Moshe*, YD, 3:43) which was actually to the religious "right" of Soloveitchik's, banning all interreligious dialogue, with no provisions for discussion between religious groups of any sort, even on general matters of common concern.

Some speculate that Soloveitchik's stance on interfaith dialogue is not only normal, given "prudential and theological" considerations, but its very normality also generated a sense of cognitive dissonance for him. In his stance, Soloveitchik is responding to the guilt he felt as a result of the clash between his traditional upbringing on the one hand, which would find interfaith dialogue odd or even sinful, and his extensive philosophical use of Christian theologians like Kierkegaard, Otto, and Barth in formulating his own Jewish philosophy, on the other. "What would they say in 'Brisk?'," one essay asks rhetorically (Singer and Sokol 1982, 255).

The immediate official reception by Catholics, however, was one of acceptance and even praise. In September 1964, *The Pilot*, the official organ of the Catholic archdiocese of Boston, published an editorial which offered measured praise and understanding of Soloveitchik's position regarding interfaith dialogue:

> Bostonians are proud to have as one of the religious leaders in this area the world-famous rabbinical scholar, Dr. Joseph Soloveitchik ... In the first paper he has ever published in English, Rabbi Soloveitchik has recently made a commentary on the present relations of Jews and Christians, with clear reference to the work of Vatican Council II on this topic; His words are worth pondering by all who have become involved in this complex but thoroughly hopeful matter.

While any summary is an injustice to the revered Rabbi's careful reasoning and exact language, one may say that the paper provides a warning to Jews—in the words and manner of the prophets—not to forget the unique commitment of their religion of covenant and its enduring claims upon them. At the same time, Christians are reminded of the necessity of seeing the Jewish faith not merely in its relation to Christian belief but also in its uniquely Jewish aspects. In making these delicate points Rabbi Soloveitchik writes with power and pride, with candor and persuasion, with understanding and friendliness.[12]

Official Catholic public response to Soloveitchik's stance was one of understanding, and his fear regarding the claim that "it has never happened in the history of the Catholic Church that it has made a concession without requesting reciprocity" (Sklarin 2009, 361) was not realized. In October 1965, the Catholic Church concluded their convocation and issued their *Declaration on Relations of the Church to Non-Christian Religions*, known as *Nostra Aetate* ("In Our Time"). The resultant, somewhat conciliatory, statement did indeed change the Church's official attitude toward the Jews for the better:[13]

> [W]hat happened in His passion cannot be charged against all the Jews, without distinction, then alive, nor against the Jews of today ... the Jews should not be presented as rejected or accursed by God ...

> Furthermore, in her rejection of every persecution against any man, the Church, mindful of the patrimony she shares with the Jews ... decries hatred, persecutions, displays of anti-Semitism, directed against Jews at any time and by anyone.[14]

Officially, and by almost[15] all accounts, at all echelons of Jewish-Catholic relations, formal and informal, matters have greatly improved. On the Jewish side, while Soloveitchik barred his followers from entering into dialogue with the Church over this (or any other theological) issue, other Jewish leaders were engaging. Abraham Joshua Heschel, perhaps most well known for his involvement with the American civil rights movement in the 1960s, was working closely with Bea to formulate a statement that the Catholic Church would adopt.[16] He did this while worrying that he was not representative of all Jews, specifically that there was insufficient buy-in from the Orthodox. Heschel's essay "From Mission to Dialogue" is partially a response to a position like Soloveitchik's. Though Heschel taught in the Jewish Theological Seminary and was identified with the Conservative Jewish movement in the United States, like Soloveitchik he hailed from a respected traditional rabbinic family and was well steeped in religious and halakhic discourse.

The goal of Heschel's essay is to find a religious basis for interreligious dialogue on moral and spiritual matters. He argued that as opposed to yesteryear, Jews are no longer in spiritual isolation. Judaism is now a normal member of the world community of religions, and such a position comes with the responsibility to interact with others. It also comes with the opportunity to unite against common foes such as nihilism and the marginalization of religion in the public sphere.

Some years later, the Orthodox Jewish philosopher and theologian Michael Wyschogrod, who had been a student of Soloveitchik, put forward a different criticism of the stance in "Confrontation." He argues that it is curious that Soloveitchik readily allowed for interreligious dialogue on matters of general human and ethical concern while prohibiting dialogue on matters spiritual. After all, he reasons, "[I]f in fact there is no distinction, for the man of faith, between the secular and the sacred order, then how can we prescribe cooperation about secular but not about sacred matters?" (Wyschogrod 1986). How can a Halakhic Man, in other words, disentangle the sacred from the secular in a way that allows him to have dialogue about one and not the other?[17] How can Jews and Christians avoid talking theology when God and His Will are the lens through which they both see the world? How else can a man of faith justify his actions if not by appealing to his faith? If called to comment as a Jew, to what can he appeal? If he appeals to anything but his faith, he is not speaking as a Jew. Later on, Wyschogrod goes so far as to suggest that this criticism is so trenchant that Soloveitchik must have designed his argument to be so fallacious, and transparently so, that it indeed permits by implication, that which internal Jewish political concerns barred him from permitting openly (Wyschogrod 1991, 156–57).

Wyschogrod makes a number of additional arguments. First, he understands that there is an unbridgeable gap between religions, just as there are gaps between man and wife, yet Judaism still demands marriage so that we can reach out and alleviate one another's loneliness. Moreover, not communicating is not a neutral position, and man can only peacefully coexist with others when there is communication. A lack of communication can only be a harbinger for violence.

Wyschogrod, employing an argument reminiscent of Hermann Cohen's anti-Zionist argument, further argues that Jews are chosen for the purpose of bringing salvation to humanity. They are required to promote the Noahide laws. But how can Jews do that if they cannot communicate with others? How can good moral non-Jews who desire a relationship with the God of Israel initiate one if they can have no religious contact with the people of Israel?

A further position, intermediate between Wyschogrod and Feinstein's, is inspired by a concern of A. J. Heschel. Though Heschel advocated for interfaith dialogue, he acknowledged a number of concerns that were picked up by later scholars who attempted a less strict interpretation of Soloveitchik's position. Heschel was worried that if interfaith dialogue were to be permitted or encouraged, some would engage in it despite a lack of competence or commitment. Unqualified people would presume to speak on behalf of Jews and Judaism without authorization from Jewish communal bodies, knowledge of relevant Jewish thought, or understanding the real nature of Jewish problems. Such dialogue would be, at best, counter-productive, and possibly even seriously harmful to Jewish interests. David Hartman, whose own institution has sponsored interfaith dialogues, Wyschogrod (1986), and others (e.g., Greenberg 2004) take this to be Soloveitchik's central concern (Hartman 2001, ch. 5) in what Daniel Rynhold calls the "political interpretation" of "Confrontation" (Rynhold 2003). Thus, they argue, Soloveitchik was not concerned to ban interfaith dialogue *per se* but rather to ensure its quality and efficacy.[18]

Similarly, Eugene Korn argues that the biggest problem with interfaith dialogue is not *whether* to participate but rather *who* should participate (Korn 2005, 309). He argues further that Soloveitchik's reasons, even if they once had force, no longer apply. They were applicable in an earlier point in Jewish history, but no longer. Soloveitchik could not have conceived of the transformation that the Church would undergo after its adoption of *Nostra Aetate*, rendering the historical and doctrinal arguments moot. Nor could he have predicted the nature of the transformation that religious dialogue had taken in the subsequent years. Nonetheless, he too accepts the preconditions that Soloveitchik advocates and concedes that only people of deep faith who are steeped in the tradition ought to participate in theological dialogue with governing bodies of other faiths.[19]

This is an ongoing discussion even among those firmly entrenched in the mainstream of contemporary Modern Orthodox Jewry. People continue to weigh in both in defense of and in opposition to the stance taken in "Confrontation," and it is a debate that shows no signs of disappearing.[20]

Interfaith dialogue appears as less of a concern for Israeli rabbis than American rabbis (former students of Soloveitchik notwithstanding). Figures such as Michael Wyschogrod, Eugene Korn, and Shlomo Riskin, all of whom were at some point affiliated with YU, felt compelled to justify their openness to interfaith dialogue. For Israeli rabbis, however, interfaith dis-cussion seems to have become a routine part of diplomacy between sover-eign states (Korn 2010, 427). Rabbi She'ar Yashuv Cohen, the former Chief Rabbi of the city of Haifa, was frequently called upon by the Israeli Chief Rabbinate to participate in interfaith dialogue, largely with the Vatican but also with Islamic bodies. Cohen believes that such discussion requires ha-lakhic justification and insists on certain constraints upon any discussion with the Vatican: no proselytizing and no debate on religious fundamentals (Frish 2017, 295–306). The halakhic justification Cohen provides looks very Soloveitchikian. He explicates what he sees as Judaism's two seemingly conflicting missions: *yihud* and *ya'ud*. On the one hand, the Jewish nation is to be particularistic, unique, and separate (as described, e.g., in the first paragraph of the *Aleinu* prayer). On the other hand, it is to "repair" the world (as described in the second paragraph of the same prayer) and be universalistic (Frish 2017, 295–96). But despite the superficial relationship with Soloveitchik's style, Soloveitchik's influence in this matter does not extend to Israel, and we can only speculate what precedent he would have set had he ended up as their Chief Rabbi.

Notes

1 Though it certainly factors into Soloveitchik's reasoning, the earlier history of Jewish-Christian discussion is far more complicated and fraught that can be presented here. However, it may be interesting to note that Elijah Zvi Soloveitchik (1805–1881), the brother of Soloveitchik's great-great-grandfather, wrote a commentary on the gospels attempting to harmonize Judaism and Christianity (Soloveitchik 2019). (Discussed in Brill 2010a, 90ff as an "inclusivist" text.) We have no indication that Soloveitchik was aware of this.

2 The RCA included at that point approximately 900 rabbis serving almost two million worshippers. Soloveitchik's affiliation with the RCA dates back to 1950 when he was appointed honorary chairman of its Halakhah Commission. For details of Soloveitchik's relationship with the RCA, see Bernstein (1984, 19).

3 The interview was published in *HaDoar* on 5/15/61. Relevant excerpts are translated in *CCC* (247–48).

4 There were Jews who were ready to reciprocate. "The head of all Reform temples solemnly informed a convention that the spirit of ecumenisms works both ways and that therefore we Jews must reciprocate by accepting the central figure of Christianity as a 'positive and prophetic spirit in the stream of Jewish tradition'" (Sklarin 2009, 370, quoting Norman Lamm).

5 For some historical context, see Feigelson (2015, ch. 4).

6 This approach to the argument in "Confrontation" is due to Korn (2005). See Brill (2012) for an introduction to the spectrum of views on the compatibility of Judaism and other religions including the view derived from "Confrontation."

7 See Brill (2012, 94–98) for discussion.

8 Throughout, Soloveitchik makes no distinction between Catholicism, Protestantism, or other forms of Christianity, though there can be little doubt that he was aware of the general doctrinal differences and their respective histories of anti-Semitism.

9 Much has been said about this caveat. See Brill (2012, 113) for discussion of Obadiah Seforno's similar, but not identical position. See also the discussion in Kaplan (1999a, 298–300).

10 See also *CCC* (259–61, 267, 268).

11 Feinstein's opposition to interfaith discussion was the predominant view among the ultra-Orthodox, most exemplified perhaps by Aron Kotler's (the head of the Lakewood Yeshiva) frequent invectives against Orthodox participation, and Soloveitchik's, in particular.

12 This is from the excerpt republished by the Jewish Telegraphic Agency (JTA). Minor punctuation anomalies have been corrected. The JTA also published Soloveitchik's original statement released to the rabbis a few days earlier.

13 Schachter (1994, 15–16n18) gives additional insight into how Soloveitchik understood the Catholic Church's motive for *Nostra Aetate*. The Church's faulting of the Jewish people of all generations for killing their God was because so long as there are Jews who do not believe in Jesus, it prevents his return. In the 1960s, however, confident in a prophecy predicting Jesus's resurrection at the end of the second millennium (and with a huge advertising budget aimed at proselytizing to the Jews), the Vatican felt there was no justification for blaming the Jews for his death.

14 *Nostra Aetate* can be accessed at: www.vatican.va/archive/hist_councils/ii_vatican_council/documents/vat-ii_decl_19651028_nostra-aetate_en.html.
15 See, however, the qualification in West (2014, 104–5).
16 Our discussion of Heschel is indebted to Kimelman (2004) and Orenstein (2011).
17 Kaplan (1999a, 304–6) understands Soloveitchik as addressing this question in "Confrontation." He argues that Soloveitchik distinguishes between religious theological dialogue and religious humanitarian dialogue.
18 Rutishauser (2010, 434–39) argues for a reading of "Confrontation" in which Soloveitchik is not against all religious interfaith dialogue, only that certain conditions be placed upon it.
19 Korn (2010, 414n12) notes that Soloveitchik's writings often reference Christian thought and theologians, and Soloveitchik delivered *TLMOF* at St. John's seminary in Brighton, Massachusetts, before it was published. Additionally, at a memorial conference for Michael Wyschogrod at Baruch College a number of the panelists claimed to have heard from Wyschogrod that Soloveitchik said to him in the context of interfaith dialogue that he was not worried about Wyschogrod participating in such dialogue but was worried that someone less qualified would attempt such discussion (https://baruch.mediaspace.kaltura.com/media/1_dnc8rfnl 1:55:30). Moreover, when Irving Greenberg, another student of Soloveitchik, actually participated in official interfaith discussions, he exchanged letters with Soloveitchik and explained that he feared that he had disobeyed his teacher. Soloveitchik responded that "[y]ou are certainly entitled to your opinion as much as I am to mine. I have never demanded conformity or compliance even from my children. I believe in freedom of opinion and freedom of action ..." (Feigelson 2015, 107ff; cf. Kaplan 1999a).
20 For example, Shlomo Riskin's defense of his own center for interfaith discussion: cjcuc.org/site/2012/08/30/is-christian-jewish-theological-dialogue-permitted-a-postscript-to-rav-joseph-b-solovetichiks-article-confrontation/ and David Berger's response and defense of the standard reading of "Confrontation" in his "*Emunah be-rishut ha-yahid*" here: https://musaf-shabbat.com/2012/11/16/ אמונה-ברשות-היחיד-דד-ברגר. Berger's response to Korn's essay can be found here: https://www.bc.edu/content/dam/files/research_sites/cjl/texts/center/conferences/soloveitchik/Berger_23Nov03.htm. See also Novak (1989, ch. 1), Johnston (1999), Breger (2005), Morgan (2015), White (2018), and Brill (2012) for critique and analysis.

7   Soloveitchik's philosophical legacy
Where to go from here

David Singer (Singer 1987, 75) advances what seems a fair criticism of *Halakhic Mind*. Why, he asks, is there no Soloveitchik school of thought or "Soloveitchik program" or anyone who can be said to be *philosophically* Soloveitchikian? Why are there no students and followers building on Soloveitchik's writing? Many people study his work and analyze this or that aspect of his thought, but there is nothing constituting a school of thought. Why have so few people absorbed his method, refined his approach, and advanced or applied it in any way? In a criticism now over thirty years old, only moderate efforts toward addressing it can be found.

Singer implies that it is Soloveitchik's fault for not generating such a school because his work is inadequately systematic (75). While we agree that there is no Soloveitchik philosophical school, we disagree that it is for want of systematicity that none exists. We hope this book goes some way toward conspicuously displaying the systematicity of Soloveitchik's philosophical program. In this final chapter, we offer some suggestions that, if seriously pursued, may go some way toward furthering Soloveitchik's philosophical program. We highlight some questions whose answers may help round out the picture that Soloveitchik began painting for us and which can potentially take his work in new directions.

What would count as a Soloveitchik school of philosophical thought? Soloveitchik has many students who have addressed his work. There is a large and growing secondary literature. Admittedly, much of it does not so much advance Soloveitchik's program as it tries to clarify and contextualize it. The secondary literature so far largely involves looking at individual or pairs of essays by Soloveitchik and explicating their meaning with respect to some detail or another. Sometimes it involves picking out themes that run throughout the various writing and looking for a clear view Soloveitchik is advocating. Some literature contrasts pairs of work by Soloveitchik and tries to explain or explain away differences (Finkelman 2014). This book notes examples of each of these types of study that are common enough in scholarship about historical philosophers. But these alone do not constitute advancing a school of thought.

The secondary literature also includes books and essays that compare Soloveitchik's writings to those of other thinkers such as Hermann Cohen (e.g., Munk 1992; Kaplan 1996), Emmanuel Levinas (e.g., Kessler 2002), Søren

Kierkegaard (e.g., Oppenheim 1998; Possen 2012), Martin Heidegger (see references in Shatz 2017, 166n85), Eliezer Berkovits (e.g., Bedzow 2009), Martin Buber (e.g., Birnbaum 1977; Berger 1998; Blidstein 2012; Ross 2014), A. J. Heschel (e.g., Zuesse 1994; Kimelman 2004), Franz Rosenzweig (e.g., Cohen 2016), Max Scheler (e.g., Ozar 2016), A. I. Kook (e.g., Saks 2006b), and Yeshayahu Leibowitz (e.g., Sagi 1992, 1997, Koller 2020, ch4). Soloveitchik was well versed in the history of philosophy and theology, and to the reader familiar with both his works and the relevant historical figures, it is easy to see how Soloveitchik drew on them and reacted against them. (It is also easy to see how later thinkers drew on Soloveitchik's work.) We attempted to clarify some of the most important of these relationships in this book. Much still remains to be done sorting out exactly how Soloveitchik draws on thinkers like William James, Wilhelm Dilthey, Karl Barth, and others. We dedicated a few paragraphs to each, but that is hardly sufficient. A recent work on Soloveitchik and Nietzsche (Rynhold and Harris 2018) connects the two philosophers in numerous interesting ways. Perhaps even more importantly, David Shatz (2017, 167) notes that the Jewish sources Soloveitchik draws upon have also received inadequate scholarly attention, and this strikes us as a serious scholarly lacuna as well. Perhaps Soloveitchik is generally considerably more transparent with his Rabbinic sources that scholars have found little to add. Weiss (2018) traces how Judah Halevi's thought is reflected in Soloveitchik's, but Soloveitchik's scope is orders of magnitude wider.

Another line of research may be to study the evolution of Soloveitchik's thought. His stance on Zionism suggests that his view evolved from when he was younger, to the post-Holocaust years. Similarly, his stance on religious Jews vis-à-vis secular Jews evolved with the realities of the State of Israel. Alan Brill also notes that Soloveitchik's stance on Biblical criticism, especially in *TLMOF*, underwent some change from the time it was first conceived and delivered as an oral address to the time it saw print. But while all this is of significant scholarly interest, it does not advance Soloveitchik's philosophical program.

David Shatz (2017, 178–96) asks what Soloveitchik can now say *to us* and provides five points of departure: Does our current understanding of the history and evolution of Halakhah affect how we see Soloveitchik's philosophical usage of the Halakha? Is the critique of contemporary religion found throughout Soloveitchik's works still relevant, given how much religious life has since changed? How does Soloveitchik explain Judaism to the world while denying that a religious understanding can be communicated? Should Soloveitchik's Zionist works be reevaluated in light of changing attitudes and realities about the State of Israel? (To which we would add, should Soloveitchik's stance on interreligious dialogue be reevaluated in light of the changing attitudes of Jews and members of other religions?) Does modern science, archaeology, epistemology, textual criticism, etc. impact how Soloveitchik's philosophical ideas withstand the test of time?

These important questions notwithstanding, Singer's criticism stands. Did Soloveitchik leave a clear enough program which leaves room for his students and followers to expand upon? Is there room for any enlargement of the program? Is there a place where Soloveitchik's program can be filled in, expanded, updated, tweaked, advanced, or applied to new areas of thought? Or, should we say that Soloveitchik left us with a novel and sophisticated answer to the *ta'amei ha-mitzvot* problem and little more?

While Soloveitchik's theory stands on its own, any philosophical approach to a problem can at least be judged by showing how it answers questions or solves problems that other theories fail to. Does Soloveitchik's analysis of the *ta'amei ha-mitzvot* problem fare better than other theories in handling nonrational commandments like *shatnez*, the prohibition against wearing garments made of wool and linen?

We believe that Soloveitchik's philosophical agenda can be furthered. To do so we must first solve a few outstanding problems. We submit the following preliminary and admittedly speculative prompts to begin discussion in this matter and to encourage the exploration of open questions.

Soloveitchik and Biblical criticism

We hope that we have shown earlier (Chapter 4) that Soloveitchik had a coherent philosophical program whose aim is to address the *ta'amei ha-mitzvot* problem. *Inter alia*, he also addressed a wide range of standard philosophical questions incidental to his main thesis. For example, he discussed the nature of God (see, e.g., Chapter 4, Section "'Catharsis': a methodological interlude"), the problem of evil (e.g., *KDD*, Chapters 1 and 2), and religious pluralism (e.g., in "Confrontation"). On the other hand, Soloveitchik only addressed obliquely and in passing some questions that other philosophers and theologians, Jewish and not, had discussed at great length. For example, Soloveitchik did not discuss at length traditional arguments for the existence of God, save for implicitly endorsing arguments from religious experience. He also has little new to say about the immortality of the soul or the challenge of determinism to free will.

Soloveitchik also failed to address in a comprehensive manner the challenges posed by Biblical criticism toward the integrity of the Pentateuch, Judaism's most sacred text. In our discussion of *TLMOF* (Chapter 4, Section "The lonely man of faith"), we briefly discussed Biblical criticism as conceived by Hobbes and Spinoza and the documentary hypothesis as articulated by Wellhausen.

Two Orthodox Jewish scholars, contemporaries of Soloveitchik, David Tzvi Hoffman (1843–1921) and Ḥayyim Heller (1880–1960), attempted to disprove the documentary hypothesis: Ḥayyim Heller (1911) in his *Untersuchungen ueber die Peschitta zur gesamten hebräischen Bibel* and David Tzvi Hoffman (1928) in his *Ra'yot Makhri'ot Neged Velhauzen*. While both these works point out major errors in Wellhausen's work—perhaps even embarrassing ones—neither succeeded in definitively refuting the documentary hypothesis, certainly not to the satisfaction of later scholars.

Theological beliefs about the integrity of the Bible prevent most Orthodox Jews from accepting the documentary hypothesis. How then should they understand the Bible's seemingly conflicting accounts of the same events? Soloveitchik and his slightly later contemporary Mordechai Breuer (1921–2007) solve this by attributing the conflicting narratives to the dialectical natures of God and man: Soloveitchik, regarding the two narratives of Adam's creation, to the dialectical nature of *man;* Breuer, regarding conflicting narratives in general, to the dialectical nature of *God.*

In *TLMOF* Soloveitchik writes:

> I have never been seriously troubled by the problem of the Biblical doctrine of creation vis-à-vis the scientific story of evolution ... nor have I been perturbed by the confrontation of the mechanistic interpretation of the human mind with the Biblical spiritual concept of man ... *Moreover, I have not even been troubled by the theories of Biblical criticism which contradict the very foundation upon which the sanctity and integrity of the Scriptures rest* ... (7, *italics* added).

Why was Soloveitchik untroubled "by the theories of Biblical criticism which contradict the very foundation upon which the sanctity and integrity of the Scriptures rest"? Two pages later in *TLMOF* Soloveitchik continues:

> We all know that the Bible offers two accounts of the creation of man. We are also aware of the theory suggested by Bible critics attributing these two accounts to two different traditions and sources. Of course, since we do unreservedly accept the unity and integrity of the Scriptures and their divine character, *we reject this hypothesis which is based, like much Biblical criticism, on literary categories invented by modern man,*[1] *ignoring completely the eidetic-noetic content of the Biblical story.* It is, of course, true that the two accounts of the creation of man differ considerably. This incongruity was not discovered by the Bible critics. Our sages of old were aware of it. However, the answer lies not in an alleged dual tradition but in dual man, not in an imaginary contradiction between two versions but in a real contradiction in the nature of man. The two accounts deal with two Adams, two men, two fathers of mankind, two types, two representatives of humanity, and it is no wonder that they are not identical ... (9–10, *italics* added).

Soloveitchik dismisses Biblical criticism[2] as based on "literary categories invented by modern man." Geoffrey H. Hartman (1994, 341), among others, challenges Soloveitchik's offhand dismissal of Biblical criticism:

> What [Soloveitchik] says about the literary is both minimal and wrong. The Higher Criticism, he alleges, based itself on "literary categories invented by modern man." Now contemporary critical theories do use

stylistic criteria to distinguish sources, but no literary scholar would stop there ... The unity of Scripture supported explicitly and unreservedly by Soloveitchik obviously suggests different criteria and forms of analysis. To discover them is also a task of contemporary literary theory.

An earlier 1959 source sheds some light on Soloveitchik's dismissal of Biblical criticism. Alan Brill summarizes a lecture[3] by Soloveitchik which he believes is a proto-version of *TLMOF*. Consider a key statement (edited by the present authors for clarity):

> The Bible is my book-of-knowledge ... Bible critics already pointed out that the two accounts of the creation of man [in Genesis 1:27 and Genesis 2:18] differ. They claim [that statements which contradict each other reflect] two [different] sources. *They make one mistake. They do not try to solve the problem philosophically. [Umberto] Casutto said they substituted source criticism for philosophic ideas* ... I tell you this not because I am a rabbi ... and not because of fundamentalism. I like to understand the text. The text is about how from estrangement we came to communication, and how fellowship came into being. The text expresses it as metaphor and symbolically as "taking a rib" and "sleep" to express these two aspects of loneliness and fellowship ... I am not interested in the source, rather the literary structure for the two accounts ... The two are contradictory and Judaism accepts both; man is created alone and together. There are two theories about society: the individual and the communal ... God is not a marriage broker. "He was asleep" means that the removal was not in consultation with Adam, but rather the original intention of creation; nature itself has the contradiction of alone and together (*italics* added).

In the above, Soloveitchik argues that in their attempt to understand the Bible, critics resort to an easy solution: that seemingly conflicting texts represent different source documents subsequently combined by an editor into a single document. Soloveitchik argues that this whole approach is misguided. Jewish sages throughout the ages have been aware that the Bible contains duplicate and seemingly contradictory statements, and Jewish sages have offered ways to resolve these anomalies. Soloveitchik sees himself as continuing in the footsteps of the sages but in his own unique way. He offers, in our case, an explanation that enlightens us about the dialectical nature of man. In the conflicting accounts of the creation of Adam, Soloveitchik sees the Bible imparting a philosophic truth—man is full of contradictions. Man strives to develop and create, but man also strives to find meaning. Man is a lonely person interested primarily in himself, but man also seeks companionship with a woman, and he creates communities for the benefit of its members. Soloveitchik dissolves this problem by claiming there is a philosophical solution regarding the human condition rather than a literary textual one.

Brill suggests that the 1959 lecture had originally addressed the question of Biblical criticism in more detail: "[T]hese ... lectures are essential tools to show what motivated his thinking: they elaborate his thought, they explicate his sources, and by contrast they show what his final resolution in 1966 rejected" (ibid). He may have originally had more to say about Biblical criticism itself but ultimately stopped short of addressing it in a systematic manner. Further research is necessary to understand why.

Soloveitchik's Orthodox contemporaries, besides Cassuto, offered other solutions. While Soloveitchik reconciles the two accounts of Adam's creation as reflecting the dialectical nature of *man*, Mordechai Breuer's approach to Biblical criticism[4] is based on his understanding of the dialectical nature of *God*. Breuer, like Soloveitchik, concedes that there are many problematic passages in the Bible. Jewish sages throughout the generations were aware of these anomalies and offered various solutions. Unlike Soloveitchik, however, Breuer believes that the conflicting passages do represent different ways of understanding the Biblical messages. These conflicting texts are not, as claimed by Biblical critics, the result of different source documents combined by a later editor but rather a result of the dialectical nature of God who expresses Himself in different ways, each based on a different one of His attributes. (Soloveitchik makes a similar claim. See, e.g., Chapter 4, Section "'Catharsis': a methodological interlude.")

Jewish sages (and some non-Jewish thinkers like Barth) understood that God, a perfect unity, nevertheless contains within Himself conflicting attributes. He is merciful toward man, and yet He is also exacting in his judgment of man. These conflicting attributes of God are implied in the names used by the Bible to refer to Him. Elohim implies a God who is unbending (as are the laws of nature) and strict in His judgment of man. Tetragrammaton implies a God who reveals himself to man and who is merciful toward him.

The opening verse of the Bible refers to God as Elohim, a name that implies strict judgment. Yet *Genesis* 2:4 refers to God as Tetragrammaton Elohim, a God who acts with both mercy and strict judgment. The sages explain this shift from Elohim to Tetragrammaton Elohim as contrasting reality with the ideal. It would have been ideal that man be judged immediately (i.e., punished or rewarded for his deeds). In reality, this could not work. A compromise or fusion of these two approaches was necessary. Rashi (*Genesis* 1:1, s.v. *Bara Elohim*) expresses this as follows: "Initially, the thought was to create the world with the attribute of strict justice. Seeing that the world could not exist, He gave preference to the attribute of mercy and partnered it with the attribute of strict justice."

Breuer notes that the Jewish sage Aryeh Leib ben Asher Gunzberg (the "Shaagat Aryeh" ca. 1695–1785) used the principles of Biblical criticism to explain contradictions within the text of Chronicles.[5] Ezra did not write this book on his own, but rather he copied accounts from the various texts at his disposal, preferring not to alter them. While this approach may be acceptable to many traditional Jews when dealing with conflicting passages within Chronicles, it cannot be used for analyzing the Torah (i.e., the Pentateuch), which Judaism understands as being identical to the Torah passed down from Moses. Here is where Breuer gets creative.

A Midrash states that God "looked" at His Torah and used it as a "blueprint" to create the world (*Genesis Rabbah* 1:1). God, because of His dialectical nature, had different understandings of the world he wished to create, each understanding based on a different one of His Own attributes. When God created the world, he "looked" at these conflicting accounts and created it in a way that is true to all these contradictory accounts. The role of one who studies the Torah is to understand each of the different accounts on their own. The actual historic event reflected by the combination of these different accounts, however, cannot be determined by analyzing and combining the different messages; this is the role of Midrash.[6]

In summary, both Soloveitchik and Breuer reject the claim that conflicting narratives in the Bible (the Pentateuch) are the result of different source documents. Rather, they see the conflicting narratives as reflecting the dialectical nature of God and man. Breuer stresses the dialectical nature of God, while Soloveitchik, specifically regarding the narratives of Adam's creation, stresses the dialectical nature of man.

In one sense Breuer's approach reflects the fruitfulness of Soloveitchik. Appealing to the dialectical nature of God, ultimately allowing this to explain the dialectical nature of man, is appealing, but it is not likely to placate Biblical critics.

The details of Halakhic Man's phenomenological experience

To grasp the unique phenomenology of Halakhic Man, we need to understand two things: categories of experience and subjective phenomenological feelings. Spelling out the full set of uniquely halakhic categories is a daunting task, if it is even possible. Each Halakhah specified in the codes of law, the responsa literature, and even in oral parts of the halakhic tradition and presumably certain halakhot in combination are expressed in terms of the halakhic categories they presume. Each of these numerous categories can be meticulously delineated in proper Brisker fashion so that we have a clear conceptual analysis of each category. Soloveitchik frequently refers to these categories and often speaks of Hayyim Brisker's analysis of one or another of them and his great accomplishment in creating or explicating the nature of the halakhic categories. Many of these cases are famous, such as the analysis of the halakhic concept of a "contract." Moreover, all of Soloveitchik's writing is presumably expressed in such terms. After all, one cannot, not without great difficulty anyway, express oneself in categories of experience that are not one's own.

Spelling out all halakhic categories completely (if it is even possible) would provide some insight into how Halakhic Man sees the world and would also set the vocabulary with which one can write about Halakhic Man. The *Encyclopedia Talmudit*, which spells out the scope of numerous halakhic concepts, should be useful in doing this. Also incidentally useful is the growing philosophical literature on concepts and the psychological literature on category formation (e.g., in Margolis and Laurence 1999) on the nature of categories themselves.

But presuming that those who write about Halakhic Man are well enough versed in Halakhah to express themselves in such terms, we ought to think about the second ingredient that goes into the description of Halakhic Man: the phenomenological feelings that emerge from thinking in these categories combined with the actual practice of Halakhah. Soloveitchik tells us about halakhot and sets of halakhot that give rise to particular feelings and phenomenological experiences. We saw this, for example, in Soloveitchik's treatment of the laws of prayer, mourning, and repentance, and other places.

Soloveitchik distinguishes between halakhot in which the *kiyyum* of the mitzvah is separate from the *ma'aseh* of the mitzvah. In other words, Soloveitchik is sometimes explicit about the fact that the act of performing a mitzvah helps stimulate a separate feeling that is its fulfillment. Each fulfillment is part of Halakhic Man's phenomenological situation. But there must be an important sense in which each individual Halakhah, even those whose fulfillment is not separate from its act, generates (or perhaps presupposes) certain feelings. At the very least the ontology of the object used, say the fact that certain monies or goods are inherently *tzedaka* (charity), partially constitutes the way a Halakhic Man perceives the world.

Can a program be spelled out that explains more thoroughly than Soloveitchik did how Halakhic Man sees the world, beyond the broad sweeping ways described in *Halakhic Man*? Can each individual Halakhah be spelled out in terms of the ontology it creates and the phenomenology it gives rise to? Some halakhot lend themselves easily to such analysis (such as *tzitzit*), and others seem not to. Can we make sense of the sum total of Halakhah in these terms? In other words, is it possible to get the details of the phenomenology in a finer grained way than Soloveitchik provides it?

Second, can we also get the details of the nature of the dialectic personality? As we understand Soloveitchik, fulfilling the mitzvot gives rise to a unique phenomenological outlook. This outlook ends up being paradoxical or at least contradictory in various ways. Specifically, it is conflicted in a way that Soloveitchik attributes to being able to specify that some parts of the outlook are characteristic of one kind of personality, while other parts are characteristic of an opposing personality type.

Some clarification, however, is needed. Soloveitchik spells out what some individual mitzvot do. But we do not know what each mitzvah does or how it contributes to the whole personality. Do some mitzvot give rise to Religious Man's traits and others give rise to Cognitive Man's? Do some cause us to advance toward God and others to retreat? Do some inspire awe while others fear? Or, is the story more complicated? Do some parts of certain mitzvot cause one set of personality traits to emerge while others give rise to another set? Or, is the situation more holistic? Is there something about the cycle of mitzvot or the cycle of life that the mitzvot interact with that collectively causes one to become a Halakhic Man? If so, it is only in retrospect that we can "deconstruct" the personality of Halakhic Man and see the underlying Religious Man and Cognitive Man that comprise him. After all, it hardly seems like it can be the case that there is some set of mitzvot such that if one keeps that set and ignores the others, he will emerge from that experience with the phenomenology of a Cognitive Man. So it only makes sense that all halakhot work together to forge a Halakhic Man.

Halakhic Man provides broad phenomenological answers to general questions about the high-level religious mindset of Halakhic Man. But is it possible to work out the details? Are there other aspects of Halakhic Man beyond the distinctly religious (or spiritual) that can be described so that we get a fuller picture of the nuanced thinking of Halakhic Man?

Spelling out the details of course presumes that the endeavor of a non-Halakhic Man spelling out the phenomenology of Halakhic Man makes sense. Is there a case to be made that it takes a Halakhic Man to know a Halakhic Man, so to speak? Soloveitchik's program is a unique form of spiritual autobiography, one that claims to apply to individuals who undertake similar spiritual exercises and intellectual endeavors. Is there a philosophically objective way of talking about Halakhic Man's phenomenology, or can it only be done from a first-person perspective? If the latter, the program implied by *Halakhic Man* is attempting to do the impossible and faces challenges related to those pointed out by Nagel (1979, esp 160–85). Nagel argues that it is essentially impossible to come to a scientific understanding of any subjective entity, as in doing so, the best one can hope to understand is what it is like to be you trying to understand someone or something else. Our challenge then is to ask if analyzing a Halakhic Man is really possible, and if so, can such an analysis be understood by anyone else? And, can it be done completely in a way that provides all the details we would want in a philosophical analysis?

Halakhic Man for the twenty-first century

Soloveitchik, as we understand him, wrote using a vocabulary that seems outdated from the perspective of twenty-first-century personality psychology. Personality psychology has taken a different turn and rarely offers the kind of straightforward breakdown of idealized personalities, though phenomenological descriptions of aspects of perception are still sometimes written by philosophers. The program of understanding the nature and personality of Halakhic Man should be updated in light of modern philosophical psychology and philosophy and psychology of religion. The intellectual context and milieu in which Soloveitchik wrote was in many ways a dead end in the history of psychology. Though we know of no straight refutation of his program, the specific vocabulary he used and the specific theoretical model of human personality Soloveitchik employs are no longer in vogue. Psychologists do not think of human personalities in precisely the same way today. Is there nonetheless a contemporary paradigm in psychology from which we can make sense of Soloveitchik's work? Is there a way to revive the paradigm so that it is more in line with contemporary philosophical and psychological thinking?

To some extent, we can look to personality psychology or perhaps the burgeoning field of psychology of religion to undertake Soloveitchik's stated program. Lately, numerous studies have been performed by experimental psychologists examining questions about religious rituals and their psychological effects. A study might inquire whether prayer or praying impacts an individual's judgment in a specific way (e.g., Abbema and Koole 2017). These studies are, in effect, correlating objective acts of prayer with subjective psychological experience. With sufficient ingenuity, there is nothing in principle to prevent research psychologists from similarly examining Halakhah to understand what effect it has on a halakhic personality. Such studies should be able to move scholarship away from autobiographical reflection and *a priori* psychological analysis about the nature of the halakhic personality to a more thorough scientific correlation of the full spectrum of Jewish religious rituals and the respective subjective or neural counterpart.

Another avenue of approach may be to think about Soloveitchik's work in terms of subsequent developments in philosophy. Soloveitchik's relationship with his philosophical predecessors is becoming increasingly well studied. It can also be philosophically fruitful to explore philosophical connections with his contemporaries and successors with whom he did not and could not interact. For example, in a discussion of Soloveitchik's critique of interfaith dialogue, where we contextualized the discussion in the context of Kuhn's notion of incommensurable paradigms, W. V. O. Quine (1960) argued against the idea that it is possible to translate from one language to another when one language is completely unknown ("radical translation" as, say, linguistic anthropologists attempt) because we can never be sure that we are getting the translation exactly correct. There are too many possible meanings that could be intended by the native speaker in certain contexts. We may want to explore if and how this speaks to Soloveitchik's stance on interreligious dialogue as well. Can Soloveitchik's argument for the incommensurability of religion (or their respective discourses) be recast in Quinean radical translation terms? Should it be recast this way? How intimately, too, is this tied to the idea that the conceptual categories or Halakhic Man are unique to him, and would Soloveitchik have to argue that those with different categories cannot make sense of what he is like either?

The twentieth-century philosopher Donald Davidson's well-known argument against the very idea of a conceptual scheme (Davidson 1974) attacks a related argument in a way that can challenge both Soloveitchik's argument for religious incommensurability and also the core point of his entire philosophical program. Davidson argues that "conceptual schemes" are generally incoherent, and especially the idea of incommensurable conceptual schemes. Do Davidson's arguments pose challenges for either Soloveitchik's typological approach to idealized Jewish phenomenology or to his approach to incommensurability of religions? Can the large secondary literature on Davidson's conceptual schemes be put in fruitful discussion with Soloveitchik's approach?

Are all Halakhic Men similar?

Halakhah is not static. It evolves over time and differs in significant ways from one community to another. Moreover, Soloveitchik believed that creating new halakhic concepts is one of Halakhic Man's tasks. We would, therefore, expect Halakhic Man's subjective religious experiences and ontology to similarly differ over time and from one geographic area to another. We may wish to study, for example, how the ontology of a Halakhic Man who is a product of the *Shulḥan Arukh* differs from one who is a product of the *Shulḥan Arukh* with the glosses of Rema (R. Moshe Isserles), or more starkly by Maimonides' *Mishneh Torah*. Meaning, it is possible to possess a complete coherent halakhically acceptable worldview that is different from some other complete halakhic system. If so, two people can possess different sets of halakhic ontological concepts. How radical a difference does this make in the macro-level worldview as articulated in the personality literature? To the extent that there are actual Halakhic Men, would it not be certain that Maimonides would differ from the Gaon of Vilna, who was separated by hundreds of years and miles? Presumably, the latter had halakhic categories; the former did not. How are these Halakhic Men different, and how do these differences manifest themselves?

This question is particularly acute in light of the nature of the Brisker method. Often the Brisker method relies on understanding the underlying pervasive categories that a particular halakhic thinker has, as opposed to the categories that another halakhic thinker employs. The Brisker method often clarifies the nature of how an individual sees a Halakhah to explain various views of that person and accounts for widespread disagreement between halakhic thinkers. If there is halakhic disagreement that is based on differing perspectives of the nature of particular halakhot or because their conceptual schema are in opposition, we should be concerned to discover how they differ as Halakhic Men. If they do not differ in their capacity as Halakhic Men, what challenge does this give either to the account of the emergence of Halakhic Man or the particular phenomenology of Halakhic Men in general?

A more general version of this question can be posed as follows: How sensitive is Soloveitchik's account of religious phenomenology to his view of Halakhah? Recalling our earlier discussion of the history and nature of Halakhah, should a proponent of this approach apply it elsewhere? Does Soloveitchik provide a good model for understanding Jewish religious spirituality in general or only for the restricted way that he understands it? Can this model apply to what he would call "more liberal forms of Judaism"?

Moreover, on Soloveitchik's own understanding of Halakhah (which may differ from other accounts), different individuals have different halakhic obligations. Priests (*kohanim*), for example, have certain halakhic obligations that nonpriests do not. (Soloveitchik was a Levite. Levites have their own specific religious obligations.) So while their halakhic ontology might be the same as other members of their religious community, the commandments they fulfill differ. Each commandment according to Soloveitchik gives rise to certain feelings and experiences. Does that create different types of Halakhic Men?

Priests nowadays anyway are only minimally significant as their religious obligations, and hence differences, are minor. But consider women (see Borowitz 1983, 243). As Soloveitchik's Orthodox traditionalism sees it, there is a whole class of commandments not binding upon Jewish women. Women are not obligated in most commandments requiring that a positive action be taken (as opposed to a prohibition against doing something) and which are time-dependent. For example, women are exempt from wearing *tzitzit*, the ritual fringes, discussed in Chapter 4, Section "Development," because that is a commandment requiring an action—putting on the garment—and is time-bound because the commandment only applies during daytime and not at night. Similarly, for *tefillin*. Importantly for Soloveitchik, most prayer (though perhaps not all) falls under this category as well. Women are thus not obligated in most prayer. The prayer experience, however, is vital to the shaping of the religious consciousness of Halakhic Man. And even if some women undertake to pray according to the standard liturgy, they are not fulfilling the same halakhic obligation. Women have some halakhic obligations that men do not. Those too presumably give rise to feelings and phenomenological expressions. Additionally, women are not obligated in the study of Torah. Given the radically different set of obligations Soloveitchik must think the sexes have, can women be "Halakhic Men" at all? Some scholarship attempts to understand Soloveitchik's stance on women and women's issues,[7] but much work remains. Perhaps scholars should consider the unique nature of Halakhic Woman to explore ways in which one's sex and gender might matter for Soloveitchik's approach.

Alternatively, is it possible that despite the certain differences in halakhic categories, the essence of Halakhic Man lies in something more stable? Is the halakhic system or methodology mostly responsible for the phenomenology of Halakhic Man, with some categories of experience playing negligible roles in the larger phenomenological picture? Understanding these issues can shed light on core themes of Soloveitchik's thought and can go far toward advancing his program.

Can other typologies be spelled out?

A core feature of Soloveitchik's philosophical writing is his exploration of Biblical personalities in service of highlighting the dual nature of their personalities.

We have seen numerous examples of this in the figures of Adam, Abraham, Jacob, Joseph, Moses, and others. Soloveitchik's sketches suggest that many other Biblical personalities, like Esther, can be thought of in similar terms. But is there a reason that such a program cannot be more thoroughly executed? For example, can a school or style of Soloveitchik thought provide further analyses of Biblical characters, say those of Noah, Samuel, Isaiah, Solomon, or Amos? Does the Bible provide us with suitable and adequate material for such a treatment? If so, can they be similarly understood? If not, why?

Further, though Soloveitchik stresses the importance of studying the Pentateuch (e.g., in *Unique Experience*), and he makes use of some examples from the remainder of the Hebrew Bible, can we similarly see the dialectical personalities of Halakhic Men in Talmudic characters? After all, it seems odd, at least it begs to be explained, that Soloveitchik, the man for whom the Halakhah is paramount, makes the majority of his points about dual personalities using Biblical figures.

The Talmud provides ample biographical materials for personality sketches. Are they amenable to the same treatment Soloveitchik provides for Biblical characters? The Talmuds contain much information about many individuals such as Rabbi Akiba, Abbaye, Rabba, Rabbi Meir, and Ravina. There is much more information about some of them than is provided in the Bible about Adam.

Soloveitchik does show that the Talmud can be mined for his philosophical purposes. For example, when speaking about the halakhic assumption that repentance is possible for everyone, he presents two slightly different versions of the story about the famous sage-turned-heretic Elisha ben Abuya–also known as Aḥer, the "Other"–for whom it appears that repentance is not possible. The story relates that Elisha ben Abuya was once violating the laws of Sabbath when his student Rabbi Meir asked him to repent. According to the Palestinian Talmud, he replied that he heard a Heavenly voice declare "Return O backsliding children, except for Elisha ben Abuya." According to the Balbyloinian Talmud, however, the Heavenly voice declared, "Return O backsliding children, except for Aḥer." Soloveitchik favors the latter version, that of the Babylonian Talmud. Only the alter-ego Aḥer, "the great logician and dialectician" cannot repent (*Five Addresses*, 198, translation modified by authors) but the true Tanna, Elisha ben Abuya can!

By Soloveitchik's standards, this is an odd case of describing a dialectic personality, but it is a case nonetheless. Certainly, there are clearer cases in the Talmuds of individuals who live with conflicting personalities they are forced to reconcile.

Soloveitchik contrasts the personalities of pairs of individuals, like Mordechai and Esther, or Moses and Aaron, to make points about dialectical opposites. There are a large number of cases in the Talmuds where pairs of individuals are known as *bar plugtot*, dialectical opponents. Throughout the Talmud, these pairs disagree on hosts of halakhic issues, and they are often ascribed conflicting personalities, learning styles, or other attributes. Such pairs include the School of Hillel and the School of Shammai, R. Akiva and R. Yishmael, R. Yohanan and Resh Lakish, Abbaye and Rava, and Rav Zevid and Rav Papa. Their arguments are fertile ground on which the Brisker method can be used to explicate the key features and conceptual differences that underlie their respective positions. They are also obvious choices for a Soloveitchikian analysis of opposing personalities. Is it possible to treat Talmudic personalities the way Soloveitchik has treated Biblical characters?

It is clear that sometimes Soloveitchik thinks of Talmudic characters in terms of their applicable dialectical features. Consider the Talmudic Tanna R. Ḥanina b. Dosa. During a fundraising dinner in 1942 for the Lubavitch Yeshiva Tomchei Tmimim, Soloveitchik compared Yosef Yitzchak Schneersohn–the "previous" Lubavitcher Rebbe with whom he was then sharing a dais–to Ḥanina b. Dosa. On the one hand, Ḥanina b. Dosa was able to rule over nature and command vinegar to burn. On the other hand, when he found himself in a desolate city, he had trouble getting others to help him bring a stone back to Jerusalem. So too, the analogy went, Schneersohn successfully employed superhuman efforts on behalf of Russian Jews to help them withstand Czarist edicts, and yet now he was dependent on a fundraiser to keep his yeshiva financially afloat (Schachter 2001, 182–86). But this tale is merely a rudimentary comparison, hardly a philosophical analysis.

It is possible that these pairs were part of the motivation for Soloveitchik's analysis of the biblical pairs, though Soloveitchik never explicitly tells us.

We can suggest a few reasons why Soloveitchik did not define the personality of many more Talmudic sages. Perhaps the Bible, and its characters, has more universal appeal or is better known than the Talmud and its characters.

Or, a case can be made that Soloveitchik felt he did not need to look to the Talmud. Biblical characters lived pre-Rabbinic Judaism. Turning them into Halakhic Men or even quasi-Halakhic Men is challenging and requires ingenuity, imagination, and creativity–a challenge Soloveitchik may have relished. It also helped Soloveitchik level the playing field. By turning Biblical characters into Halakhic Men or quasi-Halakhic Men, Biblical characters, Zugot and Tannaim, Amoraim, Rabbanim Savoraim, Geonim, Rishonim, and Aḥaronim, can then all be viewed as comprising a continuous chain of the Mesorah—a theme important to Soloveitchik.

Recall that Soloveitchik explained that every Halakhic Man (as a student and as a teacher; as a recipient and as a transmitter) is part of a chain of Mesorah starting at Sinai (and perhaps even earlier, back to Abraham and even Adam) and continuing to the last generation in eschatological times. Turning a Tanna or an Amorah into a Halakhic Man with a dialectical personality is not something Soloveitchik needed to do. They are Halakhic Men by definition. On the other hand, showing that Biblical characters are Halakhic Men has them partaking in the same chain of tradition, something that may not be obvious given that they are pre-Rabbinic.

How each Mitzvah might strengthen our relationship with God (i.e., provide a sense of spirituality)

Along the lines of criticism put forth by Schleiermacher and Otto (see Chapter 4, Section "Schleiermacher and Otto"), many people view halakhic Judaism as lacking in spirituality.[8] To them, and in accordance with an old stereotype, Judaism is a collection of commandments which need to be performed but do nothing to help us develop a relationship with the Divine. There is some apparent substance to this charge. Halakhah is generally thought to tell us that when we perform any of the vast majority of the Biblical commandments, we need only have in mind that we are doing so because God commanded us. No other thought or intent is necessary or expected. This criticism is particularly sharp with respect to ḥukim, commandments which have no apparent reason or purpose.

Soloveitchik can appear sympathetic with this Halakhic statement but adds that when a Halakhic Man performs a mitzvah, he does so within the context of the wealth of detailed halakhic information in his mind, which in turn evokes within him certain sentiments and subjective religious experiences.

Soloveitchik explains that for many commandments there is the act, the *ma'aseh ha-mitzvah*, and its fulfillment, the *kiyyum ha-mitzvah*. Normally, the act and the fulfillment happen simultaneously. For example, on Passover, when we eat matzah, we simultaneously fulfill the mitzvah. What Soloveitchik calls "experiential" commandments, however, are not fulfilled until one internalizes certain values or experiences. Kaplan (2007b, 80–81) summarizes four of Soloveitchik's examples: prayer, mourning, repentance, and enjoying the festivals.[9] Prayer is performed by the recitation of the liturgical text but is fulfilled by an awareness of standing before the Divine. Repentance is performed by the verbal recitation of the confession, the *vidduy*, but fulfilled by acknowledging past sins, regretting them, resolving for the future, and returning to God. Rejoicing on the festival is performed by eating—while the Temple existed—the meat of the holiday peace offering (and nowadays by eating meat and drinking wine) but fulfilled by an inward sense of rejoicing before God. Mourning is performed by engaging in certain rites but fulfilled when one undergoes certain experiences of pain and grief, and by a sense that the encounter with death has cut him off from God. Each of these examples, as Kaplan (2007b, 81) points out, evokes not only emotional experiences but also a special type of awareness and relationship with God.

Soloveitchik has thus provided us with an explanation of how four commandments evoke subjective experiences of the Divine. What about all the other commandments, especially those we recognize as nonrational (see Sztuden 2018b, 66–67)? Do they evoke any connection to God?

In *Halakhic Mind* while discussing Maimonides' project of providing a rationale for mitzvot, *ta'amei ha-mitzvot*, Soloveitchik provides us with three additional examples, from Maimonides' halakhic work—the *Mishneh*

Torah, of mitzvot which evoke a connection to God: blowing the Shofar on Rosh Hashanah, purification by immersion, and observing the Sabbath. The blowing of the Shofar evokes memories of the Creator, the need to examine past deeds, and a return to God in repentance. Purification by immersion in a ritual bath evokes the symbolic role ascribed to water in Jewish religious consciousness, a cleansing of the mind, and a return to God. Envisioning Sabbath as the incarnation of the mystery of creation, in Soloveitchik's words, penetrates Infinity itself.

Soloveitchik has thus provided us with additional examples, derived from *Mishneh Torah,* showing how a Halakhic Man, by performing a halakhic commandment, has a subjective experience of relating to the Divine. Can additional examples of mitzvot that evoke a subjective experience of God be extracted from the *Mishneh Torah* or any other work? If *Mishneh Torah* does not suffice, can the Talmud and other halakhic sources be interrogated? Can we ever achieve the ideal and identify the religious and perhaps mysterious experience of the Divine evoked by each and every mitzvah? The religious experience was very important to Soloveitchik and central to his life.[10] He would have expected us to do all that we can to imbue each and every facet of Halakhah and Jewish life with religious experiences.

> To this end there is only a single source from which a Jewish philosophical Weltanschauung could emerge; the objective order—the Halakhah. In passing onward from the Halakhah and other objective constructs to a limitless subjective flux, we might possibly penetrate the basic structure of our religious consciousness. We might also evolve cognitive tendencies and aspects of our world interpretation and gradually grasp the mysteries of the religious halakhic act.
>
> (Halakhic Mind, 101, emphasis added)

Notes

1 Soloveitchik does not elaborate as to which "literary categories invented by modern man" he is referring. Berman (2020, xxiv, 13–42), writing many years later, makes a similar point and includes history, fact, and fiction as constructs of our own time and place. Berman explains, "When we are speaking of *history, fact* and *fiction*, we must realize that we are utilizing modern categories of thought—categories that the modern mind has constructed. We think that history simply means a discussion of past events with factual accuracy. We assume that this history has existed for, well, all of history. But it has not. The concept *history* itself has a history and we need to understand how it came to be" (xxiv).
2 For an introduction to Biblical criticism and the Modern Orthodox approach, see Zelcer (2008). For an example of Modern Orthodoxy grappling with the challenges of Biblical criticism, see Goldstein Saks (1999).
3 https://kavvanah.wordpress.com/2012/08/16/rav-soloveitchik-religious-definitions-of-man-and-his-social-institutions-1959-part-4-of-7/ references an audio recording of the original lecture.

4 Breuer (1998) contains forty-four examples of his techniques addressing conflicting texts in Genesis. The Introduction (pp. 11–19) (which is also translated into English) lays out his general approach to Biblical criticism.

5 Additions to *Gevurat Ari, Yoma* 54a, s.v. *Teyuvta.*

6 For an analysis and examples of Breuer's approach to Biblical criticism, see Ekstein (1999).

7 Wolosky (2003) and Rudavsky (2007) explore *TLMOF* from a feminist perspective. A comprehensive discussion of Soloveitchik on women's issues is a scholarly desiderata. Beside Soloveitchik's discussion of the Rebbitzin of Talne, his stance on women's issues can be found, among other places, in the essays collected in *Family Redeemed;* in his stance on teaching Talmud to women (see, e.g., CCC, 93 and Saul Berman's recollections at https://thelehrhaus.com/commentary/forty-years-later-the-rav%E2%80%99s-opening-shiur-at-the-stern-college-for-women-beit-midrash/); remarks on the role of a wife (Wurzburger, 1994, 18)); the phenomenology of pregnancy (Ben Pazi, 2016); Halakhic rulings on divorce (see, e.g., CCC, 216–217); women and prayer (see Rakeffet-Rothkoff (1999, vol. 2, 36), Ziegler (2001, 85–87), Twersky (1998)); and on synagogue officers and Rabbis (see, e.g., Ziegler (1998, 22–23), Medoff (2008, 105, 109)).

8 Note also Isadore Twersky's criticism of "extreme talmudism" discussed in Singer and Sokol (1982, 264ff).

9 In *Noraos Harav* (vol. 10, 90) Soloveitchik specifically places the recitation of the *Shema* prayer in this category.

10 See, for example, Horwitz (1996, 48) "In our days the paths are generally divided as if there is no overlap between the religious experience and the scientific approach. Soloveitchik seeks to unite them showing that scientific man, the ideal scientist, is also the man of faith who lives the religious experience." See also Zelcer (2011).

Bibliography

Numerous works have been published under Soloveitchik's name; some he published himself, some were edited and published posthumously, some are philosophical, some are Talmudic, and others are purely halakhic. There are also collections of letters, lectures, lecture notes, compilations, recordings, and recollections (including a rather large collection housed on yutorah.org) as well as still unpublished material in scholarly archives and private hands. What follows is first a list of Soloveitchik's major works, most of which have been addressed or at least mentioned in this book. We should note that the oral lore and gossip surrounding many of Soloveitchik's publications tell an interesting story itself. In many cases, all original manuscripts were lost after publication; in another Soloveitchik is alleged to have disavowed authorship of a book published in his name; in another, Soloveitchik himself approved enhancements of a translator; in another it is disputed whether Soloveitchik or his father wrote a particular essay, and a purported letter of Soloveitchik has turned up which scholars have adamantly declared to be a forgery. The casual reader should take note and the scholar cautioned. We have used our best judgment about what to address and where to exercise more caution.

We do not have a comprehensive bibliography of Soloveitchik's output or the secondary literature on Soloveitchik's life or his work. Providing those are scholarly tasks unto themselves and projects exist to provide them. When possible, references are to accessible English versions.

Following Soloveitchik's works, we list books and articles referenced in the text and a small number of other works we found valuable.

For ease of reference, Soloveitchik's works are referred to by a one- or two-word abbreviation or acronym in parentheses preceding each entry. They are alphabetized according to the abbreviations.

Soloveitchik's works

(Abraham's Journey). 2008. *Abraham's Journey: Reflections of the Life of the Founding Patriarch*, edited by David Shatz, Joel B. Wolowelsky, and Reuven Ziegler. Jersey City: Ktav.
(Adam Eve). *"Adam and Eve." Conspectus*, 137–42.

(Address Parents). *"Address to the Parents at Maimonides School."* Delivered on November 15, 1971. Published in a special issue of the school newsletter *Kol Rambam, Legacy* in October 1993.

(AFTYSS). 2008. *And from There You Shall Seek. 2008.* Translated by Naomi Goldblum. Jersey City: Ktav. Originally published in 1978 as *U-Vikkashtem mi-Sham* in *Hadarom* 47, 1–83.

(Ahavat ha-Torah). 1976. "Al Ahavat ha-Torah u-Geulat Nefesh ha-Dor." In *Be-Sod ha-Yaḥid ve-ha-Yaḥad,* edited by Pinchas Peli. Jerusalem: Orot. (Partial translation available at https://www.torahmusings.com/2018/07/on-the-love-of-torah-and-the-redemption-of-this-generations-soul/. A full translation is forthcoming by the Toras hoRav Foundation.)

(Al ha-Tefilah). 2011. *Al ha-Tefilah: Shiuruv shel ha-Rav Yosef Dov ha-Levi Soloveitchik zt"l.* Edited and translated by Reuven Grodner. Jerusalem: OU Press. (See *On Prayer.*)

(Aseret ha-Dibrot) (Aseret ha-Dibrot). *"Aseret ha-Dibrot."Conspectus,* 111–19.

(Ben-Gurion letter). Soloveitchik, Joseph B., and Ḥayyim Heller. 2013. "To David Ben-Gurion." February 3, 1959. In *Jewish Identity: Who is a Jew? Modern Responses and Opinions on the Registration of Children of Mixed Marriages,* edited by Sidney B. Hoenig, 116–17. Jersey City: Ktav.

(Catharsis) 1978 (Catharsis). 1978. "Catharsis." *Tradition 17*(2): 38–54.

(CCC). 2005. *Community, Covenant and Commitment: Selected Letters and Communications,* edited by Nathaniel Helfgot. Ktav.

"The Community." *Tradition 17*(2): 7–24.

(Confrontation). 1964. "Confrontation." *Tradition 6*(2): 5–29. (See also *Interfaith Relationships.*)

(Conspectus). 1974. *Shiurei HaRav: A Conspectus of the Public Lectures of Rabbi Joseph B. Soloveitchik,*edited by Joseph Epstein. Hoboken: Ktav.

(Days Deliverance). 2007. *Days of Deliverance: Essays on Purim and Hanukkah,* edited by Eli D. Clark, Joel B. Wolowelsky, and Reuven Ziegler. Jersey City: Ktav.

(Emergence Ethical). 2005. *The Emergence of Ethical Man,* edited by Michael Berger. Jersey City: Ktav.

(Eulogy Gold). 1982. "Nos'ei ha-Tzitz ve-ha-Ḥoshen." *Divrei Hagut ve-Ha'arakha.* Jerusalem: World Zionist Organization.

(Eulogy Grodzinski). 1940. "Extracts from Rabbi Joseph B. Soloveitchik of Boston's Eulogy for Rav Chaim Ozer Grodzinski OB"M at the Gathering of Agudath Yisroel in Cincinnati, Ohio." *Hapardes 14*(7): 5–9.

(Eulogy Heller). *"A Eulogy for R. Hayyim Heller."* Conspectus, 46–65.

(Eulogy Rebbe). *"A Eulogy for the Talner Rebbe."* Conspectus, 66–81.

(Eulogy Rebbitzen). 1978. "A Tribute to the Rebbitzen of Talne." *Tradition 17*(2): 73–83.

(Eulogy Velvele). 1976. *"Ma Dodekh Mi-Dod."* In Be-Sod ha Yaḥid ve-ha Yaḥad, edited by Pinchas H. Peli. Jerusalem. In 1981, Be-Sod ha-Yaḥid ve-ha-Yaḥad, 189–254, at 220–35. Reprinted in *Divrei Hagut ve-Ha'arakhah.* Jerusalem: World Zionist Organization, 1982: 57–97, at 79–85. Partial English translation in Saks 1999.

(Family Redeemed). 2002. *Family Redeemed: Essays on Family Relationships,* edited by David Shatz and Joel B. Wolowelsky. Jersey City: Ktav.

(Festivals Freedom). 2006. *Festivals of Freedom: Essays on Pesach and the Haggadah,* edited by Joel B. Wolowelsky and Reuven Ziegler. Jersey City: Ktav.

(First Rebellion). *"The First Rebellion against Torah Authority."* Conspectus, 97–110.

(Five Addresses). 1982/3. *The Rav Speaks: Five Addresses by Rabbi Joseph B. Soloveitchik.* Jerusalem: Tal Orot Institute. (Originally *Four Addresses.* 1974.)

(Halakhah Aggadah). 1944. "Kuntres Halakhah Ve-Aggadah." *Musaf Ha-Pardes* 17(1): 22–44.

(Halakhic Man). 1983. *Halakhic Man.* Translated by Lawrence Kaplan. Philadelphia: Jewish Publication Society. Originally published in Hebrew as *Ish ha-Halakhah* in *Talpiot* (1(3–4), 651–735) in 1944. Reprinted with other Hebrew works by Soloveitchik in *Be-Sod ha-Yahid ve-ha-Yahad* Pinchas Peli (ed.) (Jerusalem, 1976). Reprinted again in 1979 with *"U-Vikkashtem mi-Sham,"* in *Ish ha-Halakhah: Galui ve-Nistar* (Jerusalem).

(Halakhic Mind). 1986. *The Halakhic Mind: An Essay on Jewish Tradition and Modern Thought.* New York: Free Press. London: Collier Macmillan Publishers.

(Halakhic Morality). 2017. *Halakhic Morality: Essays on Ethics and Mesorah*, edited by Joel B. Wolowelsky and Reuven Ziegler. Toras HoRav Foundation; Jerusalem and New Milford: Maggid Books.

(Insights Esther). *"Insights into M'gillat Esther."* Conspectus 167–74.

(Interfaith Relationships). 1967. "On Interfaith Relationships." *Published as an addendum to "Confrontation" in A Treasury of Tradition*, edited by Norman Lamm and Walter S. Wurzburger, 78–80. Hebrew Publishing Company.

(KDD). 2006. *Kol Dodi Dofek: Listen-My Beloved Knocks*, edited by Jeffrey R. Woolf. Translated by David Z. Gordon. New York: Yeshiva University. A shorter version was originally delivered in Yiddish by Soloveitchik in May 1956 to the Religious Zionists of America on the occasion of the eighth anniversary of Israel's independence. It was subsequently rewritten in Hebrew and published as "Torah U-Meluchah." Jerusalem, 1961.

(Lectures Genesis). 2019. "Rabbi Joseph B. Soloveitchik's Lectures on Genesis, I through V." Edited by Meir Triebitz. *Hakirah, vol. 27,* 35–69.

(Lectures Relationship). Forthcoming. "Letures of Rabbi Dr. J. B. Soloveitchik: The relationship between halakhah, aggadah, and kabbalah." Edited by Robert Blau. In *Hakirah, vol. 31.*

(Lord Righteous). 2006 *The Lord is Righteous in all His Ways: Reflections on the Tish'ah be-Av Kinot*, edited by Jacob J. Schacter. Jersey City: Ktav.

(Majesty Humility). 1978. "Majesty and Humility." *Tradition* 17(2): 25–37.

(Maimonides Course). 2016. *Maimonides, Between Philosophy and Halakhah: Rabbi Joseph B. Soloveitchik's Lectures on the Guide of the Perplexed at the Bernard Revel Graduate School (1950–51)*, edited by Lawrence J. Kaplan. Brooklyn: Ktav; Jerusalem: Urim.

(M'Pi HaShemuah). 1992. "M'Pi HaShemuah MiMaran HaGRY"D Soloveitchik ShLIT"A." *Mesorah 7:* 5–76. (Elul 5752).

(Nature Man) (Nature Man). *"On the Nature of Man."* Conspectus, 143–147.

(Noraos Harav). *Noraos HaRav. 16 vols*, edited by B. David Schreiber. http://www.noraosharav.com/.

(On Prayer). 2011. *On Prayer: Lectures of ha-Rav Yosef Dov Soloveitchik, ztz"l*, Annotated, translated and edited by Reuven Grodner. New York: OU Press.

(On Repentance). 1984. *On Repentance: The Thoughts and Oral Discourses of Rabbi Joseph B. Soloveitchik*, edited and translated by Pinchas H. Peli. New York: Paulist Press. Reprinted in 1984 by Northvale, NJ: Aronson.

(OOTW). 2003. *Out of the Whirlwind: Essays on Mourning, Suffering and the Human Condition*, edited by David Shatz, Joel B. Wolowelsky, and Reuven Ziegler. Jersey City: Ktav.

(Redemption Prayer). 1978. "Redemption, Prayer and Talmud Torah." *Tradition* 17(2): 55–72.

(Reine Denken). 1932. *Das reine Denken und die Seinskonstituierung bei Hermann Cohen*. Dissertation. University of Berlin.

(Sacred Profane). 1966. "Sacred and Profane." *In Sacred and Profane, Kodesh and Chol in World Perspective, Gesher* 3(1): 5–29. Reprinted with expanded notes in *Jewish Thought*, 3(1) 55–82, 1993. In *Conspectus* 4–32.

(Seating Sanctification). 1965. "On Seating and Sanctification." In *The Sanctity of the Synagogue*, edited by Baruch Litvin. New York: Union of Orthodox Jewish Congregations of America. The complete original typescript including references omitted in the printed version can be found at: https://seforimblog.com/2018/11/conservative-conversions-some/.

(Seder Meal). *"The Seder Meal." Conspectus*, 163–66.

(Shiurim Abba). 2005. *Shiurim le-Zekher Abba Mari, Z"l (Lectures in Memory of My Father, OB"M)*. Jerusalem: Mosad Harav.

(Shnei Sugei). 2002. *"Shnei Sugei Masorah" ("Two Types of Tradition")*. *Shiurim Abba*.

(TLMOF). 1965. "The Lonely Man of Faith." *Tradition* 7(2): 5–67. Reprinted as a monograph by New York: Doubleday Press, 1992.

(Unique Experience). *"The Unique Experience of Judaism" Conspectus*, 126–36.

(Vision and Leadership). 2013. *Vision and Leadership: Reflections on Joseph and Moses*, edited by David Shatz, Joel B. Wolowelsky, and Reuven Ziegler. Jersey City: Ktav.

(Worship Heart). 2003. *Worship of the Heart: Essays on Jewish Prayer*, edited by David Shatz, Joel B. Wolowelsky, and Shalom Carmy. New York: Ktav.

(Yemey Zikkaron). 1986. *Yemey Zikkaron*. Translated by Moshe Kroneh. Jerusalem: World Zionist Organization.

Secondary works and references

Abbema, Marieke Meijer-van, and Sander Koole. 2017. "After God's Image: Prayer Leads People with Positive God Beliefs to Read Less hostility in Others' Eyes." *Religion, Brain, Behavior* 7(3): 206–22.

Agus, Jacob B. 1954. *Guideposts in Modern Judaism*. New York: Bloch Publishing Co.

Amaru, Joshua. 2005. "Prayer and the Beauty of God: Rav Soloveitchik on Prayer and Aesthetics." *The Torah u-Madda Journal* 13: 148–76.

Aristotle, Jonathan Barnes, ed. 1984. *The Complete Works of Aristotle*. Princeton, NJ: Princeton University Press.

Austin, J. L. 1962. *How To Do Things With Words*. Cambridge: Harvard University Press.

Aviner, Shlomo Chaim. 1980. *"Beirurim be-Inyan 'She-Lo Ya'alu ke-Ḥoma'."* Jerusalem: *Noam* 20: 1–29.

Baeck, Leo, and Walter Kaufmann, trans. 1958. *Judaism and Christianity*. Philadelphia: The Jewish Publication Society.

Barth, Karl, and Edwyn C. Hoskyns, trans. 1933. *Epistle to the Romans*. New York: Oxford.

Batnitzky, Leora. 2011. *How Judaism Became a Religion: An Introduction to Modern Jewish Thought.* Princeton, NJ: Princeton University Press.

Batnitzky, Leora, and Yonatan Y. Brafman, eds. 2018. *Jewish Legal Theories: Writings on State Religion, and Morality.* Waltham, MA: Brandeis University Press.

Bedzow, Ira. 2009. *Halakhic Man, Authentic Jew: Modern Expressions of Orthodox Thought from Rabbi Joseph B. Soloveitchik and Eliezer Berkovits.* New York: Urim.

Beiser, Frederick C. 2018. *Hermann Cohen: An Intellectual Biography.* New York: Oxford University Press.

Ben Pazi, Hanoch. 2016. "Phenomenology of Pregnancy, Maternity, and Parenthood in the writings of R. Joseph Soloveitchik and Emmanuel Lévinas: Philosophical readings of Jewish sources." *Judaica 72*(3): 387–412.

Berger, Michael S. 1998. "*U-Vikashtem mi-Sham*: Rabbi Joseph B. Soloveitchik's response to Martin Buber's Religious Existentialism." *Modern Judaism 18*(2): 93–118.

Berkovits, Eliezer. 1962. *A Jewish Critique of the Philosophy of Martin Buber.* New York: Yeshiva University.

Berkovits, Eliezer. 1974. *Major Themes in Modern Philosophies of Judaism.* New York: Ktav Publishing House, Inc.

Berkovitz, Jay R. 2017. "Rabbinic Culture and the Historical Development of Halakhah." In *The Cambridge History of Judaism*, edited by J. Karp and A. Sutcliffe, 349–77. Cambridge: Cambridge University Press.

Berman, Joshua. 2020. *Ani Maamin: Biblical Criticism, Historical Truth, and the Thirteen Principles of Faith.* New Milford: Koren Publishers.

Berman, Julius. 2008. "The Rav—How He Developed P'sak and his Views on Da'at Torah." In *Mentor of Generations: Reflections on Rabbi Joseph B. Soloveitchik*, edited by Zev Eleff, 133–41. Jersey City: Ktav.

Berman, Saul J. 2008. "The Approach of the Rav to P'sak and Public Policy." In *Mentor of Generations: Reflections on Rabbi Joseph B. Soloveitchik*, edited by Zev Eleff, 61–66. Jersey City: Ktav.

Bernstein, Eliezer Zalman. 1984. "Ha-Rav ve-Histadrut ha-Rabbanan." In *Sefer Yovel: le-Kavod Moreinu ha-Gaon Rabbi Yosef Dov Soloveitchik Shlit"a*, edited by Shaul Israeli, Norman Lamm, and Yitzchak Raphael. 2 vols, 18–29. Jerusalem and New York: Mossad Harav Kook, Yeshiva University.

Besdin, Abraham R. 1981. *Reflections of the Rav: Lessons in Jewish Thought adapted from Lectures of Rabbi Joseph B. Soloveitchik.* Jerusalem: Jewish Agency.

Besdin, Abraham R. 1989. *Man of Faith in the Modern World: Reflections of the Rav. Lessons in Jewish Thought adapted from Lectures of Rabbi Joseph B. Soloveitchik.* vol. 2. Hoboken: Ktav.

Biale, David, David Assaf, Benjamin Brown, Uriel Gellman, Samuel C. Heilman, Moshe Rosman, Gadi Sagiv, and Marcin Wodziński. 2018. *Hasidism: A New History.* Princeton: Princeton University Press.

Bierman, Michael A., ed. 2003. *Memories of a Giant: Eulogies in Memory of Rabbi Dr. Joseph B Soloveitchik zt"l.* Jerusalem and New York: Urim.

Birnbaum, Ruth. 1977. "The Man of Dialogue and the Man of Halakhah." *Judaism 26*(1): 52–62.

Blau, Alter Asher Yesha'yah. 1993. *Efneh ve-Eshne [A collection of lectures from R. Yosef Dov ha-Levi Soloveitchik].* New York: Yeshiva University Press.

Blau, Robert. 2008. "The Rav at Revel—The Rav at RIETS." *Mentor of Generations: Reflections on Rabbi Joseph B. Soloveitchik*, edited by Zev Eleff. Jersey City: Ktav.

Blau, Yitzchak. 1997. "Creative Repentance: On Rabbi Soloveitchik's Concept of Teshuva." In *Exploring the Thought of Rabbi J. B. Soloveitchik,* edited by M. Angel, 263–274. New Jersey: Ktav.

Blidstein, Gerald J. 1996. "On the Halakhic Thought of Rabbi Joseph B. Soloveitchik: The Norms and Nature of Mourning." *Tradition 30*(4): 115–30.

Blidstein, Gerald J. 1997. "On the Jewish People in the Writings of Rabbi Joseph Solovetchik." In *Exploring the Thought of Rabbi J. B. Soloveitchik*, edited by M. Angel, 293–324. New Jersey: Ktav.

Blidstein, Gerald J. 2012. *Society and Self: On the Writings of Rabbi Joseph B. Soloveitchik*. New York: OU Press.

Blidstein, Gerald J. 2015. "Rabbi Soloveitchik's Abraham." *Tradition 48*(4): 18–23.

Borowitz, Eugene. 1966. "The Typological Theology of Rabbi Joseph B. Soloveitchik." *Judaism 15*: 203–10.

Borowitz, Eugene. 1983. "A Theology of Modern Orthodoxy: Rabbi Joseph B. Soloveitchik." In *Choices in Modern Jewish Thought*, 218–242. New York: Behrman House.

Boylan, Stanley. 1996. "Learning with the Rav: Learning from the Rav." *Tradition 30*(4): 131–44.

Brafman, Yonatan Yisrael. 2014. *Critical Philosophy of Halakha (Jewish Law): The Justification of Halakhic Norms and Authority*. PhD Thesis. Columbia University.

Breger, Marshall. 2005. *"A Reassessment of Rav Soloveitchik's Essay on Interfaith Dialogue: 'Confrontation'."* *Studies in Christian-Jewish Relations, vol. 1*, 151–69. Center for Christian-Jewish Learning at Boston College.

Breuer, Mordechai, and Yosef Ofer, eds. 1998. *Pirqe Bereshit*. 2 vols. Alon Shevut: Tevunot Press.

Brill, Alan. 2006. "Elements of Dialectical Theology in Rabbi Soloveitchik's View of Torah Study." In *Study and Knowledge in Jewish Thought*, edited by Howard Kreisel, vol. 1, 265–96. Beer Sheva: Ben-Gurion University The Negev.

Brill, Alan. 2010a. *Judaism and Other Religions: Models of understanding*. New York: Palgrave.

Brill, Alan. 2010b. *"Nitzaḥon le-Lo Kerav: Gishah Dialektikit le-Tarbut be-Haguto shel Ha-Rav Soloveitchik."* In *Rav ba-Olam he-Ḥadash*, edited by Avinoam Rosenak and Naftali Rothenberg, 118–44. Jerusalem: The Van Leer Jerusalem Institute and Magnes Press.

Brill, Alan. 2012. *Judaism and World Religions: Encountering Christianity, Islam, and Eastern Traditions*. New York: Palgrave.

Brooks, David. 2015. *The Road to Character*. New York: Random House.

Brunner, Emil, and Olive Wyon, trans. 1941. *The Divine Imperative*. Philadelphia: The Westminster Press.

Carmy, Shalom. 1997a. "Of Eagles' Flight and Snail's Pace." *Tradition 29*(1): 21–31.

Carmy, Shalom. 1997b. "Pluralism and the Category of the Ethical." In *Exploring the Thought of Rabbi Joseph B. Soloveitchik*, edited by Marc D. Angel, 325–46. New Jersey: Ktav.

Carmy, Shalom. 2018. "'In Many Respects God was Closer to Abraham than He was to Moses,' Themes in *Emergence of Ethical Man*." In *Scholarly Man of Faith: Studies in the Thought and Writings of Rabbi Joseph B. Soloveitchik*, edited by Ephraim Kanarfogel and Dov Schwartz, 11–26. Urim Publications and Ktav.

Charlop, Zevulun. 2003. "Wherever You Find His Greatness, There You Will Find His Humility." In *Memories of a Giant: Eulogies in Memory of Rabbi Dr. Joseph Soloveitchik zt"l*. Edited by Michael A. Bierman. Jerusalem: Urim.

Chomsky, Noam. 1968. *Language and Mind*. New York: Harcourt Brace Janovich.

Cohen, Gerson. 1967. *Sefer ha-qabbalah: The Book of Tradition by Abraham Ibn Da'ud*. Philadelphia: Jewish Publication Society.

Cohen, Hermann. 1995. *Religion of Reason Out of the Sources of Judaism: Jewish Philosophy of Religion and a Jewish Ethics*. Atlanta: Scholars Press.

Cohen, Hermann, and A. S. Bruckstein, trans. 2004. *Hermann Cohen's Ethics of Maimonides*. University of Wisconsin Press.

Cohen, Hermann, and Eva Jospe, trans. and ed. 1971. *Reason and Hope: Selections from the Jewish Writings of Hermann Cohen*. New York: Norton.

Cohen, Jonathan. 2008. "Incompatible Parallels: Soloveitchik and Berkovits on religious experience and the dimension of history." *Modern Judaism* 28(2): 173–203.

Cohen, Jonathan. 2016. "The Halakhah, Sacred Events, and Time Consciousness in Rosenzweig and Soloveitchik." *Shofar* 35(1): 69–94.

Cohen, Martin S., ed. 2012. *The Observant Life: The Wisdom of Conservative Judaism for Contemporary Jews*. New York: Rabbinical Assembly.

Dahlstrom, Daniel O. 2015. "Natorp's Psychology." In *New Approaches to Neo-Kantianism*, edited by Andrea Staiti and Nicolas de Warren, 240–260. Cambridge University Press.

Dalfin, Chaim. 2016. *Rav and Rebbe*. Brooklyn: Jewish Enrichment Press.

Davidson, Donald. 1974. "On the Very Idea of a Conceptual Scheme." In *Proceedings and Addresses of the American Philosophical Association*, vol. 47, 5–20.

Davis, Joseph. 2002. "The Reception of the 'Shulḥan 'Arukh' and the Formation of Ashkenazic Jewish Identity." *AJS Review* 26(2): 251–76.

Deutsch, Shaul Shimon. 1997. *Larger than Life: The Life and Times of the Lubavitcher Rebbe Rabbi Menachem Mendel Schneerson*. 2 vols. New York: Chasidic Historical Productions.

Dilthey, W. 1977. *Ideas Concerning a Descriptive and Analytic Psychology*. In *Descriptive Psychology and Historical Understanding*. Translated by R. M. Zaner and K. L. Heiges, 35–120 The Hague: Martinus Nijhoff.

Dilthey, W., and H. P. Rickman, ed. 1979. *Selected Writings*. New York: Cambridge University Press.

Dunner, Pini, and David N. Myers. 2015. "A Haredi Attack on Rabbi Joseph Ber Soloveitchik: A battle over the Brisker Legacy from 1984." *Jewish Quarterly Review* 105(1): 131–38.

Eisenberg, Ethan, dir and prod. 2006. *Lonely Man of Faith: The Life and Legacy of Rabbi Joseph B. Soloveitchik*. Second Look Productions. Film.

Ekstein, Meir. 1999. "Rabbi Mordechai Breuer and Modern Orthodox Biblical Commentary," *Tradition* 33(3): 6–23.

Elberg, Simcha. 1960. *"Seiruvo shel HgRY"D Soloveitchik she-Lo Leheyot Muamad le-Rabbanut ha-Rashit."* *Hapardes* 34(7): 3–5.

Elon, Menachem. 1975. *The Principles of Jewish Law*, edited by Menachem Elon. Jerusalem: Hebrew University of Jerusalem.

Farber, Seth. 2001. "Reproach, Recognition and Respect: Rabbi Joseph B. Soloveitchik and Orthodoxy's Mid-Century Attitude toward non-Orthodox denominations." *American Jewish History* 89(2): 193–214.

Farber, Seth. 2004. *An American Orthodox Dreamer: Rabbi Joseph B. Soloveitchik and Boston's Maimonides School.* Hanover: University Press of New England.

Farber, Seth. 2020. "Rabbi Joseph B. Soloveitchik's Early Zionism," *Tradition 52*(2); 127–32.

Feigelson, Joshua Meir. 2015. *Relationship, Power, and Holy Secularity: Rabbi Yitz Greenberg and American Jewish Life, 1966-1983.* PhD Dissertation, Northwestern University.

Feldinger, Lauren Gelfond. 2010. "The Lonely Man of Peace." *Jerusalem Post, 22*: 18.

Feldman, Emmanuel. 1996. "The Halakhic Rebbe." *Tradition 30*(4): 1–4.

Fenton, Paul B. 1994 "Asher Zelig Margaliot." In Raphael Patai and Emanuel S. Goldsmith *Thinkers and Teachers of Modern Judaism*, 37–46. New York: Paragon House.

Finkelman, Yoel. 2014. "Theology with Fissures: Contradictions in Rabbi Joseph B. Soloveitchik's Theological writings." *Journal of Modern Jewish Studies 13*(3): 399–421.

Fishman, Aryeh. 1996. "'*Ish ha-Emunah ha-Boded' be-Prespectivah Soẓeologit.*" In *Emunah be-Zemanim Mishtanim: Al Mishnato shel ha-Rav Yosef Dov Soloveitchik*, edited by Avi Sagi, 265–74. Jerusalem: Ha-Maḥlakah le-Ḥinukh u-le-Tarbut Toraniyim ba-Golah.

Fiske, Edward B. 1972. "Rabbi's Rabbi Keeps The Law Up to Date." *The New York Times*, June 23, 39, *74*.

Forman, Paul. 1971. "Weimar Culture, Causality, and Quantum theory: Adaptation by German Physicists and Mathematicians to a Hostile Environment." *Historical Studies in the Physical Sciences, 3*: 1–115.

Fox, Marvin. 1996. "The Rav as Maspid." *Tradition 30*(4): 164–81.

Fraenkel, Abraham A., and Jiska Cohen-Mansfield, ed. 2016. *Reflections of a Jewish Mathematician in Germany.* Translated by Allison Brown. Switzerland: Springer.

Franks, Paul W. 2007. "Jewish Philosophy after Kant: The Legacy of Solomon Maimon." In *The Cambridge Companion to Modern Jewish Philosophy*, edited by Michael L. Morgan and Peter Eli Gordon, 53–79. New York: Cambridge University Press.

Freedman, Samuel G. 1999. *"Modern Orthodox Jews Have a Hero but Not All His Words." The New York Times*, May 22.

Frege, Gottlob. 1980. "On Sense and Reference." In *Translations from the Philosophical Writings of Gottlob Frege*, edited and translated by P. Geach and M. Black, 3rd ed., 36–56. Oxford: Blackwell.

Friedman, Richard Elliott. 2017. *The Exodus: How it Happened and Why it Matters.* New York: HarperOne.

Fries, Jakob Friedrich. 1805. *Wissen, Glaube und Ahndung.* Jena: J. C. G. Göpferdt.

Frimmer, Aryeh, and Dov Frimmer. 1998. "Women's Prayer Services–Theory and Practice." *Tradition 32*(2): 5–118.

Frish, Yechiel, and Yedidya HaCohen. 2017. *Rabbi Shear Yashuv Cohen: Between War and Peace.* Translated by Irene Lancaster. Jerusalem and New York: Urim Publications.

Genack, Menachem. 1998. "Walking with Ramban." In *Rabbi Joseph B. Soloveitchik: Man of Halacha, Man of Faith*, edited by Menachem D. Genack. Hoboken: Ktav.

Genack, Menachem. 2018. "The Rav and the Brisker Derech: A Unique Method." *Jewish Action*, *78*(3): 36–38.

Goldberg, Hillel. 2010. *Between Berlin and Slobodka: Jewish Transition Figures from Eastern Europe, Augmented Edition*, Updated Edition. Jersey City: Ktav.

Goldman, Eliezer. 1996. "Teshuva u-Zeman be-Hagut ha-Rav Soloveitchik." In *Emunah be-Zemanim Mishtanim: Al Mishnato shel ha-Rav Yosef Dov Soloveitchik*, edited by Avi Sagi, 175–89. Jerusalem: Ha-Maḥlakah le-Ḥinukh u-le-Tarbut Toraniyim ba-Golah.

Goldschmidt, Tyron. 2014. "Jewish Responses to the Problem of Evil." *Philosophy Compass 9*(12): 894–905.

Goldstein Saks, Ilana. 1999. *"Encounters between Torah Min Hashamayim and Biblical Criticism." Atid* 98: 1–36.

Gopin, Mendi. 2006. *Davening with the Rav: My Rabbi and My Rebbe*. Jersey City: Ktav Publishers.

Gorelik, Moshe S. 2008. "A Titan among Giants." In *Mentor of Generations: Reflections on Rabbi Joseph B. Soloveitchik*, edited by Zev Eleff. Jersey City: Ktav.

Greenberg, Irving. 2004. *For the Sake of Heaven and Earth: The new encounter between Judaism and Christianity*. Philadelphia: Jewish Publication Society.

Greenblatt, Matis. 2003. "Faith and Intellect: The Impact of the Rav." In *Memories of a Giant: Eulogies in Memory of Rabbi Dr. Joseph Soloveitchik zt"l*, edited by Michael A. Bierman. Jerusalem: Urim.

Giuliani, Massimo. 2008. "On the Jewish-Christian Dialogue: Halakhic Guidance of Rabbi Joseph B. Soloveitchik." *Keshet 6*(1–2): 69–74.

Hain, Kenneth. 2003. "The Rav as Darshan." In *Memories of a Giant: Eulogies in Memory of Rabbi Dr. Joseph Soloveitchik zt"l*, edited by Michael A. Bierman. Jerusalem: Urim.

Halivni, David Weiss. 1986. *Midrash, Mishnah, and Gemara: The Jewish Predilection for Justified Law*. Cambridge, Massachusettts and London: Harvard University Press.

Hartman, David. 1978. "Soloveitchik's Response to Modernity: Reflections on 'The Lonely Man of Faith'." In *Joy and Responsibility*, 198–231. Shalom Hartman Institute: Jerusalem.

Hartman, David. 1989. "The Halakhic Hero: Rabbi Joseph Soloveitchik, Halakhic Hero." *Modern Judaism 9*(3): 249–73.

Hartman, David. 2001. *Love and Terror in the God Encounter: The Theological Legacy of Rabbi Joseph B. Soloveitchik*. Jewish Lights.

Hartman, David. 2003. "Prayer and Religious Consciousness: An analysis of Jewish Prayer in the Works of Joseph B. Soloveitchik, Yeshayahu Leibowitz, and Abraham Joshua Heschel." *Modern Judaism 23*(2): 105–25.

Hartman, Geoffrey H. 1994. "Midrash as Law and Literature." *The Journal of Religion 74*(3): 338–55.

Harvey, Zev. 1996. *"He'arot al ha-Rav Soloveitchik ve-ha-Filosofiah Ha-Rambamit."* In *Emunah be-Zemanim Mishtanim: Al Mishnato shel ha-Rav Yosef Dov Soloveitchik*, edited by Avi Sagi, 95–107. Jerusalem: Ha-Maḥlakah le-Ḥinukh u-le-Tarbut Toraniyim ba-Golah.

Hazony, Yoram. 2012. "The Rav's Bombshell." *Commentary 2012* (April): 48–55.

Hecht, Neil S., B. S. Jackson, A. M. Rabello, D. Piattelli, and S. M. Passamaneck. 1996. *An Introduction to the History and Sources of Jewish Law*. London: Oxford University Press.

Helfgot, Nathaniel. 2009. "From the Rav's Pen: Selected Letters." In *Rav Chesed: Essays in Honor of Rabbi Dr. Haskel Lookstein*, edited by Rafael Medoff. 2 vols. Jersey City: Ktav.

Heller, Ḥayyim. 1911. *Untersuchungen über die Peschitta zur gesamten hebräischen Bibel*. Berlin: Itzkowski.

Henkin, Eitam. 2018. *Ta'arokh Lefanei Shulḥan: Ḥaiyav Zemanov u-Mefalo shel Ha-RY"M Epshtein Ba'al Arukh ha-Shulḥan*. Jerusalem: Koren Publishers/Maggid.

Herskowitz, Daniel. 2015. "Rabbi Joseph B. Soloveitchik's Endorsement and Critique of Volkish Thought." *Journal of Modern Jewish Studies 14*(3): 373–90.

Heschel A. J. 1955. *God in Search of Man: A Philosophy of Judaism*. New York: Farrar, Straus and Giroux.

Heschel, A. J. 1962. *Torah min HaShamayim BeAspeclaria shel HaDorot*, vol. 2. London: Soncino Press. 1965, vol. 3. Jerusalem: Jewish Theological Seminary of America.

Heschel, A. J. 1996. *Moral Grandeur and Spiritual Audacity*. New York: Farrar, Straus and Giroux.

Hirsch, Samson Raphael, and Bernard Drachman, trans. 1969. *The Nineteen Letters*. New York: Feldheim.

Holzer, David. 2009a. *The Rav Thinking Aloud: Transcripts of Personal Conversations with Rabbi Joseph B. Soloveitchik*. HolzerSeforim.

Holzer, David. 2009b. *The Rav Thinking Aloud on the Parsha, Sefer Bereishis: Transcripts of Shiurim from Rabbi Joseph B. Soloveitchik*. HolzerSeforim.

Horwitz, Rivka. 1996. *"Yaḥaso shel ha-Rav Soloveitchik le-Ḥaviyah ha-Datit u-li-Mistorin."* In *Emunah be-Zemanim Mishtanim: Al Mishnato shel ha-Rav Yosef Dov Soloveitchik*, edited by Avi Sagi, 45–74. Jerusalem: Ha-Maḥlakah le-Ḥinukh u-le-Tarbut Toraniyim ba-Golah.

Hume, David. 1999. *An Enquiry concerning Human Understanding*, edited by Tom L. Beauchamp. New York: Oxford University Press.

Husserl, Edmund, and W. R. Boyce Gibson, trans. 2002. *Ideas: General Introduction to Pure Phenomenology*. London: Routledge.

Hyatt, David. 2014. "Tolerance and Pluralism in the Philosophical Writings of Rabbi Joseph B. Soloveitchik." *Ciências da Religião: história e sociedade 12*(2): 133–50.

Inbari, Motti. 2016. *Jewish Radical Ultra-Orthodoxy Confronts Modernity, Zionism and Women's Equality*. New York: Cambridge University Press.

James, William. 1912. *A Pluralistic Universe*. London: Longmans, Green and Co.

James, William. 2004. *The Varieties of Religious Experience*. New York: Barnes and Noble. (originally published 1902).

Johnston, Murray. 1999. *Engagement and Dialogue. Pluralism in the Thought of Joseph B. Soloveitchik*. MA Thesis, McGill University.

Jung, Carl. 1971. *Psychological Types*. New Jersey: Princeton University Press.

Kamenetsky, Nathan. 2002. *Making of a Godol: A Study of Episodes in the Lives of Great Torah Personalities, 2 vols*. Jerusalem: Hamesorah Publishers.

Kanarfogel, Ephraim. 2018. "The History of the Tosafists and their Literary Corpus According to Rav Soloveitchik's Interpretation of the *Qinot* for *Tisha B'Av*." In *Scholarly Man of Faith: Studies in the Thought and Writings of Rabbi Joseph B. Soloveitchik*, edited by Ephraim Kanarfogel and Dov Schwartz, 75–108. Urim Publications and Ktav.

Kant, Immanuel. 1902. *Prolegomena to any Future Metaphysics.* Chicago: Open Court.
Kant, Immanuel, and Mary Gregor, trans. 1997. *Critique of Practical Reason.* New York: Cambridge University Press.
Kant, Immanuel, and Werner S. Pluhar, trans. 2009. *Religion Within the Bounds of Bare Reason.* Indianapolis: Hackett.
Kant, Immanuel, and Norman Kemp Smith, trans. 2003. *Critique of Pure Reason.* Revised ed. Palgrave.
Kaplan, Lawrence. 1973. "The Religious Philosophy of Rabbi Joseph B. Soloveitchik." *Tradition 14*(2): 43–64.
Kaplan, Lawrence. 1984–5. *"Degamim shel ha-Adam ha-Dati ha-Edeali be-Hagut ha-Rav Yosef Dov Soloveitchik."* *Jerusalem Studies in Jewish Thought 4*(3–4): 327–39.
Kaplan, Lawrence. 1987. "Rabbi Joseph B. Soloveitchik's Philosophy of Halakhah." *The Jewish Law Annual 7*: 139–197.
Kaplan, Lawrence. 1992. "The Ḥazon Ish: Ḥaredi Critic of Traditional Orthodoxy." In *The Uses of Tradition: Jewish Continuity in the Modern Era*, edited by Jack Wertheimer, 145–73. New York: Jewish Theological Seminary Press.
Kaplan, Lawrence. 1996. *"Motivim Kabbaliyim be-Hagoto shel ha-Rav Soloveitchik: Mashmautiyim oh Eturiyim?"* In *Emunah be-Zemanim Mishtanim: Al Mishnato shel ha-Rav Yosef Dov Soloveitchik*, edited by Avi Sagi, 75–90. Jerusalem: Ha-Maḥlakah le-Ḥinukh u-le-Tarbut Toraniyim ba-Golah.
Kaplan, Lawrence. 1998. "The Multi-faceted Legacy of Rabbi Joseph B. Soloveitchik." *BDD 7*: 51–86.
Kaplan, Lawrence. 1999a. "Revisionism and the Rav." *Judaism 48*(3): 290–311.
Kaplan, Lawrence. 1999b. "Rabbi Abraham Isaac Kook, Rabbi Joseph B. Soloveitchik, and Dr. Isaac Breuer on Jewish Identity and the Jewish National Revival." In *Jewish Identity in the Postmodern Age*, edited by C. Selengut, 47–66. St. Paul, MN: Paragon.
Kaplan, Lawrence. 2000. "Hermann Cohen's Theory of Sacrifice in 'Religion of Reason out of the Sources of Judaism'." In *"Religion of Reason out of the Sources of Judaism": Tradition and the Concept of Origin in Hermann Cohen's Later Work*, edited by Helmut Holzhey, Gabriel Motzkin, and Hartwig Wiedebach, 191–204. Hildesheim: Georg Olms Verlag.
Kaplan, Lawrence. 2006. "Hermann Cohen and Joseph Soloveitchik on repentance." *Journal of Jewish Thought and Philosophy 13*: 213–58.
Kaplan, Lawrence J. 2007a. "Joseph Soloveitchik and Halakhic Man." In *The Cambridge Companion to Modern Jewish Philosophy*, edited by Michael L. Morgan and Peter Eli Gordon, 209–33. New York: Cambridge University Press.
Kaplan, Lawrence J. 2007b. "Review Essay: *Worship of the Heart: Essays on Prayer. By Rabbi Joseph B. Soloveitchik.*" *Ḥakirah 5*: 79–114.
Kaplan, Lawrence. 2010a. "From Cooperation to Conflict: Rabbi Professor Emanuel Rackman, Rav Joseph B. Soloveitchik, and the evolution of American modern Orthodoxy." *Modern Judaism 30*(1): 46–68.
Kaplan, Lawrence. 2010b. *"Ish he-Emunah ha-Boded le-Rav Soloveitchik be-Maḥashavah ha-Ortoduksit-Modernit."* In *Rav ba-Olam he-Ḥadash*, edited by Avinoam Rosenak and Naftali Rothenberg, 147–176. Jerusalem: Magnes Press and Van Leer Institute.
Kaplan, Lawrence. 2013. "Exposition as High Art: Review of *Society and Self: On the Writings of Rabbi Joseph B. Soloveitchik.*" *Ḥakirah 15*: 61–107.

Kasher, Menachem M. 1968. *HaTekufah HaGedolah*. Jerusalem: Torah Shelemah Institute.

Kashkin, Yisrael. 2012. "My Long Lonely Journey to the Rav." *Tradition* 45(4): 47–59.

Katz, Steven T., ed. 1975. *Jewish Philosophers*. Jerusalem: Keter.

Kelly, Eugene. 1977. *Max Scheler*. Boston: Twayne Publishers.

Kessler, Seymour. 2002. "Soloveitchik and Levinas: Pathways to the Other." *Judaism* 51(4): 440–56.

Kierkegaard, Søren. 1985. *Fear and Trembling*. London: Penguin.

Kierkegaard, Søren, Howard V. Hong, and Edna H. Hong, eds. 1987. *Either/Or*. New Jersey: Princeton University Press.

Kimelman, Reuven. 2004. "Rabbis Joseph B. Soloveitchik and Abraham Joshua Heschel on Jewish-Christian Relations." *The Edah Journal* 4(2): 1–21.

Klein, Felix. 1911. *The Evanston Colloquium: Lectures on Mathematics*. New York: American Mathematical Society.

Klein, Isaac. 1979. *A Guide to Jewish Religious Practice*. New York: Jewish Theological Seminary of America.

Koenigsberg, Eliakim. 2007. *Sefer MercerShiurei Ha-Rav al Inyanei Aveilut u-Tishah b-Av*. Jerusalem: Mesorah.

Kolbrener, William. 1996. "No 'elsewhere': Fish, Soloveitchik, and the unavoidability of interpretation." *Literature and Theology* 10(2): 171–90.

Kolbrener, William. 1997. "Towards a Genuine Jewish Philosophy: *Halakhic Mind*'s new philosophy of religion." In *Exploring the Thought of Rabbi Joseph B. Soloveitchik*, edited by Marc D Angel, 179–206. New Jersey: Ktav.

Kolbrener, William. 2015. "On Abandoning Aristotle: Love in Psychoanalysis and Jewish Philosophy." In *Answering a Question with a Question: Contemporary psychoanalysis and Jewish thought: A tradition of inquiry*, edited by Lewis Aron and Libby Henik, 65–98. Brighton, MA: Academic Studies Press.

Kolbrener, William. 2016. *The Last Rabbi: Joseph Soloveitchik and Talmudic Tradition*. Indiana University Press.

Koller, Aaron. 2020. *Unbinding Isaac: The Significance of the Akedah for Modern Jewish Thought*. Philadelphia: Jewish Publication Society.

Koltun-Fromm, Ken. 2012. "America." In *The Cambridge History of Jewish Philosophy, Vol 2: The Modern Era*, edited by Martin Kavka, Zachary Braiterman, and David Novak, 128–53. Cambridge University Press.

Korn, Eugene. 2005. "The Man of Faith and Religious Dialogue: Revisiting 'Confrontation'." *Modern Judaism* 25(3): 290–315.

Korn, Yitzhak Dov. 2010. "*HaRav Soloveitchik ve-ha-Dialog ha-Te'alogi le-Or Te'alogiot Katoliot Akhshavit*." In *Rav Ba-Olam he-Ḥadash*, edited by Avinoam Rosenak and Naftali Rothenberg, 410–33. Jerusalem: The Van Leer Jerusalem Institute and Magnes Press.

Krauss, Simcha. 2000. "The Rav: On Zionism, Universalism and Feminism." *Tradition* 34(2): 24–39.

Kuhn, Thomas. 1962. *The Structure of Scientific Revolutions*. Chicago: University of Chicago Press.

Kurzweil, Z'vi. 1982. "Universalism in the Philosophy of Rabbi Joseph B. Soloveitchik." *Judaism* 31(4): 459–71.

Lamm, Norman. 1993. "A Eulogy for the Rav." *Tradition* 28(1): 4–17.

Lang, Berel. 2007. "Evil, Suffering, and the Holocaust." In *The Cambridge Companion to Modern Jewish Philosophy*, edited by Michael L. Morgan and Peter Eli Gordon, 277–299. New York: Cambridge University Press.

Leibowitz, Yeshayahu. 1955. "*HaRaMBaM - HaAdam HaAbrahami.*" *Beterem*, August 1, *1955*; 20–23. Published in English as Elvin Kose (Tr.), "Maimonides – The Abrahamic Man," in *Judaism* (6) 1957: 148–54.

Leibowitz, Yeshayahu. 1992. *Judaism, Human Values, and the Jewish State*, edited by Eliezer Goldman. Cambridge, MA: Harvard University Press.

Levenson, Alan. 1994. "Jewish Responses to Modern Biblical Criticism: Some Reflections and a Course Proposal." *Shofar 12*(3): 100–14.

Lewit, Tonja. 1931. *Die Entwicklung des jüdischen Volksbildungswesens in Polen.* Wilna: Druckerei J. Lewin.

Lewittes, Mendell. 1987. *Principles and Development of Jewish Law: Concepts and History of Rabbinic Jurisprudence from Its Inception to Modern Times.* New York, NY: Bloch Publishing Company.

Liadi, Shneur Zalman of. 1969. *Likutei Amarim (Tanya) by Rabbi Schneur Zalman of Liadi. Translated from the Hebrew, with an Introduction.* Brooklyn, NY: Kehot Publication Society.

Lichtenstein, Aharon. 1963. "R. Joseph Soloveitchik." In *Great Jewish Thinkers of the Twentieth Century, Vol. 3*, edited by Simon Noveck, 281–97. Clinton: B'nai Brith Department of Adult Jewish Education.

Lichtenstein, Aharon. 1996. "The Rav at Jubilee: An Appreciation." *Tradition 30*(4): 45–57.

Lichtenstein, Aharon. 2003. *Leaves of Faith: The World of Jewish Learning.* Jersey City, NJ: Ktav.

Lichtenstein, Mosheh. 2000. "'What' Hath Brisk Wrought: The Brisker Derekh Revisited." *Torah u-Madda 9*: 1–18.

Lichtenstein, Tovah. 2011. "Reflections on the Influence of the Rov on the American Jewish Community." *Tradition 44*(4): 7–22.

Lookstein, Haskel. 2003. "Our Rebbe: A Sermon of Tribute to Rabbi Joseph B. Soloveitchik." In *Memories of a Giant: Eulogies in Memory of Rabbi Dr. Joseph Soloveitchik zt"l*, edited by Michael A. Bierman. Jerusalem: Urim.

Luft, Sebastian. 2010. "Reconstruction and Reduction: Natorp and Husserl on Method and the Question of Subjectivity." In *Neo-Kantianism in Contemporary Philosophy*, edited by R. Makkreel and S. Luft, 59–91. Bloomington and Indianapolis: Indiana University Press.

Lustiger, Arnold. 2016-7. "The Kabbalistic Underpinnings of U-vikkashtem mi-Sham." *The Torah U-Madda Journal 17*: 174–84.

Lyčka, Milan. 1995a. "Human Typology in the Works of Rabbi Joseph B. Soloveitchik." *Listy filologické CXVIII*: 267–83.

Lyčka, Milan. 1995b. "The Land and its Sanctification in the Teaching of Rabbi Joseph B. Soloveitchik." In *Landgabe. Festschrift für Jan Heller zum 70. Geburtstag*, edited by M Prudký, 245–50. Praha: Oikoymenh.

Lyčka, Milan. 2003. ""You shall be Holy..." Joseph B. Soloveitchik's Concept of the Sacred." *Focus Pragensis 3*: 7–27.

Maier, Heinrich. 1913. *Sokrates: sein Werk und seine geschichtliche Stellung*, Mohr: Tübingen.

Margolis, Eric and Laurence, Stephen. 1999. *Concepts: Core Readings.* Cambridge: MIT Press.

Medoff, Rafael. 2008. *Rav Chese Wurzburgerd: The Life and Times of Rabbi Haskel Lookstein.* Jersey City: Ktav.

Meiselman, Moshe. 1998. "The Rav, Feminism and Public Policy: An Insider's View." *Tradition 33*(1): 5–30.

Meiselman, Shulamith. 1995. *The Soloveitchik Heritage: A Daughter's Memoir.* Hoboken: Ktav.

Mendelssohn, Moses. 1975. *Selections from His writings,* edited and translated by Eva Jospe. New York: Viking Press.

Mercer, Christia. 2020. "Empowering Philosophy." *Proceedings and Addresses of The American Philosophical Association (94)*: 68–96.

Millen, Rochelle L. 2004. "Like Pebbles on the Seashore: J. B. Soloveitchik on Suffering." *Modern Judaism 24*(2): 150–64.

Mirsky, Yehudah. 2014. *Rav Kook: Mystic in a Time of Revolution.* New Haven: Yale University Press.

Morgan, Fred. 2015. "Jewish Perspectives on Jewish-Christian Dialogue Over Five Decades." *European Judaism 48*(2): 3–22.

Moynahan, Gregory B. 2003. "Hermann Cohen's *Das Prinzip der Infinitesimalmethode und Seine Geschichte,* Ernst Cassirer, and the Politics of Science in Wilhelmine Germany." *Perspectives in Science 11*(1): 35–75.

Munk, Reinier. 1992. "Joseph B. Soloveitchik on Hermann Cohen's Logik der reinen Erkenntnis." In *Torah and Wisdom: Studies in Jewish Philosophy, Kabbalah, and Halakhah: Essays in Honor of Arthur Hyman,* edited by Ruth Link-Salinger, 147–63. New York: Shengold.

Munk, Reinier. 1996. *The Rationale of Halakhic Man: Joseph B. Soloveitchik's conception of Jewish thought.* Netherlands: J. C. Gieben.

Munk, Reinier. 1999. "The Intellect is the Bond Between Us and Him: Joseph B. Soloveitchik in Divine Names and Communion with God through the Intellect." *The Journal of Jewish Thought and Philosophy 9*: 107–26.

Nadler, Allan. 1993. "Soloveitchik's Halakhic Man: Not a Mithnagged." *Modern Judaism 13*(2): 119–47.

Nagel, Thomas. 1979. *Mortal Question.* New York: Cambridge University Press.

Natorp, Paul. 1912. *Allgemeine Psychologie nach kritischer Methode.* Tübingen: J. C. B. Mohr (P. Siebeck).

Natorp, Paul. 2015. "On the Objective and Subjective Grounding of Knowledge." In *The Neo-Kantian Reader,* edited by Sebastian Luft, 164–179. New York: Routledge. Originally published in 1887 as "Über objective und subjective Begründung der Erkenntnis."

Nietzsche, F., and Francis Golffing, trans. 1956. *The Birth of Tragedy and The Genealogy of Morals.* New York: Doubleday.

Novak, David. 1989. *Jewish-Christian Dialogue: A Jewish Justification.* New York: Oxford University Press.

Oppenheim, Michael. 1998. "Kierkegaard and Soloveitchik." *Judaism 37*(1): 29–49.

Orenstein, David. 2011. *The Views of Rabbi Moses Feinstein, Rabbi Abraham Joshua Heschel, and Rabbi Joseph B. Soloveitchik on Interfaith Dialogue.* Master's Thesis, Brandeis University.

Otto, Rudolf, and John W. Harvey, trans. 1923. *The Idea of the Holy: An Inquiry into the Non-Rational Factor in the Idea of the Divine and its Relation to the Rational.* London: Oxford University Press.

Ozar, Alex S. 2016. "The emergence of Max Scheler: Understanding Rabbi Joseph Soloveitchik's Philosophical Anthropology." *Harvard Theological Review 109*(2): 178.

Pappas, Nickolas, and Mark Zelcer. 2013. "Plato's Menexenus as a History That Falls into Patterns." *Ancient Philosophy 33*: 19–31.

Paul, L. A. 2016. *Transformative Experience.* New York: Oxford University Press.

Pick, Shlomo H. 2009. "Who Is Halakhic Man?" *Review of Rabbinic Judaism 12*(2): 245–72.

Poma, Andrea. 2006. *Yearning for Form and Other Essays on Hermann Cohen's Thought.* Netherlands: Springer.

Poma, Andrea. 2007. "Hermann Cohen: Judaism and Critical Idealism." In *The Cambridge Companion to Modern Jewish Philosophy*, edited by Michael L. Morgan and Peter Eli Gordon, 80–101. New York: Cambridge University Press.

Possen, David D. 2012. "J. B. Soloveitchik: Between Neo-Kantianism and Kierkegaardian Existentialism." In *Kierkegaard's Influence on Theology: Tome III, Catholic and Jewish Theology*, edited by Jon Stewart. Farnham: Ashgate.

Potok, Chaim 1967. *The Chosen.* New York: Fawcett.

Putnam, Hilary. 2008. *Jewish Philosophy as a Guide to Life.* Bloomington, IN: Indiana University Press.

Quine, W. V. O. 1960. *Word and Object.* Cambridge: MIT Press.

Rakeffet-Rothkoff, Aaron. 1996. "*Biyografya shel ha-Rav Yosef Dov ha-Levi Soloveitchik.*" In *Emunah be-Zemanim Mishtanim: Al Mishnato shel ha-Rav Yosef Dov Soloveitchik*, edited by Avi Sagi, 17–41. Jerusalem: Ha-Maḥlakah le-Ḥinukh u-le-Tarbut Toraniyim ba-Golah.

Rakeffet-Rothkoff, Aaron. 1998. "Rabbi Joseph B. Soloveitchik: The Early Years." In *Rabbi Joseph B. Soloveitchik: Man of Halacha, Man of Faith*, edited by Menachem D. Genack. Hoboken: Ktav.

Rakeffet-Rothkoff, Aaron. 1999. *The Rav: The World of Rabbi Joseph B. Soloveitchik.* 2 vols. Ktav.

Rakeffet-Rothkoff, Aaron. 2013. *"The Religious Zionism of Rav Soloveitchik."* Jewish Press 5/1/2013: http://www.jewishpress.com/indepth/front-page/the-religious-zionism-of-rav-soloveitchik/2013/05/01/0/.

Ravitzky, Aviezer. 1986. "Rabbi J. B. Soloveitchik on Human Knowledge: Between Maimonidean and Neo-Kantian Philosophy." *Modern Judaism 6*(2): 157–88.

Ravitzky, Aviezer. 1998. "Munkács and Jerusalem: Ultra-Orthodox Opposition to Zionism and Agudaism." In *Zionism and Religion*, edited by Shmuel Almog, Jehuda Reinharz, and Anita Shapira, 67–89. Hanover, NH: Brandeis University Press.

Ravitzky, Aviezer. 2005. "Covenant of Faith or Covenant of Fate?" In *Creation and Re-Creation in Jewish Thought: Festschrift in Honor of Joseph Dan on the Occasion of his Seventieth Birthday*, edited by Rachel Elior and Peter Schafer, 271–308. Tubingen: Mohr Siebeck.

Riskin, Shlomo. 2010. *Listening to God: Inspirational Stories for My Grandchildren.* New Milford: Maggid.

Rosenberg, Danny. 2012. "The Jewish Athlete of Faith: On the limit of sport." In *Jews in the Gym*, edited by Leonard Jay Greenspoon, 79–96. Indiana: Purdue University Press.

Rosensweig, Bernard. 1998. "The Rav as Communal Leader." In *Rabbi Joseph B. Soloveitchik: Man of Halacha, Man of Faith*, edited by Menachem D. Genack, 210–17. Hoboken: Ktav.

Rosenak, Avinoam. 1996. "Filosofiya u-Maḥshevet ha-Halakhah: Keri'a be-Shiurei ha-Talmud shel ha-Rav Y"D Soloveitchik l-Ohr Modellim NeoKantianim." In *Emunah be-Zemanim Mishtanim: Al Mishnato shel ha-Rav Yosef Dov Soloveitchik*, edited by Avi Sagi, 275–306. Jerusalem: Ha-Maḥlakah le-Ḥinukh u-le-Tarbut Toraniyim ba-Golah.

Rosenak, Michael, and Avinoam Rosenak. 2009. "Rabbi Joseph B. Soloveitchik and Aspects of Jewish Educational Philosophy: Explorations in His Philosophical Writings." *Journal of Jewish Education 75*: 114–29.

Ross, Nicham. 2014. *"Teguvato shel 'Ish ha-Emunah ha-Boded' le-Torat 'Ani—Atah': Bein Martin Buber le-Rav Soloveitchik."* *Zehut 5*: 47–74.

Ross, Tamar. 2004. *Expanding the Palace of Torah: Orthodoxy and feminism.* Wlatham: MA, Brandeis University Press.

Ross, Tamar. 2015. "Orthodoxy and the Challenge of Biblical Criticism: Some Reflections on the Importance of Asking the Right Question." *Journal of Modern Jewish Studies 14*: 6–26.

Rotenstreich, Nathan. 1984. *Jews and German Philosophy: The Polemics of Emancipation.* New York: Schocken Books.

Roth, Sol. 1989. "The Halakha as a Theoretical Construction." In *Of Scholars, Savants, and Their Texts: Studies in Religious Thought: Essays in Honor of Arthur Hyman*, edited by Ruth Link-Salinger, 201–08. New York: Peter Lang.

Rudavsky, Tamar. 2007. "Feminism and Modern Jewish Philosophy." In *The Cambridge Companion to Modern Jewish Philosophy*, edited by Michael L. Morgan and Peter Eli Gordon, 324–48. New York: Cambridge University Press.

Rutishauser, Christian M. 2010. *"Gishato Shel HaRav Soloveitchik le-Mifgash Yehudi-Notzri: Ikronot u-Gevulot ha-Petiḥot."* In *Rav ba-Olam he-Ḥadash*, edited by Avinoam Rosenak and Naftali Rothenberg, 435–45. Jerusalem: The Van Leer Jerusalem Institute and Magnes Press.

Rutishauser, Christian M. 2013. *The Human Condition and the Thought of Rabbi Joseph B. Soloveitchik.* Jersey City: Ktav.

Rynhold, Daniel. 2003. "The Philosophical Foundations of Soloveitchik's Critique of Interfaith Dialogue." *The Harvard Theological Review 96*(1): 101–20.

Rynhold, Daniel. 2005. *Two Models of Jewish Philosophy: Justifying One's Practices.* New York: Oxford University Press.

Rynhold, Daniel. 2012–13. "Letting the Facts Get in the Way of a Good Thesis: On interpreting R. Soloveitchik's philosophical method." *The Torah u-Madda Journal 16*: 52–77.

Rynhold, Daniel, and Michael J. Harris. 2018. *Nietzsche, Soloveitchik, and Contemporary Jewish Philosophy.* New York: Cambridge University Press.

Sagi, Avi. 1992. "Ha-Rav Soloveitchik U-Prof. Leibowitz Ke-Teoretikanim Shel Ha-Halakha." *Daat 29*: 131–48.

Sagi, Avi. 1997. "Contending with Modernity: Scripture in the Thought of Yeshayahu Leibowitz and Joseph Soloveitchik." *The Journal of Religion 77*(3): 421–41.

Sagi, Avi. 2012. "Reflections on the Challenges Confronting the Philosophy of Halakhah." In *The Cambridge History of Jewish Philosophy: The Modern Era,* edited by Martin Kavka, Zachary Braiterman, and David Novak, 501–18. New York: Cambridge University Press.

Sagi, Avi, and Dov Schwartz. 2019. *Religious Zionism and the Six-Day War: From realism to messianism*. Translated by Batya Stein. New York: Routledge.

Saiman, Chaim. 2007. "Legal Theology: The Turn to Conceptualism in Nineteenth-Century Jewish Law." *Journal of Law and Religion, 21*(1): 39–100.

Saiman, Chaim N. 2018. *Halakhah: The Rabbinic Idea of Law*. NJ: Princeton University Press.

Saks, Jeffrey. 1999. "Rabbi Joseph B. Soloveitchik on the Brisker Method." *Tradition 33*(2): 50–60.

Saks, Jeffrey. 2002. "An Index to Rabbi Joseph B. Soloveitchik's *Halakhic Man*." *Torah U-Madda 11*: 107–22.

Saks, Jeffrey. 2006a. "Rabbi Joseph B. Soloveitchik and the Israeli Chief Rabbinate: Biographical notes (1959–1960)." *B. D. D. 17*: 45–68.

Saks, Jeffrey. 2006b. "Rabbi Soloveitchik Meets Rav Kook." *Tradition 39*(3): 90–96.

Sacks, Jonathan. 1997. "Rabbi Joseph B. Soloveitchik's Early Epistemology." In *Exploring the Thought of Rabbi Joseph B. Soloveitchik*, edited by Marc D Angel, 209–25. New Jersey: Ktav.

Sacks, Jonathan. 2003. "A Hesped in Honor of Rav Yosef Soloveitchik." In *Memories of a Giant: Eulogies in Memory of Rabbi Dr. Joseph B. Soloveitchik*, edited by Michael A. Bierman. Jerusalem: Urim Publications.

Sacks, Jonathan. 2011. *The Great Partnership: Science, Religion and the Search for Meaning*. New York: Schocken Press.

Samuelson, Norbert M. (ed.). 1987. *Studies in Jewish Philosophy: Collected essays of the Academy for Jewish Philosophy, 1980–1985*. Lanham, MD: University Press of America.

Samuelson, Norbert M. 1989. *An Introduction to Modern Jewish Philosophy*. Albany: SUNY Press.

Schachter, Hershel. 1994. *Nefesh ha-Rav*. Jerusalem: Reishis Yerushalayim.

Schachter, Hershel. 2001. *Me-Peninei ha-Rav*. New York: Flatbush Beth Hamedrosh.

Schachter, Hershel. 2010. *Divrei ha-Rav*. New York: OU Press.

Schacter, Jacob J. 1998. "Facing the Truths of History." *Torah U-Madda 8*: 200–76.

Schacter, Jacob J. 2006. "Religious Zionism and the Meaning of Redemption." *Tradition 39*(3): 54–58.

Scheler, Max. 1980. *Die Wissensformen und die Gesellschaft*. 3rd ed. Bern: Francke Verlag.

Scheler, Max, and Bernard Noble, trans. 1960. *On the Eternal in Man*. London: SCM Press.

Scheler, Max, and M. S. Frings, ed. and trans. 1987. *Person and Self-Value: Three Essays*. Dordrecht: Martinus Nijhoff Publishers.

Scheler, Max, Manfred Frings, and Roger L. Funk, trans. 1973. *Formalism in Ethics and Non-Formal Ethics of Values*. Evanston: Northwestern University Press.

Schirn, Matthias. 2014. "Frege on Quantities and Real Numbers in Consideration of the Theories of Cantor, Russell and Others." In *Formalism and beyond: On the Nature of Mathematical Discourse*, edited by Godehard Link. Berlin: De Gruyter.

Schleiermacher, F. 1988. *On Religion: Speeches to its Cultured Despisers*. New York: Cambridge University Press.

Schopenhauer, A. 1969. *World as Will and Representation*. New York: Dover.

Schwartz, Dov. 1996. *"Mishnato shel ha-Rav Y"D Soloveitchik be-Re'i ha-Hagut ha-Ziyonit - ha-Datit: ha-Ḥelon ve-ha-Medinah."* In *Emunah be-Zemanim Mishtanim: Al Mishnato shel ha-Rav Yosef Dov Soloveitchik*, edited by Avi Sagi, 123–145. Jerusalem: Ha-Maḥlakah le-Ḥinukh u-le-Tarbut Toraniyim ba-Golah.

Schwartz, Dov. 2006. *"Kol Dodi Dofek*: A Religious-Zionist Alternative." *Tradition* 39(3): 59–72.

Schwartz, Dov. 2012. *From Phenomenology to Existentialism: The Philosophy of Rabbi Joseph B. Soloveitchik*. vol 2. Leiden: Brill.

Schwartz, Dov 2017. "Investigations into R. Joseph Dov Soloveitchik's Philosophy in the Light of his Posthumously Published Writing." In *In the Path of the Hebrew Book: From Sefer Yesira to R. Soloveitchik's Writings*, edited by Dov Schwartz and Gila Prebor, 333–54. Alei Sefer: Ramat Gan 2017.

Schwartz, Dov. 2019. *Rabbi Joseph Dov Soloveitchik on the Experience of Prayer*. Boston: Academic Studies Press.

Schwartz, Dov, and Batya Stein, trans. 2002. *Faith at The Crossroads: A Theological Profile of Religious Zionism*. Leiden: Brill.

Schwartz, Dov, and Batya Stein, trans. 2007. *Religion or Halakha: The Philosophy of Rabbi Joseph B. Soloveitchik*. Leiden: Brill.

Schwartz, Dov, and Batya Stein, trans. 2012. "The Phenomenology of Faith: R. Soloveitchik's analysis in *And From There You Shall Seek.*" In *Jewish Philosophy: Perspectives and Retrospectives*, edited by Raphael Jospe and Dov Schwartz, 279–314. Boston: Academic Studies Press.

Searle, John. 1995. *The Construction of Social Reality*. New York: Penguin.

Seeskin, Kenneth. 1997. "Jewish neo-Kantianism: Hermann Cohen." In *History of Jewish Philosophy*, edited by Daniel H. Frank and Oliver Leaman, 786–98. New York: Routledge.

Segal, Sanford L. 2003. *Mathematicians Under the Nazis*. Princeton, NJ: Princeton University Press.

Shakh, Elazar Menaḥem Man. 1990. *Mikhtavim u-Ma'amarim me-Maran ha-Gaon Rabbi Elazar Menaḥem Man Shakh, shlit"a*. vol. 4. Bnei Brak.

Shapiro, Marc B. 1997. "The Brisker Method Reconsidered." *Tradition 31*(3): 78–102.

Shatz, David. 1996. "The Traveler's Route Home: Rabbi Joseph B. Soloveitchik and the Unending Dialectic," *Jewish Action 57*(1): 16–19.

Shatz, David. 2002. *From the Depths I Have Called to You: Jewish Reflections on September 11th and Contemporary Terror*. New York: Yeshiva University Press.

Shatz, David. 2003. "The Rav's Philosophical Legacy." In *Memories of a Giant: Eulogies in Memory of Rabbi Dr. Joseph B. Soloveitchik*, edited by Michael A. Bierman. Jerusalem: Urim Publications.

Shatz, David. 2008a. "A Framework for Reading *Ish ha-Halakhah*," In *Turim: Studies in Jewish History and Literature Presented to Dr. Bernard Lander*, edited by Michael A. Shmidman. 2 vols. New York: Touro College Press.

Shatz, David. 2008b. "The Rav and Torah u-Madda." In *Mentor of Generations: Reflections on Rabbi Joseph B. Soloveitchik*, edited by Zev Eleff. Jersey City: Ktav.

Shatz, David. 2009. *Jewish Thought in Dialogue: Essays on Thinkers, Theologies, and Moral Theories*. Brighton: Academic Studies Press.

Shatz, David. 2013. "Constructing a Jewish Theodicy." In *The Blackwell Companion to the Problem of Evil*, edited by Justin P. McBrayer and Daniel Howard-Snyder, 309–25. Malden: Wiley-Blackwell.

Shatz, David. 2015. "The Muted Messiah: The Aversion to Messianic Forms of Zionism in Modern Orthodox Thought." In *Rethinking the Messianic Idea in Judaism*, edited by Michael L. Morgan and Steven Weitzman. Bloomington: Indiana University Press.

Shatz, David. 2018. "Contemporary Scholarship on Rabbi Soloveitchik's Thought: Where We Are, Where We Can Go." In *Scholarly Man of Faith: Studies in the Thought and Writings of Rabbi Joseph B. Soloveitchik,*edited by Ephraim Kanarfogel and Dov Schwartz, 135–96. Urim Publications and Ktav.

Sherlo, Yuval (Cherlow, Yuval). 1999/2000. *Joined Together in Your Hand: From Dialectic to Harmony in the Thought of Rabbi Joseph B. Soloveitchik (Heb)*. Alon Shvut: Hegyonut Press. (Revised edition 2002).

Shihor, Rachel. 1978. "On the Problem of Halacha's Status in Judaism: A study of the attitude of Rabbi Josef Dov Halevi Soloveitchik." *Forum 30–31*: 149–53.

Singer, Aharon. 1994. "Soloveitchik's Lonely Man of Faith." In *Thinkers and Teachers of Modern Judaism*, edited by Raphael Patai and Emanuel S. Goldsmith, 103–19, New York: Paragon House.

Singer, David. 1987. *"Enlightened Orthodoxy," Review of The Halakhic Mind. Commentary* 83:1 January: 73–76.

Singer, David. 1989. "The New Orthodox Theology." *Modern Judaism 9*(1): 35–54.

Singer, David and Moshe Sokol. 1982. "Joseph Soloveitchik: Lonely Man of Faith." *Modern Judaism 2*(3): 227–72.

Sklarin, Yigal. 2009. "Rushing in Where Angels Fear to Tread: Rabbi Joseph B. Soloveitchik, the Rabbinical Council of America, Modern Orthodox Jewry and the Second Vatican Council." *Modern Judaism 29*(3): 351–58.

Sokol, Moshe, ed. 1992. *Rabbinic Authority and Personal Autonomy*. Northvale, N.J: Jason Aronson.

Sokol, Moshe. 1999. "Is there a 'Halakhic' Response to the Problem of Evil?". *The Harvard Theological Review 92*(3): 311–23.

Sokol, Moshe. 2007. "Master or Slave? Rabbi Joseph B. Soloveitchik on Human Autonomy in the Presence of God." In *Turim: Studies in Jewish History and Literature Presented to Dr. Bernard Lander*, edited by Michael Shmidman, 275–330. Jersey City, NJ: Touro College Press/Ktav.

Sokol, Moshe. 2010. "Transcending Time: Elements of Romanticism in the Thought of Rabbi Joseph B. Soloveitchik." *Modern Judaism 30*(3): 233–46.

Solomon, Norman. 1993. *The Analytic Movement: Hayyim Soloveitchik and his Circle*. Atlanta: Scholars Press.

Solomon, Norman. 2012. *Torah from Heaven: The Reconstruction of Faith*. London: Littman.

Soloveitchik, Elijah Zvi, Levy, Jordan Gayle, Salovey, Peter, and Magid, Shaul. 2019. *The Bible, the Talmud, and the New Testament: Elijah Zvi Soloveitchik's Commentary to the Gospels*. United States: University of Pennsylvania Press.

Soloveitchik, Haym. 1994. "Rupture and Reconstruction: The Transformation of Contemporary Orthodoxy," *Tradition 28*(4): 64–130.

Soloveitchik, Moshe. 2010. "Mikhtav min ha-Rav Soloveitchik el ha-Rav Dov Katz." *Ḥakirah 9*: 19–23.

Sommers, Fred. 2006. "How the Rav Stayed with Me." In *My Yeshiva College: 75 Years of Memories*, edited by Menachem Butler and Zev Nagel, 122–26. Yashar Books.

Spiegel, Irving. 1964. *"Rabbi Says Faiths Are Not Related."* The New York Times, August 16.

Spero, Shubert. 2009 *Aspects of Rabbi Joseph B. Soloveitchik's Philosophy of Judaism: An Analytic Approach*. Jersey City, NY: Ktav.

Spinoza, Benedict, and R. H. M. Elwes, trans. 1951. *A Theologico-Political Treatise*. New York: Dover.

Spranger, Eduard, and Paul J. W. Pigors, trans. 1928. *Types of Men: The Psychology and Ethics of Personality*. Halle: Max Niemeyer Verlag.

Statman, Dani. 1996. *"Hibutim be-Tefisato ha-Mosarit shel ha-Rav Soloveitchik."* In *Emunah be-Zemanim Mishtanim: Al Mishnato shel ha-Rav Yosef Dov Soloveitchik*, edited by Avi Sagi, 249–264. Jerusalem: Ha-Maḥlakah le-Ḥinukh u-le-Tarbut Toraniyim ba-Golah.

Steinsaltz (Even-Israel), Adin. 2014. *My Rebbe*. New Milford, CT: Koren publishers.

Stern, Josef. 1998. *Problems and Parables of Law: Maimonides and Nachmanides on Reasons for the Commandments*. Albany: State University of New York Press.

Strohminger, Nina, and Shaun Nichols. 2014. "The Essential Moral Self." *Cognition 131*: 159–71.

Sztuden, Alex. 2010. "Grief and Joy in the Writings of Rabbi Soloveitchik." *Tradition 43*(4): 37–55; 2011, 44(3): 9–32; 2012, 45(2): 67–79.

Sztuden, Alex. 2018a. God of Abraham, God of Aristotle: Soloveitchik's Reading of the *Guide of the Perplexed." Journal of Jewish Thought and Philosophy 26*: 212–32.

Sztuden, Alex. 2018b. "The Identity of Love and Cognition in the Thought of R. Joseph Soloveitchik." In *Scholarly Man of Faith: Studies in the Thought and Writings of Rabbi Joseph B. Soloveitchik*, edited by Ephraim Kanarfogel and Dov Schwartz, 49–74. Urim Publications and Ktav.

Teitelbaum, Joel. 1961. *"Ma'amar Shalosh Shevuot."* In *Va-Yoel Moshe*, 21–194. Brooklyn: Beit Maschar Seforim "Yerushalayim".

Turner, Yosef. 2010. *"'Ha-Meḥashev ha-Halakhti' ke-Diyun be-Teḥum ha-Filosofiya shel ha-Dat ve-Hashlakhotav ha-Yehudiyot."* In *Rav ba-Olam he-Ḥadash*, edited by Avinoam Rosenak and Naftali Rothenberg, 42–55. Jerusalem: The Van Leer Jerusalem Institute and Magnes Press.

Turner, Yossi. 2014. "Sacrifice and Repentance: The Religious Thought of Hermann Cohen, Frans Rosenzweig, and Joseph B. Soloveitchik." In *The Actuality of Sacrifice: Past and Present*, edited by Alberdina Houtman, Marcel Poorthuis, Joshua Schwartz, and Yossi Turner. Leiden: Brill.

Twersky, Isadore. 1962. *Rabad of Posquières: A Twelfth Century Talmudist*. Cambridge, MA: Harvard University Press.

Twersky, Mayer. 1996. "A Glimpse of the Rav." *Tradition 30*(4): 79–114.

Twersky, Mayer. 1998. "Halakhic Values and Halakhic Decisions: Rav Soloveitchik's Pesak regarding women's prayer groups." *Tradition 32*(3): 5–18.

Urbach, Ephraim E. 1975. *The Sages: Their Concepts and Beliefs*. Cambridge, MA: Harvard University Press.

Washofsky, Mark (ed.). 2010. *Reform Responsa for the Twenty-First Century: She'eilot Ut'shuvot*, 2 vols. New York: CCAR Press.

Waxman, Chaim I. 2010. *"Maḥashavah, Tarbut, Ḥevratit u-Mivneh: Ha-Rav*

Soloveitchik ke-Manhig Ortodoksiyah Modernit." In *Rav ba-Olam he-Hadash,* edited by Avinoam Rosenak and Naftali Rothenberg, 363–86. Jerusalem: The Van Leer Jerusalem Institute and Magnes Press.

Weiss, Shira. 2018. "Biblical Hermeneutics in the Thought of R. Soloveitchik: A Preliminary Appraisal of the Influence of R. Yehudah Halevi." In *Scholarly Man of Faith: Studies in the Thought and Writings of Rabbi Joseph B. Soloveitchik,* edited by Ephraim Kanarfogel and Dov Schwartz, 27–48. Urim Publications and Ktav.

Wellhausen, Julius. 1885. *Prolegomena to the History of Ancient Israel.* Edinburgh: Adam and Charles Black.

West, Angela. 2014. "Soloveitchik's 'no' to Interfaith Dialogue." *European Judaism* 47(2): 95–106.

White, Tanya. 2018. "Between Soloveitchik, Greenberg and Meir: The Evolution of Interfaith Thought." In *A Torah Giant: The intellectual legacy of Rabbi Dr. Irving (Yitz) Greenberg,* edited by Shmuly Yanklowitz. New York: Ktav Publishing.

Windelband, W. 1892. *Geschichte der Philosophie.* Freiburg: J. C. B. Mohr. *(Published in 1905 in English as History of Philosophy.* New York: Macmillan.

Wittgenstein, Ludwig. 1958. *Philosophical Investigations.* New Jersey: Prentice Hall.

Wittgenstein, Ludwig. 1966. *Lectures and Conversations on Aesthetics, Psychology, and Religious Belief.* University of California Press.

Wolfson, Elliot. 2015. "Eternal Duration and Temporal Compresence: The influence of Ḥabad on Joseph B. Soloveitchik." In *The Value of the Particular: Lessons from Judaism and the Modern Jewish Experience,* edited by Michael Zank and Ingrid Anderson. Leiden: Brill.

Wolosky, Shira. 2003. "The Lonely Woman of faith." *Judaism 52*(1/2): 3–18.

Wolowelsky, Joel B. 1996. "Communal and Individual Mourning Dynamics within Traditional Jewish Law." *Death Studies 20*: 469–80.

Woolf, Jeffrey R. 2012. "Time Awareness as a Source of Spirituality in the Thought of Rabbi Joseph B. Soloveitchik." *Modern Judaism 32*(1): 54–75.

Wurzburger, Walter S. 1984. "*Ha-Metaḥ ha-De'alekti beyn 'Ish ha-Halakhah' u-beyn 'Ish he-Emunah ha-Boded'.*" In *Sefer Yovel: le-Kavod Moreinu ha-Gaon Rabbi Yosef Dov Soloveitchik Shlit"a,* edited by Shaul Israeli, Norman Lamm, Yitzchak Raphael. 2 vols, 18–29. Jerusalem and New York: Mossad Harav Kook, Yeshiva University.

Wurzburger, Walter S. 1994. "Rav Joseph B. Soloveitchik as Posek of Post-Modern Orthodoxy." *Tradition 29*(1) : 5–20.

Wurzburger, Walter S. 1996. "*Ha-Yesodot ha-Filosofi'im be-Mishnato ha-Ziyonit-Datit shel Ha-Rav Soloveitchik.*" In *Emunah be-Zemanim Mishtanim: Al Mishnato shel ha-Rav Yosef Dov Soloveitchik,* edited by Avi Sagi, 111–22. Jerusalem: Ha-Maḥlakah le-Ḥinukh u-le-Tarbut Toraniyim ba-Golah.

Wurzburger, Walter S. 1997. "The Centrality of Creativity in the Thought of Rabbi Joseph B. Soloveitchik." In *Exploring the Thought of Rabbi Joseph B. Soloveitchik,* edited by Marc D Angel, 277–89. New Jersey: Ktav.

Wyschogrod, Michael. 1983. *The Body of Faith.* New York: The Seabury Press.

Wyschogrod, Michael. 1986. "Orthodox Judaism and Jewish Christian Dialogue." https://www.bc.edu/content/dam/files/research_sites/cjl/texts/center/conferences/soloveitchik/sol_wyscho.htm.

Wyschogrod, Michael. 1991. "A Jewish View of Christianity." In *Toward a Theological Encounter: Jewish Understandings of Christianity,* edited by Leon

Klenicki, 104–119. New York: Paulist Press. Reprinted in R. Kendall Soulen (ed.). 2004. *Abraham's Promise: Judaism and Christian Relations*, 149–64. Grand Rapids, MI: Eerdmans Publishing.

Zelcer, Heshey. 2002. *A Guide to the Jerusalem Talmud.* Universal Publishers.

Zelcer, Heshey. 2008. "Review Essay 'Modern Scholarship in the Study of Torah: Contributions and Limitations' and 'Yirat Shamayim: The Awe, Reverence and Fear of God'." *Hakirah 8*: 141–56.

Zelcer, Heshey. 2011. "The Mystical Spirituality of Rabbi Joseph B. Soloveitchik." *Ḥakirah 11*: 135–48.

Zelcer, Heshey. 2012. "Shemoneh Esreh in Eretz Yisrael ca. 220–250 CE." *Ḥakirah 14*: 79–121.

Zelcer, Heshey. 2017. "Review Essay: Rabbi Soloveitchik's Lectures on the Guide." *Ḥakirah 22*: 35–47.

Zelcer, Heshey and M. Zelcer. 2017. "A Note on the Original Title for *The Halakhic Mind.*" *Ḥakirah 23*: 73–80.

Zelcer, Mark. 2009. "Critical notice of Hilary Putnam's *Jewish Philosophy as a Guide to Life.*" *The Philosophical Forum XL*(3): 425–34.

Zevin, Shlomo Yosef. 2007. *Ishim Ve-Shitot.* Jerusalem: Kol Mevaser.

Ziegler, Aharon. 1998. *Halakhic Positions of Rabbi Joseph B. Soloveitchik.* New York: Ktav Publishing. Vol II, 2001; Vol III, 2004; Vol IV 2007; Vol V 2012; and Vol VI 2013.

Ziegler, Reuven. 2012. *Majesty and Humility: The Thought of Rabbi Joseph B. Soloveitchik.* New York: OU Press; Jerusalem: Urim.

Zeitlin, Hillel. 1913. "Be-Hevyon ha-Neshama." *Netivot*, 205–235. Warsaw: Ahisefer.

Zivan, Gili. 1996. "*Ha-Ḥaviya ha-Datit al-pi HaRav Soloveitchik.*" In *Emunah be-Zemanim Mishtanim: Al Mishnato shel ha-Rav Yosef Dov Soloveitchik*, edited by Avi Sagi, 219–48. Jerusalem: Ha-Maḥlakah le-Ḥinukh u-le-Tarbut Toraniyim ba-Golah.

Zuesse, Evan M. 1994. "The Gate to God's Presence in Heschel, Buber, and Soloveitchik." In *Thinkers and Teachers of Modern Judaism*, edited by Raphael Patai and Emanuel S. Goldsmith, 121–49. New York: Paragon House.

Index

Made in the USA
Monee, IL
09 April 2023

31593074R00149